THE OFFICIAL
BIBLE
BRILLIANT

Trivia Book

Questions, Puzzles, *and* Quizzes
from Genesis *to* Revelation

Timothy E. Parker

Revell

a division of Baker Publishing Group
Grand Rapids, Michigan

© 2016 by Timothy E. Parker

Published by Revell
a division of Baker Publishing Group
P.O. Box 6287, Grand Rapids, MI 49516-6287
www.revellbooks.com

Printed in the United States of America

Library of Congress Cataloging-in-Publication Data
Names: Parker, Timothy E., author.
Title: The official Bible brilliant trivia book : questions, puzzles, and quizzes from Genesis to Revelation / Timothy E. Parker.
Description: Grand Rapids : Revell, 2016. | Includes bibliographical references.
Identifiers: LCCN 2016011272 | ISBN 9780800727062 (pbk.)
Subjects: LCSH: Bible—Miscellanea. | Bible games and puzzles.
Classification: LCC BS612 .P28 2016 | DDC 220—dc23
LC record available at http://lccn.loc.gov/2016011272

Scripture quotations are from the King James Version of the Bible.

16 17 18 19 20 21 22   7 6 5 4 3 2 1

To all those seeking a deeper relationship with Jesus Christ,
the one true God

Contents

Section 2: The Advanced Section

Section 3: The Bible Brilliant Section

Section 4: The Bonus Section

Before You Begin

It is time to become brilliant in the knowledge of God's Word, the richness of the biblical past and the prophetic future. To get the true benefits of this book, you may have to go through it more than once. The goal is to challenge you in multiple ways, using multiple strategies and a wide array of exercises, puzzles, and quizzes, to get you to the highest level of Bible knowledge, a level I call Bible brilliant.

Joshua 1:8 states, "This book of the law shall not depart out of thy mouth; but thou shalt meditate therein day and night, that thou mayest observe to do according to all that is written therein: for then thou shalt make thy way prosperous, and then thou shalt have good success." Although this book uses clever games, word play, and trivia to increase your overall Bible knowledge, its goal is no trivial matter. It behooves every believer to know as much about the Lord and his Word as humanly possible. *Bible Brilliant* will be overwhelmingly helpful in that endeavor.

There are at least two unique features of this book. One is a score card in the back of the book on which you can mark your scores for each exercise. A perfect score is 12,909 points, but there are also 2,475 bonus points available. A final score of 11,529 points or better qualifies you as Bible brilliant, a level achieved only by the finest Bible scholars. You can reach that level.

The second unique feature is this: there is no penalty for doing the same exercise repeatedly until you feel comfortable and competent with it. This is not a race given to the swift; the victory will come to those who endure to the end. Feel free to do any exercise any amount of times and record only your highest score.

It is far more important for you to learn and know the information in the exercises than to complete the exercises quickly. In fact, I strongly recommend that you never time yourself in any challenge presented but take your time and focus on retaining correct answers.

This is an open-book book. That means you may use your own Bible to find answers. It is always a good thing to have the Good Book open, and you are never penalized in any way for referencing your own Bible as you seek answers to the thousands of questions presented.

Some of the exercises are easy, and some are maddeningly difficult. However, they all have one purpose, and that is to teach the Word of God and bring you to the highest levels of Bible understanding and true knowledge.

THE MUST-KNOW SECTION

This section deals with Bible information, facts, and questions and answers that you absolutely must know to become Bible brilliant. (Answers begin on page 560.)

All human discoveries seem to be made only for the purpose of confirming more and more strongly the truths contained in the sacred Scriptures.

Sir William Herschel

Do Not Be Fooled

This is a simple true or false test to get things started. Award yourself 10 points on the score card in the back of this book for each correct true or false answer. Complete the entire test before checking your answers.

1. _____ The phrase "This too shall pass" is in the Bible.

2. _____ Eve bit into the forbidden apple in the Garden of Eden.

3. _____ "Spare the rod, spoil the child" is a biblical teaching on child raising.

4. _____ "God works in mysterious ways" is from the book of Proverbs.

5. _____ One of the most-quoted Bible verses is "Cleanliness is next to godliness."

6. _____ Three wise men visited Jesus on the day of his birth.

7. _____ "The Little Drummer Boy" Christmas song is based on the boy drummer in Micah.

8. _____ According to the book that bears his name, Jonah was in the belly of a whale for three days and three nights.

9. _____ Satan took the form of a serpent when he tempted Eve in the Garden of Eden.

10. _____ "God helps those who help themselves" is in the book of Psalms.

11. _____ "Money is the root of all evil" is a classic Bible verse concerning placing money above God.

12. _____ Jesus Christ himself said, "To thine own self be true."

13. _____ The apostle Paul said, "Love the sinner, hate the sin."

14. _____ The wise men visited the baby Jesus in the manger.

15. _____ There was one set of the Ten Commandments given to Moses.

2

The Essentials

To be truly Bible brilliant, you must have a strong, fundamental knowledge of the basics of the Bible. You may retake the following quiz as often as necessary and record only your highest score on the score card. You earn 2 points per correct answer.

1. What is the Bible's very first verse?
2. Who was the mother of Jesus?
3. What garden was the home of Adam and Eve?
4. What type of creature tricked Eve into eating forbidden fruit?
5. What was the method of execution the Romans used to kill Jesus?
6. What are the wages of sin, according to the Bible?
7. What was the name of Moses's brother?
8. What crime did Cain commit?
9. Who was thrown into a den of lions?
10. Man was made in whose image?
11. How does the Lord's Prayer start?
12. What did Jesus use to feed five thousand people?
13. What part of Adam's body did God use to create Eve?
14. What is the only sin that cannot be forgiven?

15. From what substance did God create man?

16. The ark was built to save humankind from what disaster?

17. When accused of knowing Jesus, who denied him three times?

18. What was placed on the head of Jesus Christ before his crucifixion?

19. Who lied to God when questioned about the whereabouts of his brother?

20. The Ten Commandments were written on what material?

21. How many apostles followed Jesus?

22. Who was directed by an angel to go see the baby Jesus?

23. What is the second book of the Bible?

24. Before David became king, what was his occupation?

25. What is the first book of the Bible?

26. What is the first book of the New Testament?

27. How did David kill Goliath?

28. Where was the "wilderness" in which John the Baptist preached?

29. What was written at the top of Jesus's cross?

30. In what did Jesus sleep after his birth?

31. Who was willing to offer his son as a sacrifice to the Lord?

32. What was miraculous about Jesus's mother?

33. After Noah built the ark, for how many days and nights did it rain?

34. Who was placed in an ark of bulrushes and placed in a river by his mother?

35. What curious thing happened to Jonah?

36. How was Ruth related to Naomi?

37. To whom was Mary engaged when she became pregnant with Jesus?

38. What book of the Bible contains hymns written by David?

39. What animals drowned themselves in the sea when demons cast out by Jesus entered them?

40. What psalm begins, "The LORD is my shepherd"?

41. Who wrote the majority of the letters that form a large part of the New Testament?

42. What wicked things did Joseph's brothers do to him and to get rid of him?

43. Who was the father of King David?

44. Who was the father of Solomon?

45. What is the final book of the Bible?

46. What is the last word of the Bible?

47. How many individual books are in the Bible?

48. What humble act did Jesus do for his disciples at the Last Supper?

49. What was the name of Adam and Eve's first son?

50. How long did it take the Lord to make the heaven and the earth?

Books of the Bible

The following exercise will help you learn the precise order of all sixty-six books of the Holy Scriptures without fail. For each question, simply fill in the name of the Bible book in its proper place in the list.

After mastering this exercise, which may take several attempts, you will know not only the precise order of the books as they appear in the Bible but also such facts as the twentieth book is Proverbs and the forty-fifth book is Romans.

You will be filling in 186 various blanks for the sixty-six Bible books during this exercise. Award yourself 1 point per blank. You may do this exercise as many times as necessary and record only your best score.

1.
 1. Genesis
 2.
 3. Leviticus
 4.
 5. Deuteronomy

2.
 1.
 2. Exodus
 3. Leviticus
 4. Numbers
 5.

3.
1. Genesis
2. Exodus
3.
4. Numbers
5.

4.
1. Genesis
2.
3.
4. Numbers
5. Deuteronomy

5.
3. Leviticus
4.
5. Deuteronomy
6.
7. Judges
8. Ruth

6.
4. Numbers
5.
6. Joshua
7.
8.
9. 1 Samuel
10. 2 Samuel

7.
4. Numbers
5. Deuteronomy
6. Joshua
7.
8. Ruth
9.
10. 2 Samuel

8.
4. Numbers
5.
6. Joshua
7. Judges
8.
9. 1 Samuel
10.

9.
4. Numbers
5. Deuteronomy
6.
7. Judges
8.
9. 1 Samuel
10. 2 Samuel

10.
7. Judges
8.
9. 1 Samuel
10.
11. 1 Kings
12.
13. 1 Chronicles

11.
7. Judges
8. Ruth
9.
10. 2 Samuel
11.
12. 2 Kings
13.

12.
7. Judges
8. Ruth
9. 1 Samuel
10.
11. 1 Kings
12.
13. 1 Chronicles

13.
7. Judges
8.
9. 1 Samuel
10. 2 Samuel
11.
12. 2 Kings
13.

14.
11. 1 Kings
12.
13. 1 Chronicles
14. 2 Chronicles
15.
16. Nehemiah
17. Esther
18.
19. Psalms
20. Proverbs

15.
11. 1 Kings
12. 2 Kings
13. 1 Chronicles
14. 2 Chronicles
15.
16. Nehemiah
17.
18. Job
19.
20. Proverbs

16.
11. 1 Kings
12. 2 Kings
13. 1 Chronicles
14. 2 Chronicles
15. Ezra
16.
17. Esther
18. Job
19. Psalms
20.

17.
11. 1 Kings
12. 2 Kings
13. 1 Chronicles
14. 2 Chronicles
15.
16. Nehemiah
17. Esther
18.
19. Psalms
20.

18.

11. 1 Kings
12.
13. 1 Chronicles
14. 2 Chronicles
15.
16. Nehemiah
17.
18. Job
19. Psalms
20.

19.

11.
12. 2 Kings
13. 1 Chronicles
14. 2 Chronicles
15. Ezra
16.
17. Esther
18. Job
19.
20. Proverbs

20.

17.
18. Job
19. Psalms
20.
21. Ecclesiastes
22.
23. Isaiah
24. Jeremiah
25. Lamentations

21.

17. Esther
18. Job
19.
20. Proverbs
21.
22. Song of Solomon
23.
24. Jeremiah
25. Lamentations

22.

17.
18. Job
19. Psalms
20. Proverbs
21.
22. Song of Solomon
23. Isaiah
24.
25. Lamentations

23.

17. Esther
18.
19. Psalms
20. Proverbs
21. Ecclesiastes
22.
23. Isaiah
24. Jeremiah
25.

24.
20.
21. Ecclesiastes
22.
23. Isaiah
24. Jeremiah
25. Lamentations
26.
27. Daniel
28. Hosea
29.
30. Amos

25.
20. Proverbs
21. Ecclesiastes
22.
23. Isaiah
24. Jeremiah
25.
26. Ezekiel
27. Daniel
28. Hosea
29. Joel
30.

26.
20. Proverbs
21. Ecclesiastes
22. Song of Solomon
23.
24. Jeremiah
25. Lamentations
26.
27. Daniel
28.
29. Joel
30. Amos

27.
20.
21. Ecclesiastes
22. Song of Solomon
23. Isaiah
24.
25. Lamentations
26. Ezekiel
27.
28. Hosea
29. Joel
30.

28.
20. Proverbs
21. Ecclesiastes
22.
23. Isaiah
24. Jeremiah
25.
26. Ezekiel
27. Daniel
28. Hosea
29.
30. Amos

29.
20. Proverbs
21. Ecclesiastes
22. Song of Solomon
23.
24. Jeremiah
25. Lamentations
26.
27.
28. Hosea
29.
30. Amos

30.
20.
21. Ecclesiastes
22. Song of Solomon
23. Isaiah
24.
25. Lamentations
26. Ezekiel
27.
28. Hosea
29. Joel
30.

31.
26.
27. Daniel
28. Hosea
29.
30. Amos
31. Obadiah
32.
33. Micah
34.
35. Habakkuk

32.
26. Ezekiel
27. Daniel
28.
29. Joel
30. Amos
31.
32. Jonah
33.
34. Nahum
35. Habakkuk

33.
26.
27. Daniel
28. Hosea
29. Joel
30. Amos
31.
32. Jonah
33. Micah
34.
35. Habakkuk

34.
26. Ezekiel
27.
28. Hosea
29. Joel
30. Amos
31. Obadiah
32.
33. Micah
34. Nahum
35.

35.
30. Amos
31. Obadiah
32.
33. Micah
34. Nahum
35.
36. Zephaniah
37.
38. Zechariah
39. Malachi

36.
30. Amos
31. Obadiah
32. Jonah
33.
34. Nahum
35. Habakkuk
36.
37. Haggai
38. Zechariah
39.

38.
30. Amos
31. Obadiah
32.
33. Micah
34. Nahum
35.
36. Zephaniah
37.
38. Zechariah
39. Malachi

37.
30. Amos
31.
32. Jonah
33. Micah
34.
35. Habakkuk
36. Zephaniah
37.
38. Zechariah
39.

39.
30.
31. Obadiah
32. Jonah
33.
34. Nahum
35. Habakkuk
36.
37. Haggai
38.
39. Malachi

Fill in each of the twenty-seven books of the New Testament as necessary to create a perfect order.

40.
40. Matthew
41. Mark
42.
43. John
44. Acts (of the Apostles)

41.
40.
41. Mark
42. Luke
43.
44. Acts

42.

40. Matthew
41.
42. Luke
43. John
44.

43.

40. Matthew
41.
42. Luke
43.
44. Acts
45.
46.
47.
48. Galatians
49.
50. Philippians
51. Colossians
52. 1 Thessalonians

44.

43. John
44.
45. Romans
46. 1 Corinthians
47.
48. Galatians
49. Ephesians
50.

45.

43.
44.
45. Romans
46.
47. 2 Corinthians
48.
49. Ephesians
50. Philippians

46.

43. John
44. Acts
45.
46. 1 Corinthians
47. 2 Corinthians
48.
49. Ephesians
50. Philippians
51.
52. 1 Thessalonians
53.

47.

47.
48. Galatians
49.
50. Philippians
51.
52. 1 Thessalonians
53. 2 Thessalonians
54. 1 Timothy
55.
56. Titus

48.
49. Ephesians
50.
51. Colossians
52.
53. 2 Thessalonians

49.
49.
50. Philippians
51.
52. 1 Thessalonians
53. 2 Thessalonians
54. 1 Timothy
55. 2 Timothy
56.
57. Philemon
58.
59. James

50.
49. Ephesians
50.
51. Colossians
52. 1 Thessalonians
53.
54. 1 Timothy
55. 2 Timothy
56. Titus
57.
58. Hebrews
59.

51.
49.
50. Philippians
51. Colossians
52. 1 Thessalonians
53. 2 Thessalonians
54.
55.
56. Titus
57.
58. Hebrews
59.

52.
50.
51.
52. 1 Thessalonians
53. 2 Thessalonians
54. 1 Timothy
55. 2 Timothy
56.
57. Philemon
58. Hebrews
59.
60. 1 Peter

53.
53.
54. 1 Timothy
55. 2 Timothy
56. Titus
57.
58. Hebrews
59. James
60.

54.
50. Philippians
51. Colossians
52. 1 Thessalonians
53.
54. 1 Timothy
55.
56. Titus
57. Philemon
58.
59. James

55.
57. Philemon
58. Hebrews
59.
60. 1 Peter
61. 2 Peter
62.

56.
54. 1 Timothy
55.
56.
57. Philemon
58. Hebrews
59. James
60.
61. 2 Peter
62.

57.
61.
62. 1 John
63. 2 John
64.

58.
58.
59. James
60.
61. 2 Peter
62.
63. 2 John
64.
65. Jude

59.
59.
60. 1 Peter
61. 2 Peter
62. 1 John
63. 2 John
64. 3 John
65.
66. Revelation

60.
56.
57. Philemon
58.
59. James
60. 1 Peter
61.
62. 1 John
63. 2 John
64.
65. Jude
66.

Did You Know?
(Set 1)

Here is our first set of astonishing facts found by close study of the Holy Scriptures.

- The book of Esther is the only book in the Bible that does not mention the word *God*.
- The Israelites crossed the Red Sea at night, not during the day. The Lord created a "pillar" of a cloud to provide light for the Israelites, while the Egyptians saw only darkness (Exodus 14:19–22).
- There will be no marriages in heaven (Matthew 22:30; Mark 12:25; Luke 20:34–35).
- Luke 19:23 speaks about putting money in the bank to allow it to earn interest.
- Hebrews 13:2 instructs us to always show hospitality to strangers because we may unknowingly be helping an angel.
- Although Joshua wrote the book of Joshua, he could not have written Joshua 24:29–33, which describes his death and Israel after his death.

5

The Ultimate Books
of the Bible Test

Give yourself 5 points for each correct answer.

1. The first book of the Bible is _____.
2. The third book of the Bible is _____.
3. The fifth book of the Bible is _____.
4. The eighth book of the Bible is _____.
5. The ninth book of the Bible is _____.
6. The twelfth book of the Bible is _____.
7. The fifteenth book of the Bible is _____.
8. The eighteenth book of the Bible is _____.
9. The twenty-first book of the Bible is _____.
10. The twenty-second book of the Bible is _____.
11. The twenty-fifth book of the Bible is _____.
12. The twenty-eighth book of the Bible is _____.
13. The thirtieth book of the Bible is _____.
14. The thirty-first book of the Bible is _____.
15. The thirty-third book of the Bible is _____.
16. The thirty-fifth book of the Bible is _____.

17. The thirty-eighth book of the Bible is _____.

18. The last book of the Old Testament is _____.

19. The first book of the New Testament is _____.

20. The third book of the New Testament is _____.

21. The fifth book of the New Testament is _____.

22. The seventh book of the New Testament is _____.

23. The tenth book of the New Testament is _____.

24. The twelfth book of the New Testament is _____.

25. The fourteenth book of the New Testament is _____.

26. The sixteenth book of the New Testament is _____.

27. The twentieth book of the New Testament is _____.

28. The twenty-second book of the New Testament is _____.

29. The twenty-fifth book of the New Testament is _____.

30. The last book of the Bible is _____.

Facts about the King James Bible

The following are facts that the truly Bible brilliant know. You may award yourself 5 points for each of the multiple-choice answers you get correct.

1. The Bible was written over a period of approximately how many years?
   A. 200 years
   B. 800 years
   C. 1,600 years

2. What number is closest to the approximate number of men believed to have been inspired by God to write the Bible?
   A. 8
   B. 40
   C. 620

3. How many books are in the Bible?
   A. 27
   B. 39
   C. 66

4. How many books are in the Old Testament?

   A. 25

   B. 39

   C. 44

5. How many books are in the New Testament?

   A. 12

   B. 20

   C. 27

6. How many books of the Bible are not divided into chapters?

   A. 1

   B. 3

   C. 5

7. What is the longest chapter of the Bible?

   A. Psalm 119

   B. Job 3

   C. Revelation 2

8. How many verses does the longest chapter of the Bible contain?

   A. 89

   B. 101

   C. 176

9. What is the longest book of the Bible?

   A. Genesis

   B. Psalms

   C. John

10. How many chapters does the longest book of the Bible contain?

    A. 99

    B. 150

    C. 201

11. What is the shortest book of the Bible?
    A. 1 Peter
    B. 3 John
    C. Jude

12. What is the longest verse of the Bible?
    A. Esther 8:9
    B. Psalm 13:3
    C. Revelation 1:2

13. How many words does the longest verse of the Bible contain?
    A. 90
    B. 152
    C. 301

14. What is the shortest verse of the Bible?
    A. God is.
    B. Jesus wept.
    C. Time stood still.

15. "Thus saith the Lord" appears approximately how many times in the Bible?
    A. 102 times
    B. 387 times
    C. 876 times

16. Worldwide, the Bible has been translated into how many languages?
    A. About 120
    B. About 550
    C. Over 1,200

Did You Know?
(Set 2)

Here are more interesting facts from the Bible.

- Gabriel, Michael, Lucifer, and Abaddon/Apollyon are the only angels mentioned by name in the Bible (Isaiah 14:12; Luke 19:1; Revelation 12:7).
- The apostle Paul was once stoned so thoroughly that his attackers thought he was dead, stopped the stoning, and dragged him out of the city (Acts 14:8–20).
- God ordered Isaiah to walk around stark naked for three years (Isaiah 20:1–4).
- There was a window on Noah's ark (Genesis 6:16).
- The Ten Commandments had writing on both sides of the tablets (Exodus 32:15).
- God caused Aaron's rod to sprout buds that blossomed, producing almonds (Numbers 17:8).
- Jesus, who promises to "come quickly" in the second coming, issues the final promise in the Bible (Revelation 22:20).

8

450 Key Verses

Knowing key Scripture passages is essential to becoming a Bible scholar. In this important exercise, you are given 450 verses with one key word missing. If you fill in the missing word correctly, you may reward yourself with 2 points.

1. John 3:16
   For God so loved the world that he gave his only begotten Son, that whosoever _____ in him should not perish, but have everlasting life.

2. John 1:1
   In the beginning was the _____, and the Word was with God, and the Word was God.

3. John 14:6
   Jesus saith unto him, I am the way, the truth, and the life: no man cometh unto the _____, but by me.

4. Matthew 28:19
   Go ye therefore, and teach all _____, baptizing them in the name of the Father, and of the Son, and of the Holy Ghost.

5. Romans 3:23
   For all have _____, and come short of the glory of God.

6. Ephesians 2:8

For by _____ are ye saved through faith; and that not of yourselves: it is the gift of God.

7. Genesis 1:1

In the _____ God created the heaven and the earth.

8. Acts 1:8

But ye shall receive _____, after that the Holy Ghost is come upon you: and ye shall be witnesses unto me both in Jerusalem, and in all Judaea, and in Samaria, and unto the uttermost part of the earth.

9. 2 Timothy 3:16

_____ scripture is given by inspiration of God, and is profitable for doctrine, for reproof, for correction, for instruction in righteousness.

10. Romans 10:9

That if thou shalt confess with thy mouth the Lord _____, and shalt believe in thine heart that God hath raised him from the dead, thou shalt be saved.

11. Romans 6:23

For the wages of sin is _____; but the gift of God is eternal life through Jesus Christ our Lord.

12. Acts 2:38

Then Peter said unto them, _____, and be baptized every one of you in the name of Jesus Christ for the remission of sins, and ye shall receive the gift of the Holy Ghost.

13. John 1:12

But as many as received him, to them gave he power to become the sons of God, even to them that _____ on his name.

14. Romans 8:28

And we know that all things work together for _____ to them that love God, to them who are the called according to his purpose.

15. John 1:9

That was the true _____, which lighteth every man that cometh into the world.

16. Genesis 1:26

And God said, Let us make man in our _____, after our likeness: and let them have dominion over the fish of the sea, and over the fowl of the air, and over the cattle, and over all the earth, and over every creeping thing that creepeth upon the earth.

17. Romans 12:1

I beseech you therefore, brethren, by the mercies of God, that ye present your _____ a living sacrifice, holy, acceptable unto God, which is your reasonable service.

18. Romans 5:8

But God commendeth his love toward us, in that, while we were yet _____, Christ died for us.

19. Matthew 28:18

And Jesus came and spake unto them, saying, All _____ is given unto me in heaven and in earth.

20. John 3:3

Jesus answered and said unto him, Verily, verily, I say unto thee, Except a man be _____ again, he cannot see the kingdom of God.

21. Mark 16:15

And he said unto them, Go ye into all the world, and preach the _____ to every creature.

22. John 10:10

The _____ cometh not, but for to steal, and to kill, and to destroy: I am come that they might have life, and that they might have it more abundantly.

23. John 1:14

And the _____ was made flesh, and dwelt among us, (and we beheld his glory, the glory as of the only begotten of the Father,) full of grace and truth.

24. Acts 4:12

Neither is there _____ in any other: for there is none other name under heaven given among men, whereby we must be saved.

25. Acts 2:42

And they continued stedfastly in the apostles' doctrine and fellowship, and in breaking of bread, and in _____.

26. Galatians 5:22

But the fruit of the _____ is love, joy, peace, longsuffering, gentleness, goodness, faith.

27. Proverbs 3:5

_____ in the LORD with all thine heart; and lean not unto thine own understanding.

28. Jeremiah 29:11

For I know the thoughts that I think toward you, saith the LORD, thoughts of peace, and not of _____, to give you an expected end.

29. Titus 3:5

Not by works of righteousness which we have done, but according to his mercy he _____ us, by the washing of regeneration, and renewing of the Holy Ghost.

30. Romans 12:2

And be not conformed to this _____: but be ye transformed by the renewing of your mind, that ye may prove what is that good, and acceptable, and perfect, will of God.

31. John 14:1

Let not your heart be _____: ye believe in God, believe also in me.

32. John 4:1

When therefore the Lord knew how the Pharisees had heard that Jesus made and _____ more disciples than John.

33. Ephesians 4:11

And he gave some, apostles; and some, prophets; and some, _____; and some, pastors and teachers.

34. Romans 5:12

    Wherefore, as by one man _____ entered into the world, and death by sin; and so death passed upon all men, for that all have sinned.

35. Matthew 11:28

    Come unto me, all ye that labour and are heavy laden, and I will give you _____.

36. Romans 5:1

    Therefore being justified by _____, we have peace with God through our Lord Jesus Christ.

37. Genesis 1:27

    So God _____ man in his own image, in the image of God created he him; male and female created he them.

38. Romans 1:16

    For I am not ashamed of the _____ of Christ: for it is the power of God unto salvation to every one that believeth; to the Jew first, and also to the Greek.

39. 1 John 1:9

    If we confess our sins, he is faithful and just to forgive us our sins, and to _____ us from all unrighteousness.

40. Acts 2:1

    And when the day of _____ was fully come, they were all with one accord in one place.

41. 2 Corinthians 5:17

    Therefore if any man be in _____, he is a new creature: old things are passed away; behold, all things are become new.

42. Hebrews 11:1

    Now _____ is the substance of things hoped for, the evidence of things not seen.

43. 2 Timothy 2:15

    Study to shew thyself _____ unto God, a workman that needeth not to be ashamed, rightly dividing the word of truth.

44. Romans 8:1

There is therefore now no _____ to them which are in Christ Jesus, who walk not after the flesh, but after the Spirit.

45. Romans 10:13

For whosoever shall call upon the name of the Lord shall be _____.

46. John 8:32

And ye shall know the truth, and the truth shall make you _____.

47. Isaiah 9:6

For unto us a child is born, unto us a son is given: and the _____ shall be upon his shoulder: and his name shall be called Wonderful, Counsellor, The mighty God, The everlasting Father, The Prince of Peace.

48. John 14:15

If ye _____ me, keep my commandments.

49. Deuteronomy 6:4

Hear, O Israel: The LORD our God is _____ LORD.

50. John 13:34

A new _____ I give unto you, That ye love one another; as I have loved you, that ye also love one another.

51. John 4:24

God is a Spirit: and they that worship him must worship him in spirit and in _____.

52. Philippians 4:13

I can do all things through _____ which strengtheneth me.

53. Ephesians 2:1

And you hath he quickened, who were dead in trespasses and _____.

54. John 14:16

And I will pray the _____, and he shall give you another Comforter, that he may abide with you for ever.

55. Genesis 1:2
And the earth was without form, and void; and _____ was upon the face of the deep. And the Spirit of God moved upon the face of the waters.

56. Hebrews 4:12
For the word of God is quick, and powerful, and sharper than any twoedged sword, piercing even to the dividing asunder of soul and _____, and of the joints and marrow, and is a discerner of the thoughts and intents of the heart.

57. James 5:16
_____ your faults one to another, and pray one for another, that ye may be healed. The effectual fervent prayer of a righteous man availeth much.

58. Isaiah 7:14
Therefore the Lord himself shall give you a sign; Behold, a _____ shall conceive, and bear a son, and shall call his name Immanuel.

59. John 1:7
The same came for a witness, to bear witness of the Light, that all men through him might _____.

60. John 3:5
Jesus answered, Verily, verily, I say unto thee, Except a man be born of _____ and of the Spirit, he cannot enter into the kingdom of God.

61. Philippians 2:5
Let this _____ be in you, which was also in Christ Jesus.

62. John 1:29
The next day John seeth Jesus coming unto him, and saith, Behold the Lamb of God, which taketh away the _____ of the world.

63. Romans 1:18

    For the _____ of God is revealed from heaven against all ungodliness and unrighteousness of men, who hold the truth in unrighteousness.

64. Philippians 4:6

    Be careful for _____; but in every thing by prayer and supplication with thanksgiving let your requests be made known unto God.

65. Hebrews 12:1

    Wherefore seeing we also are compassed about with so great a cloud of _____, let us lay aside every weight, and the sin which doth so easily beset us, and let us run with patience the race that is set before us.

66. John 1:3

    All things were _____ by him; and without him was not any thing made that was made.

67. Matthew 16:18

    And I say also unto thee, That thou art Peter, and upon this _____ I will build my church; and the gates of hell shall not prevail against it.

68. Galatians 2:20

    I am _____ with Christ: nevertheless I live; yet not I, but Christ liveth in me: and the life which I now live in the flesh I live by the faith of the Son of God, who loved me, and gave himself for me.

69. Matthew 25:31

    When the Son of man shall come in his glory, and all the holy angels with him, then shall he sit upon the _____ of his glory.

70. Matthew 5:17

    Think not that I am come to destroy the law, or the prophets: I am not come to destroy, but to _____.

71. Romans 10:17

So then _____ cometh by hearing, and hearing by the word of God.

72. Matthew 6:33

But seek ye first the kingdom of God, and his _____; and all these things shall be added unto you.

73. Luke 4:18

The _____ of the Lord is upon me, because he hath anointed me to preach the gospel to the poor; he hath sent me to heal the brokenhearted, to preach deliverance to the captives, and recovering of sight to the blind, to set at liberty them that are bruised.

74. John 16:13

Howbeit when he, the Spirit of _____, is come, he will guide you into all truth: for he shall not speak of himself; but whatsoever he shall hear, that shall he speak: and he will shew you things to come.

75. Acts 20:28

Take heed therefore unto yourselves, and to all the flock, over the which the Holy Ghost hath made you overseers, to feed the church of God, which he hath purchased with his own _____.

76. Titus 2:11

For the grace of God that bringeth _____ hath appeared to all men.

77. John 8:44

Ye are of your father the devil, and the lusts of your father ye will do. He was a murderer from the beginning, and abode not in the _____, because there is no truth in him. When he speaketh a lie, he speaketh of his own: for he is a liar, and the father of it.

78. Ephesians 6:10
    Finally, my brethren, be strong in the Lord, and in the
    _____ of his might.

79. Romans 13:1
    Let every soul be subject unto the higher powers. For there is
    no power but of _____: the powers that be are ordained
    of God.

80. John 2:15
    And when he had made a scourge of small cords, he drove
    them all out of the temple, and the sheep, and the oxen; and
    poured out the changers' money, and overthrew the _____.

81. Mark 16:16
    He that believeth and is _____ shall be saved; but he that
    believeth not shall be damned.

82. Romans 3:10
    As it is written, There is none _____, no, not one.

83. Genesis 3:15
    And I will put enmity between thee and the _____, and
    between thy seed and her seed; it shall bruise thy head, and
    thou shalt bruise his heel.

84. Hebrews 11:6
    But without _____ it is impossible to please him: for he
    that cometh to God must believe that he is, and that he is a
    rewarder of them that diligently seek him.

85. John 14:26
    But the Comforter, which is the Holy Ghost, whom the
    _____ will send in my name, he shall teach you all things,
    and bring all things to your remembrance, whatsoever I have
    said unto you.

86. John 5:24
    Verily, verily, I say unto you, He that heareth my word, and
    believeth on him that sent me, hath everlasting life, and shall
    not come into condemnation; but is passed from _____
    unto life.

87. Joel 2:28
    And it shall come to pass afterward, that I will pour out my
    _____ upon all flesh; and your sons and your daughters
    shall prophesy, your old men shall dream dreams, your young
    men shall see visions.

88. Genesis 1:11
    And God said, Let the earth bring forth grass, the herb yield-
    ing seed, and the fruit tree yielding fruit after his _____,
    whose seed is in itself, upon the earth: and it was so.

89. James 1:2
    My brethren, count it all _____ when ye fall into divers
    temptations.

90. Colossians 1:15
    Who is the image of the invisible God, the _____ of every
    creature.

91. Matthew 22:37
    Jesus said unto him, Thou shalt love the Lord thy God with
    all thy heart, and with all thy soul, and with all thy _____.

92. Titus 2:13
    Looking for that blessed _____, and the glorious appear-
    ing of the great God and our Saviour Jesus Christ.

93. Philippians 4:8
    Finally, brethren, whatsoever things are true, whatsoever things
    are honest, whatsoever things are just, whatsoever things
    are pure, whatsoever things are lovely, whatsoever things are
    of good report; if there be any virtue, and if there be any
    _____, think on these things.

94. Acts 1:9
    And when he had spoken these things, while they beheld, he
    was taken up; and a _____ received him out of their sight.

95. John 4:7
    There cometh a woman of _____ to draw water: Jesus
    saith unto her, Give me to drink.

96. Micah 6:8

He hath shewed thee, O man, what is good; and what doth the LORD require of thee, but to do justly, and to love mercy, and to walk _____ with thy God?

97. John 17:17

_____ them through thy truth: thy word is truth.

98. Acts 20:7

And upon the first day of the week, when the disciples came together to break bread, _____ preached unto them, ready to depart on the morrow; and continued his speech until midnight.

99. Acts 16:31

And they said, Believe on the Lord Jesus Christ, and thou shalt be saved, and thy _____.

100. John 11:25

Jesus said unto her, I am the _____, and the life: he that believeth in me, though he were dead, yet shall he live.

101. John 8:58

Jesus said unto them, Verily, verily, I say unto you, Before _____ was, I am.

102. Acts 2:4

And they were all filled with the Holy Ghost, and began to speak with other _____, as the Spirit gave them utterance.

103. John 15:5

I am the vine, ye are the _____: He that abideth in me, and I in him, the same bringeth forth much fruit: for without me ye can do nothing.

104. Acts 2:41

Then they that gladly received his word were _____: and the same day there were added unto them about three thousand souls.

105. Proverbs 22:6

Train up a _____ in the way he should go: and when he is old, he will not depart from it.

106. Genesis 3:1

Now the _____ was more subtil than any beast of the field which the LORD God had made. And he said unto the woman, Yea, hath God said, Ye shall not eat of every tree of the garden?

107. James 1:5

If any of you lacks _____, let him ask of God, that giveth to all men liberally, and upbraideth not; and it shall be given him.

108. Hebrews 1:1

God, who at sundry times and in divers manners spake in time past unto the fathers by the _____.

109. 2 John 1:2

For the _____ sake, which dwelleth in us, and shall be with us for ever.

110. John 17:3

And this is life _____, that they might know thee the only true God, and Jesus Christ, whom thou hast sent.

111. John 5:7

The impotent man answered him, Sir, I have no man, when the _____ is troubled, to put me into the pool: but while I am coming, another steppeth down before me.

112. John 8:31

Then said Jesus to those Jews which believed on him, If ye continue in my word, then are ye my _____ indeed.

113. Luke 1:4

That thou mightest know the certainty of those things, wherein thou hast been _____.

114. Revelation 3:20

Behold, I stand at the door, and knock: if any man hear my _____, and open the door, I will come in to him, and will sup with him, and he with me.

115. 1 Peter 2:3

If so be ye have _____ that the Lord is gracious.

116. John 10:30

I and my _____ are one.

117. 1 Peter 3:15

But sanctify the Lord God in your hearts: and be ready always to give an answer to every man that asketh you a reason of the _____ that is in you with meekness and fear.

118. Matthew 7:21

Not every one that saith unto me, Lord, Lord, shall enter into the kingdom of heaven; but he that doeth the _____ of my Father which is in heaven.

119. John 3:18

He that believeth on him is not condemned: but he that believeth not is condemned already, because he hath not believed in the name of the only _____ Son of God.

120. Genesis 12:1

Now the LORD had said unto _____, Get thee out of thy country, and from thy kindred, and from thy father's house, unto a land that I will shew thee.

121. John 3:8

The wind bloweth where it listeth, and thou hearest the sound thereof, but canst not tell whence it cometh, and whither it goeth: so is every one that is born of the _____.

122. John 15:1

I am the true _____, and my Father is the husbandman.

123. Genesis 2:7

And the LORD God formed man of the dust of the ground, and breathed into his nostrils the breath of _____; and man became a living soul.

124. Genesis 1:3

And God said, _____ there be light: and there was light.

125. John 8:12

Then spake Jesus again unto them, saying, I am the _____ of the world: he that followeth me shall not walk in darkness, but shall have the light of life.

126. 1 Peter 2:9

But ye are a _____ generation, a royal priesthood, an holy nation, a peculiar people; that ye should shew forth the praises of him who hath called you out of darkness into his marvellous light.

127. Luke 1:26

And in the _____ month the angel Gabriel was sent from God unto a city of Galilee, named Nazareth.

128. Hebrews 9:27

And as it is appointed unto men once to die, but after this the _____.

129. John 3:2

The same came to Jesus by night, and said unto him, _____, we know that thou art a teacher come from God: for no man can do these miracles that thou doest, except God be with him.

130. Matthew 5:14

Ye are the _____ of the world. A city that is set on an hill cannot be hid.

131. Exodus 3:14

And God said unto _____, I Am That I Am: and he said, Thus shalt thou say unto the children of Israel, I Am hath sent me unto you.

132. 1 Corinthians 6:9

Know ye not that the unrighteous shall not inherit the kingdom of God? Be not _____: neither fornicators, nor idolaters, nor adulterers, nor effeminate, nor abusers of themselves with mankind.

133. Luke 10:25

And, behold, a certain lawyer stood up, and tempted him, saying, Master, what shall I do to inherit eternal _____?

134. Matthew 7:7

_____, and it shall be given you; seek, and ye shall find; knock, and it shall be opened unto you.

135. Ephesians 1:3

_____ be the God and Father of our Lord Jesus Christ, who hath blessed us with all spiritual blessings in heavenly places in Christ.

136. Matthew 1:18

Now the _____ of Jesus Christ was on this wise: When as his mother Mary was espoused to Joseph, before they came together, she was found with child of the Holy Ghost.

137. Romans 1:20

For the invisible things of him from the creation of the world are clearly seen, being understood by the things that are made, even his eternal power and Godhead; so that they are without _____.

138. John 8:9

And they which heard it, being convicted by their own conscience, went out one by one, beginning at the eldest, even unto the last: and _____ was left alone, and the woman standing in the midst.

139. John 1:5

And the _____ shineth in darkness; and the darkness comprehended it not.

140. 1 Thessalonians 4:13

But I would not have you to be ignorant, brethren, concerning them which are asleep, that ye sorrow not, even as others which have no _____.

141. Hebrews 13:5

Let your conversation be without covetousness; and be content with such things as ye have: for he hath said, I will never leave thee, nor _____ thee.

142. 1 John 4:1

Beloved, believe not every _____, but try the spirits whether they are of God: because many false prophets are gone out into the world.

143. James 1:17

Every good _____ and every perfect gift is from above, and cometh down from the Father of lights, with whom is no variableness, neither shadow of turning.

144. Matthew 6:19

Lay not up for yourselves _____ upon earth, where moth and rust doth corrupt, and where thieves break through and steal.

145. Isaiah 61:1

The Spirit of the Lord GOD is upon me; because the LORD hath anointed me to _____ good tidings unto the meek; he hath sent me to bind up the brokenhearted, to proclaim liberty to the captives, and the opening of the prison to them that are bound.

146. Galatians 3:28

There is neither Jew nor Greek, there is neither bond nor free, there is neither male nor female: for ye are all _____ in Christ Jesus.

147. 2 Peter 3:9

The Lord is not slack concerning his _____, as some men count slackness; but is longsuffering to us-ward, not willing that any should perish, but that all should come to repentance.

148. Acts 1:11

Which also said, Ye men of Galilee, why stand ye gazing up into heaven? this same _____, which is taken up from you into heaven, shall so come in like manner as ye have seen him go into heaven.

149. James 5:14

Is any _____ among you? let him call for the elders of the church; and let them pray over him, anointing him with oil in the name of the Lord.

150. John 3:36

He that believeth on the _____ hath everlasting life: and he that believeth not the Son shall not see life; but the wrath of God abideth on him.

151. Ephesians 6:12

For we wrestle not against flesh and blood, but against _____, against powers, against the rulers of the darkness of this world, against spiritual wickedness in high places.

152. Matthew 6:9

After this manner therefore _____ ye: Our Father which art in heaven, Hallowed be thy name.

153. Acts 3:19

_____ ye therefore, and be converted, that your sins may be blotted out, when the times of refreshing shall come from the presence of the Lord.

154. James 2:14

What doth it profit, my brethren, though a man say he hath faith, and have not works? can _____ save him?

155. Isaiah 40:31

But they that wait upon the _____ shall renew their strength; they shall mount up with wings as eagles; they shall run, and not be weary; and they shall walk, and not faint.

156. John 3:17

For God sent not his Son into the world to condemn the world; but that the world through him might be _____.

157. Luke 1:35

And the _____ answered and said unto her, The Holy Ghost shall come upon thee, and the power of the Highest shall overshadow thee: therefore also that holy thing which shall be born of thee shall be called the Son of God.

158. Genesis 1:28

And God blessed them, and God said unto them, Be _____, and multiply, and replenish the earth, and subdue it: and have dominion over the fish of the sea, and over the fowl of the air, and over every living thing that moveth upon the earth.

159. Ephesians 2:10

For we are his _____, created in Christ Jesus unto good works, which God hath before ordained that we should walk in them.

160. 2 Corinthians 5:21

For he hath made him to be _____ for us, who knew no sin; that we might be made the righteousness of God in him.

161. Romans 6:1

What shall we say then? Shall we continue in sin, that _____ may abound?

162. Ephesians 1:13

In whom ye also trusted, after that ye heard the word of truth, the gospel of your _____: in whom also after that ye believed, ye were sealed with that holy Spirit of promise.

163. Romans 6:3

Know ye not, that so many of us as were baptized into Jesus Christ were baptized into his _____?

164. Matthew 18:15

Moreover if thy _____ shall trespass against thee, go and tell him his fault between thee and him alone: if he shall hear thee, thou hast gained thy brother.

165. 1 John 4:5

They are of the _____: therefore speak they of the world, and the world heareth them.

166. James 1:27

Pure religion and undefiled before God and the Father is this, To visit the fatherless and _____ in their affliction, and to keep himself unspotted from the world.

167. John 16:33

These things I have spoken unto you, that in me ye might have peace. In the world ye shall have tribulation: but be of good cheer; I have _____ the world.

168. John 5:28

Marvel not at this: for the hour is coming, in the which all that are in the _____ shall hear his voice.

169. John 5:39

Search the _____; for in them ye think ye have eternal life: and they are they which testify of me.

170. Titus 2:3

The aged _____ likewise, that they be in behaviour as becometh holiness, not false accusers, not given to much wine, teachers of good things.

171. John 4:23

But the hour cometh, and now is, when the true _____ shall worship the Father in spirit and in truth: for the Father seeketh such to worship him.

172. Matthew 7:1

_____ not, that ye be not judged.

173. 1 Timothy 2:5

For there is one God, and one _____ between God and men, the man Christ Jesus.

174. Matthew 4:1

Then was Jesus led up of the Spirit into the _____ to be tempted of the devil.

175. John 1:18

No man hath seen _____ at any time, the only begotten Son, which is in the bosom of the Father, he hath declared him.

176. Ephesians 4:1

I therefore, the _____ of the Lord, beseech you that ye walk worthy of the vocation wherewith ye are called.

177. Ephesians 5:18
     And be not drunk with wine, wherein is excess; but be filled
     with the _____.

178. Ephesians 5:22
     Wives, _____ yourselves unto your own husbands, as unto
     the Lord.

179. Revelation 21:1
     And I saw a new heaven and a new earth: for the first heaven
     and the first earth were passed away; and there was no more
     _____.

180. 2 Peter 3:4
     And saying, Where is the promise of his _____? for since
     the fathers fell asleep, all things continue as they were from
     the beginning of the creation.

181. John 6:44
     No man can come to me, except the _____ which hath
     sent me draw him: and I will raise him up at the last day.

182. John 20:19
     Then the same day at evening, being the first day of the
     week, when the doors were shut where the _____ were
     assembled for fear of the Jews, came Jesus and stood in the
     midst, and saith unto them, Peace be unto you.

183. Psalm 119:105
     Thy word is a _____ unto my feet, and a light unto my
     path.

184. Genesis 2:18
     And the LORD God said, It is not good that the _____
     should be alone; I will make him an help meet for him.

185. 1 John 1:7
     But if we walk in the light, as he is in the light, we have
     _____ one with another, and the blood of Jesus Christ
     his Son cleanseth us from all sin.

186. 1 Corinthians 15:3
    For I delivered unto you first of all that which I also received, how that Christ died for our _____ according to the scriptures.

187. Isaiah 53:5
    But he was _____ for our transgressions, he was bruised for our iniquities: the chastisement of our peace was upon him; and with his stripes we are healed.

188. Ephesians 1:7
    In whom we have _____ through his blood, the forgiveness of sins, according to the riches of his grace.

189. Ephesians 5:25
    Husbands, love your wives, even as Christ also loved the _____, and gave himself for it.

190. Romans 8:9
    But ye are not in the _____, but in the Spirit, if so be that the Spirit of God dwell in you. Now if any man have not the Spirit of Christ, he is none of his.

191. John 15:13
    Greater _____ hath no man than this, that a man lay down his life for his friends.

192. Galatians 5:16
    This I say then, Walk in the _____, and ye shall not fulfil the lust of the flesh.

193. John 3:14
    And as _____ lifted up the serpent in the wilderness, even so must the Son of man be lifted up.

194. John 3:4
    Nicodemus saith unto him, How can a man be _____ when he is old? can he enter the second time into his mother's womb, and be born?

195. Matthew 7:13
    Enter ye in at the strait _____: for wide is the gate, and broad is the way, that leadeth to destruction, and many there be which go in thereat.

196. James 1:22
    But be ye doers of the word, and not hearers only, _____ your own selves.

197. Genesis 2:24
    Therefore shall a man leave his father and his mother, and shall cleave unto his _____: and they shall be one flesh.

198. John 10:27
    My _____ hear my voice, and I know them, and they follow me.

199. Colossians 1:16
    For by him were all things _____, that are in heaven, and that are in earth, visible and invisible, whether they be thrones, or dominions, or principalities, or powers: all things were created by him, and for him.

200. Colossians 3:1
    If ye then be risen with _____, seek those things which are above, where Christ sitteth on the right hand of God.

201. Acts 17:30
    And the times of this ignorance God winked at; but now commandeth all men every where to _____.

202. John 16:7
    Nevertheless I tell you the truth; It is expedient for you that I go away: for if I go not away, the _____ will not come unto you; but if I depart, I will send him unto you.

203. 1 Peter 3:18
    For Christ also hath once suffered for _____, the just for the unjust, that he might bring us to God, being put to death in the flesh, but quickened by the Spirit.

204. Hebrews 10:25
    Not forsaking the _____ of ourselves together, as the manner of some is; but exhorting one another: and so much the more, as ye see the day approaching.

205. John 2:2
And both Jesus was called, and his disciples, to the _____.

206. Matthew 7:8
For every one that asketh receiveth; and he that seeketh findeth; and to him that knocketh it shall be _____.

207. Matthew 5:13
Ye are the salt of the _____: but if the salt have lost his savour, wherewith shall it be salted? it is thenceforth good for nothing, but to be cast out, and to be trodden under foot of men.

208. James 4:7
_____ yourselves therefore to God. Resist the devil, and he will flee from you.

209. John 10:11
I am the good shepherd: the good shepherd giveth his _____ for the sheep.

210. 1 Peter 2:24
Who his own self bare our sins in his own body on the tree, that we, being dead to sins, should live unto righteousness: by whose _____ ye were healed.

211. John 14:27
Peace I leave with you, my peace I give unto you: not as the _____ giveth, give I unto you. Let not your heart be troubled, neither let it be afraid.

212. John 6:37
All that the _____ giveth me shall come to me; and him that cometh to me I will in no wise cast out.

213. Acts 6:12
And they stirred up the people, and the _____, and the scribes, and came upon him, and caught him, and brought him to the council.

214. Romans 8:26

Likewise the Spirit also helpeth our _____: for we know not what we should pray for as we ought: but the Spirit itself maketh intercession for us with groanings which cannot be uttered.

215. John 20:1

The first day of the week cometh Mary _____ early, when it was yet dark, unto the sepulchre, and seeth the stone taken away from the sepulchre.

216. John 6:7

Philip answered him, Two hundred pennyworth of bread is not sufficient for them, that every one of them may take a _____.

217. Luke 14:1

And it came to pass, as he went into the house of one of the chief Pharisees to eat bread on the _____ day, that they watched him.

218. Romans 8:29

For whom he did foreknow, he also did predestinate to be conformed to the _____ of his Son, that he might be the firstborn among many brethren.

219. John 5:19

Then answered Jesus and said unto them, Verily, verily, I say unto you, The Son can do nothing of himself, but what he seeth the _____ do: for what things soever he doeth, these also doeth the Son likewise.

220. Jeremiah 17:9

The heart is _____ above all things, and desperately wicked: who can know it?

221. 1 John 4:7

Beloved, let us love one another: for love is of God; and every one that loveth is born of _____, and knoweth God.

222. Exodus 1:5

And all the souls that came out of the loins of _____ were seventy souls: for Joseph was in Egypt already.

223. 1 John 2:15

Love not the world, neither the things that are in the world. If any man love the world, the love of the _____ is not in him.

224. 2 Peter 1:20

Knowing this first, that no prophecy of the _____ is of any private interpretation.

225. Colossians 3:12

Put on therefore, as the elect of God, holy and beloved, bowels of mercies, kindness, humbleness of _____, meekness, longsuffering.

226. John 15:26

But when the Comforter is come, whom I will send unto you from the Father, even the Spirit of truth, which proceedeth from the Father, he shall _____ of me.

227. John 17:20

Neither _____ I for these alone, but for them also which shall believe on me through their word.

228. 1 John 3:1

Behold, what manner of _____ the Father hath bestowed upon us, that we should be called the sons of God: therefore the world knoweth us not, because it knew him not.

229. Acts 10:34

Then _____ opened his mouth, and said, Of a truth I perceive that God is no respecter of persons.

230. Matthew 2:1

Now when Jesus was born in Bethlehem of Judaea in the days of _____ the king, behold, there came wise men from the east to Jerusalem.

231. Titus 1:5

For this cause left I thee in Crete, that thou shouldest set in order the things that are wanting, and ordain _____ in every city, as I had appointed thee.

232. Acts 17:10

And the brethren immediately sent away Paul and _____ by night unto Berea: who coming thither went into the synagogue of the Jews.

233. Luke 9:23

And he said to them all, If any man will come after me, let him deny himself, and take up his _____ daily, and follow me.

234. Galatians 3:26

For ye are all the children of God by _____ in Christ Jesus.

235. 1 John 2:1

My little children, these things write I unto you, that ye sin not. And if any man sin, we have an advocate with the Father, Jesus Christ the _____.

236. 1 Peter 5:8

Be _____, be vigilant; because your adversary the devil, as a roaring lion, walketh about, seeking whom he may devour.

237. 2 Corinthians 1:2

Grace be to you and _____ from God our Father, and from the Lord Jesus Christ.

238. Hebrews 4:15

For we have not an high _____ which cannot be touched with the feeling of our infirmities; but was in all points tempted like as we are, yet without sin.

239. Hebrews 1:3

Who being the brightness of his glory, and the express image of his person, and upholding all things by the _____ of his power, when he had by himself purged our sins, sat down on the right hand of the Majesty on high.

240. Galatians 5:1

Stand fast therefore in the liberty wherewith Christ hath made us _____, and be not entangled again with the yoke of bondage.

241. John 4:10

Jesus answered and said unto her, If thou knewest the
_____ of God, and who it is that saith to thee, Give me
to drink; thou wouldest have asked of him, and he would
have given thee living water.

242. John 5:14

Afterward Jesus findeth him in the temple, and said unto
him, Behold, thou art made whole: _____ no more, lest
a worse thing come unto thee.

243. Isaiah 14:12

How art thou fallen from heaven, O _____, son of the
morning! how art thou cut down to the ground, which didst
weaken the nations!

244. Hebrews 13:8

Jesus Christ the same yesterday, and to day, and _____.

245. Galatians 3:4

Have ye suffered so many things in _____? if it be yet in
vain.

246. Colossians 3:16

Let the word of Christ dwell in you richly in all wisdom;
teaching and admonishing one another in psalms and hymns
and spiritual _____, singing with grace in your hearts to
the Lord.

247. John 7:37

In the last day, that great day of the feast, Jesus stood and
cried, saying, If any man _____, let him come unto me,
and drink.

248. Joshua 24:15

And if it seem evil unto you to _____ the LORD, choose
you this day whom ye will serve; whether the gods which
your fathers served that were on the other side of the flood,
or the gods of the Amorites, in whose land ye dwell: but as
for me and my house, we will serve the LORD.

249. Matthew 5.16

Let your _____ so shine before men, that they may see your good works, and glorify your Father which is in heaven.

250. Romans 8:14

For as many as are _____ by the Spirit of God, they are the sons of God.

251. 2 Chronicles 1:2

Then _____ spake unto all Israel, to the captains of thousands and of hundreds, and to the judges, and to every governor in all Israel, the chief of the fathers.

252. Luke 11:1

And it came to pass, that, as he was praying in a certain place, when he ceased, one of his disciples said unto him, Lord, teach us to pray, as _____ also taught his disciples.

253. Luke 10:38

Now it came to pass, as they went, that he entered into a certain village: and a certain woman named _____ received him into her house.

254. Romans 8:31

What shall we then say to these things? If God be for us, who can be _____ us?

255. John 13:1

Now before the feast of the _____, when Jesus knew that his hour was come that he should depart out of this world unto the Father, having loved his own which were in the world, he loved them unto the end.

256. John 1:4

In him was life; and the life was the _____ of men.

257. Philippians 2:12

Wherefore, my beloved, as ye have always obeyed, not as in my presence only, but now much more in my absence, work out your own salvation with _____ and trembling.

258. John 14:23

Jesus answered and said unto him, If a man love me, he will keep my _____: and my Father will love him, and we will come unto him, and make our abode with him.

259. John 16:8

And when he is come, he will reprove the world of sin, and of righteousness, and of _____.

260. 2 Peter 1:21

For the _____ came not in old time by the will of man: but holy men of God spake as they were moved by the Holy Ghost.

261. 1 John 1:8

If we say that we have no _____, we deceive ourselves, and the truth is not in us.

262. Luke 18:1

And he spake a parable unto them to this end, that men ought always to _____, and not to faint.

263. James 2:3

And ye have respect to him that weareth the gay clothing, and say unto him, Sit thou here in a good place; and say to the poor, Stand thou there, or sit here under my _____.

264. Philippians 1:6

Being confident of this very thing, that he which hath begun a good _____ in you will perform it until the day of Jesus Christ.

265. Matthew 7:15

Beware of false _____, which come to you in sheep's clothing, but inwardly they are ravening wolves.

266. John 2:19

Jesus answered and said unto them, Destroy this _____, and in three days I will raise it up.

267. Exodus 20:8

Remember the _____ day, to keep it holy.

268. Hebrews 10:24

And let us consider one another to provoke unto _____ and to good works.

269. John 14:2

In my Father's _____ are many mansions: if it were not so, I would have told you. I go to prepare a place for you.

270. Galatians 6:7

Be not deceived; God is not _____: for whatsoever a man soweth, that shall he also reap.

271. Romans 6:4

Therefore we are buried with him by baptism into death: that like as Christ was raised up from the dead by the glory of the Father, even so we also should walk in newness of _____.

272. Matthew 5:7

Blessed are the _____: for they shall obtain mercy.

273. Galatians 5:19

Now the works of the flesh are manifest, which are these; _____, fornication, uncleanness, lasciviousness.

274. John 2:18

Then answered the _____ and said unto him, What sign shewest thou unto us, seeing that thou doest these things?

275. 1 Peter 1:3

Blessed be the God and Father of our Lord Jesus Christ, which according to his abundant _____ hath begotten us again unto a lively hope by the resurrection of Jesus Christ from the dead.

276. 1 Corinthians 13:4

Charity suffereth long, and is kind; charity envieth not; charity vaunteth not itself, is not _____ up.

277. John 6:35

And Jesus said unto them, I am the _____ of life: he that cometh to me shall never hunger; and he that believeth on me shall never thirst.

278. Acts 9:1

And Saul, yet breathing out threatenings and slaughter against the _____ of the Lord, went unto the high priest.

279. Jude 1:2

Mercy unto you, and peace, and love, be _____.

280. Ephesians 1:4

According as he hath chosen us in him before the foundation of the _____, that we should be holy and without blame before him in love.

281. John 21:15

So when they had dined, _____ saith to Simon Peter, Simon, son of Jonas, lovest thou me more than these? He saith unto him, Yea, Lord; thou knowest that I love thee. He saith unto him, Feed my lambs.

282. John 5:13

And he that was healed wist not who it was: for _____ had conveyed himself away, a multitude being in that place.

283. 2 Corinthians 6:14

Be ye not unequally yoked together with _____: for what fellowship hath righteousness with unrighteousness? and what communion hath light with darkness?

284. Matthew 6:25

Therefore I say unto you, Take no thought for your _____, what ye shall eat, or what ye shall drink; nor yet for your body, what ye shall put on. Is not the life more than meat, and the body than raiment?

285. Romans 1:6

Among whom are ye also the _____ of Jesus Christ.

286. Isaiah 53:4

Surely he hath borne our griefs, and carried our _____: yet we did esteem him stricken, smitten of God, and afflicted.

287. Ephesians 1:22

And hath put all things under his _____, and gave him to be the head over all things to the church.

288. Matthew 1:21
     And she shall bring forth a son, and thou shalt call his name
     Jesus: for he shall save his _____ from their sins.

289. 1 John 1:1
     That which was from the _____, which we have heard,
     which we have seen with our eyes, which we have looked
     upon, and our hands have handled, of the Word of life.

290. Ephesians 3:20
     Now unto him that is able to do exceeding abundantly above
     all that we ask or _____, according to the power that
     worketh in us.

291. Galatians 4:4
     But when the fulness of the time was come, God sent forth
     his Son, made of a woman, made under the _____.

292. Hebrews 12:2
     Looking unto _____ the author and finisher of our faith;
     who for the joy that was set before him endured the cross,
     despising the shame, and is set down at the right hand of
     the throne of God.

293. John 16:17
     Then said some of his disciples among themselves, What
     is this that he saith unto us, A little while, and ye shall not
     see me: and again, a little while, and ye shall see me: and,
     Because I go to the _____?

294. John 5:11
     He answered them, He that made me whole, the same said
     unto me, Take up thy bed, and _____.

295. Luke 4:1
     And Jesus being full of the Holy Ghost returned from Jordan,
     and was led by the Spirit into the _____.

296. Acts 2:22
     Ye men of Israel, hear these words; Jesus of Nazareth, a
     man approved of God among you by _____ and wonders
     and signs, which God did by him in the midst of you, as ye
     yourselves also know.

297. Luke 1:1

Forasmuch as _____ have taken in hand to set forth in order a declaration of those things which are most surely believed among us.

298. Romans 8:18

For I reckon that the sufferings of this present time are not worthy to be compared with the _____ which shall be revealed in us.

299. Acts 17:26

And hath made of one blood all _____ of men for to dwell on all the face of the earth, and hath determined the times before appointed, and the bounds of their habitation.

300. John 20:21

Then said Jesus to them again, _____ be unto you: as my Father hath sent me, even so send I you.

301. Matthew 5:3

Blessed are the poor in _____: for theirs is the kingdom of heaven.

302. Colossians 1:13

Who hath delivered us from the power of _____, and hath translated us into the kingdom of his dear Son.

303. Luke 10:1

After these things the LORD appointed other _____ also, and sent them two and two before his face into every city and place, whither he himself would come.

304. Luke 7:36

And one of the _____ desired him that he would eat with him. And he went into the Pharisee's house, and sat down to meat.

305. Luke 1:7

And they had no child, because that _____ was barren, and they both were now well stricken in years.

306. Isaiah 6:1

In the year that king _____ died I saw also the LORD sitting upon a throne, high and lifted up, and his train filled the temple.

307. Revelation 20:11

And I saw a great white _____, and him that sat on it, from whose face the earth and the heaven fled away; and there was found no place for them.

308. Romans 1:26

For this cause God gave them up unto vile affections: for even their women did change the natural use into that which is against _____.

309. Mark 1:15

And saying, The time is fulfilled, and the kingdom of God is at hand: _____ ye, and believe the gospel.

310. Leviticus 20:13

If a man also lie with mankind, as he lieth with a woman, both of them have committed an _____: they shall surely be put to death; their blood shall be upon them.

311. Ephesians 5:21

Submitting yourselves one to another in the fear of _____.

312. 1 Corinthians 6:19

What? know ye not that your body is the _____ of the Holy Ghost which is in you, which ye have of God, and ye are not your own?

313. Luke 19:10

For the Son of man is come to seek and to _____ that which was lost.

314. Matthew 28:20

_____ them to observe all things whatsoever I have commanded you: and, lo, I am with you always, even unto the end of the world.

315. Luke 24:1

Now upon the first day of the week, very early in the morning, they came unto the _____, bringing the spices which they had prepared, and certain others with them.

316. Hebrews 4:14

Seeing then that we have a great high _____, that is passed into the heavens, Jesus the Son of God, let us hold fast our profession.

317. 2 Chronicles 7:14

If my people, which are called by my _____, shall humble themselves, and pray, and seek my face, and turn from their wicked ways; then will I hear from heaven, and will forgive their sin, and will heal their land.

318. 1 John 3:2

Beloved, now are we the sons of _____, and it doth not yet appear what we shall be: but we know that, when he shall appear, we shall be like him; for we shall see him as he is.

319. 1 Corinthians 15:1

Moreover, brethren, I declare unto you the _____ which I preached unto you, which also ye have received, and wherein ye stand.

320. John 14:12

Verily, verily, I say unto you, He that believeth on me, the works that I do shall he do also; and greater works than these shall he do; because I go unto my _____.

321. Mark 1:14

Now after that John was put in _____, Jesus came into Galilee, preaching the gospel of the kingdom of God.

322. 2 Timothy 3:1

This know also, that in the last days perilous _____ shall come.

323. John 15:16

Ye have not chosen me, but I have chosen you, and ordained you, that ye should go and bring forth _____, and that your fruit should remain: that whatsoever ye shall ask of the Father in my name, he may give it you.

324. Exodus 20:3

Thou shalt have no other _____ before me.

325. Acts 2:37

Now when they heard this, they were pricked in their heart, and said unto _____ and to the rest of the apostles, Men and brethren, what shall we do?

326. Luke 23:34

Then said Jesus, Father, _____ them; for they know not what they do. And they parted his raiment, and cast lots.

327. Matthew 7:12

Therefore all things whatsoever ye would that _____ should do to you, do ye even so to them: for this is the law and the prophets.

328. Matthew 6:24

No man can serve two _____: for either he will hate the one, and love the other; or else he will hold to the one, and despise the other. Ye cannot serve God and mammon.

329. Matthew 6:1

Take heed that ye do not your alms before men, to be seen of them: otherwise ye have no reward of your Father which is in _____.

330. Mark 1:1

The beginning of the gospel of Jesus Christ, the _____ of God.

331. Jeremiah 31:31

Behold, the days come, saith the LORD, that I will make a new _____ with the house of Israel, and with the house of Judah.

332. James 5:6

     Ye have _____ and killed the just; and he doth not resist
     you.

333. Philippians 4:19

     But my God shall supply all your need according to his
     _____ in glory by Christ Jesus.

334. Matthew 18:20

     For where two or three are gathered together in my _____,
     there am I in the midst of them.

335. Daniel 9:24

     Seventy weeks are determined upon thy people and upon
     thy holy city, to finish the transgression, and to make an end
     of _____, and to make reconciliation for iniquity, and to
     bring in everlasting righteousness, and to seal up the vision
     and prophecy, and to anoint the most Holy.

336. James 4:6

     But he giveth more grace. Wherefore he saith, God resisteth
     the _____, but giveth grace unto the humble.

337. Mark 16:17

     And these signs shall follow them that believe; In my name
     shall they cast out devils; they shall speak with new _____.

338. Revelation 19:11

     And I saw _____ opened, and behold a white horse; and
     he that sat upon him was called Faithful and True, and in
     righteousness he doth judge and make war.

339. Psalm 19:1

     The heavens declare the glory of God; and the _____
     sheweth his handywork.

340. John 1:6

     There was a man sent from God, whose name was _____.

341. 1 Corinthians 10:13

     There hath no _____ taken you but such as is common
     to man: but God is faithful, who will not suffer you to be
     tempted above that ye are able; but will with the temptation
     also make a way to escape, that ye may be able to bear it.

342. Luke 6:27
But I say unto you which hear, Love your _____, do good to them which hate you.

343. Matthew 24:14
And this gospel of the kingdom shall be preached in all the world for a witness unto all nations; and then shall the _____ come.

344. Matthew 4:4
But he answered and said, It is _____, Man shall not live by bread alone, but by every word that proceedeth out of the mouth of God.

345. 2 Timothy 3:15
And that from a child thou hast known the holy scriptures, which are able to make thee _____ unto salvation through faith which is in Christ Jesus.

346. Acts 5:3
But Peter said, Ananias, why hath _____ filled thine heart to lie to the Holy Ghost, and to keep back part of the price of the land?

347. Matthew 5:38
Ye have heard that it hath been said, An eye for an eye, and a tooth for a _____.

348. Colossians 2:9
For in _____ dwelleth all the fulness of the Godhead bodily.

349. Colossians 2:8
Beware lest any man spoil you through philosophy and vain deceit, after the tradition of men, after the rudiments of the _____, and not after Christ.

350. Galatians 6:1
Brethren, if a man be overtaken in a fault, ye which are spiritual, restore such an one in the spirit of meekness; considering thyself, lest thou also be _____.

351. John 1:11
     He came unto his own, and his own _____ him not.

352. Hebrews 12:14
     Follow _____ with all men, and holiness, without which
     no man shall see the Lord.

353. John 3:19
     And this is the condemnation, that _____ is come into
     the world, and men loved darkness rather than light, because
     their deeds were evil.

354. Mark 12:30
     And thou shalt love the Lord thy God with all thy heart, and
     with all thy _____, and with all thy mind, and with all
     thy strength: this is the first commandment.

355. Daniel 9:27
     And he shall confirm the covenant with many for one week:
     and in the midst of the week he shall cause the sacrifice and
     the oblation to cease, and for the overspreading of _____
     he shall make it desolate, even until the consummation, and
     that determined shall be poured upon the desolate.

356. Ecclesiastes 3:1
     To every thing there is a _____, and a time to every pur-
     pose under the heaven.

357. Acts 2:17
     And it shall come to pass in the last days, saith God, I will
     pour out of my Spirit upon all flesh: and your sons and your
     daughters shall _____, and your young men shall see vi-
     sions, and your old men shall dream dreams.

358. Acts 1:4
     And, being assembled together with them, commanded them
     that they should not depart from _____, but wait for the
     promise of the Father, which, saith he, ye have heard of me.

359. Luke 1:10
     And the whole multitude of the people were praying without
     at the time of _____.

360. Philippians 2:6

Who, being in the form of God, thought it not robbery to be _____ with God.

361. Matthew 1:23

Behold, a _____ shall be with child, and shall bring forth a son, and they shall call his name Emmanuel, which being interpreted is, God with us.

362. Philippians 4:4

_____ in the Lord always: and again I say, Rejoice.

363. Luke 12:14

And he said unto him, Man, who made me a _____ or a divider over you?

364. Luke 6:38

Give, and it shall be given unto you; good measure, pressed down, and shaken together, and running over, shall men give into your _____. For with the same measure that ye mete withal it shall be measured to you again.

365. Romans 3:21

But now the righteousness of God without the _____ is manifested, being witnessed by the law and the prophets.

366. John 13:35

By this shall all men know that ye are my disciples, if ye have _____ one to another.

367. Romans 15:4

For whatsoever things were written aforetime were written for our learning, that we through patience and comfort of the _____ might have hope.

368. 1 John 4:8

He that loveth not knoweth not God; for God is _____.

369. 1 John 2:2

And he is the propitiation for our sins: and not for ours only, but also for the sins of the whole _____.

370. James 4:4

     Ye adulterers and adulteresses, know ye not that the friend-
     ship of the world is enmity with God? whosoever therefore
     will be a friend of the world is the _____ of God.

371. 1 Thessalonians 4:16

     For the Lord himself shall descend from heaven with a shout,
     with the voice of the archangel, and with the _____ of
     God: and the dead in Christ shall rise first.

372. 1 Corinthians 1:18

     For the preaching of the _____ is to them that perish fool-
     ishness; but unto us which are saved it is the power of God.

373. John 15:12

     This is my _____, That ye love one another, as I have
     loved you.

374. 2 Timothy 1:2

     To _____, my dearly beloved son: Grace, mercy, and peace,
     from God the Father and Christ Jesus our Lord.

375. 1 Corinthians 13:1

     Though I speak with the _____ of men and of angels,
     and have not charity, I am become as sounding brass, or a
     tinkling cymbal.

376. Job 1:6

     Now there was a day when the sons of God came to pres-
     ent themselves before the LORD, and _____ came also
     among them.

377. James 1:13

     Let no man say when he is _____, I am tempted of God:
     for God cannot be tempted with evil, neither tempteth he
     any man.

378. 1 Timothy 4:1

     Now the _____ speaketh expressly, that in the latter times
     some shall depart from the faith, giving heed to seducing
     spirits, and doctrines of devils.

379. Ephesians 2:19
Now therefore ye are no more strangers and foreigners, but fellowcitizens with the saints, and of the _____ of God.

380. Acts 13:1
Now there were in the church that was at _____ certain prophets and teachers; as Barnabas, and Simeon that was called Niger, and Lucius of Cyrene, and Manaen, which had been brought up with Herod the tetrarch, and Saul.

381. John 10:28
And I give unto them eternal life; and they shall never _____, neither shall any man pluck them out of my hand.

382. James 1:19
Wherefore, my beloved brethren, let every man be swift to hear, slow to speak, slow to _____.

383. Galatians 1:6
I marvel that ye are so soon removed from him that called you into the grace of _____ unto another gospel.

384. Acts 10:38
How God anointed Jesus of Nazareth with the Holy Ghost and with _____; who went about doing good, and healing all that were oppressed of the devil; for God was with him.

385. 2 Peter 1:3
According as his divine power hath given unto us all things that pertain unto life and _____, through the knowledge of him that hath called us to glory and virtue.

386. Hebrews 11:12
Therefore sprang there even of one, and him as good as _____, so many as the stars of the sky in multitude, and as the sand which is by the sea shore innumerable.

387. Acts 8:26
And the angel of the Lord spake unto _____, saying, Arise, and go toward the south unto the way that goeth down from Jerusalem unto Gaza, which is desert.

388. Luke 22:19

And he took _____, and gave thanks, and brake it, and gave unto them, saying, This is my body which is given for you: this do in remembrance of me.

389. Luke 5:1

And it came to pass, that, as the people pressed upon him to hear the _____ of God, he stood by the lake of Gennesaret.

390. Colossians 1:18

And he is the head of the body, the _____: who is the beginning, the firstborn from the dead; that in all things he might have the preeminence.

391. John 2:3

And when they wanted wine, the _____ of Jesus saith unto him, They have no wine.

392. 1 Corinthians 12:12

For as the body is one, and hath many members, and all the members of that one body, being many, are one body: so also is _____.

393. Acts 5:29

Then _____ and the other apostles answered and said, We ought to obey God rather than men.

394. Luke 13:3

I tell you, Nay: but, except ye _____, ye shall all likewise perish.

395. Matthew 25:41

Then shall he say also unto them on the left hand, Depart from me, ye cursed, into everlasting _____, prepared for the devil and his angels.

396. Matthew 1:1

The book of the generation of Jesus Christ, the son of _____, the son of Abraham.

397. John 17:21

That they all may be one; as thou, Father, art in me, and I in thee, that they also may be one in us: that the _____ may believe that thou hast sent me.

398. James 5:13

    Is any among you afflicted? let him _____. Is any merry? let him sing psalms.

399. James 1:12

    _____ is the man that endureth temptation: for when he is tried, he shall receive the crown of life, which the Lord hath promised to them that love him.

400. Romans 5:6

    For when we were yet without strength, in due time Christ died for the _____.

401. John 4:19

    The woman saith unto him, Sir, I perceive that thou art a

    _____.

402. 2 Timothy 1:7

    For God hath not given us the spirit of _____; but of power, and of love, and of a sound mind.

403. Matthew 25:14

    For the kingdom of heaven is as a man travelling into a far country, who called his own _____, and delivered unto them his goods.

404. James 2:19

    Thou believest that there is one _____; thou doest well: the devils also believe, and tremble.

405. Acts 1:6

    When they therefore were come together, they asked of him, saying, Lord, wilt thou at this time restore again the kingdom to _____?

406. Luke 18:9

    And he spake this parable unto certain which trusted in themselves that they were _____, and despised others.

407. Luke 13:10

    And he was teaching in one of the synagogues on the

    _____.

408. Isaiah 64:6

But we are all as an _____ thing, and all our righteous-nesses are as filthy rags; and we all do fade as a leaf; and our iniquities, like the wind, have taken us away.

409. Luke 6:7

And the scribes and Pharisees watched him, whether he would heal on the _____ day; that they might find an accusation against him.

410. Genesis 1:31

And God saw every thing that he had made, and, behold, it was very good. And the evening and the morning were the _____ day.

411. Acts 4:32

And the multitude of them that believed were of one heart and of one soul: neither said any of them that ought of the things which he _____ was his own; but they had all things common.

412. Acts 2:36

Therefore let all the house of Israel know assuredly, that God hath made the same _____, whom ye have crucified, both Lord and Christ.

413. Luke 24:44

And he said unto them, These are the words which I spake unto you, while I was yet with you, that all things must be fulfilled, which were written in the law of _____, and in the prophets, and in the psalms, concerning me.

414. Luke 1:12

And when Zacharias saw him, he was troubled, and _____ fell upon him.

415. Revelation 21:8

But the fearful, and _____, and the abominable, and mur-derers, and whoremongers, and sorcerers, and idolaters, and all liars, shall have their part in the lake which burneth with fire and brimstone: which is the second death.

416. 2 Peter 2:1
But there were false _____ also among the people, even as there shall be false teachers among you, who privily shall bring in damnable heresies, even denying the Lord that bought them, and bring upon themselves swift destruction.

417. James 1:7
For let not that man think that he shall _____ any thing of the Lord.

418. Hebrews 7:25
Wherefore he is able also to _____ them to the uttermost that come unto God by him, seeing he ever liveth to make intercession for them.

419. Mark 12:29
And Jesus answered him, The first of all the commandments is, Hear, O _____; The Lord our God is one Lord.

420. John 18:36
Jesus answered, My _____ is not of this world: if my kingdom were of this world, then would my servants fight, that I should not be delivered to the Jews: but now is my kingdom not from hence.

421. Psalm 1:1
_____ is the man that walketh not in the counsel of the ungodly, nor standeth in the way of sinners, nor sitteth in the seat of the scornful.

422. Romans 12:3
For I say, through the grace given unto me, to every man that is among you, not to think of himself more highly than he ought to think; but to think soberly, according as God hath dealt to every man the measure of _____.

423. John 15:7
If ye abide in me, and my words abide in you, ye shall _____ what ye will, and it shall be done unto you.

424. Mark 16:9

Now when Jesus was risen early the first day of the week, he appeared first to Mary Magdalene, out of whom he had cast _____ devils.

425. Matthew 28:1

In the end of the sabbath, as it began to dawn toward the first day of the week, came Mary Magdalene and the other _____ to see the sepulchre.

426. John 14:9

Jesus saith unto him, Have I been so long time with you, and yet hast thou not known me, Philip? he that hath seen me hath seen the Father; and how sayest thou then, Show us the _____?

427. John 4:18

For thou hast had _____ husbands; and he whom thou now hast is not thy husband: in that saidst thou truly.

428. Mark 10:45

For even the Son of man came not to be ministered unto, but to minister, and to give his life a _____ for many.

429. James 3:1

My brethren, be not many _____, knowing that we shall receive the greater condemnation.

430. Acts 5:1

But a certain man named _____, with Sapphira his wife, sold a possession.

431. John 6:8

One of his disciples, _____, Simon Peter's brother, saith unto him.

432. Leviticus 19:18

Thou shalt not avenge, nor bear any _____ against the children of thy people, but thou shalt love thy neighbour as thyself: I am the LORD.

433. **John 19:30**
    When Jesus therefore had received the vinegar, he said, It is finished: and he bowed his head, and gave up the _____.

434. **Mark 16:1**
    And when the sabbath was past, Mary Magdalene, and Mary the mother of James, and _____, had bought sweet spices, that they might come and anoint him.

435. **1 John 1:5**
    This then is the message which we have heard of him, and declare unto you, that God is _____, and in him is no darkness at all.

136. **Matthew 5:48**
    Be ye therefore _____, even as your Father which is in heaven is perfect.

437. **Philippians 3:20**
    For our conversation is in _____; from whence also we look for the Saviour, the Lord Jesus Christ.

438. **John 3:6**
    That which is born of the _____ is flesh; and that which is born of the Spirit is spirit.

439. **Matthew 10:34**
    Think not that I am come to send peace on earth: I came not to send peace, but a _____.

440. **Hosea 4:6**
    My people are destroyed for lack of knowledge: because thou hast rejected _____, I will also reject thee, that thou shalt be no priest to me: seeing thou hast forgotten the law of thy God, I will also forget thy children.

441. **Isaiah 53:6**
    All we like sheep have gone astray; we have turned every one to his own way; and the LORD hath laid on him the _____ of us all.

442. James 1:11

For the sun is no sooner risen with a burning heat, but it withereth the grass, and the flower thereof falleth, and the grace of the fashion of it perisheth: so also shall the _____ man fade away in his ways.

443. Acts 17:28

For in him we live, and move, and have our being; as certain also of your own poets have said, For we are also his

_____.

444. 1 Peter 4:10

As every man hath received the gift, even so minister the same one to another, as good _____ of the manifold grace of God.

445. 1 Peter 3:5

For after this manner in the old time the holy _____ also, who trusted in God, adorned themselves, being in subjection unto their own husbands.

446. 1 Thessalonians 2:3

For our exhortation was not of _____, nor of uncleanness, nor in guile.

447. Philippians 2:3

Let nothing be done through strife or vainglory; but in lowliness of _____ let each esteem other better than themselves.

448. Ephesians 6:1

Children, obey your _____ in the Lord: for this is right.

449. John 1:2

The same was in the _____, with God.

450. Isaiah 55:8

For my thoughts are not your _____, neither are your ways my ways, saith the LORD.

9

Did You Know?
(Set 3)

Here are more facts that amaze.

- The youngest book of the Old Testament is the book of Malachi, written approximately 400 BC.
- Delilah did not cut Samson's hair. She called someone else to do it (Judges 16:19).
- There is a city named Sin in the book of Ezekiel (30:15).
- Although ivory is mentioned thirteen times in the Bible, elephants, the source of the ivory, are not mentioned at all.
- The longest single sentence in the King James Bible features the genealogy of Jesus and spans sixteen verses from Luke 3:23 all the way through Luke 3:38.
- There are at least five women named Mary in the New Testament.
- An unidentified son of a prophet once told a man to strike him. The man refused to strike the prophet's son and was told that because he refused, he would be killed by a lion. He was indeed killed in a lion attack (1 Kings 20:35–36).

10

The Ten Plagues Inflicted on Egypt

To be Bible brilliant and not just Bible literate, you must have a thorough understanding of the ten plagues God inflicted on Egypt in Exodus 7:14–12:30. God sent the plagues as a warning that there is only one true God. The Egyptians worshiped a multitude of false gods, and the Lord used the plagues to prove that nothing worshiped in Egypt could save them from his demonstrative power.

This tutorial will explain the ten plagues and their order. This section concludes with seven fill-in-the-blank questions to test your knowledge of the ten plagues.

Plague 1: Water Turned into Blood

God turned water throughout Egypt into blood. Fish and river animals died, and the Nile River reeked. The account of the first plague is in Exodus 7:14–25.

Plague 2: Frogs

The Lord saturated the land of Egypt with an abundance of frogs. Later, in yet another display of his power, God supernaturally killed the frogs, filling Egypt with the stench of their death. The full account of the second plague is in Exodus 8:1–15.

Plague 3: Lice

God sent an infestation of the wingless, biting parasites known as lice. The infestation was so thick that, according to Exodus 8:17, "All the dust of the land became lice throughout all the land of Egypt." The full account is in Exodus 8:16–19.

Plague 4: Flies

God sent massive, intrusive swarms of flies upon Egypt. Flies covered the ground, harassed the people, and invaded all the Egyptian homes. To prove he was God alone and that this plague was only for Egyptians, no flies invaded Goshen, where God's people, the Israelites, lived. This account is in Exodus 8:20–32.

Plague 5: Death of Livestock

God killed Egypt's cattle, horses, donkeys, camels, oxen, and sheep during the fifth plague. No livestock of the Israelites died during this time. This plague is detailed in Exodus 9:1–7.

Plague 6: Boils

God sent the sixth plague to Egypt without any warning. The sixth plague resulted in festering boils on all the Egyptians and an incurable itch. The boils were so bad that Pharaoh's magicians could not stand before Moses. The account of this plague is in Exodus 9:8–12.

Plague 7: Hailstorm

God provided prior warning before unleashing the worst hailstorm in Egypt's existence. The entire account is in Exodus 9:13–34.

Plague 8: Locusts

God sent swarms of locusts into Egypt that were so dense the land became dark because of them. Yet no locusts intruded into Goshen, where the Israelites were safe from the infestation. The account is in Exodus 10:1–20.

Plague 9: Darkness

Darkness "which may be felt" covered Egypt for three days. The darkness was so intense that, according to Exodus 10:21–23, people could not see each other. The Israelites, however, enjoyed light as usual.

Plague 10: Death of All Firstborn

The firstborn of the Egyptian people and the firstborn of their beasts were slain in the tenth and final plague. All deaths occurred in a single night. To show a clear distinction between the Egyptians and God's beloved Israelites, the Lord said the Israelites' peace on that historically gruesome night would be so complete that not even an Israelite dog would bark at a person or animal. The account is in Exodus 11:1–8; 12:21–30.

In the following exercise, take your time and try to fill in the missing plagues in the lists. In each case, the list is in order. This will help you to learn not only the plagues but also the order in which they occurred. Give yourself 10 points for each of the twenty-eight blanks you fill in correctly.

1.
   1.
   2. Frogs
   3. Lice

2.
   4. Flies
   5.
   6. Boils

3.
   7. Hailstorm
   8. Locusts
   9.
   10. Death of all firstborn

4.
   1.
   2. Frogs
   3. Lice
   4.
   5.
   6. Boils
   7. Hailstorm
   8.
   9.
   10. Death of all firstborn

5.
   1. Water turned into blood
   2.
   3.
   4. Flies
   5. Death of livestock

   6.
   7.
   8. Locusts
   9. Darkness
   10. Death of all firstborn

6.
   1. Water turned into blood
   2.
   3.
   4.
   5. Death of livestock
   6.
   7.
   8. Locusts
   9.
   10. Death of all firstborn

You knew this was coming. Try to fill in each plague in the order in which it occurred.

7.
   1.
   2.
   3.
   4.
   5.
   6.
   7.
   8.
   9.
   10.

ALL ABOUT MONEY

In the following exercises that teach God's wisdom in money affairs, take the words under each Scripture passage and put them in the appropriate blanks. By studying which word goes into which blank, you will learn what God desires us to know about money. Give yourself 2 points for each passage you complete accurately.

Any repeats of passages throughout the various money topics are intentional.

11

Maintaining Budgets

1. Proverbs 6:6–8

   Go to the ant, thou _____; consider her ways, and be wise: Which having no _____, overseer, or ruler, Provideth her meat in the summer, and gathereth her food in the _____.

   guide   sluggard   harvest

2. Proverbs 21:5

   The _____ of the _____ tend only to plenteousness; but of every one that is _____ only to want.

   diligent   hasty   thoughts

3. Proverbs 22:3

   A prudent man _____ the evil, and _____ himself: but the _____ pass on, and are _____.

   punished   simple   foreseeth   hideth

4. Proverbs 24:3–4

   Through _____ is an house builded; and by understanding it is established: And by _____ shall the _____ be _____ with all precious and _____ riches.

   pleasant   wisdom   knowledge   chambers   filled

5. Proverbs 25:28

   He that hath no _____ over his own _____ is like a _____ that is broken down, and without _____.

   spirit   rule   walls   city

6. Proverbs 27:12 (This passage is nearly identical to the one in number 3, Proverbs 22:3. Their close proximity to each other in the Bible indicates that this is a vitally important idea.)
A _____ man foreseeth the _____, and hideth _____; but the simple _____ on, and are punished.

> evil   prudent   pass   himself

7. Proverbs 27:23
Be thou _____ to know the state of thy _____, and _____ well to thy _____.

> look   flocks   herds   diligent

8. Proverbs 27:26
The _____ are for thy _____, and the goats are the _____ of the _____.

> price   field   clothing   lambs

9. Luke 14:28–30
For which of you, intending to _____ a _____, sitteth not down first, and counteth the cost, whether he have sufficient to _____ it? Lest haply, after he hath laid the _____, and is not able to finish it, all that behold it begin to _____ him, Saying, This man began to build, and was not able to finish.

> finish   tower   build   foundation   mock

10. 1 Corinthians 16:2
Upon the first day of the _____ let every one of you _____ by him in store, as God hath _____ him, that there be no _____ when I come.

> prospered   week   gatherings   lay

12

Debt

1. Exodus 22:14

   And if a man _____ ought of his neighbour, and it be
   _____, or _____, the owner thereof being not with it,
   he shall surely make it _____.

   hurt   die   good   borrow

2. Deuteronomy 15:6

   For the LORD thy God blesseth thee, as he _____ thee:
   and thou shalt lend unto many _____, but thou shalt not
   _____; and thou shalt _____ over many nations, but
   they shall not reign over thee.

   reign   nations   promised   borrow

3. Deuteronomy 28:12

   The LORD shall open unto thee his good _____, the
   _____ to give the rain unto thy land in his _____,
   and to bless all the work of thine _____: and thou shalt
   lend unto many _____, and thou shalt not borrow.

   season   heaven   nations   hand   treasure

4. 2 Kings 4:7

   Then she came and told the man of _____. And he said,
   Go, sell the _____, and pay thy _____, and live thou
   and thy _____ of the rest.

   debt   children   oil   God

5. Psalm 37:21

The wicked borroweth, and _____ not again: but the _____ sheweth _____, and giveth.

payeth   righteous   mercy

6. Proverbs 22:7

The _____ ruleth over the _____, and the _____ is servant to the _____.

poor   lender   borrower   rich

7. Proverbs 22:26–27

Be not thou one of them that strike _____, or of them that are _____ for _____. If thou hast _____ to pay, why should he take away thy _____ from under thee?

sureties   bed   nothing   hands   debts

8. Ecclesiastes 5:5

_____ is it that thou shouldest not _____, than that thou shouldest vow and not _____.

pay   vow   better

9. Romans 13:8

Owe no _____ any thing, but to love one _____: for he that loveth another hath fulfilled the _____.

law   another   man

13

Wealth

1. Exodus 23:12
   Six days thou shalt do thy work, and on the _____ day thou shalt rest: that thine _____ and thine ass may rest, and the son of thy _____, and the _____, may be _____.

   <u>refreshed   handmaid   ox   stranger   seventh</u>

2. Proverbs 12:11
   He that tilleth his _____ shall be satisfied with _____: but he that followeth _____ persons is _____ of understanding.

   <u>vain   void   land   bread</u>

3. Proverbs 13:11
   _____ gotten by _____ shall be _____: but he that gathereth by labour shall _____.

   <u>increase   vanity   diminished   wealth</u>

4. Proverbs 14:15
   The _____ believeth every _____: but the prudent _____ looketh _____ to his going.

   <u>man   simple   word   well</u>

5. Proverbs 19:2

Also, that the soul be without _____, it is not _____;
and he that hasteth with his _____ _____.

feet   sinneth   knowledge   good

6. Proverbs 21:5

The _____ of the _____ _____ only to plenteousness; but of _____ one that is _____ only to want.

diligent   hasty   thoughts   tend   every

7. Proverbs 23:4

_____ not to be _____: cease from _____ own
_____.

rich   wisdom   thine   labour

8. Proverbs 28:19–20

He that tilleth his land shall have plenty of _____: but he
that followeth after _____ persons shall have _____
enough. A faithful man shall abound with blessings: but he
that maketh haste to be _____ shall not be _____.

innocent   poverty   vain   bread   rich

Did You Know?
(Set 4)

Here are more interesting facts from the Holy Scriptures.

- A ball is mentioned only once in the Bible. It occurs in Isaiah 22:18.
- When the Israelites wandered in the desert for forty years, God supernaturally prevented their clothes and sandals from wearing out (Deuteronomy 29:5).
- God actually sings (Zephaniah 3:17).
- When the dove released by Noah returned to the ark, it did not return with an olive branch. It was an olive leaf (Genesis 8:11).
- According to Matthew 22:15–16, the Pharisees had their own disciples.
- Abraham not only had a son with his wife, Sarah, but also had several sons with his concubine (Genesis 25:6).

Being Happy
with What You Have

1. Psalm 23:1
   The _____ is my _____; I shall not _____.

2. Ecclesiastes 5:10
   He that loveth _____ shall not be satisfied with silver; nor
   he that loveth _____ with _____: this is also _____.

3. Matthew 6:31–33
   Therefore take no _____, saying, What shall we eat?
   or, What shall we _____? or, Wherewithal shall we be
   _____? (For after all these things do the _____ seek:)
   for your heavenly Father knoweth that ye have need of all
   these things. But seek ye first the kingdom of God, and his
   _____; and all these things shall be added unto you.

4. Luke 3:14
   And the _____ likewise demanded of him, saying, And
   what shall we do? And he said unto them, Do _____ to
   no man, neither accuse any _____; and be content with
   your _____.

5. Philippians 4:11–13

Not that I speak in respect of want: for I have learned, in whatsoever _____ I am, therewith to be _____. I know both how to be abased, and I know how to abound: every where and in all things I am _____ both to be full and to be _____, both to abound and to suffer need. I can do all things through _____ which strengtheneth me.

content   hungry   state   instructed   Christ

6. 1 Thessalonians 4:11

And that ye study to be _____, and to do your own _____, and to work with your own _____, as we _____ you.

quiet   business   commanded   hands

7. 1 Timothy 6:6

But _____ with _____ is great _____.

gain   godliness   contentment

8. 1 Timothy 6:7–10

For we brought nothing into this world, and it is certain we can carry nothing out. And having food and _____ let us be therewith content. But they that will be rich fall into temptation and a snare, and into many _____ and hurtful _____, which drown men in _____ and perdition. For the love of money is the root of all evil: which while some coveted after, they have erred from the _____, and pierced themselves through with many _____.

faith   raiment   lusts   foolish   destruction   sorrows

9. Hebrews 13:5

Let your _____ be without covetousness; and be content with such things as ye have: for he hath said, I will _____ leave thee, nor _____ thee.

forsake   conversation   never

10. James 4:1–3

From whence come _____ and fightings among you? come they not hence, even of your lusts that _____ in your _____? Ye lust, and have not: ye kill, and desire to have, and cannot obtain: ye fight and war, yet ye have not, because ye ask not. Ye _____, and receive not, because ye ask amiss, that ye may _____ it upon your lusts.

consume   ask   members   wars   war

16

Giving and Being Generous

1. Deuteronomy 15:10
   Thou shalt surely give him, and thine _____ shall not
   be grieved when thou givest unto him: because that for this
   thing the _____ thy God shall _____ thee in all thy
   _____, and in all that thou puttest thine _____ unto.

   hand   bless   works   heart   Lord

2. Deuteronomy 16:17
   Every _____ shall give as he is able, according to the
   _____ of the Lord thy _____ which he hath given
   _____.

   thee   man   God   blessing

3. 1 Chronicles 29:9
   Then the _____ rejoiced, for that they offered willingly,
   because with perfect _____ they offered willingly to the
   _____: and _____ the _____ also rejoiced with
   great joy.

   Lord   David   people   heart   king

4. Proverbs 3:9–10
   Honour the Lord with thy _____, and with the _____
   of all thine increase: So shall thy _____ be filled with
   plenty, and thy _____ shall burst out with new _____.

   presses   firstfruits   wine   substance   barns

5. Proverbs 3:27

Withhold not _____ from them to whom it is _____, when it is in the _____ of thine _____ to do it.

> hand   power   good   due

6. Proverbs 11:24–25

There is that _____, and yet _____; and there is that withholdeth more than is meet, but it tendeth to poverty. The liberal _____ shall be made _____: and he that watereth shall be _____ also himself.

> increaseth   fat   scattereth   soul   watered

7. Proverbs 21:26

He _____ _____ all the _____ long: but the righteous giveth and _____ not.

> day   coveteth   spareth   greedily

8. Proverbs 22:9

He that hath a bountiful _____ shall be _____; for he giveth of his _____ to the _____.

> bread   poor   eye   blessed

9. Proverbs 28:27

He that giveth unto the _____ shall not _____: but he that hideth his _____ shall have many a _____.

> lack   eyes   curse   poor

10. Malachi 3:10

Bring ye all the tithes into the _____, that there may be meat in mine house, and prove me now herewith, saith the _____ of _____, if I will not open you the windows of heaven, and pour you out a _____, that there shall not be _____ enough to receive it.

> blessing   storehouse   hosts   room   LORD

11. Matthew 6:3–4

But when thou doest _____, let not thy left _____ know what thy right hand doeth: That thine alms may be in _____: and thy _____ which seeth in secret himself shall reward _____ openly.

> secret   alms   Father   thee   hand

12. Mark 12:41–44

And Jesus sat over against the _____, and beheld how the people _____ money into the treasury: and many that were rich cast in much. And there came a certain poor widow, and she threw in two mites, which make a farthing. And he called unto him his disciples, and saith unto them, Verily I say unto you, That this poor widow hath cast more in, than all they which have cast into the treasury: For all they did cast in of their _____; but she of her want did cast in all that she had, even all her _____.

cast   living   treasury   abundance

13. Luke 3:11

He _____ and saith unto them, He that hath two _____, let him _____ to him that hath _____; and he that hath _____, let him do likewise.

meat   coats   impart   answereth   none

14. Luke 6:30

Give to every _____ that asketh of _____; and of him that taketh away thy _____ ask them not again.

thee   man   goods

15. Luke 6:38

Give, and it shall be given unto you; good measure, pressed down, and _____ together, and _____ over, shall men give into your _____. For with the same measure that ye mete withal it shall be _____ to you again.

measured   shaken   running   bosom

16. Acts 20:35

I have shewed you all _____, how that so _____ ye ought to support the weak, and to remember the words of the Lord _____, how he said, It is more _____ to give than to receive.

labouring   blessed   Jesus   things

17. Romans 12:8

Or he that exhorteth, on _____: he that giveth, let him do it with _____; he that ruleth, with _____; he that sheweth mercy, with _____.

diligence   cheerfulness   exhortation   simplicity

18. 2 Corinthians 9:6–8

But this I say, He which _____ sparingly shall reap also sparingly; and he which soweth bountifully shall reap also bountifully. Every man according as he purposeth in his _____, so let him give; not _____, or of necessity: for God loveth a cheerful giver. And God is able to make all grace _____ toward you; that ye, always having all _____ in all things, may abound to every good _____.

grudgingly   heart   soweth   abound   work   sufficiency

19. 2 Corinthians 9:10

Now he that ministereth _____ to the sower both minister _____ for your _____, and multiply your seed sown, and increase the _____ of your righteousness.

fruits   seed   food   bread

20. Galatians 6:7

Be not deceived; _____ is not _____: for whatsoever a man _____, that shall he also _____.

reap   God   mocked   soweth

21. Philippians 4:15–17

Now ye Philippians know also, that in the beginning of the _____, when I departed from Macedonia, no _____ communicated with me as concerning giving and receiving, but ye only. For even in Thessalonica ye sent once and again unto my _____. Not because I desire a gift: but I desire _____ that may _____ to your _____.

account   church   necessity   abound   fruit   gospel

22. James 2:15–16

If a brother or _____ be naked, and destitute of daily _____, And one of you say unto them, Depart in peace, be ye warmed and _____; notwithstanding ye give them not those things which are needful to the _____; what doth it _____?

filled   body   sister   food   profit

17

Receiving

Note that there are far more passages on giving than on receiving.

1. Ecclesiastes 5:19
   Every man also to whom _____ hath given riches and wealth, and hath given him power to eat thereof, and to take his _____, and to rejoice in his _____; this is the _____ of God.

   labour   God   gift   portion

2. John 3:27
   _____ answered and said, A _____ can receive _____, except it be given him from _____.

   man   John   heaven   nothing

3. Acts 20:35
   I have shewed you all things, how that so _____ ye ought to support the _____, and to remember the _____ of the Lord Jesus, how he said, It is more _____ to give than to receive.

   words   blessed   labouring   weak

4. 1 Corinthians 9:10–11
   Or saith he it altogether for our sakes? For our sakes, no doubt, this is _____: that he that _____ should plow in hope; and that he that _____ in hope should be partaker

of his hope. If we have sown unto you spiritual _____, is it a great thing if we shall reap your _____ things?

written   thresheth   things   ploweth   carnal

5. 1 Timothy 5:18

For the _____ saith, thou shalt not _____ the _____ that treadeth out the corn. And, The _____ is worthy of his _____.

labourer   reward   muzzle   scripture   ox

Running a Business

1. Leviticus 19:13

   _____ shalt not defraud thy _____, neither rob him: the _____ of him that is hired shall not abide with _____ all night until the _____.

   > neighbour   thou   wages   morning   thee

2. Deuteronomy 25:13–15

   Thou shalt not have in thy _____ divers weights, a great and a small. Thou shalt not have in thine house divers measures, a great and a small. But thou shalt have a _____ and just _____, a perfect and just _____ shalt thou have: that thy days may be lengthened in the land which the LORD thy _____ giveth thee.

   > measure   bag   weight   God   perfect

3. Job 31:13–14

   If I did despise the cause of my _____ or of my maidservant, when they contended with me; What then shall I do when God _____ up? and when he _____, what shall I answer him?

   > riseth   visiteth   manservant

4. Psalm 112:5

   A good man sheweth _____, and _____: he will guide his _____ with _____.

   > affairs   favour   discretion   lendeth

5. Proverbs 10:4

He becometh _____ that _____ with a slack _____:
but the hand of the _____ maketh rich.

dealeth   diligent   poor   hand

6. Proverbs 11:1

A false _____ is _____ to the _____: but a just
weight is his _____.

delight   abomination   LORD   balance

7. Proverbs 13:4

The _____ of the _____ desireth, and hath _____:
but the soul of the diligent shall be made _____.

sluggard   soul   fat   nothing

8. Proverbs 13:11

_____ gotten by _____ shall be diminished: but he
that gathereth by _____ shall _____

labour   vanity   wealth   increase

9. Proverbs 16:8

_____ is a little with _____ than great _____ without _____.

revenues   right   righteousness   better

10. Proverbs 22:16

He that _____ the _____ to increase his _____, and
he that giveth to the _____, shall surely come to want.

riches   oppresseth   rich   poor

11. Jeremiah 22:13

Woe unto him that _____ his house by unrighteousness,
and his chambers by wrong; that useth his neighbour's
_____ without _____, and giveth him not for his
_____.

wages   work   buildeth   service

12. Malachi 3:5

    And I will come near to you to judgment; and I will be a swift witness against the sorcerers, and against the _____, and against false _____, and against those that oppress the _____ in his wages, the widow, and the fatherless, and that turn aside the stranger from his right, and _____ not me, saith the LORD of _____.

    hosts   fear   adulterers   hireling   swearers

13. Luke 16:10

    He that is faithful in that which is _____ is _____ also in much: and he that is _____ in the least is unjust also in _____.

    faithful   unjust   much   least

14. Ephesians 6:9

    And, ye masters, do the same _____ unto them, forbearing threatening: knowing that your _____ also is in _____; neither is there respect of _____ with him.

    heaven   Master   persons   things

15. Colossians 4:1

    _____, give unto your _____ that which is just and equal; knowing that ye also have a _____ in _____.

    servants   heaven   Master   masters

16. James 5:4

    Behold, the hire of the _____ who have reaped down your _____, which is of you kept back by _____, crieth: and the _____ of them which have reaped are entered into the ears of the _____ of sabaoth.

    cries   labourers   Lord   fields   fraud

19

Investing

1. Proverbs 13:11
   _____ gotten by _____ shall be _____: but he that gathereth by _____ shall increase.

   > diminished   vanity   labour   wealth

2. Proverbs 15:22
   Without _____ _____ are disappointed: but in the _____ of counsellors they are _____.

   > multitude   counsel   established   purposes

3. Proverbs 19:2
   Also, that the _____ be without _____, it is not _____; and he that hasteth with his feet _____.

   > good   knowledge   soul   sinneth

4. Proverbs 24:27
   Prepare thy _____ without, and make it fit for thyself in the _____; and afterwards _____ thine _____.

   > house   field   work   build

5. Proverbs 28:20
   A faithful _____ shall abound with _____: but he that maketh _____ to be _____ shall not be _____.

   > blessings   rich   man   haste   innocent

6. Ecclesiastes 11:2

Give a portion to _____, and also to eight; for _____ knowest not what _____ shall be upon the _____.

evil · earth   seven   thou

God's Provisions

1. 1 Kings 17:13–16

   And Elijah said unto her, Fear not; go and do as thou hast said: but make me thereof a little cake first, and bring it unto me, and after make for thee and for thy _____ . For thus saith the Lord God of _____, The barrel of meal shall not waste, neither shall the cruse of oil fail, until the day that the Lord sendeth rain upon the earth. And she went and did according to the saying of _____: and she, and he, and her _____, did eat many days. And the barrel of _____ wasted not, neither did the cruse of oil fail, according to the word of the Lord, which he spake by Elijah.

   > meal   house   Elijah   Israel   son

2. Nehemiah 6:9

   For they all made us _____, saying, Their _____ shall be _____ from the work, that it be not done. Now _____, O God, strengthen my hands.

   > therefore   afraid   hands   weakened

3. Psalm 37:25

   I have been _____, and now am _____; yet have I not seen the righteous forsaken, nor his _____ begging _____.

   > old   bread   young   seed

4. Matthew 6:31–32

Therefore take no thought, saying, What shall we eat? or, What shall we drink? or, Wherewithal shall we be _____? (For after all these things do the _____ seek:) for your heavenly _____ knoweth that ye have need of all these _____.

Father   things   Gentiles   clothed

5. Matthew 7:11

If ye then, being _____, know how to give good gifts unto your _____, how much more shall your _____ which is in _____ give good things to them that ask him?

heaven   evil   children   Father

6. Luke 12:7

But even the very _____ of your _____ are all _____. Fear not therefore: ye are of more _____ than many _____.

value   sparrows   head   hairs   numbered

7. John 21:6

And he said unto them, _____ the _____ on the _____ side of the _____, and ye shall find. They cast therefore, and now they were not able to draw it for the multitude of _____.

net   ship   fishes   cast   right

8. 2 Corinthians 9:8

And God is able to make all _____ abound toward you; that ye, always having _____ _____ in all things, may _____ to every good _____.

all   abound   work   grace   sufficiency

9. Philippians 4:19

But my _____ shall supply all your need according to his _____ in _____ by Christ _____.

Jesus   God   riches   glory

21

Lending

1. Exodus 22:25

   If thou lend _____ to any of my _____ that is poor by thee, _____ shalt not be to him as an usurer, neither shalt thou lay upon him _____.

   > people   usury   money   thou

2. Leviticus 25:35–37

   And if thy brother be _____ poor, and fallen in _____ with thee; then thou shalt relieve him: yea, though he be a stranger, or a _____; that he may live with thee. Take thou no usury of him, or increase: but fear thy God; that thy _____ may live with thee. Thou shalt not give him thy _____ upon usury, nor lend him thy _____ for increase.

   > sojourner   waxen   decay   victuals   money   brother

3. Deuteronomy 15:8

   But thou shalt open thine _____ wide unto him, and shalt surely lend him _____ for his _____, in that which he _____.

   > need   hand   wanteth   sufficient

4. Deuteronomy 23:19–20

Thou shalt not _____ upon usury to thy _____; usury of money, usury of victuals, usury of any thing that is lent upon usury: Unto a _____ thou mayest lend upon usury; but unto thy brother thou shalt not lend upon usury: that the LORD thy _____ may _____ thee in all that thou settest thine _____ to in the land whither thou goest to possess it.

> stranger   God   bless   brother   lend   hand

5. Deuteronomy 24:10

When thou dost _____ thy _____ any thing, thou shalt not go into his _____ to fetch his _____.

> pledge   house   brother   lend

6. Psalm 15:5

He that putteth not out his _____ to _____, nor taketh reward against the _____. He that doeth these _____ shall never be _____.

> things   moved   usury   money   innocent

7. Psalm 37:26

_____ is ever _____, and lendeth; and his _____ is _____.

> merciful   seed   blessed   he

8. Psalm 112:5

A good _____ _____ favour, and _____: he will guide his affairs with _____.

> lendeth   discretion   sheweth   man

9. Proverbs 3:27–28

Withhold not good from them to whom it is due, when it is in the _____ of thine _____ to do it. Say not unto thy _____, Go, and come again, and to morrow I will give; when thou hast it by _____.

> neighbour   power   thee   hand

10. Proverbs 28:8

He that by _____ and unjust gain _____ his _____,
he shall gather it for him that will pity the _____.

> poor   increaseth   substance   usury

11. Matthew 5:42

Give to him that _____ _____, and from him that
would _____ of thee turn not _____ away.

> thou   asketh   borrow   thee

12. Luke 6:35

But love ye your _____, and do good, and lend, hoping
for _____ again; and your reward shall be _____, and
ye shall be the _____ of the _____: for he is kind unto
the unthankful and to the _____.

> Highest   children   evil   enemies   great   nothing

22

Planning for the Future

1. Genesis 41:34–36

   Let _____ do this, and let him appoint officers over the land, and take up the fifth part of the land of _____ in the seven plenteous _____. And let them gather all the food of those good years that come, and lay up corn under the _____ of Pharaoh, and let them keep food in the _____. And that food shall be for store to the land against the seven years of _____, which shall be in the land of Egypt; that the land perish not through the famine.

   Egypt   famine   years   Pharaoh   hand   cities

2. Proverbs 1:1

   The _____ of _____ the son of _____, king of _____.

   Israel   Solomon   David   proverbs

3. Proverbs 13:16

   _____ _____ _____ dealeth with knowledge: but a _____ layeth open his _____.

   fool   folly   man   every   prudent

4. Proverbs 13:19

   The desire _____ is _____ to the _____: but it is abomination to _____ to depart from _____.

   accomplished   soul   sweet   evil   fools

5. Proverbs 15:22

Without _____ purposes are _____: but in the multitude of _____ they are _____.

disappointed   counsel   established   counsellors

6. Proverbs 16:1

The preparations of the _____ in _____, and the
_____ of the _____, is from the _____.

tongue   LORD   man   heart   answer

7. Proverbs 16:9

A man's _____ deviseth his _____: but the _____
directeth his _____.

LORD   steps   heart   way

8. Proverbs 20:18

Every _____ is established by _____: and with good
_____ make _____.

advice   war   counsel   purpose

9. Proverbs 22:3

A prudent _____ foreseeth the _____, and hideth himself: but the _____ _____ on, and are _____.

pass   evil   man   simple   punished

10. Proverbs 24:3–4

Through wisdom is an _____ builded; and by understanding it is established: And by _____ shall the _____
be filled with all precious and _____ _____.

house   riches   pleasant   knowledge   chambers

11. Proverbs 24:27

Prepare _____ work without, and make it _____ for
thyself in the _____; and afterwards build thine _____.

field   house   thy   fit

12. Proverbs 27:23

Be _____ diligent to know the _____ of thy _____,
and look well to thy _____.

herds   flocks   state   thou

13. Ecclesiastes 10:2

A _____ man's _____ is at his right _____; but a _____ heart at his _____.

left   wise   heart   hand   fool's

14. Luke 12:16–21

And he spake a _____ unto them, saying, The ground of a certain rich man brought forth plentifully: And he thought within himself, saying, What shall I do, because I have no room where to bestow my fruits? And he said, This will I do: I will pull down my barns, and build greater; and there will I bestow all my _____ and my goods. And I will say to my soul, _____, thou hast much goods laid up for many years; take thine ease, eat, drink, and be merry. But God said unto him, Thou fool, this night thy soul shall be required of thee: then whose shall those things be, which thou hast _____? So is he that layeth up _____ for himself, and is not _____ toward God.

fruits   rich   provided   parable   Soul   treasure

15. Luke 14:28–30

For which of you, intending to build a _____, sitteth not down first, and counteth the cost, whether he have sufficient to finish it? Lest haply, after he hath laid the _____, and is not able to finish it, all that behold it begin to _____ him, Saying, This man began to build, and was not able to _____.

mock   finish   tower   foundation

16. 1 Corinthians 16:1–2

Now concerning the _____ for the _____, as I have given order to the _____ of Galatia, even so do ye. Upon the first day of the _____ let every one of you lay by him

in store, as God hath _____ him, that there be no gatherings when I come.

prospered   churches   collection   saints   week

17. 1 Timothy 6:7
For we brought _____ into this _____, and it is
_____ we can carry nothing _____.

nothing   world   out   certain

23

The Love of Money

1. Mark 4:19

   And the cares of this _____, and the deceitfulness of _____, and the _____ of other things entering in, _____ the word, and it becometh _____.

   unfruitful   world   lusts   riches   choke

2. Mark 8:36

   For what shall it _____ a man, if he shall gain the whole _____, and _____ his own _____?

   soul   profit   world   lose

3. 1 Timothy 6:9–11

   But they that will be rich fall into _____ and a snare, and into many foolish and hurtful _____, which drown men in _____ and perdition. For the love of money is the root of all evil: which while some coveted after, they have erred from the faith, and pierced themselves through with many sorrows. But thou, O man of God, flee these things; and follow after _____, godliness, faith, love, _____, _____.

   destruction   temptation   righteousness   lusts   meekness   patience

24

Being Truly Prosperous

1. Genesis 26:12

   Then Isaac sowed in that _____, and received in the same _____ an _____: and the LORD _____ him.

   land   year   blessed   hundredfold

2. Genesis 39:3

   And his _____ saw that the LORD was with him, and that the _____ made all that he did to _____ in his _____.

   LORD   hand   master   prosper

3. Deuteronomy 8:18

   But thou shalt _____ the LORD thy God: for it is he that giveth thee _____ to get _____, that he may establish his _____ which he sware unto thy _____, as it is this day.

   fathers   wealth   power   remember   covenant

4. Deuteronomy 15:10

   _____ shalt surely give him, and thine heart shall not be _____ when thou givest unto him: because that for this thing the LORD thy God shall _____ thee in all thy _____, and in all that thou puttest thine _____ unto.

   bless   works   grieved   thou   hand

5. Deuteronomy 24:19

When thou cuttest down thine _____ in thy field, and hast forgot a _____ in the field, thou shalt not go again to _____ it: it shall be for the stranger, for the fatherless, and for the widow: that the _____ thy God may bless thee in all the _____ of thine hands.

> harvest   work   fetch   LORD   sheaf

6. Deuteronomy 30:8–10

And thou shalt return and obey the voice of the LORD, and do all his commandments which I command thee this day. And the LORD thy God will make thee plenteous in every _____ of thine hand, in the fruit of thy body, and in the fruit of thy _____, and in the fruit of thy land, for good: for the LORD will again rejoice over thee for good, as he rejoiced over thy _____: If thou shalt hearken unto the _____ of the LORD thy God, to keep his _____ and his statutes which are written in this book of the law, and if thou turn unto the LORD thy God with all thine heart, and with all thy _____.

> commandments   soul   cattle   work   voice   fathers

7. Joshua 1:8

This book of the law shall not depart out of thy _____; but thou shalt meditate therein day and _____, that thou mayest observe to do according to all that is _____ therein: for then thou shalt make thy way prosperous, and then thou shalt have good _____.

> written   success   mouth   night

8. 1 Chronicles 22:12

Only the _____ give thee wisdom and understanding, and give thee _____ concerning Israel, that thou mayest keep the _____ of the LORD thy _____.

> law   God   LORD   charge

9. 2 Chronicles 31:20

And thus did _____ throughout all _____, and wrought that which was good and right and truth before the _____ his _____.

Judah   Lord   God   Hezekiah

10. Psalm 1:1–3

Blessed is the man that walketh not in the counsel of the _____, nor standeth in the way of sinners, nor sitteth in the seat of the _____. But his delight is in the law of the Lord; and in his law doth he meditate day and night. And he shall be like a _____ planted by the rivers of _____, that bringeth forth his fruit in his season; his leaf also shall not wither; and whatsoever he doeth shall _____.

ungodly   tree   prosper   water   scornful

11. Psalm 35:27

Let them shout for joy, and be glad, that favour my _____ cause: yea, let them say continually, Let the Lord be _____, which hath pleasure in the _____ of his _____.

servant   magnified   righteous   prosperity

12. Jeremiah 17:8

For he shall be as a _____ planted by the _____, and that spreadeth out her roots by the _____, and shall not see when heat cometh, but her leaf shall be _____; and shall not be careful in the year of _____, neither shall cease from yielding fruit.

green   drought   waters   tree   river

13. Malachi 3:10

Bring ye all the _____ into the storehouse, that there may be meat in mine _____, and prove me now herewith, saith the _____ of _____, if I will not open you the windows of _____, and pour you out a _____, that there shall not be room enough to receive it.

blessing   Lord   hosts   house   tithes   heaven

14. 3 John 1:2

_____, I wish above all things that thou mayest _____
and be in _____, even as thy _____ prospereth.

prosper   health   soul   beloved

25

Being a Good Steward over One's Money

1. Genesis 2:15

   And the LORD God _____ the _____, and put him
   into the _____ of _____ to dress it and to _____ it.

   > Eden   garden   man   keep   took

2. Deuteronomy 10:14

   _____, the _____ and the heaven of _____ is the
   LORD's thy God, the _____ also, with all that therein is.

   > heavens   earth   heaven   behold

3. Luke 12:42–44

   And the Lord said, Who then is that faithful and wise _____,
   whom his lord shall make _____ over his _____, to give
   them their portion of _____ in due season? Blessed is that
   _____, whom his lord when he cometh shall find so doing.
   Of a truth I say unto you, that he will make him ruler over
   all that he hath.

   > steward   ruler   household   meat   servant

4. Luke 12:47–48

And that _____, which knew his lord's will, and prepared not himself, neither did according to his will, shall
be beaten with many stripes. But he that knew not, and did
commit things worthy of _____, shall be _____ with
few stripes. For unto _____ much is given, of him shall
be much required: and to whom men have _____ much,
of him they will ask the more.

committed   stripes   servant   whomsoever   beaten

5. Luke 16:9–11

And I say unto you, Make to yourselves _____ of the
mammon of unrighteousness; that, when ye fail, they may
receive you into everlasting habitations. He that is faithful
in that which is least is _____ also in much: and he that
is _____ in the least is unjust also in much. If therefore
ye have not been faithful in the unrighteous _____, who
will commit to your trust the true _____?

unjust   mammon   faithful   friends   riches

6. Romans 14:8

For whether we live, we live unto the Lord; and whether we
_____, we die unto the _____: whether we _____
therefore, or die, we are the _____.

Lord's   die   live   Lord

26

Saving

1. Proverbs 21:5

   The _____ of the diligent _____ only to plenteousness; but of every one that is _____ only to _____.

   hasty   thoughts   tend   want

2. Proverbs 21:20

   There is _____ to be desired and _____ in the dwelling of the _____; but a foolish man _____ it up.

   oil   treasure   wise   spendeth

3. Proverbs 27:12

   A _____ man foreseeth the _____, and hideth himself; but the _____ pass on, and are _____.

   evil   prudent   punished   simple

4. Proverbs 30:25

   The ants are a _____ not strong, yet they prepare their meat in the _____.

   summer   people

5. 1 Corinthians 16:2

   Upon the first _____ of the _____ let every one of you lay by him in store, as _____ hath prospered him, that there be no _____ when I come.

   God   week   day   gatherings

27

Tithing

1. Genesis 14:20
   And blessed be the most high _____, which hath delivered _____ enemies into thy _____. And he gave him _____ of all.

   > thine   tithes   God   hand

2. Genesis 28:20–22
   And _____ vowed a vow, saying, If God will be with me, and will keep me in this way that I go, and will give me _____ to eat, and raiment to put on, So that I come again to my father's _____ in peace; then shall the LORD be my God: And this stone, which I have set for a _____, shall be God's house: and of all that thou shalt give me I will surely give the _____ unto thee.

   > house   tenth   bread   Jacob   pillar

3. Exodus 23:19
   The first of the _____ of thy _____ thou shalt bring into the _____ of the LORD thy God. Thou shalt not seethe a _____ in his mother's _____.

   > milk   land   firstfruits   house   kid

4. Leviticus 27:30

And all the _____ of the _____, whether of the _____ of the land, or of the fruit of the tree, is the LORD's: it is holy unto the _____.

land   seed   LORD   tithe

5. Numbers 18:26

Thus speak unto the _____, and say unto them, When ye take of the children of _____ the tithes which I have given you from them for your _____, then ye shall offer up an heave offering of it for the LORD, even a tenth part of the _____.

tithe   Levites   Israel   inheritance

6. Deuteronomy 14:22–23

Thou shalt truly _____ all the increase of thy seed, that the field bringeth forth _____ by year. And thou shalt eat before the LORD thy God, in the place which he shall choose to place his _____ there, the tithe of thy _____, of thy wine, and of thine oil, and the _____ of thy herds and of thy _____; that thou mayest learn to fear the LORD thy God always.

year   tithe   flocks   firstlings   corn   name

7. Deuteronomy 14:28

At the end of _____ _____ thou shalt bring forth all the tithe of thine _____ the same _____, and shalt lay it up within thy _____.

increase   three   years   gates   year

8. Deuteronomy 26:12

When thou hast made an end of _____ all the tithes of thine increase the third year, which is the year of tithing, and hast given it unto the _____, the _____, the _____, and the _____, that they may eat within thy gates, and be filled.

widow   stranger   fatherless   Levite   tithing

9. 2 Chronicles 31:5
   And as soon as the _____ came abroad, the children
   of _____ brought in abundance the firstfruits of corn,
   _____, and oil, and honey, and of all the increase of the
   field; and the _____ of all things brought they in _____.

   abundantly   tithe   commandment   Israel   wine

10. Nehemiah 10:38
    And the priest the son of _____ shall be with the _____,
    when the Levites take _____: and the Levites shall bring
    up the tithe of the tithes unto the _____ of our God, to
    the chambers, into the _____ house.

    treasure   Aaron   Levites   house   tithes

11. Proverbs 3:9–10
    Honour the _____ with thy substance, and with the first-
    fruits of all thine increase: So shall thy _____ be filled with
    _____, and thy presses shall burst out with new _____.

    plenty   LORD   wine   barns

12. Ezekiel 44:30
    And the first of all the _____ of all things, and every
    oblation of all, of every sort of your oblations, shall be the
    priest's: ye shall also give unto the _____ the first of your
    _____, that he may cause the _____ to rest in thine
    house.

    priest   dough   firstfruits   blessing

13. Amos 4:4
    Come to _____, and transgress; at Gilgal multiply _____;
    and bring your _____ every morning, and your _____
    after three years.

    transgression   sacrifices   Bethel   tithes

14. Malachi 3:8
    Will a man _____ God? Yet ye have _____ me. But
    ye say, Wherein have we robbed _____? In _____ and
    _____.

    robbed   rob   offerings   tithes   thee

15. Matthew 23:23

Woe unto you, scribes and _____, hypocrites! for ye pay tithe of mint and anise and _____, and have omitted the _____ matters of the law, _____, mercy, and faith: these ought ye to have done, and not to leave the other _____.

cummin   undone   weightier   Pharisees   judgment

16. 1 Corinthians 16:1–2

Now concerning the collection for the _____, as I have given order to the _____ of _____, even so do ye. Upon the first day of the _____ let every one of you lay by him in store, as _____ hath prospered him, that there be no gatherings when I come.

God   saints   churches   Galatia   week

17. Hebrews 7:4

Now consider how great this _____ was, unto whom even the _____ _____ gave the tenth of the _____.

spoils   patriarch   man   Abraham

28

Ultimate Success

1. Deuteronomy 30:9

   And the Lord thy God will make thee plenteous in every work of thine _____, in the fruit of thy body, and in the _____ of thy cattle, and in the fruit of thy land, for good: for the Lord will again _____ over thee for good, as he rejoiced over thy _____.

   fathers   rejoice   hand   fruit

2. Joshua 1:8

   This book of the law shall not depart out of thy _____; but thou shalt _____ therein day and _____, that thou mayest observe to do according to all that is written therein: for then thou shalt make thy way _____, and then thou shalt have good _____.

   prosperous   mouth   meditate   night   success

3. Nehemiah 2:20

   Then _____ I them, and said unto them, The God of _____, he will prosper us; therefore we his servants will arise and _____: but ye have no _____, nor right, nor memorial, in Jerusalem.

   build   portion   answered   heaven

4. Psalm 1:1–3

   Blessed is the man that _____ not in the counsel of the ungodly, nor standeth in the way of sinners, nor sitteth in

the seat of the scornful. But his _____ is in the law of the
LORD; and in his law doth he _____ day and night. And
he shall be like a tree planted by the _____ of water, that
bringeth forth his fruit in his season; his leaf also shall not
_____; and whatsoever he doeth shall _____.

> prosper   rivers   wither   walketh   delight   meditate

5. Psalm 37:4
Delight _____ also in the _____: and he shall give thee
the _____ of thine _____.

> desires   thyself   heart   LORD

6. Proverbs 22:29
Seest thou a _____ diligent in his _____? he shall stand
before _____; he shall not stand before mean _____.

> men   business   kings   man

7. Proverbs 22:4
By _____ and the _____ of the LORD are _____,
and honour, and _____.

> riches   life   humility   fear

8. Isaiah 1:19
If ye be _____ and _____, ye shall eat the _____
of the _____.

> good   land   obedient   willing

9. Matthew 6:24
No man can _____ two _____: for either he will hate
the one, and _____ the other; or else he will hold to
the one, and _____ the other. Ye cannot serve God and
_____.

> despise   love   mammon   masters   serve

10. Matthew 23:12
And _____ shall exalt himself shall be _____; and he
that shall _____ himself shall be _____.

> abased   humble   exalted   whosoever

11. Luke 9:48

And said unto them, _____ shall receive this child in my _____ receiveth me: and whosoever shall receive me receiveth him that sent me: for he that is least among _____ all, the same shall be _____.

> name   great   Whosoever   you

12. Ephesians 3:20

Now unto him that is able to do exceeding abundantly above all that we _____ or _____, according to the _____ that _____ in us.

> think   power   ask   worketh

29

Did You Know?
(Set 5)

Here are more little-known, interesting facts from the Bible.

- The reason the Bible states in several places that people were "going up" to Jerusalem is because Jerusalem sat on a high hill. People had to climb the hill regardless of the direction from which they approached.

- Everyone spoke the same language until God scrambled the languages at the tower of Babel (Genesis 11:1–9).

- There is an altar named Ed mentioned in Joshua 22:34.

- Earrings were the only gold items Aaron used to construct the false idol, the golden calf (Exodus 32:2–4).

- Six of the false gods mentioned in the Bible are female: Anammelech of 2 Kings 17:31; Asherah (grove) of Judges 3:7 NKJV; Diana (Artemis) of Acts 19:24; Ashtoreth of 1 Kings 11:5; queen of Heaven (Ishtar) of Jeremiah 7:18; and Succothbenoth of 2 Kings 17:30.

- The book of Job was likely written before the book of Exodus, although Exodus is the Bible's second book after Genesis.

- In 2 Kings 17:4, there is a king named So.

SPECIALIZED MULTIPLE-CHOICE TRIVIA

Next is a large array of multiple-choice trivia by topic. Give yourself 1 point for each correct answer. Record your scores for each topic on the score card, and as always, you may repeat any or all of the quizzes as many times as necessary.

Take your time. This is not a race, and your ability to retain this information is greatly enhanced if you meditate on each answer.

30

All about Food

1. Who ate locusts in the wilderness?
   A. Matthew
   B. Paul
   C. John the Baptist
   D. Peter

2. Who traded his birthright for his brother's bread and lentil stew?
   A. Jacob
   B. David
   C. Joseph
   D. Esau

3. Who had a baker who baked pastries for him?
   A. The pharaoh in Moses's time
   B. The pharaoh in Joseph's time
   C. Samson
   D. Gideon

4. Who was tricked when his non-hairy son dressed in hairy gloves and presented him with a meal?
   A. Jacob
   B. Esau
   C. Isaac
   D. Israel

5. What did Ezekiel's scroll taste like?
   A. Candy
   B. Honey
   C. Fish
   D. Wafers

6. What judge of Israel prepared a delicious meal for an angel?
   A. Gideon
   B. Samson
   C. Ehud
   D. Deborah

7. What book of the Bible describes Canaan as a land flowing with milk and honey?
   A. Genesis
   B. Exodus
   C. Leviticus
   D. Judges

8. What animal was killed for food when the prodigal son returned home?
   A. A hog
   B. A rooster
   C. A turkey
   D. The fatted calf

9. Where did the Hebrews feast on cucumbers, melons, leeks, onions, and garlic?
   A. Jerusalem
   B. Bethlehem
   C. Egypt
   D. Gilead

10. Who ate honey out of a lion's carcass?
    A. David
    B. Elijah
    C. Saul
    D. Samson

11. What prophet made deadly stew edible again?
    A. Elijah
    B. Elisha
    C. Jeremiah
    D. Obadiah

12. What miraculous food fed the Israelites in the desert?
    A. Potatoes
    B. Manna
    C. Fish
    D. Five loaves of bread

31

From Sweet to Bitter

1. Who ate a book that was originally sweet but turned bitter?
   A. Peter
   B. Mark
   C. Thomas
   D. John

2. Who presented a riddle about finding something sweet in a lion's carcass?
   A. Elijah
   B. Elisha
   C. Samson
   D. Joel

3. According to Proverbs, what kind of bread is sweet to a man?
   A. Bread of deceit
   B. Bread of idleness
   C. Bread of comfort
   D. Bread of humbleness

4. What kind of grape sets the children's teeth on edge, according to Jeremiah?
   A. Red
   B. Green
   C. Sour
   D. Sweet

5. What type of herbs were the Israelites supposed to eat with the Passover meal?

   A. None

   B. Sweet herbs

   C. Bitter herbs

   D. Sour herbs

6. According to Proverbs, what kind of water is sweet?

   A. Purified water

   B. Rain water

   C. River water

   D. Stolen water

7. What did Moses do to make the bitter waters of Marah drinkable?

   A. He threw a piece of wood in the water.

   B. He poured some honey in the water.

   C. He prayed over the water.

   D. He fasted several days.

8. After his resurrection, what did Jesus say his followers would be able to drink?

   A. Juice

   B. Milk

   C. Water

   D. Poison

9. What strange thing did Moses make the people of Israel drink?

   A. Cane sugar

   B. Honey

   C. Silver

   D. Gold dust

10. According to Proverbs, what sort of person thinks bitter things are sweet?

    A. A conceited person

    B. A prideful person

    C. A hungry person

    D. A loving person

32

Residential Area

1. What Genesis ship captain lived in a tent?
   A. Job
   B. Jonah
   C. Noah
   D. Nehemiah

2. Who stored Goliath's armor in his tent?
   A. Saul
   B. Jonathan
   C. Michal
   D. David

3. Who did Noah say would live in the tents of Shem?
   A. Japheth
   B. Ham
   C. Job
   D. Joel

4. Who took riches from Jericho and buried them in his tent?
   A. Amber
   B. Achan
   C. Uriah
   D. Aaron

5. Who took his wife to his mother's tent on their wedding night?
   A. Ishmael
   B. Isaac
   C. Jacob
   D. Esau

6. Who was "the father of such as dwell in tents"?
   A. Jabal
   B. Jacob
   C. Joseph
   D. Jonah

7. Who compared her dark skin to the darkness of the tents of Kedar?
   A. The woman in the Song of Solomon
   B. Eve
   C. Lydia
   D. The woman at the well

8. What prophet said, "The LORD also shall save the tents of Judah"?
   A. Nehemiah
   B. Jeremiah
   C. Zechariah
   D. Obadiah

9. Who murdered both an Israelite man and a Moabite woman inside a tent?
   A. Phinehas
   B. Naaman
   C. Jacob
   D. Abner

10. Who commanded his descendants to live in tents forever?
    A. David
    B. Jonadab
    C. Japheth
    D. Jabal

11. Who robbed the tents of the Syrians after the army fled their camp?
    A. The Samaritans
    B. The Jebusites
    C. The Levites
    D. The Benjamites

12. What prophet saw "the tents of Cushan in affliction"?
    A. Elijah
    B. Elisha
    C. Habakkuk
    D. Samuel

33

Kiddie Land

1. Who was the first child mentioned in the Bible?
   A. Cain
   B. Abel
   C. Seth
   D. Ham

2. Who was Noah's youngest son?
   A. Shem
   B. Japheth
   C. Ham
   D. Benjamin

3. What king was the youngest of eight brothers?
   A. Saul
   B. David
   C. Solomon
   D. Ahab

4. Who was the youngest son of Joseph?
   A. Manassah
   B. Ephraim
   C. Malachi
   D. Jair

5. Who of the following was not a son of Adam?

   A. Cain

   B. Abel

   C. Seth

   D. Ahab

6. Who died giving birth to Benjamin?

   A. Rebekah

   B. Rachel

   C. Rhoda

   D. Rahab

7. What judge had seventy sons?

   A. Samson

   B. Gideon

   C. Deborah

   D. Samuel

8. What king of Judah had twenty-eight sons and sixty daughters?

   A. Rehoboam

   B. David

   C. Solomon

   D. Saul

9. Who advised young Christians to stop thinking as children think?

   A. Peter

   B. Paul

   C. Pilate

   D. John

10. What king was severely distressed over the death of his wayward son?

   A. Saul

   B. Solomon

   C. David

   D. Heman

34

Did You Know?
(Set 6)

Prepare to be amazed by the following Bible facts.

- Approximately forty men wrote the Bible over a sixteen-hundred-year period. The time of the writing dates from 1500 BC to approximately AD 100.

- The Red Sea was not the only waterway parted by God. He also parted the Jordan River for Elijah and Elisha (2 Kings 2:7–9).

- Pontius Pilate and King Herod were bitter enemies until they became friends during Jesus's persecution (Luke 23:12).

- In the Gospels, Jesus is called the "Son of man" over seventy-five times.

- David kept Goliath's armor in his tent as a souvenir after slaying him (1 Samuel 17:54).

- Abraham was not circumcised until he was ninety-nine years old (Genesis 17:24).

- The place where Jesus was crucified, "the place of a skull," contained a garden (John 19:17–18, 41).

Window Display

1. Who died falling out of a window during one of Paul's sermons?
   A. Eutychus
   B. Esau
   C. Ephraim
   D. Naphtali

2. Who released two birds out of the window of a ship?
   A. Jacob
   B. Esau
   C. Noah
   D. David

3. Who was embarrassed when she looked out of her window and saw her husband dancing?
   A. Martha
   B. Michal
   C. Melissa
   D. Mary

4. Whose wife helped him escape the clutches of Saul via a window?
   A. David's
   B. Samuel's
   C. Uriah's
   D. Absalom's

5. What prophet commanded that a king shoot arrows out of a window?
   A. Elisha
   B. Elijah
   C. Ezra
   D. Ezekiel

6. Where did Paul escape a threat against his life by being let down by the wall in a basket?
   A. Damascus
   B. Corinth
   C. Ephesus
   D. Rome

7. What king peered out of his window and spotted Isaac and Rebekah being affectionate?
   A. David
   B. Saul
   C. Abimelech
   D. Solomon

8. What queen was hurled out of a window by her servants?
   A. Michal
   B. Rizpah
   C. Maachah
   D. Jezebel

9. Who saw a young man being approached by a prostitute while looking through his window?
   A. Solomon
   B. David
   C. Saul
   D. Absalom

10. What windows would be opened for people who tithed, according to the book of Malachi?
    A. Many blessings
    B. Windows of heaven
    C. Joyful windows
    D. Prayerful windows

36

That Makes Scents

1. What aromatic substance was brought to the baby Jesus?
   A. Ginger
   B. Frankincense
   C. Cinnamon
   D. Palm leaves

2. Whose harem contained women who were purified with various perfumes?
   A. King Herod
   B. King Ahaz
   C. King Josiah
   D. King Ahasuerus

3. In the Gospel of John, who anointed Jesus's feet with spikenard, an expensive ointment?
   A. Mary Magdalene
   B. Mary, mother of Jesus
   C. Mary, sister of Lazarus
   D. Mary, a nurse

4. In the Gospel of Luke, where was Jesus when a sinful woman poured an alabaster jar of perfume on his feet?
   A. At the home of Simon the Pharisee
   B. At Peter's house
   C. At the home of John and James
   D. In Bethlehem

5. What book of the Bible mentions a woman using spikenard, calamus, and various perfumes?

    A. Proverbs

    B. Psalms

    C. Song of Solomon

    D. Esther

6. Who perfumed her bed with myrrh, aloes, and cinnamon?

    A. The bride

    B. The harlot

    C. The mother

    D. The virtuous woman

7. What man used myrrh and frankincense as perfumes?

    A. Solomon

    B. David

    C. Saul

    D. Jonathan

8. What prophet refused to use anointing oils during mourning?

    A. Elijah

    B. Daniel

    C. Jonah

    D. Joel

9. According to the book of Proverbs, ointment and perfume do what?

    A. Help people to love everybody

    B. Rejoice the heart

    C. Make peace in the valley

    D. Bring laughter

10. What two prophets denounced women applying makeup?

    A. Elijah and Elisha

    B. Jonah and Joel

    C. Samuel and Josiah

    D. Jeremiah and Ezekiel

37

Nighty-Night

1. Who met a man who wrestled him all night?
   A. Jacob
   B. Jonah
   C. Jeremiah
   D. Joshua

2. Who passed through Egypt one night visiting nearly every household?
   A. Pharaoh
   B. The Lord
   C. Aaron
   D. Moses

3. Who paid a late-night visit to the young Samuel?
   A. Eli
   B. The Lord
   C. Moses
   D. Hannah

4. Who came to Peter in the dead of night and released him from prison?
   A. Rhoda
   B. The Lord
   C. An angel
   D. A guard

5. Who was visited by an angel who assured him he would be safe aboard a storm-ravaged ship?
   A. Jonah
   B. Peter
   C. Paul
   D. Judas

6. What Pharisee visited Jesus late at night?
   A. Cephas
   B. Gamaliel
   C. Paul
   D. Nicodemus

7. Who was mistakenly thought to be a spirit when spotted late one night?
   A. An angel
   B. Jesus
   C. Paul
   D. Peter

8. Who brought some officers of the chief priest to a late-night visit with Jesus?
   A. Nicodemus
   B. Philip
   C. Peter
   D. Judas

9. Who stole Saul's spear after creeping into his camp late one night?
   A. Jonathan
   B. David
   C. Uriah
   D. Samuel

10. Who visited a medium at night?
    A. David
    B. Samuel
    C. Saul
    D. Moses

11. Who attacked a Midianite camp late one night?
    A. Joshua and his men
    B. Gideon and his men
    C. David and his men
    D. Saul and his men

Wedding Bells

1. Who was the first man mentioned in the Bible to have more than one wife?
   A. Adam
   B. Lamech
   C. Moses
   D. Seth

2. Who married both Rachel and Leah?
   A. Lamech
   B. Abdon
   C. Jotham
   D. Jacob

3. Whose father's wives were named Hannah and Peninnah?
   A. Jacob's
   B. Samuel's
   C. Abraham's
   D. Isaac's

4. What king was married to Ahinoam?
   A. Josiah
   B. Saul
   C. David
   D. Solomon

5. Mahlon and Boaz were the husbands of what woman?

   A. Orpah

   B. Ruth

   C. Naomi

   D. Rachel

6. Who married two of Judah's sons?

   A. Rachel

   B. Leah

   C. Rebekah

   D. Tamar

7. What king of Judah had fourteen wives?

   A. Abijah

   B. Aaron

   C. Uzziah

   D. Saul

8. What judge of Israel surrendered his Philistine wife to a friend?

   A. Samson

   B. Othniel

   C. Ehud

   D. Gideon

39

Farming

1. Who planted the first garden?
   A. Adam
   B. Solomon
   C. Noah
   D. God

2. Who of the following was a farmer?
   A. Jacob
   B. Job
   C. Paul
   D. Stephen

3. What king planted many vineyards, gardens, and orchards?
   A. Pharaoh
   B. David
   C. Saul
   D. Solomon

4. What judge was also a farmer of grain?
   A. Gideon
   B. Othniel
   C. Deborah
   D. Joel

5. Who was the first man to plant a vineyard?
   A. Adam
   B. Cain
   C. Enoch
   D. Noah

6. What farmer and ancestor of David married a Moabite woman?
   A. Elimelech
   B. Ahaziah
   C. Boaz
   D. Ehud

7. Who was a farmer in Gerar and received a hundredfold harvest?
   A. Jacob
   B. Isaac
   C. Abraham
   D. Noah

8. What king of Judah enjoyed farming?
   A. Uzziah
   B. Ahaziah
   C. Amaziah
   D. Uriah

9. Who had a vineyard that was coveted by Ahab?
   A. Naaman
   B. Naboth
   C. Obadiah
   D. Omri

10. David commanded Ziba to farm for what lame man?
    A. Naaman
    B. Hezekiah
    C. Mephibosheth
    D. Jeroboam

40

Rulers

1. What king made a famous ruling that involved cutting a baby in two?
   A. David
   B. Pharaoh
   C. Solomon
   D. Saul

2. Who was the first king to reign in Jerusalem?
   A. Saul
   B. David
   C. Ahasuerus
   D. Pharaoh

3. What wicked ruler ordered the infant boys of Bethlehem to be slaughtered?
   A. Pharaoh
   B. Saul
   C. Archelaus
   D. Herod

4. What ruler ordered that Daniel be thrown into the lions' den?
   A. Nebuchadnezzar
   B. Belshazzar
   C. Darius
   D. Ahasuerus

5. What king of Judah was hobbled by a foot disease in his old age?
   A. Asa
   B. Rehoboam
   C. Abijah
   D. Jehoshaphat

6. What young shepherd boy was anointed by Samuel in front of his brothers?
   A. Solomon
   B. David
   C. Joseph
   D. Josiah

7. What imprisoned man interpreted the dreams of the Egyptian pharaoh?
   A. Jacob
   B. Moses
   C. Joseph
   D. Reuben

8. What wise king became allies with Egypt when he married Pharaoh's daughter?
   A. Jeroboam II
   B. Solomon
   C. Menahem
   D. Saul

9. What man led in the conquering of thirty-one kings and their empires?
   A. Samson
   B. David
   C. Joshua
   D. Elisha

10. What king of Moab commanded that prophet Balaam go and curse Israel?
    A. Balak
    B. Ahaziah
    C. Pharaoh
    D. Saul

11. What son of Gideon (Jerubbaal) became king in Shechem?
    A. Joash
    B. Ezekiel
    C. Abimelech
    D. Abiezer

12. What king of the Amalekites was captured by Saul and severed into pieces by Samuel?
    A. Omri
    B. Agag
    C. Jehu
    D. Ahab

13. David sought refuge with what Philistine king after fleeing from Saul?
    A. Achish
    B. Saul
    C. Hoshea
    D. Elah

41

The Apostles

1. What was Peter's original name?
   A. Philip
   B. Levi
   C. Simon
   D. Epaphras

2. Who was with Jesus at the transfiguration?
   A. Matthew
   B. John
   C. Mark
   D. Luke

3. Who healed Aeneas, a paralytic?
   A. Paul
   B. Stephen
   C. Peter
   D. Jesus

4. Who brought Greeks to Jesus?
   A. Andrew
   B. James
   C. Thaddaeus
   D. Matthew

42

Doorway

1. Who shut the door of Noah's ark?
   A. Noah
   B. Ham
   C. Shem
   D. God

2. What is to be lifted up to allow entry of the King of glory?
   A. The doors and the gates
   B. The gates and the everlasting doors
   C. The windows of heaven
   D. The doorposts and the windows

3. Who healed a lame man at the temple's Beautiful Gate?
   A. Paul and Silas
   B. John the Baptist
   C. Peter and John
   D. Paul and Barnabas

4. What were the Israelites commanded to apply to their doorposts at the first Passover?
   A. Lamb's blood
   B. Goat's blood
   C. Wine
   D. Manna

5. God spoke to what person about the gates of death?

    A. Jacob

    B. Jonah

    C. Job

    D. Jeremiah

6. What brave soldier elected to sleep in front of the king's palace door instead of going home?

    A. Uriah

    B. Uzziah

    C. Eliab

    D. Naboth

7. According to Moses, where were the words of God to be written?

    A. On doorposts and gates

    B. On the wall

    C. Out of the window

    D. In the street

8. Who removed the huge doors from the gate of Gaza and hauled them all the way to a hill at Hebron?

    A. David

    B. Solomon

    C. Samson

    D. Jabal

9. What gate of Jerusalem was rebuilt under the direction of Nehemiah?

    A. The ox gate

    B. The sheep gate

    C. The chicken gate

    D. The large gate

10. What king removed the gold from the doors of the temple
    and gave it to the king of Assyria?
    A. Jeremiah
    B. Nehemiah
    C. Hezekiah
    D. Isaiah

11. In Revelation, how many gates does the city have?
    A. 10
    B. 11
    C. 12
    D. 13

43

In the Military

1. Who was sleeping between two soldiers when miraculously rescued from prison?
   A. Paul
   B. John
   C. Peter
   D. Timothy

2. What leper commanded Syrian troops?
   A. Nathan
   B. Nathanael
   C. Nethaniah
   D. Naaman

3. Where was Jesus when a Roman officer asked him to heal his faithful servant?
   A. Bethsaida
   B. Capernaum
   C. Cana
   D. Tiberias

4. What Roman soldier was kind to Paul on Paul's voyage to Rome?
   A. Pontius
   B. Julius
   C. Onesimus
   D. Felix

5. What Israelite soldier gave Joshua an enthusiastic report about the land of Canaan?
   A. Jephunneh
   B. Othniel
   C. Caleb
   D. Nun

6. What Hittite soldier was put on the front lines of battle specifically to allow David to have his widow?
   A. Amaziah
   B. Uzziah
   C. Uriah
   D. Ahaziah

7. What soldier supported David during Absalom's rebellion?
   A. Goliath
   B. Ittai
   C. Obededom
   D. Zeruiah

8. What soldier led a revolt against King Elah and made himself the new king?
   A. Zichri
   B. Zophar
   C. Zimri
   D. Zerubbabel

9. Who commanded the rebel army when Absalom rebelled against David?
   A. Ahasuerus
   B. Amasa
   C. Amram
   D. Aristarchus

44

Women and Rulers

1. Who became David's wife and gave him a son named Solomon?
   A. Jezebel
   B. Abigail
   C. Bathsheba
   D. Delilah

2. What king of Israel had Rizpah as his concubine?
   A. David
   B. Saul
   C. Solomon
   D. Jeroboam

3. Who plotted to have John the Baptist beheaded?
   A. Euodias
   B. Eunice
   C. Herodias
   D. Hannah

4. What princess led Ahab into the depths of idolatry?
   A. Salome
   B. Jezebel
   C. Bithiah
   D. Serah

5. What queen traveled a great distance to meet Solomon face-to-face?
   A. Queen Vashti
   B. Queen Esther
   C. The queen of Sheba
   D. Queen Maachah

6. Who was replaced by a foreign woman after defiling her royal husband?
   A. Esther
   B. Deborah
   C. Vashti
   D. Claudia

7. After Nabal died, who became David's wife?
   A. Bathsheba
   B. Abigail
   C. Baara
   D. Abijah

8. Who was ousted as queen mother for making a false idol?
   A. Maachah
   B. Herodias
   C. Asenath
   D. Cleopatra

9. Philip witnessed to an Ethiopian eunuch who was the servant of what queen?
   A. Queen Herodias
   B. Queen Candace
   C. Queen Nitocris
   D. Queen Esther

10. What daughter of Ahab tried to destroy the entire line of Judah?
    A. Jemima
    B. Myrrina
    C. Huldah
    D. Athaliah

45

Hair Apparent

1. What famous figure never had a haircut until his mistress had his head shaved?
   A. Othniel
   B. Barak
   C. Samson
   D. Joseph

2. What apostle, along with four other men, purified himself by shaving his head?
   A. Joseph
   B. Paul
   C. Jonathan
   D. James

3. What king of Babylon once lived in the wilderness and let his hair grow wild?
   A. Daniel
   B. Nebuchadnezzar
   C. Elijah
   D. Naaman

4. Who is mentioned in the book of Genesis as being very hairy?
   A. Noah
   B. Abraham
   C. Esau
   D. Joseph

5. What prophet was described as a very hairy man?
   A. Elisha
   B. Hosea
   C. Elijah
   D. Amos

6. What man, stricken by grief, shaved his head after he learned his children had been killed?
   A. Noah
   B. Naaman
   C. David
   D. Job

7. Who was forbidden to "round the corners of your heads"?
   A. Greeks
   B. Chaldeans
   C. The children of Israel
   D. Egyptians

8. Who was the only man in the Bible referred to as being naturally bald?
   A. Elijah
   B. Jacob
   C. Elisha
   D. Esau

9. What type of person had to shave all his hair twice, six days apart?
   A. An epileptic
   B. A blind man
   C. A leper
   D. A paralytic

10. What type of people could neither shave their heads nor let their hair grow long?
    A. Pharisees
    B. Prophets
    C. Levite priests
    D. Scribes

11. God told what prophet to shave his head and beard?
    A. Isaiah
    B. Jeremiah
    C. Ezekiel
    D. Daniel

46

Anointment

1. Who was anointed by the Holy Ghost?
   A. Moses
   B. Peter
   C. Joseph
   D. Jesus

2. Who anointed the tabernacle with oil?
   A. Aaron
   B. Bezaleel
   C. Moses
   D. Solomon

3. Who anointed a stone before dedicating it to God?
   A. Esau
   B. Jacob
   C. Aaron
   D. Joseph

4. Who told the early Christians that God had "given the earnest of the Spirit in our hearts"?
   A. Peter
   B. John
   C. James
   D. Paul

5. What man and his sons were anointed by Moses with the blood of a ram?
   A. Elijah and his sons
   B. Caleb and his sons
   C. Aaron and his sons
   D. Joshua and his sons

6. What well-respected judge anointed Saul?
   A. David
   B. Deborah
   C. Othniel
   D. Samuel

7. According to James, who should anoint a sick believer with oil?
   A. The saved
   B. The deacons
   C. The elders
   D. The scribes

8. What king of Persia was regarded to be God's anointed one?
   A. Ahasuerus
   B. Cyrus
   C. Alexander
   D. Belshazzar

9. What priest anointed Solomon king?
   A. Aaron
   B. Zadok
   C. Melchizedek
   D. Joshua

The Swift

1. What boy raced to the Philistine camp to challenge the feared Philistine warrior?
   A. Samuel
   B. Jesus
   C. David
   D. Solomon

2. What height-challenged man ran to see Jesus but could not because he was too short?
   A. Bartimaeus
   B. Peter
   C. Zacchaeus
   D. John

3. What combative man ran to meet his brother and kissed him after a long time apart?
   A. Esau
   B. Benjamin
   C. James
   D. Abel

4. What prophet outran a king's chariot and its team of horses?
   A. Isaiah
   B. Jeremiah
   C. Elijah
   D. Zedekiah

5. In the plains of Mamre, who ran to meet the Lord?
   A. Noah
   B. Abraham
   C. Moses
   D. Joshua

6. What man ran to meet Abraham's servant at the well?
   A. Isaac
   B. Jacob
   C. Laban
   D. Abimelech

7. Who sent Cushi to run to David with the news of Absalom's death?
   A. Joab
   B. Jonathan
   C. Joram
   D. Jethro

8. What encroacher to the throne of Israel found fifty men to run before him?
   A. Adonijah
   B. Samson
   C. Zerubbabel
   D. David

9. What man, a servant of the prophet Elisha, ran to meet the woman of Shunem?
   A. Shemariah
   B. Nebajoth
   C. Caleb
   D. Gehazi

48

Special Women

1. Who was the only female judge of Israel?
   A. Deborah
   B. Sarah
   C. Rebekah
   D. Ruth

2. What cousin of Mary gave birth to John the Baptist?
   A. Elisabeth
   B. Anna
   C. Bernice
   D. Herodias

3. What prophetess was the sister of Moses and Aaron?
   A. Sarah
   B. Miriam
   C. Deborah
   D. Rebekah

4. What Jewish girl married an emperor and helped save her people from certain extermination?
   A. Ruth
   B. Naomi
   C. Esther
   D. Deborah

5. What deceitful princess of the Zidonians married Ahab?
   A. Ruth
   B. Bathsheba
   C. Esther
   D. Jezebel

6. What wife of David was once married to Nabal?
   A. Hildah
   B. Azubah
   C. Abigail
   D. Ahinoam

7. What harlot helped save the lives of Joshua's spies?
   A. Bathsheba
   B. Leah
   C. Hodiah
   D. Rahab

8. What wife of David was the mother of the disobedient Adonijah?
   A. Abigail
   B. Bathsheba
   C. Michal
   D. Haggith

9. Who protected the corpses of her slaughtered children from birds and various animals?
   A. Rizpah
   B. Baara
   C. Bathsheba
   D. Reumah

10. What prophetess consoled the king while severely criticizing the people of Judah?
    A. Deborah
    B. Naomi
    C. Huldah
    D. Miriam

49

Funny Money

1. What was Judas paid to betray Jesus?
   A. Thirty pieces of silver
   B. A sack of grains
   C. The key to the temple
   D. An official position in the palace

2. What ruler required tribute during Jesus's time on earth?
   A. Caesar
   B. Caiaphas
   C. Agrippa
   D. Archelaus

3. What publican (tax collector) climbed a tree to see Jesus?
   A. Zacchaeus
   B. Matthew
   C. Peter
   D. James

4. Who made Jesus a feast that had many publicans (tax collectors) as guests?
   A. John
   B. Zacchaeus
   C. Levi
   D. Peter

5. Who suggested that the Egyptians be taxed one-fifth of their produce in order to prepare for an upcoming famine?
   A. Reuben
   B. Benjamin
   C. Joseph
   D. Simeon

6. Who kept Paul in prison, hoping to receive a bribe for his release?
   A. Felix
   B. Stephen
   C. Barnabas
   D. Elymas

7. Who placed a tax on the entire Persian empire?
   A. Ahasuerus
   B. Xerxes
   C. Pharaoh
   D. Pekahiah

8. Who taxed the Israelites to pay off a debt to Pul, the king of Assyria?
   A. Pharaoh
   B. Menahem
   C. Joram
   D. Omri

9. What king of Israel became a servant and gave presents to King Shalmaneser of Assyria?
   A. David
   B. Elah
   C. Zechariah
   D. Hoshea

10. What Persian king gave tax exemptions to the priests and Levites?
   A. Jeroboam
   B. Pharaoh
   C. Artaxerxes
   D. Saul

50

Fly High

1. What cannot be tamed even though all birds can be tamed, according to James?
   A. The mind
   B. The tongue
   C. The heart
   D. The soul

2. The Holy Spirit took the form of what bird at Jesus's baptism?
   A. Raven
   B. Pigeon
   C. Dove
   D. Eagle

3. How many of each species of bird was Noah commanded to take on to the ark?
   A. 1
   B. 3
   C. 5
   D. 7

4. Who had a vision that featured a woman with eagle's wings flying to the desert?
   A. John
   B. Paul
   C. James
   D. Peter

5. What bird was supplied in abundance to feed the Israelites in the wilderness?
   A. Eagle
   B. Quail
   C. Dove
   D. Raven

6. What parable of Jesus featured greedy birds?
   A. The tares
   B. The prodigal son
   C. The sower
   D. The great supper

51

What's That I Hear?

1. What apostle spoke to the Pentecost crowd in a loud voice?
   A. Peter
   B. Stephen
   C. John
   D. Judas

2. Who heard a voice talking of the fall of Babylon?
   A. John
   B. Barnabas
   C. Bartholomew
   D. Bildad

3. "This is my beloved Son, in whom I am well pleased" was spoken at what important event?
   A. Paul's conversion
   B. Jesus's baptism
   C. Peter's release from jail
   D. Jesus's ascension

4. Who heard the voice of those who had been slaughtered for proclaiming God's Word?
   A. Paul
   B. Elam
   C. John
   D. Caleb

5. Who heard the voice of God after he ran away from Queen Jezebel?
   A. Elisha
   B. David
   C. Elijah
   D. Gomer

6. What boy was sleeping near the ark of the covenant when he heard the voice of God?
   A. David
   B. Obededom
   C. Amaziah
   D. Samuel

7. What trees are broken by the power of God's voice, according to the book of Psalms?
   A. Sycamore trees
   B. Fig trees
   C. Cedars of Lebanon
   D. Lilies of the field

8. Whom did Isaiah tell that the king of Assyria had raised his voice up against God?
   A. Zechariah
   B. Hophni
   C. Zebediah
   D. Hezekiah

9. Who cried out upon seeing a vision of Samuel?
   A. Samuel's mother, Hannah
   B. Elkanah
   C. The witch of Endor
   D. King Saul

52

Did You Know?
(Set 7)

Here are more facts for the Bible brilliant.

- The apostle Paul spoke both Greek and Hebrew (Acts 21:37–40).
- God once gave Moses leprosy for a short time (Exodus 4:6–7).
- The devastating earthquake mentioned in Amos 1:1 has been verified by modern geologists.
- Nowhere in the Bible does it specifically state or imply that Mary Magdalene was a prostitute.
- If one goes by the total number of words, Luke wrote more of the New Testament than Paul did.
- Moses could not have written the last chapter of Deuteronomy because he was dead. Joshua is thought to have finished the book.

The Story of Joseph

1. How many of Joseph's brothers traveled to Egypt to buy grain?
   A. 12
   B. 10
   C. 11
   D. 6

2. Which brother of Joseph did not go down to buy grain in Egypt?
   A. Reuben
   B. Benjamin
   C. Levi
   D. Judah

3. How many days did Joseph keep his brothers in prison?
   A. 3
   B. 14
   C. 20
   D. 1

4. Which of Joseph's brothers did Joseph keep tied up until Benjamin was brought back?
   A. Reuben
   B. Manasseh
   C. Levi
   D. Simeon

5. What did Joseph command to be placed in his brothers' sacks along with grain?
   A. Money
   B. Manna
   C. Quails
   D. Sword

6. When Joseph's brothers returned, what did Joseph command to be placed in Benjamin's sack?
   A. Golden candle stick
   B. Silver cup
   C. Bronze caver
   D. Golden ring

7. What did Joseph say the man who was found in possession of the silver cup would become?
   A. His successor
   B. His friend
   C. His servant
   D. His betrayer

8. During the seven years of famine, Joseph let his father and brothers dwell in what land?
   A. Hushim
   B. Goshen
   C. Beulah
   D. Moab

9. What did Pharaoh tell Joseph that his father and his household should eat?
   A. Milk and honeycomb
   B. From the fat of the land
   C. Manna
   D. Whatever they could find

10. How old was Joseph when he died?
    A. 99 years old
    B. 100 years old
    C. 110 years old
    D. 120 years old

11. What did Joseph name his first son?
    A. Jacob
    B. Ephraim
    C. Benjamin
    D. Manasseh

12. How many pieces of silver did Joseph give to his brother Benjamin?
    A. 100
    B. 1,000
    C. 300
    D. 3,000

Have a Laugh

1. Who was laughed at for saying that a dead girl was only asleep?
   A. Paul
   B. Jesus
   C. Peter
   D. Jairus

2. What elderly man laughed at God's promise that he would father a child in his old age?
   A. Noah
   B. Methuselah
   C. Abraham
   D. Saul

3. Who danced with great enthusiasm when the ark of the covenant was brought to Jerusalem?
   A. David
   B. Solomon
   C. Obed
   D. Uzziah

4. Who laughed when told that she would bear a son in her old age?
   A. Rebekah
   B. Anna
   C. Leah
   D. Sarah

5. After the exodus, the Israelites danced in front of what graven image?

    A. A molten calf

    B. Baal

    C. A dual-horned unicorn

    D. The Semel carved image

6. What elderly woman said, "God hath made me to laugh, so that all that hear will laugh with me"?

    A. Eve

    B. Rebekah

    C. Leah

    D. Sarah

7. In the Beatitudes, to whom did Jesus promise laughter?

    A. Those who mourn

    B. Those who are sad

    C. Those who weep

    D. Those who hunger

8. Whose daughter danced after his victory over the Ammonites?

    A. Jacob's

    B. Job's

    C. Jochebed's

    D. Jephthah's

9. Who was preoccupied with dancing when David caught them?

    A. Moabites

    B. Canaanites

    C. Amalekites

    D. Philistines

10. Who laughed when he learned of Nehemiah's plans to rebuild Jerusalem?

    A. Sanballat

    B. Eliashib

    C. Shallum

    D. Benaiah

55

Anything Goes

1. To whom did Jesus say, "It is written again, Thou shalt not tempt the Lord thy God"?
   A. Peter
   B. Judas
   C. The devil
   D. Michael

2. When Joseph, the earthly father of Jesus, took the infant and Mary into the night, where did they go?
   A. Jerusalem
   B. Bethlehem
   C. Nazareth
   D. Egypt

3. When Jesus went into Peter's house, what was Peter's mother-in-law sick with?
   A. Leprosy
   B. Paralysis
   C. A fever
   D. An issuance of blood

4. Who was a personal servant to Moses?
   A. Caleb
   B. Joshua
   C. Aaron
   D. Jethro

5. What book of the Bible explains that a virtuous woman is more valuable than rubies?
   A. Ecclesiastes
   B. Job
   C. Psalms
   D. Proverbs

6. What crime was Jesus charged with by the high priest?
   A. Murder
   B. Blasphemy
   C. Thievery
   D. Adultery

7. Who was rewarded with the ring from King Ahasuerus of Persia?
   A. Mordecai
   B. Zeresh
   C. Adalia
   D. Esther

8. Who was David's oldest brother?
   A. Eli
   B. Adonijah
   C. Eliab
   D. Amaziah

9. Who risked her life to keep her royal nephew alive?
   A. Jehosheba
   B. Jochebed
   C. Deborah
   D. Dorcas

10. Who called herself Marah, which means "bitter"?
    A. Naomi
    B. Martha
    C. Lois
    D. Ruth

11. What apostle was exiled to the island of Patmos?
    A. Peter
    B. John
    C. James
    D. Andrew

12. What was the profession of Paul, Aquila, and Priscilla?
    A. Fishing
    B. Farming
    C. Shepherding
    D. Tentmaking

13. What prophet was thrown overboard during a powerful storm?
    A. Peter
    B. Jonah
    C. Paul
    D. Isaiah

14. Who had a daughter named Jemima?
    A. Moses
    B. Hosea
    C. Job
    D. Noah

15. Persecuted Christians were scattered throughout Judea and Samaria after the death of what person?
    A. John the Baptist
    B. Herod
    C. Stephen
    D. Judas

16. What two tribes of Israel were both descended from an Egyptian woman?
    A. Benjamin and Judah
    B. Manasseh and Ephraim
    C. Dan and Naphtali
    D. Reuben and Simeon

17. What king of Israel had a vast amount of his territory taken away by an Assyrian king?
    A. Ahab
    B. Jehoash
    C. Pekah
    D. Jehu

18. What did Jesus put on the eyes of the blind man at the pool of Siloam?
    A. Water
    B. Clay
    C. Speck
    D. Mote

19. What father of a dozen sons became blind in his old age?
    A. Jacob
    B. Isaac
    C. Abraham
    D. Job

20. What blind man of Jericho was healed by Jesus?
    A. Zacchaeus
    B. Elymas
    C. Barsabas
    D. Bartimaeus

21. What king repented after hearing the preaching of Jonah?
    A. The king of Persia
    B. The king of Nineveh
    C. The king of Syria
    D. The king of Assyria

22. What great Greek teacher who taught in the synagogue at Ephesus was himself taught by Aquila and Priscilla?
    A. Gamaliel
    B. Paul
    C. Apollos
    D. Peter

23. Whose Passover decree was laughed at by the men of Israel?
    A. Isaiah
    B. Saul
    C. Hezekiah
    D. David

24. Who rebuilt Ramah in order to keep people from coming and going to Judah?
    A. Baasha
    B. Nehemiah
    C. Jeroboam I
    D. Joram

25. What king of Judah reigned for only two years before being murdered by his own court officials?
    A. Zimri
    B. Amon
    C. Baasha
    D. Shallum

26. Who hid in a cave to escape Saul's wrath?
    A. David
    B. Solomon
    C. Jonathan
    D. Samuel

27. Who was reluctant to have Jesus wash his feet?
    A. Paul
    B. John
    C. James
    D. Peter

28. What brother of Jesus was called an apostle by Paul?
    A. John
    B. James
    C. Andrew
    D. Philip

29. Who infamously crafted a false idol, a golden calf?
    A. Moses
    B. Aaron
    C. Elijah
    D. Esau

30. Which of Saul's grandsons had crippling infirmities in his feet?
    A. Samuel
    B. Jonathan
    C. Kish
    D. Mephibosheth

31. The victory over Samaria of what Syrian king caused a famine so great that Samarians had to survive through cannibalism?
    A. Benhadad
    B. Menahem
    C. Joash
    D. Amaziah

32. What elderly woman recognized that the baby Jesus was the Messiah?
    A. Priscilla
    B. Salome
    C. Anna
    D. Drusilla

33. Who asked Jesus for the type of water that would quench her thirst forever?
    A. The crippled woman
    B. Mary Magdalene
    C. The Samaritan woman
    D. Martha

34. Who pretended to be her husband's sister while in Egypt?
    A. Lot's wife
    B. Abram's wife, Sarai
    C. Jochebed
    D. Joseph's sister

35. What king's claim to fame was an enormous iron bed?
    A. Og
    B. Goliath
    C. Baasha
    D. Shallum

36. Who was cursed to be Israel's servants during the time of Joshua?
    A. Amorites
    B. Hittites
    C. Levites
    D. Hivites

37. Who masquerades as an angel of light, according to Paul?
    A. Michael
    B. Elymas
    C. Satan
    D. The witch of Endor

38. What king commanded that Ahimelech and some other priests be executed because they had plotted with David?
    A. Zimri
    B. Joram
    C. Pekah
    D. Saul

39. What woman ran from the empty tomb of Jesus to tell the disciples?
    A. Joanna
    B. Mary Magdalene
    C. Salome
    D. Martha

40. What king vowed loyalty to David while trying his best to kill him at the same time?
    A. Samuel
    B. Solomon
    C. Jeroboam I
    D. Saul

41. What prophet condemned those who stockpiled stolen goods?
    A. Isaiah
    B. Habakkuk
    C. Micah
    D. Jonah

42. In what parable are the servants of a landowner assaulted?
    A. The tares
    B. The hidden treasure
    C. The lost coin
    D. The wicked husbandmen

43. What king of Judah married the daughter of the sinful Ahab?
    A. Zimri
    B. Pekah
    C. Jehoram
    D. Solomon

44. In what parable are servants supplied with money to invest?
    A. The sower
    B. The talents
    C. The creditor and two debtors
    D. The minas

45. What harlot was saved from a burning city, and her family with her?
    A. Jezebel
    B. Bathsheba
    C. The witch of Endor
    D. Rahab

46. Who was in exile three years after he had his brother Amnon killed?
    A. Elijah
    B. Absalom
    C. David
    D. Achish

47. What king of Judah became king at age seven and was helped greatly by priest Jehoiada?
    A. Jehoash
    B. Joram
    C. Josiah
    D. Hoshea

48. Who had a vision in which one angel ran to meet another?
    A. Isaiah
    B. Seraiah
    C. Zechariah
    D. Balaam

49. What king of Moab was known for being a farmer of sheep?
    A. Ahaziah
    B. Jeroboam II
    C. Solomon
    D. Mesha

50. How many books comprise the New Testament?
    A. 22
    B. 25
    C. 27
    D. 33

Priests

1. What severe penalty was handed out in Israel for disobeying a priest?
   - A. Imprisonment
   - B. Daily confession for a year
   - C. Death
   - D. Daily offering of a badger for a year

2. What was etched on the twelve stones in the high priest's breastplate?
   - A. The names of the kings of Israel
   - B. The names of the tribes of Israel
   - C. Elohim
   - D. Yahweh

3. What priest was said to have had no mother or father?
   - A. Ezekiel
   - B. Melchisedec
   - C. Joshua
   - D. Ananias

4. What priest was called "King of peace"?
   - A. Zacharias
   - B. Melchisedec
   - C. Zadok
   - D. Ezra

5. What priest chastised a woman because he thought she had
   been drinking at the tabernacle?
   A. Eli
   B. Abiathar
   C. Joshua
   D. Phinehas

6. What king ousted all the priests who had been appointed to
   serve pagan gods?
   A. David
   B. Jehu
   C. Shallum
   D. Josiah

7. What greedy priest was infamous for keeping the sacrificial
   meat all to himself?
   A. Ahimelech
   B. Aaron
   C. Phinehas
   D. Caiaphas

8. What priest located in Midian trained Moses in how to ad-
   minister justice among the Hebrews?
   A. Aaron
   B. Jethro
   C. Aleazar
   D. Eli

57

Lions' Den

1. Who saw a creature resembling a lion near the throne of God?
   A. Moses
   B. Jonathan
   C. John
   D. Samuel

2. Who envisioned a lion with eagle's wings?
   A. Jeremiah
   B. Amos
   C. Haggai
   D. Daniel

3. Who claimed to have grabbed a lion by the throat and pummeled him to death?
   A. King Hiram
   B. King Nebuchadnezzar
   C. King David
   D. King Zimri

4. What person is like a ravenous lion, according to 1 Peter?
   A. The devil
   B. Judas
   C. Herod
   D. Elymas

5. Who ripped a lion apart with his bare hands?
   A. Joshua
   B. Samson
   C. Jacob
   D. Ethan

6. What two men did David say were stronger than lions?
   A. Jacob and Joseph
   B. Saul and Jonathan
   C. Noah and Ham
   D. Abraham and Isaac

7. What prophet had a vision of a creature with a lion's face as one of its four sides?
   A. Isaiah
   B. Jeremiah
   C. Ezekiel
   D. Micah

8. What soldier in David's army killed a lion in a pit on a snowy day?
   A. Joab
   B. Uriah
   C. Shimei
   D. Benaiah

58

More of Anything Goes

1. Who had to shave their entire bodies as a form of consecration?
   A. Amorites
   B. Levites
   C. Philistines
   D. Gibeonites

2. A soldier of Gideon dreamed that a Midianite tent was overturned by what strange object?
   A. A grain of salt
   B. A quail from heaven
   C. A jug of milk
   D. A cake of barley bread

3. What king of Gerar took Sarah away from Abraham?
   A. Abimelech
   B. Saul
   C. Baasha
   D. Pekah

4. What wicked queen of Israel practiced witchcraft?
   A. Bathsheba
   B. Jezebel
   C. Potiphar's wife
   D. Esther

5. What leper of Bethany entertained Jesus in his home?
   A. Simeon
   B. Namaan
   C. Nadab
   D. Simon

6. What king is the author of the Song of Songs?
   A. David
   B. Solomon
   C. Moses
   D. Ahaziah

7. What king was referred to as "the Mede"?
   A. Darius
   B. Nebuchadnezzar
   C. Arioch
   D. Belshazzar

8. In the book of Ezekiel, what woman was a symbol of wicked Jerusalem?
   A. Delilah
   B. Aholibah
   C. Kezia
   D. Athaliah

9. What king sent an exiled priest back to Samaria to teach the Gentiles the proper way to follow God?
   A. The king of Assyria
   B. The king of Persia
   C. The king of Israel
   D. The king of Judah

10. What disciple outran Peter to the tomb of Jesus?
    A. John
    B. Philip
    C. Bartholomew
    D. Andrew

11. Whom did God tell to name his son Mahershalalhashbaz?
    A. Jeremiah
    B. Hosea
    C. Isaiah
    D. Iddo

12. What king of Israel was murdered while drunk?
    A. Zimri
    B. Elah
    C. Nadab
    D. Shallum

13. Who asked her son to give his father's concubine to another son?
    A. Manoah
    B. Bathsheba
    C. Deborah
    D. Rahab

14. What tribe got their wives from among the dancers at Shiloh?
    A. Dan
    B. Benjamin
    C. Naphtali
    D. Zebulun

15. Who told Job that God would fill a righteous man with laughter?
    A. Eliphaz
    B. Zophar
    C. Bildad
    D. Elihu

16. What king attacked the Israelites on their way into Canaan but was annihilated later?
    A. King Arad the Caananite
    B. King Saul
    C. The king of Syria
    D. King Joram

17. Who had a vision of a point in time when the Lord would collect the kings of the earth and put them in a pit?
   A. Jeremiah
   B. Amos
   C. Isaiah
   D. Joshua

18. What woman helped the poor in the early church?
   A. Bernice
   B. Dorcas (Tabitha)
   C. Candace
   D. Priscilla

19. The Israelites paused in their journey to the Promised Land because what woman was absent?
   A. Miriam
   B. Esther
   C. Ruth
   D. Huldah

20. Who was the last female to have dinner with King Saul?
   A. The witch of Endor
   B. Ahinoam
   C. The woman of Tekoa
   D. Merab

21. Whom did the prophet Elijah miraculously supply with food?
   A. Jezebel
   B. The widow of Zarephath
   C. Jerioth
   D. The Shulamite woman

22. What woman did Elisha warn of an approaching famine?
   A. The woman of Tishbite
   B. Ahab's wife
   C. The woman of Shunem
   D. Maachah

23. How was the adulterous woman going to be punished before she was forgiven by Jesus?

    A. Crucifixion

    B. Stoning

    C. Starvation

    D. Prison

24. In what book are the sons of God described as taking the daughters of men as wives?

    A. Genesis

    B. Exodus

    C. Leviticus

    D. Numbers

25. Where did Mary and Martha live?

    A. Samaria

    B. Bethany

    C. Jerusalem

    D. Jericho

26. There was a plot hatched against Jesus in the home of what person?

    A. Ananias

    B. Phinehas

    C. Zacharias

    D. Caiaphas

27. All the priests of Israel originated from what tribe?

    A. Judah

    B. Benjamin

    C. Levi

    D. Joseph

28. Who was the first metal worker named in the Bible?

    A. Abel

    B. Seth

    C. Noah

    D. Tubalcain

29. After Eve, who was the second woman mentioned in the Bible?
   A. Abel's wife
   B. Enoch's wife
   C. Cain's wife
   D. Adah

30. God made his first covenant with Noah and his second covenant with whom?
   A. Adam
   B. Abraham
   C. Cain
   D. Lamech

31. What was the second recorded miracle of Jesus?
   A. The raising of Lazarus
   B. Healing the man born blind
   C. Walking on the sea
   D. Healing an official's son in Cana

32. Paul first traveled with Barnabas before traveling with whom?
   A. Peter
   B. Silas
   C. Timothy
   D. John Mark

33. Who was Jacob's second son?
   A. Simeon
   B. Joseph
   C. Benjamin
   D. Dan

34. Who followed Saul as king of Israel?
   A. Samuel
   B. David
   C. Ishbosheth
   D. Jeroboam I

35. Who lived for 962 years?
    A. Seth
    B. Jared
    C. Mahalalel
    D. Lamech

36. After Solomon built the first temple in Jerusalem, who built the second?
    A. Joshua and Caleb
    B. Rehoboam and Jeroboam
    C. Asa and Abijam
    D. Zerubbabel and Jeshua

37. Who heard the voice of God speaking out of a whirlwind?
    A. Elisha
    B. Nathan
    C. Paul
    D. Job

38. Who was permanently crippled due to a servant woman dropping him as a baby?
    A. Balaam
    B. Saul's brother
    C. Mephibosheth
    D. Jonathan's grandson

39. Who committed suicide by hanging because Absalom would not follow his advice?
    A. Ahithophel
    B. Amnon
    C. Hushai
    D. Joab

40. What warrior wore a coat of mail weighing over 5,000 shekels of brass (over 125 pounds)?
    A. Goliath
    B. Samson
    C. David
    D. Methuselah

41. What did Malachi say the people of Judah were stealing from God?
    A. Idols
    B. Taxes
    C. Tithes and offerings
    D. Lands

42. When Jerusalem fell to the hands of the Babylonians, who was the king?
    A. Hezekiah
    B. Nebuchadnezzar
    C. Jeroboam II
    D. Zedekiah

43. What priest led a revolt in Judah that resulted in people tearing down their Baal temple and destroying idols?
    A. Jehoiada
    B. Asa
    C. Josiah
    D. Ahab

44. What priest dedicated the newly rebuilt walls of Jerusalem?
    A. Eleazar
    B. Pashur
    C. Zadok
    D. Eliashib

45. Who spoke the words of Joel in a sermon?
    A. John
    B. Paul
    C. Peter
    D. Thomas

46. What woman did Paul commend for her hard work?
    A. Phebe
    B. Mary
    C. Sapphira
    D. Susanna

47. Who was able to entice Herod to the point that he offered her anything she wanted?
    A. The daughter of Caiaphas
    B. Tabitha
    C. The daughter of Herodias
    D. Damaris

48. Who was told by God to name his son Loammi?
    A. Micah
    B. Amos
    C. Joel
    D. Hosea

49. What son of David tried to make himself king of Israel?
    A. Jesse
    B. Adonijah
    C. Solomon
    D. Abner

50. What Canaanite king had nine hundred chariots of iron?
    A. Hezekiah
    B. Jabin
    C. Ahaziah
    D. Pekah

51. Who was the only Egyptian queen mentioned in the Bible?
    A. Tahpenes
    B. Esther
    C. The queen of Sheba
    D. Candace

52. What was the affliction of the ten men who cried out to Jesus, begging him for mercy?
    A. Blindness
    B. Deafness
    C. Leprosy
    D. Paralysis

53. What miracle of Jesus prompted the priests to plot to have him executed?
   A. The temple tax in the fish's mouth
   B. The escape from the hostile multitude
   C. The raising of Lazarus from the dead
   D. The healing of a centurion's servant

54. What rotund king of Moab was murdered by the judge Ehud?
   A. Zimri
   B. Solomon
   C. Eglon
   D. David

55. What woman had already had five husbands and was living with another man?
   A. Martha
   B. The woman with the issue of blood
   C. Mary Magdalene
   D. The Samaritan woman

56. What woman made her living selling purple cloth?
   A. Priscilla
   B. Claudia
   C. Lydia
   D. Lois

57. What church had a sexually immoral woman named Jezebel?
   A. Ephesus
   B. Smyrna
   C. Pergamos
   D. Thyatira

58. What king's wife disguised herself in order to seek counsel with the prophet Ahijah?
   A. Potifar's
   B. Jeroboam's
   C. David's
   D. Job's

59. What two apostles were imprisoned in Jerusalem for preaching the gospel?
   A. Paul and Barnabas
   B. Peter and John
   C. Titus and Timothy
   D. Paul and Timothy

60. Who had a dream in which God warned that Jacob should not be pursued or harmed?
   A. Laban
   B. Leah
   C. Nahor
   D. Bethuel

61. What king introduced Israel to the worship of the false god Baal?
   A. Elijah
   B. Ahab
   C. Jehoshaphat
   D. Shallum

62. What king established a beauty contest in order to select a bride?
   A. Ahasuerus
   B. Malcham
   C. Joahaz
   D. Nethaniah

63. Who prophesied the destruction of Jerusalem?
   A. Peter
   B. Thomas
   C. Herod
   D. Jesus

64. Who built an altar unto the Lord and called it Jehovahnissi?
   A. Abraham
   B. Noah
   C. Moses
   D. Aaron

65. What prophet foresaw the destruction of the altars of Bethel?
    A. Nahum
    B. Joel
    C. Habakkuk
    D. Amos

66. Who murdered Shallum and replaced him on the throne of Israel?
    A. Shamar
    B. Menahem
    C. Baasha
    D. Jehoash

67. Whom did the Sanhedrin jail for disturbing the peace?
    A. Paul and Barnabas
    B. Timothy and Titus
    C. Peter and John
    D. Stephen and Silas

68. Who preached to the intellectual elite of Athens?
    A. Paul
    B. Peter
    C. Jesus
    D. Gamaliel

69. After Sodom and Gomorrah were destroyed, who gathered his daughters and lived in a cave?
    A. Abraham
    B. Caleb
    C. Elijah
    D. Lot

70. What is the fortieth book of the Bible?
    A. Haggai
    B. Malachi
    C. Luke
    D. Matthew

59

Did You Know?
(Set 8)

Ready for more astonishing facts? Help yourself.

- In the early thirteenth century, Archbishop Stephen Langton developed a system for dividing the Bible into chapters.
- At the grand dedication of God's temple, Solomon had 22,000 oxen and 120,000 sheep sacrificed (1 Kings 8:62–63).
- After the Israelites destroyed the temple of Baal, they used it as a communal latrine (draught house) (2 Kings 10:26–27).
- Luke, the only physician among the disciples, chronicled that as Jesus was praying in the Garden of Gethsemane before he was crucified, his extreme duress caused his perspiration to become like large drops of blood falling to the ground. This phenomenon is a medical condition called hematidrosis that only Luke the physician documented.
- Although dogs are mentioned in the Bible forty-one times, cats are not mentioned at all.
- God himself buried Moses in Moab, but no one knows precisely where (Deuteronomy 34:5–6).
- In Joshua 3:16, there is a town called Adam.

SCRIPTURE
FILL IN THE BLANKS

Fill in the blanks to complete the following Scripture passages. Give yourself 2 points for each correct passage.

60

Fill in the Blanks

1. Genesis 1:1
   In the _____ God created the _____ and the _____.

2. Psalm 37:4
   Delight _____ also in the _____: and he shall give thee
   the _____ of thine _____.

3. Isaiah 9:6
   For unto us a _____ is born, unto us a son is given: and
   the _____ shall be upon his shoulder: and his name shall
   be called _____, Counsellor, The mighty God, The everlasting Father, The Prince of _____.

4. Isaiah 40:28
   Hast thou not _____? hast thou not heard, that the
   _____ God, the LORD, the Creator of the ends of the
   earth, fainteth not, neither is _____? there is no searching
   of his understanding.

5. Jeremiah 29:11
   For I know the _____ that I think toward you, saith the
   _____, thoughts of peace, and not of _____, to give
   you an expected end.

6. John 3:16
   For God so _____ the _____, that he gave his only
   begotten _____, that whosoever believeth in him should
   not perish, but have everlasting _____.

7. John 15:7

If ye _____ in me, and my words abide in you, ye shall ask what ye _____, and it shall be done unto _____.

8. Romans 4:21

And being _____ persuaded that, what he had _____, he was able also to _____.

9. Romans 8:1

There is therefore now no _____ to them which are in Christ _____, who walk not after the flesh, but after the _____.

10. Romans 8:28

And we know that all things _____ together for _____ to them that _____ God, to them who are the called according to his _____.

11. 2 Corinthians 1:20

For all the _____ of God in him are yea, and in him _____, unto the _____ of God by us.

12. Ephesians 2:10

For we are his workmanship, created in Christ Jesus unto good _____, which God hath before _____ that we should walk in them.

13. Philippians 4:6–7

Be careful for _____; but in every thing by _____ and supplication with _____ let your requests be made known unto God. And the peace of God, which passeth all understanding, shall keep your hearts and _____ through Christ Jesus.

14. Philippians 4:19

But my God shall _____ all your need according to his _____ in _____ by Christ Jesus.

15. 2 Peter 1:4

Whereby are given unto us exceeding _____ and precious _____: that by these ye might be partakers of the divine _____, having escaped the corruption that is in the world through lust.

61

Scriptures on Salvation

1. John 14:6
   Jesus saith unto him, I am the _____, the truth, and the
   _____: no man cometh unto the _____, but by me.

2. Romans 3:23
   For all have _____, and come short of the _____ of
   God.

3. Romans 6:23
   For the wages of _____ is _____; but the gift of God
   is eternal _____ through Jesus Christ our Lord.

4. 2 Corinthians 5:17
   Therefore if any man be in _____, he is a new _____:
   old things are passed away; behold, all things are become
   _____.

5. Ephesians 2:8–9
   For by _____ are ye saved through _____; and that not
   of yourselves: it is the gift of God: Not of works, lest any
   man should _____.

6. Revelation 3:20
   Behold, I stand at the _____, and _____: if any man
   hear my _____, and open the door, I will come in to him,
   and will sup with him, and he with me.

62

Scriptures on Security

1. Psalm 27:1

   The _____ is my light and my _____; whom shall I fear? the LORD is the strength of my life; of whom shall I be _____?

2. Psalm 37:4

   Delight _____ also in the LORD: and he shall give thee the _____ of thine _____.

3. Proverbs 3:5–6

   Trust in the _____ with all thine heart; and lean not unto thine own _____. In all thy ways acknowledge him, and he shall direct thy _____.

4. Isaiah 40:31

   But they that _____ upon the _____ shall renew their strength; they shall mount up with wings as eagles; they shall run, and not be _____; and they shall walk, and not _____.

5. Jeremiah 29:11

   For I know the thoughts that I think toward you, saith the _____, thoughts of _____, and not of _____, to give you an expected end.

6. Lamentations 3:22–23

It is of the LORD's _____ that we are not _____, because his compassions fail not. They are new every morning: great is thy _____.

7. Matthew 11:28–30

Come unto me, all ye that labour and are heavy _____, and I will give you rest. Take my _____ upon you, and learn of me; for I am meek and lowly in _____: and ye shall find rest unto your souls. For my yoke is easy, and my burden is _____.

8. Luke 16:13

No _____ can serve two _____: for either he will hate the one, and love the other; or else he will hold to the one, and despise the other. Ye cannot serve _____ and mammon.

9. Acts 1:8

But ye shall receive _____, after that the Holy _____ is come upon you: and ye shall be witnesses unto me both in _____, and in all Judaea, and in Samaria, and unto the uttermost part of the _____.

10. Romans 8:28

And we know that all _____ work together for _____ to them that love God, to them who are the called according to his _____.

11. Romans 8:38–39

For I am persuaded, that neither _____, nor life, nor _____, nor principalities, nor powers, nor things present, nor things to come, Nor _____, nor depth, nor any other creature, shall be able to separate us from the love of God, which is in Christ Jesus our _____.

12. Romans 12:1

I beseech you therefore, _____, by the mercies of _____, that ye present your bodies a living _____, holy, acceptable unto God, which is your reasonable _____.

13. 1 Corinthians 15:58
Therefore, my beloved brethren, be ye stedfast, _____, always abounding in the _____ of the Lord, forasmuch as ye know that your labour is not in _____ in the Lord.

14. 2 Corinthians 4:18
While we _____ not at the things which are _____, but at the things which are not seen: for the things which are seen are _____; but the things which are not seen are _____.

15. 2 Corinthians 12:9
And he said unto me, My _____ is sufficient for _____: for my strength is made perfect in weakness. Most gladly therefore will I rather glory in my _____, that the power of Christ may rest upon me.

16. Galatians 2:20
I am _____ with Christ: nevertheless I live; yet not I, but Christ liveth in me: and the _____ which I now live in the flesh I live by the _____ of the Son of God, who loved me, and gave himself for me.

17. Galatians 5:22–23
But the _____ of the Spirit is love, joy, peace, _____, gentleness, goodness, _____, Meekness, temperance: against such there is no law.

18. Philippians 4:13
I can do all _____ through Christ which _____ me.

19. Colossians 3:23
And whatsoever ye do, do it _____, as to the Lord, and not unto _____.

20. Hebrews 12:1–2
Wherefore seeing we also are compassed about with so great a cloud of _____, let us lay aside every _____, and the sin which doth so easily beset us, and let us run with patience the race that is set before us, looking unto Jesus the author and finisher of our _____; who for the joy that was set before him endured the _____, despising the shame, and is set down at the right hand of the throne of God.

21. Hebrews 13:8

Jesus Christ the same _____, and to day, and for _____.

22. James 1:22

But be ye _____ of the _____, and not hearers only, deceiving your own _____.

23. James 4:7

_____ yourselves therefore to _____. Resist the devil, and he will _____ from you.

24. 2 Peter 3:9

The _____ is not slack concerning his _____, as some men count slackness; but is longsuffering to us-ward, not willing that any should _____, but that all should come to repentance.

25. 1 John 4:7–8

Beloved, let us _____ one another: for love is of God; and every one that loveth is born of God, and knoweth _____. He that loveth not knoweth not God; for God is love.

63

Scriptures on Prayer

1. Psalm 19:14
   Let the words of my _____, and the meditation of my _____, be acceptable in thy sight, O LORD, my _____, and my redeemer.

2. Psalm 50:14–15
   Offer unto God _____; and pay thy vows unto the most _____: And call upon me in the day of trouble: I will deliver thee, and thou shalt _____ me.

3. Psalm 66:17
   I cried unto him with my mouth, and he was extolled with my _____.

4. Psalm 95:2
   Let us come before his presence with _____, and make a joyful _____ unto him with psalms.

5. Psalm 118:25
   Save now, I beseech thee, O _____: O LORD, I beseech thee, send now _____:

6. Psalm 119:11
   Thy _____ have I hid in mine _____, that I might not _____ against thee.

7. Psalm 119:105

Thy word is a _____ unto my _____, and a light unto my _____.

8. Psalm 122:6

_____ for the _____ of Jerusalem: they shall prosper that _____ thee.

9. Romans 10:1

Brethren, my heart's _____ and _____ to God for Israel is, that they might be _____.

10. Romans 10:13

For _____ shall call upon the _____ of the Lord shall be _____.

11. Romans 15:30

Now I beseech you, _____, for the Lord _____ Christ's sake, and for the _____ of the Spirit, that ye strive together with me in your _____ to God for me.

12. 1 Corinthians 1:4

I thank my God always on your _____, for the _____ of God which is given you by Jesus _____.

13. 1 Corinthians 14:15

What is it then? I will pray with the _____, and I will pray with the understanding also: I will sing with the spirit, and I will _____ with the understanding also.

14. 2 Corinthians 1:11

Ye also helping together by _____ for us, that for the _____ bestowed upon us by the means of many persons thanks may be given by many on our _____.

15. Ephesians 6:18

_____ always with all prayer and _____ in the _____, and watching thereunto with all perseverance and supplication for all saints.

16. Philippians 1:3–4
    I thank my _____ upon every _____ of you, always in
    every _____ of mine for you all making request with joy.

17. Colossians 1:3
    We give thanks to God and the Father of our Lord Jesus
    Christ, _____ always for you.

18. 1 Thessalonians 5:17
    _____ without ceasing.

19. 1 Thessalonians 5:18
    In every thing give _____: for this is the will of God in
    Christ Jesus concerning _____.

20. James 1:6
    But let him ask in _____, nothing wavering. For he that
    wavereth is like a wave of the _____ driven with the wind
    and _____.

21. James 5:13–14
    Is any among you _____? let him _____. Is any merry?
    let him sing psalms. Is any sick among you? let him call for the
    elders of the _____; and let them pray over him, anointing
    him with _____ in the name of the Lord.

22. James 5:16
    _____ your faults one to another, and _____ one for
    another, that ye may be _____. The effectual fervent prayer
    of a righteous man availeth much.

64

Scriptures on Temptation

1. Matthew 6:13
   And _____ us not into _____, but deliver us from evil:
   For thine is the kingdom, and the power, and the _____,
   for ever. Amen.

2. Matthew 26:41
   Watch and _____, that ye enter not into _____: the
   spirit indeed is willing, but the _____ is weak.

3. Luke 4:13
   And when the _____ had ended all the _____, he departed from him for a _____.

4. Luke 11:4
   And _____ us our sins; for we also forgive every one that
   is _____ to us. And lead us not into _____; but deliver
   us from evil.

5. Luke 22:40
   And when he was at the _____, he said unto them, _____
   that ye enter not into temptation.

6. 1 Corinthians 7:2
   Nevertheless, to _____ fornication, let every man have his
   own _____, and let every woman have her own _____.

7. 1 Corinthians 10:13

There hath no _____ taken you but such as is common to _____: but God is _____, who will not suffer you to be tempted above that ye are able; but will with the temptation also make a way to _____, that ye may be able to bear it.

8. 1 Timothy 6:9

But they that will be _____ fall into temptation and a snare, and into many _____ and hurtful _____, which drown men in destruction and perdition.

65

Scriptures on Never Losing Faith

1. Joshua 1:9
   Have not I _____ thee? Be strong and of a good _____;
   be not afraid, neither be thou dismayed: for the LORD thy
   _____ is with thee whithersoever thou goest.

2. 2 Chronicles 15:7
   Be ye _____ therefore, and let not your _____ be weak:
   for your work shall be _____.

3. Job 19:25
   For I know that my _____ liveth, and that he shall stand
   at the latter _____ upon the _____.

4. Job 23:10
   But he knoweth the _____ that I take: when he hath tried
   _____, I shall come forth as _____.

5. Psalm 16:11
   Thou wilt shew me the _____ of life: in thy presence is
   fulness of joy; at thy right _____ there are pleasures for
   evermore.

6. Proverbs 14:12
   There is a way which seemeth _____ unto a _____,
   but the end thereof are the ways of _____.

7. Proverbs 16:7

   When a man's ways _____ the _____, he maketh even
   his enemies to be at _____ with him.

8. Proverbs 21:1

   The king's _____ is in the _____ of the LORD, as the
   rivers of _____: he turneth it whithersoever he will.

9. Proverbs 27:17

   Iron sharpeneth _____; so a man sharpeneth the countenance of his _____.

10. Isaiah 41:10

    Fear thou not; for I am with thee: be not _____; for I am
    thy God: I will strengthen thee; yea, I will help _____; yea, I
    will uphold thee with the right _____ of my righteousness.

11. Isaiah 58:1

    Cry _____, spare not, lift up thy voice like a _____,
    and shew my people their _____, and the house of Jacob
    their _____.

12. Matthew 18:18

    _____ I say unto you, Whatsoever ye shall bind on _____
    shall be bound in heaven: and whatsoever ye shall loose on
    earth shall be loosed in _____.

13. Matthew 19:26

    But _____ beheld them, and said unto them, With men
    this is _____; but with God all _____ are possible.

14. Luke 1:37

    For with God _____ shall be _____.

15. John 8:12

    Then spake _____ again unto them, saying, I am the
    _____ of the world: he that followeth me shall not walk
    in darkness, but shall have the light of _____.

16. 1 Corinthians 2:14

    But the natural _____ receiveth not the things of the
    _____ of God: for they are foolishness unto him: neither
    can he know them, because they are spiritually _____.

17. 2 Corinthians 4:1

    Therefore seeing we have this _____, as we have received
    _____, we faint not.

18. 2 Corinthians 11:3

    But I fear, lest by any means, as the _____ beguiled Eve
    through his subtilty, so your _____ should be corrupted
    from the simplicity that is in _____.

19. Galatians 6:9

    And let us not be weary in well _____: for in due season
    we shall _____, if we faint not.

20. Ephesians 4:26

    Be ye _____, and _____ not: let not the sun go down
    upon your _____.

21. Hebrews 4:12

    For the word of _____ is quick, and powerful, and sharper
    than any twoedged _____, piercing even to the dividing
    asunder of soul and _____, and of the joints and marrow,
    and is a discerner of the thoughts and intents of the _____.

22. Hebrews 11:6

    But without faith it is _____ to please _____: for he
    that cometh to God must believe that he is, and that he is a
    rewarder of them that diligently seek _____.

23. Hebrews 12:3

    For consider _____ that endured such contradiction of
    _____ against himself, lest ye be wearied and faint in
    your _____.

24. Revelation 7:1

    And after these things I saw four _____ standing on the
    four corners of the _____, holding the four winds of the
    _____, that the wind should not blow on the earth, nor
    on the sea, nor on any tree.

25. Revelation 12:11

    And they overcame him by the blood of the _____, and
    by the word of their _____; and they loved not their lives
    unto the _____.

66

Scriptures on Hope

1. Numbers 23:19
   God is not a _____, that he should _____; neither the son of man, that he should repent: hath he said, and shall he not do it? or hath he spoken, and shall he not make it _____?

2. Job 13:15
   Though he _____ me, yet will I _____ in him: but I will maintain mine own _____ before him.

3. Proverbs 24:14
   So shall the knowledge of _____ be unto thy _____: when thou hast found it, then there shall be a reward, and thy _____ shall not be cut off.

4. Proverbs 24:20
   For there shall be no reward to the _____ man; the candle of the _____ shall be put out.

5. Romans 8:24–25
   For we are saved by _____: but hope that is seen is not _____: for what a man seeth, why doth he yet hope for? But if we hope for that we see not, then do we with _____ wait for it.

6. 1 Corinthians 15:19
   If in this _____ only we have hope in _____, we are of all men most _____.

7. Hebrews 11:1

   Now _____ is the substance of things _____ for, the evidence of _____ not seen.

8. 1 Peter 1:3

   Blessed be the _____ and Father of our Lord Jesus _____, which according to his abundant mercy hath begotten us again unto a lively hope by the _____ of Jesus Christ from the _____.

67

Scriptures on Love

1. Leviticus 19:17–18
   Thou shalt not hate thy _____ in thine heart: thou shalt in any wise rebuke thy neighbour, and not suffer _____ upon him. Thou shalt not avenge, nor bear any grudge against the _____ of thy people, but thou shalt _____ thy neighbour as thyself: I am the LORD.

2. Psalm 30:5
   For his _____ endureth but a moment; in his favour is _____: weeping may endure for a _____, but joy cometh in the morning.

3. Psalm 103:8
   The _____ is merciful and _____, slow to anger, and plenteous in _____.

4. Psalm 103:13
   Like as a _____ pitieth his _____, so the LORD pitieth them that fear _____.

5. Psalm 143:8
   Cause me to hear thy lovingkindness in the _____; for in thee do I trust: cause me to know the way wherein I should _____; for I lift up my soul unto thee.

6. Proverbs 10:12
   _____ stirreth up strifes: but _____ covereth all sins.

7. Proverbs 21:21

He that followeth after _____ and mercy findeth _____, righteousness, and honour.

8. Isaiah 43:4

Since thou wast precious in my _____, thou hast been honourable, and I have loved _____: therefore will I give _____ for thee, and people for thy _____.

9. Matthew 5:44

But I say unto you, _____ your _____, bless them that curse you, do good to them that hate you, and pray for them which despitefully use you, and persecute _____.

10. Mark 12:30

And thou shalt _____ the Lord thy God with all thy _____, and with all thy soul, and with all thy mind, and with all thy strength: this is the first _____.

11. Mark 12:31

And the second is like, namely this, Thou shalt _____ thy neighbour as thyself. There is none other _____ greater than these.

12. Luke 10:27

And he answering said, _____ shalt love the Lord thy God with all thy _____, and with all thy _____, and with all thy strength, and with all thy mind; and thy neighbour as thyself.

13. John 14:21

He that hath my _____, and keepeth them, he it is that _____ me: and he that loveth me shall be loved of my _____, and I will love him, and will manifest myself to him.

14. John 15:12

This is my _____, That ye _____ one another, as I have _____ you.

15. John 15:13

Greater love hath no _____ than this, that a man lay down his _____ for his _____.

16. Romans 8:38–39

For I am _____, that neither death, nor life, nor angels, nor principalities, nor _____, nor things present, nor things to come, nor _____, nor depth, nor any other creature, shall be able to separate us from the love of _____, which is in Christ Jesus our Lord.

17. Romans 12:9

Let _____ be without dissimulation. Abhor that which is _____; cleave to that which is good.

18. Romans 12:10

Be kindly affectioned one to another with brotherly _____; in honour preferring one another.

19. Romans 13:8

Owe no man any thing, but to _____ one another: for he that loveth another hath fulfilled the _____.

20. Romans 13:10

_____ worketh no _____ to his neighbour: therefore love is the fulfilling of the law.

21. 1 Corinthians 2:9

But as it is _____, Eye hath not seen, nor ear _____, neither have entered into the heart of man, the things which God hath prepared for them that _____ him.

22. 1 Corinthians 10:24

Let no _____ seek his own, but every man another's _____.

23. 1 Corinthians 13:1

Though I speak with the _____ of men and of _____, and have not charity, I am become as sounding brass, or a tinkling _____.

24. 1 Corinthians 13:2

And though I have the gift of _____, and understand all _____, and all knowledge; and though I have all faith, so that I could remove _____, and have not charity, I am nothing.

25. 1 Corinthians 13:3

And though I bestow all my _____ to feed the poor, and though I give my _____ to be burned, and have not charity, it profiteth me _____.

26. 1 Corinthians 13:4–5

_____ suffereth long, and is kind; charity envieth not; charity vaunteth not itself, is not puffed up, doth not _____ itself unseemly, seeketh not her own, is not easily provoked, thinketh no _____.

27. 1 Corinthians 16:14

Let all your _____ be done with _____.

28. Ephesians 3:16–17

That he would grant you, according to the _____ of his _____, to be strengthened with might by his _____ in the inner man; that Christ may dwell in your hearts by faith; that ye, being rooted and grounded in _____.

29. Ephesians 4:2

With all lowliness and _____, with longsuffering, forbearing one another in _____.

30. Ephesians 4:15

But speaking the truth in _____, may grow up into him in all _____, which is the head, even _____.

31. Ephesians 5:2

And walk in love, as Christ also hath _____ us, and hath given _____ for us an offering and a sacrifice to _____ for a sweetsmelling savour.

32. Ephesians 5:25–26

_____, love your _____, even as Christ also loved the church, and gave himself for it; That he might sanctify and cleanse it with the washing of water by the word.

33. Colossians 3:14

And above all these things put on _____, which is the bond of _____.

34. 1 Thessalonians 3:12

And the Lord make you to increase and abound in _____ one toward another, and toward all _____, even as we do toward you.

35. 2 Thessalonians 3:5

And the Lord direct your _____ into the love of God, and into the _____ waiting for Christ.

36. 2 Timothy 1:7

For God hath not given us the spirit of _____; but of power, and of love, and of a sound _____.

37. 1 Peter 4:8

And above all things have fervent _____ among yourselves: for charity shall cover the multitude of _____.

38. 1 John 3:1

Behold, what manner of love the _____ hath bestowed upon _____, that we should be called the sons of God: therefore the world knoweth us not, because it knew him not.

39. 1 John 3:11

For this is the message that ye heard from the _____, that we should _____ one another.

40. 1 John 4:9

In this was manifested the _____ of God toward us, because that God sent his only begotten Son into the _____, that we might live through him.

41. 1 John 4:10

Herein is _____, not that we loved God, but that he loved us, and sent his _____ to be the propitiation for our _____.

42. 1 John 4:12

No man hath seen _____ at any time. If we love one another, God dwelleth in us, and his love is perfected in _____.

43. 1 John 4:16

And we have known and believed the _____ that God hath to us. God is _____; and he that dwelleth in love dwelleth in God, and God in him.

44. 1 John 4:18

There is no fear in love; but perfect _____ casteth out _____: because fear hath torment. He that feareth is not made perfect in _____.

45. 1 John 4:20

If a man say, I love God, and hateth his brother, he is a _____: for he that loveth not his _____ whom he hath seen, how can he love God whom he hath not seen?

46. Revelation 3:19

As many as I _____, I rebuke and _____: be zealous therefore, and repent.

68

Crossword Puzzle 1

Tackle this first of five crossword puzzles for 25 bonus points. Since crossword puzzles are difficult by nature, you are allowed three mistakes without penalty. If you solve the puzzle with only three mistakes or fewer, give yourself 25 points in the bonus column of the score card.

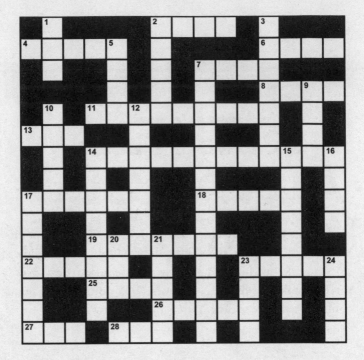

Across

2. Caspar, Balthazar and Melchior
4. Christian symbol
6. First gardener
7. Apostle to the Gentiles
8. Proverbs 19:1, Slothfulness casteth into a deep sleep; and an ___ soul shall suffer hunger
11. Chief heavenly messenger, like Gabriel
13. Daniel 7:1, In the first year of Belshazzar king of Babylon Daniel had a dream and visions of his head upon his ___
14. A gift to the infant Jesus
17. Certain man of the cloth
18. Psalm 106:16, They envied Moses also in the camp, and Aaron the ___ of the LORD
19. Adore to the fullest
22. Genesis 7:1, ___ whose nostrils was the breath of life, of all that was in the dry land, died (2 words)
23. Confidence that God's Word is true
25. Period beginning Ash Wednesday
26. Church building feature
27. Mother of Abel
28. The wages of it are death

Down

1. How great thou ___
2. Proverbs 7:1, I have perfumed my bed with ___, aloes, and cinnamon
3. Nazareth's locale
5. Revelation 8:11, And the name of the ___ is called Wormwood
7. He ordered Christ's crucifixion
9. The Ten Commandments, for example
10. Man originally called Simon
12. Thing with verses in the Bible
14. What God has given so that people can make their own choices (2 words)
15. Christmas scene
16. Twin in Genesis
17. Kind of story Jesus told
20. Genesis 11:1, And the whole earth was of ___ language
21. The enemy to us all
23. Genesis 19:24, Then the LORD rained upon Sodom and upon Gomorrah brimstone and ___
24. Psalm 9:1, The wicked shall be turned into ___, and all the nations that forget God

THE ADVANCED SECTION

This section gets into very specific and challenging questions and puzzles geared to take you to an extreme level of Bible brilliance. (Answers to section 2 begin on page 588).

> If we abide by the principles taught in the Bible, our country will go on prospering but if we and our posterity neglect its instructions and authority, no man can tell how sudden a catastrophe may overwhelm us and bury all our glory in profound obscurity.
>
> Daniel Webster, American statesman and the fourteenth United States secretary of state

69

Did You Know?
(Set 9)

Here is the ninth set of astounding biblical facts.

- Sheep are the animals mentioned most often in the Bible.
- A man named Ben-hur (son of Hur) was once an officer over Israel (1 Kings 4:7–8 NKJV).
- In his day, Moses was the most humble man on the face of the earth (Numbers 12:3).
- Zechariah 6:14 mentions a man named Hen.
- The king of Babylon tried to foretell the future by examining liver (Ezekiel 21:21).
- When the angel of the Lord delivered a pestilence upon the land of Israel, he could actually be seen in the sky holding a sword in his hand (2 Samuel 24:15–17; 1 Chronicles 21:14–17).
- King Solomon built God's temple in seven years but took thirteen years to build his own palace (1 Kings 6:38; 7:1).

SPECIALIZED TRUE OR FALSE TRIVIA

For 1 point per correct answer, tackle this section of true or false statements derived from all areas of the Bible. Some are easy, and some are quite difficult. Do one group at a time and record your score for each group on the score card.

Remember, you may do a single group as many times as necessary before posting your best score. It is far more important to be thorough and to learn this information than to finish quickly and retain little.

70

Group 1

1. _____ Isaac was the son of Abraham.

2. _____ Matthew was David's firstborn son.

3. _____ Solomon's son Shaphat became king after him.

4. _____ The apostle Paul said that a woman's long hair is her pride and joy.

5. _____ Flesh and blood is unable to inherit the kingdom of God.

6. _____ In the Bible, sin is called the sting of death.

7. _____ All believers are called to be the temple of God, according to Paul.

8. _____ Paul refers to himself as a missionary in the book of 1 Corinthians.

9. _____ David promised Bathsheba that her son Solomon would one day be governor.

10. _____ Rehoboam ruled in Judah for twenty-one years.

11. _____ King Ahab was the husband of Jezebel.

12. _____ In Samaria, Ahab built a temple for Baal.

13. _____ Elisha brought a widow's son back from the dead in Zarephath.

14. _____ Ravens brought Elijah food in a dire situation.

15. _____ On Mount Nebo, Elijah met the prophets of Baal.

16. _____ Elijah once outran a king's chariot to the town of Jezreel.

17. _____ The prophet Elijah was fed three meals by an angel.

18. _____ When Elijah fled from Jezebel, he went to Mount Horeb.

19. _____ Mount Horeb is called the mount of God.

20. _____ King Solomon had twelve thousand horsemen.

71

Group 2

1. _____ Abner was the commander of Solomon's army.

2. _____ David received permission from the Lord to build the temple.

3. _____ In Solomon's first year as king, he began to build the house of the Lord.

4. _____ Jesus is the chief cornerstone.

5. _____ The apostle Peter compared the devil to a roaring lion.

6. _____ Hannah received a son after asking God to bless her with a child.

7. _____ The first king of Israel was Saul.

8. _____ A person's hand was the part of the body that was usually anointed.

9. _____ Because King Saul acted as a priest in Samuel's place, he was rejected.

10. _____ David's father was Jesse.

11. _____ David had a skill for playing the harp.

12. _____ David boasted of killing a pig and a horse.

13. _____ Bartimaeus was healed of blindness.

14. _____ The gigantic Goliath was from the city of Ekron.

15. _____ Goliath stood over nine feet tall (six cubits and a span).

16. _____ David took seven stones from the brook before killing Goliath.

17. _____ To bring down Goliath, David used a huge sword.

18. _____ David stored Goliath's armor in his tent.

19. _____ Saul once threw a javelin at David.

20. _____ David's first wife was Michal.

72

Group 3

1. _____ The women of Israel danced when Goliath was killed by David.

2. _____ Hannah made a robe every year for her son.

3. _____ In 1 Samuel, Jonathan and David made a covenant of friendship.

4. _____ The priest of Nod gave Saul's sword to David.

5. _____ Saul massacred eighty-five priests in the town of Nazareth.

6. _____ David's wife Abigail was also married to a man named Nabal.

7. _____ At night, Saul visited a medium.

8. _____ When Samuel was a boy, he was awakened out of his sleep by the voice of God.

9. _____ Saul's bones were buried under a bridge at Jabesh.

10. _____ Saul's sons were killed by the Philistines.

11. _____ King Saul was critically wounded by Philistine arrows.

12. _____ Six of Saul's sons were killed in battle.

13. _____ Eli's sons were killed when the ark was taken.

14. _____ The ark of the covenant was taken into battle with the Philistines by Eli's sons.

15. _____ Dagon was the god of the Philistines.

16. _____ Samuel, a judge and a prophet, built an altar to the Lord at Ramah.

17. _____ Samuel's home was in the city of Ramah.

18. _____ Kish was the father of King Saul.

19. _____ Jesus Christ is the mediator between God and man.

20. _____ Paul told Timothy that Christians should lift up a symbol of the cross in prayer.

73

Group 4

1. _____ Abijah, the king of Judah, had fourteen wives.

2. _____ The Philistines brought a tribute to King Jehoshaphat.

3. _____ In a vision, the prophet Micaiah saw the Lord sitting upon a mountain.

4. _____ Solomon got the cedars for his temple from Lebanon.

5. _____ King Uzziah dug wells in the desert.

6. _____ Uzziah, the king of Judah, was a leper until he died.

7. _____ Moses disguised himself before fighting with an Egyptian.

8. _____ Paul's nationality was Greek.

9. _____ Paul suffered shipwrecks three times.

10. _____ Eve's name appears seven times in the New Testament.

11. _____ The apostle Paul fled from the soldiers of King Aretas in Damascus.

12. _____ Paul knew of a man who had been caught up into the third heaven.

13. _____ The bones of Elisha healed a man of leprosy.

14. _____ Elijah was taken to heaven in a whirlwind.

15. _____ When Elisha struck the Jordan River with Elijah's cloak, it turned red.

16. _____ Elisha was used by God to heal the waters of Gibeah with a bowl of salt.

17. _____ Hezekiah and Joshua had time altered for them.

18. _____ Josiah was only eight years old when he became king, and he reigned in Jerusalem thirty-one years.

19. _____ King Josiah was killed in Megiddo.

20. _____ Nebuchadnezzar was a ruler of Babylon.

74

Group 5

1. _____ David was the last king of Judah.
2. _____ Elisha's servant was Gehazi.
3. _____ Elisha supplied a widow with large quantities of milk and honey.
4. _____ For lying to the prophet Elisha, Gehazi was turned into a leper.
5. _____ Elisha's servant had a vision of the hills filled with horses and chariots of fire.
6. _____ Hazael murdered King Benhadad.
7. _____ The prophet Urijah was murdered for opposing King Jehoiakim.
8. _____ King Jehu ordered Jezebel's servants to toss her out the window.
9. _____ After Jezebel's death, wild horses ate her body.
10. _____ David saw his neighbor bathing on a rooftop.
11. _____ Nathan, a prophet, confronted King David about his sin of adultery.
12. _____ Absalom was David and Bathsheba's second son.
13. _____ God named Solomon Jedidiah.

14. _____ After killing his brother Amnon, Absalom fled to Geshur for three years.

15. _____ David's son Absalom was known for being an unattractive man.

16. _____ As David went up the Mount of Olives, he was barefoot and wept.

17. _____ Absalom was buried by Joab in a great pit in the forest.

18. _____ David was anointed king at Hebron.

19. _____ Saul's son Ishbosheth was made king over Israel by Abner.

20. _____ King Saul's son Ishbosheth was also known as Titus.

75

Group 6

1. _____ The wise woman of Abel saved her city by negotiating with Joab.

2. _____ Joab killed a man while kissing him.

3. _____ David moved the bones of Saul and his son Jonathan to their final place of burial.

4. _____ Saul's grandson Mephibosheth was crippled in both feet.

5. _____ While pretending to get wheat, Rechab and Baanah killed a king.

6. _____ Amorites inhabited Jerusalem before the Israelites.

7. _____ In her heart, Michal despised her husband, David.

8. _____ Jehu was the commander of David's army.

9. _____ Timothy's grandmother's name was Hilda.

10. _____ Lydia was Timothy's mother.

11. _____ Paul sent Tychicus to Ephesus.

12. _____ Four soldiers were stationed with Peter in his cell.

13. _____ Matthias succeeded Judas Iscariot as an apostle.

14. _____ Peter led a Roman soldier named Cornelius to Christ.

15. _____ Cornelius was baptized by Peter.

16. _____ Believers were first called Christians at the church in Thessalonica.

17. _____ Agabus prophesied there would be a famine in the land.

18. _____ Philip was the first apostle to be martyred.

19. _____ The first apostle to be martyred was James.

20. _____ Herod ordered the jail keepers be put to death after Peter escaped.

76

Group 7

1. _____ Herod was eaten by worms before he died.

2. _____ Peter was released from prison by an angel.

3. _____ Barnabas and Paul were deserted by Mark in Perga.

4. _____ The apostle Paul was originally known as Saul.

5. _____ Paul was stoned in the city of Lystra.

6. _____ Silas, Paul's traveling companion, was considered a prophet.

7. _____ On Paul's second missionary journey, he was accompanied by John the Baptist.

8. _____ Lydia was a seller of purple cloth.

9. _____ The Lord opened Lydia's heart to respond to Paul's message.

10. _____ Lydia was baptized by Paul and Silas.

11. _____ The Bereans were famous for writing gospel songs.

12. _____ Claudius demanded all the Jews depart from Rome.

13. _____ Crispus, a synagogue leader, was a member of the church in Corinth.

14. _____ The church in Ephesus was the scene of a burning of wicked books.

15. _____ The school of Tyrannus was in Corinth.

16. _____ John preached at Pentecost.

17. _____ Eutychus was in Assos when he fell out of a window.

18. _____ Both Paul and Peter raised people from the dead.

19. _____ Paul's hometown was Tarsus in Cilicia.

20. _____ Paul's teacher was a famous rabbi named Gamaliel.

77

Group 8

1. _____ Paul studied under Gamaliel.
2. _____ Paul's nephew came to sing Paul songs while he was imprisoned in Jerusalem.
3. _____ Forty men made an oath to fast until they had killed Paul.
4. _____ Tertullus prosecuted Paul when he was in Caesarea.
5. _____ Festus replaced Felix as governor of Judea.
6. _____ Felix, wanting to do a favor for the Jews, let Paul out of prison.
7. _____ Euroclydon was the name of a false god.
8. _____ Paul was not affected when a viper bit him.
9. _____ James healed a crippled man at the Beautiful Gate.
10. _____ Barnabas means "the son of consolation."
11. _____ Barnabas means "the son of peace."
12. _____ Bartholomew was Barnabas's original name.
13. _____ About six thousand men accepted Christ when Peter spoke on the day of Pentecost.
14. _____ A Pharisee was considered a servant.
15. _____ Gamaliel was described as a teacher of the law.
16. _____ Stephen was the first Christian to be martyred.

17. _____ Stephen was stoned to death.

18. _____ An angel carried Philip from Gaza to Azotus.

19. _____ King David tried to buy the gifts of the Holy Spirit.

20. _____ Peter was headed to Damascus to arrest Christians.

78

Group 9

1. _____ Aeneas was healed from palsy by John the Baptist.

2. _____ John the Baptist raised Dorcas from the dead.

3. _____ After the apostle Paul saw a vision of Jesus, he temporarily lost his sight.

4. _____ Before Amos was a prophet, he was a carpenter.

5. _____ Amos spoke about justice rolling down like a boulder.

6. _____ Paul told believers to set their affections on things around them.

7. _____ Paul described his friend Luke as a beloved brother.

8. _____ Nebuchadnezzar was king of Egypt.

9. _____ Before the Babylonians changed Meshach's Jewish name, it was Daniel.

10. _____ Nebuchadnezzar had worrisome dreams that kept him from sleeping.

11. _____ Nebuchadnezzar promised various gifts, rewards, and great honor to the person who could interpret his dream.

12. _____ During Belshazzar's feast, a mysterious hand wrote on the wall.

13. _____ David was the only king in the Bible referred to as "the Mede."

14. _____ King Darius ordered Daniel be thrown into the lions' den.

15. _____ Daniel would kneel and pray five times a day.

16. _____ King Darius fasted after Daniel was thrown into the lions' den.

17. _____ Daniel had a vision of a horse with eagle's wings.

18. _____ The angel Gabriel gave Daniel an understanding of the future.

19. _____ The angel Gabriel visited David while he was confessing his sins.

20. _____ When Moses died, he was 130 years old.

79

Group 10

1. _____ Eleazar succeeded his father, Aaron, as priest.

2. _____ The Israelites were commanded to bring firstborn animals to God for sacrifice.

3. _____ Og, the king of Bashan, had a bed made of iron.

4. _____ On the mountain of Nebo, Moses was given a view into the Promised Land.

5. _____ During the time of Moses, the city of Jericho was also known as the city of palm trees.

6. _____ God buried Moses in the land of Moab.

7. _____ The Israelites mourned Moses for seventy days.

8. _____ The Lord tells us to honor our mother and father.

9. _____ God described the Israelites as being stiffnecked.

10. _____ The book of Ecclesiastes says laughter is madness (NKJV).

11. _____ In Ephesians, sleepers are told to rise from the dead.

12. _____ Paul recommended the Holy Spirit as a substitute for food.

13. _____ Adah was Esther's Hebrew name.

14. _____ Esther was an orphan.

15. _____ Haman was angry with Mordecai because he stole his cattle.

16. _____ Haman planned to destroy all of the Jews.

17. _____ Tamar was the wife of Haman of Persia.

18. _____ The Egyptians made the Israelites into slaves.

19. _____ Pharaoh made a false confession to Moses and Aaron.

20. _____ God blew a strong west wind and stopped the locust plague.

Group 11

1. _____ Egypt suffered fifteen plagues that were signs of the Lord's power.

2. _____ The plague of darkness lasted in Egypt for five days.

3. _____ In Egyptian households, the firstborn was to die the night of the Passover.

4. _____ Lamb was eaten at the Passover meal.

5. _____ The Israelites were in Egypt for four hundred years.

6. _____ Egypt's army was destroyed as a result of drowning in the Red Sea.

7. _____ A huge rock hid the departing Israelites.

8. _____ The Lord used a strong east wind to part the Red Sea.

9. _____ To make the bitter waters of Marah drinkable, Moses threw a piece of wood into it.

10. _____ David was the commander of the Israelites under Moses.

11. _____ On Mount Horeb, Moses brought forth water from a rock.

12. _____ On Mount Sinai, God appeared in the form of a star.

13. _____ Moses was from the tribe of Levi.

14. _____ After killing an Egyptian, Moses fled to Moab.

15. _____ Zipporah was the wife of Moses.

16. _____ Ruth was Moses's first wife.

17. _____ As a baby, Moses was put in a basket made of beaver skin.

18. _____ Pharaoh's wife discovered the baby Moses.

19. _____ God brought the children of Israel out of the land of Egypt.

20. _____ The Ten Commandments of God were written on tablets of stone.

81

Group 12

1. _____ The ark of the covenant was made out of shittim wood.
2. _____ Goats' hair and linen were used to make the curtains in the tabernacle.
3. _____ A door separated the Holy Place from the Most Holy Place.
4. _____ Jethro was Moses's father-in-law.
5. _____ Moses saw the burning bush on Mount Everest.
6. _____ The Sabbath day was a sign of rest and completion.
7. _____ The seventh day of the week was called the Sabbath.
8. _____ Moses met with God on a mountain called Sinai.
9. _____ Noah rebuked Aaron for making a molten calf.
10. _____ Joshua was Moses's personal servant.
11. _____ Once when God passed by, Moses hid in a cave.
12. _____ Joshua fasted for forty days on Mount Sinai.
13. _____ The staff of Moses turned into a lizard.
14. _____ Moses anointed the tabernacle with oil.
15. _____ Jochebed was Moses's mother.
16. _____ The river turning into blood was the first plague in Egypt.

17. _____ The Nile River turned into wine.

18. _____ In the book of Exodus, dust was turned into a plague of lice.

19. _____ In one plague, alligators came out of the Nile River in droves.

20. _____ Moses tossed ashes into the sea to plague the Egyptians with boils.

Group 13

1. _____ Ezekiel had a vision of creatures with wheels.
2. _____ Job ate a book that tasted like honey.
3. _____ Ezekiel was encouraged to mourn the death of his wife.
4. _____ The prophet Ezekiel had a sister who died suddenly.
5. _____ Teman and Dedan were cities in Edom.
6. _____ The nation of Media dwelt in the land of Pathros.
7. _____ Mount Seir was located in Edom.
8. _____ Ezekiel had a vision of a river that had waters too deep to pass over.
9. _____ Jehovah Shammah means "the LORD is good."
10. _____ Ezekiel once dug through a wall and saw a doorway.
11. _____ When the exiles returned to Israel, the priest Jeshua rebuilt Jerusalem.
12. _____ Before Ezra left Babylonia to go to Jerusalem, he fasted.
13. _____ Arabia was the site of Mount Sinai, according to Paul.
14. _____ There are twelve fruits of the Spirit.
15. _____ Daniel found a ram caught in a thicket.
16. _____ After Noah was five hundred years old, he became the father of Shem, Ham, and Japheth.

17. _____ Melchizedek was a priest but also a farmer.

18. _____ God promised Abraham that he would be buried at a ripe old age.

19. _____ Before the flood, man was exclusively vegetarian.

20. _____ God created the world and everything in it in seven days.

Group 14

1. _____ The tower of Babel was built so the people could try to reach heaven.

2. _____ In times of famine, Abram went to Syria.

3. _____ Melchizedek was the king of Salem.

4. _____ Melchizedek was the second priest mentioned in the Bible.

5. _____ While Abram was in a deep sleep, God spoke to him.

6. _____ Abraham pleaded with the Lord to spare the city of Zoar.

7. _____ Hagar was the mother of Isaac.

8. _____ Hagar named Ishmael.

9. _____ Hagar called God "The One Who Sees."

10. _____ Hagar was approached by a demon at the well.

11. _____ The Lord changed Sarai's name to Sarah.

12. _____ Jeremiah met the Lord at the oaks of Mamre.

13. _____ Lot prepared a meal for two angels in the city of Sodom.

14. _____ Fire and brimstone rained down on the cities of Sodom and Gomorrah.

15. _____ While intoxicated, Lot was seduced by his daughters.

16. _____ Lot's wife was turned into a pillar of salt.

17. _____ God had Adam name all the animals.

18. _____ God removed Adam's collarbone to form Eve.

19. _____ God placed Adam in the Garden of Eden.

20. _____ Ishmael became a farmer.

84

Group 15

1. _____ Sarah gave birth to a daughter at ninety years of age.

2. _____ Isaac's name means "joy."

3. _____ When Isaac was born, Abraham was seventy-five years old.

4. _____ Abraham took Isaac to Mount Moriah to be sacrificed.

5. _____ Pidash, Buz, and Huz had a mother named Hagar.

6. _____ Abraham buried his wife Sarah in a cave in the field of Machpelah.

7. _____ Lot was Rebekah's father.

8. _____ Laban ran to meet Abraham's servant at the well.

9. _____ The servant of Abraham gave Rebekah gold jewelry.

10. _____ Rebekah was Isaac's sister.

11. _____ After Sarah died, Abraham's next wife was Keturah.

12. _____ Esau and Jacob were the twin sons of David and Bathsheba.

13. _____ Esau was Isaac's favorite son.

14. _____ Jacob traded bread and lentil stew for his brother's birthright.

15. _____ Isaac and Ishmael buried Abraham.

16. _____ Jacob married sisters Rachel and Leah.

17. _____ Jacob had to serve Laban a total of sixteen years in order to marry Rachel.

18. _____ Leah tricked Jacob by posing as her sister Rachel.

19. _____ Reuben was Jacob's firstborn.

20. _____ Levi was Jacob's second son.

85

Group 16

1. _____ Eve was tempted by a lizard in the Garden of Eden.
2. _____ After disobeying God, Adam blamed Satan.
3. _____ Jared was the father of Enoch.
4. _____ As a result of God's curse, the ground brought forth trees with no fruit.
5. _____ Because of Adam, God cursed the air.
6. _____ After Adam and Eve sinned, God cursed the ground so that it would bring forth thorns and thistles.
7. _____ Eve's name appears just five times in the book of Genesis.
8. _____ The entrance to Eden was guarded by cherubims.
9. _____ Cherubims and a flaming sword were placed east of the Garden of Eden.
10. _____ Jacob and Leah had six sons.
11. _____ Jacob and Laban made their covenant at Gilead.
12. _____ Laban and Jacob parted ways in Jabbok.
13. _____ Jacob gave his brother twenty donkeys as a gesture of goodwill.
14. _____ God changed Jacob's name to Gideon.
15. _____ Abraham buried Isaac.

16. _____ Joseph's brothers sold him into slavery.

17. _____ Joseph was sold as a slave and taken to Babylon.

18. _____ Joseph's mother made him a beautiful, colorful coat.

19. _____ As a baby, Zarah was marked with a scarlet thread.

20. _____ Potiphar's wife tried to seduce Joseph.

86

Group 17

1. _____ Potiphar's lying wife caused Joseph to be thrown into prison.
2. _____ Noah's grandson Canaan was cursed for his father's sins.
3. _____ Cain left Eden to live in Nod.
4. _____ Adam built the first city.
5. _____ The first city was called Cana.
6. _____ Abel was the inventor of farming.
7. _____ Seth was Cain and Abel's sibling.
8. _____ According to Eve, Jared replaced her son Abel.
9. _____ Cain killed Abel on a mountaintop.
10. _____ Cain was the first man to murder his brother.
11. _____ Joseph rode in Pharaoh's second chariot.
12. _____ Pharaoh put a silver chain on Joseph's neck.
13. _____ Joseph married the daughter of an Egyptian priest.
14. _____ Joseph married an Egyptian woman named Asenath.
15. _____ Because of famine in the land, Jacob sent his sons to Egypt.
16. _____ Joseph governed Egypt.

17. _____ Joseph accused his brothers of stealing his hat and sandals.

18. _____ Jacob lived in Egypt for twenty-five years.

19. _____ Jacob did not want to be buried in Egypt.

20. _____ Abraham was Methuselah's father.

Group 18

1. _____ When Adam died, he was 910 years old.

2. _____ Noah's ark was made of gopher wood.

3. _____ Noah's ark had three windows.

4. _____ Noah's ark had five stories.

5. _____ Noah was three hundred years old when God flooded the earth.

6. _____ When the dove returned to the ark, it was carrying a fish in its beak.

7. _____ Noah's ark landed on the mountains of Ararat.

8. _____ Noah released a sparrow from the ark.

9. _____ Earthquakes are a reminder that the world will never again be destroyed by a flood.

10. _____ Canaan was not one of Noah's sons.

11. _____ The marriage bed should be kept pure, according to the book of Hebrews.

12. _____ The Word of God is sharper than a twoedged sword, according to the book of Hebrews.

13. _____ The word *Sabbath* means "Saturday."

14. _____ Christ is the mediator of the new covenant.

15. _____ Hosea was told to name his daughter Sarah.

16. _____ David hid in caves to avoid Saul's wrath.

17. _____ God referred to the nation of Assyria as "the rod of mine anger."

18. _____ The prophet Isaiah walked around naked for three years.

19. _____ The prophet Isaiah mentioned a voice singing in the wilderness.

20. _____ Isaiah predicted that the city of Babylon would become like a helpless widow.

Group 19

1. _____ According to the prophet Isaiah, Jesus would carry the government on his shoulders.
2. _____ A double-minded man is like the grass in a field.
3. _____ Abraham was known as the friend of God.
4. _____ Before birth, Moses was ordained to be God's messenger.
5. _____ The prophet Micah is mentioned in the book of Jeremiah.
6. _____ Ephraim was described as God's firstborn son.
7. _____ Uz was the name of Job's homeland.
8. _____ Job was a farmer.
9. _____ The children of Job were killed while attending a feast.
10. _____ Zophar, Bildad, and Eliphaz laughed when they saw Job suffering.
11. _____ There was a time when Job suffered from boils.
12. _____ Job once sat in a pile of ashes.
13. _____ Job's wife urged him to curse God and die.
14. _____ Zophar spoke of a river flowing with honey.
15. _____ Job said that owls had become his companions.
16. _____ After Job's severe testing, he lived another 150 years.

17. _____ Joel spoke of an invasion of locusts.

18. _____ Philip brought Nathanael to Jesus.

19. _____ Jesus saw the disciple Peter sitting under a fig tree.

20. _____ Jesus said, "I am the good carpenter."

89

Group 20

1. _____ Mary, Martha, and Lazarus lived in Bethany.
2. _____ Lazarus was buried in a cave.
3. _____ Jesus raised Lazarus from the dead.
4. _____ Simon the Zealot brought Greeks to Jesus.
5. _____ Mary of Bethany anointed Jesus's feet with ointment.
6. _____ The woman who anointed Jesus was criticized by Judas Iscariot.
7. _____ Peter was reluctant to have Jesus wash his feet.
8. _____ Philip asked Jesus to show the disciples the Father.
9. _____ Peter cut off the arm of Malchus, the high priest's servant.
10. _____ When the soldiers crucified Jesus, they divided his clothes into six shares.
11. _____ Jesus turned water into wine.
12. _____ Jesus turned ten jars of water into wine.
13. _____ Jesus worked his first miracle in Bethlehem.
14. _____ Jesus told the servants in Cana to fill six stone water jars with sand.
15. _____ Mary Magdalene started to dance when she first saw the empty tomb.

16. _____ Rebekah called Jesus Rabboni.

17. _____ Thomas doubted the resurrection of Jesus.

18. _____ The disciple John jumped into the water to meet Jesus after his resurrection.

19. _____ Eternal life is God's promise to believers.

20. _____ Jesus told the woman at the well that he was a preacher and a fisherman.

90

Group 21

1. _____ The woman at the well had at least five husbands.

2. _____ Jesus asked the woman at the well for bread to eat.

3. _____ In the Gospel of John, the Sea of Galilee is called the Sea of Tiberias.

4. _____ Peter betrayed Jesus with a kiss.

5. _____ Satan is the father of lies.

6. _____ Peter asked his shipmates to cast him into the sea.

7. _____ Jonah was in the belly of a great fish for four days and four nights.

8. _____ In an attempt to run from the presence of the Lord, Jonah tried to flee to Tarshish.

9. _____ Jonah danced while inside a giant fish.

10. _____ Jonah proclaimed that Nineveh would be overturned in sixty days.

11. _____ Nun was Joshua's brother.

12. _____ The Euphrates is described as "the great river" in the book of Joshua.

13. _____ Joshua sent spies into Jericho.

14. _____ Joshua was 120 years old when he died.

15. _____ Joseph's bones were buried at Shechem.

16. _____ Levi was the first tribe to enter the Promised Land.

17. _____ The city of Jericho was famous for its fallen walls.

18. _____ Jephthah ran from his brothers and dwelt in the land of Tob.

19. _____ Abdon had fifty-two sons.

20. _____ Elimelech was Samson's father.

91

Group 22

1. _____ Samson ate honey from the carcass of a lion he killed.

2. _____ Samson lost his power when his hair was cut off.

3. _____ Elisha was buried with his father, Manoah.

4. _____ Achan stole eleven hundred pieces of silver from his mother.

5. _____ Micah made his son a priest over all his idols.

6. _____ Eglon, the king of Moab, was a very skinny man.

7. _____ King Eglon was slain by Ehud.

8. _____ Jael gave a captain wine and then killed him.

9. _____ Jabin was the king of the Philistines.

10. _____ Nebuchadnezzar was killed by Jael as he slept in a tent.

11. _____ Israel was once judged by the prophetess Ruth.

12. _____ Moses was commissioned by an angel to save Israel from the Midianites.

13. _____ Gideon and his men attacked Israelite soldiers late at night.

14. _____ The Midianite Zeeb was murdered at his winepress by David's army.

15. _____ Gideon defeated the Midianites with only 350 men.

16. _____ The Midianites had gold chains around the necks of their camels.

17. _____ During the time of Gideon, the Israelites experienced forty years of turmoil.

18. _____ Gideon had seventy sons.

19. _____ Goats were forbidden as food to the Israelites.

20. _____ The law instructed lepers to cover their hair at all times.

Group 23

1. _____ A ram was released into the wilderness bearing the sins of Israel.

2. _____ Moses anointed Aaron and his daughters with the blood of a ram.

3. _____ Nadab and Abihu were the sons of Moses.

4. _____ While in the temple of God, Zacharias lost his voice.

5. _____ Mary was married when Jesus was born.

6. _____ Mary was told by the angel Gabriel that her son was to be named Jesus.

7. _____ Jesus saw Satan falling as lightning from heaven.

8. _____ The eyes are called the lamp of the body.

9. _____ A singing Christian causes angels to rejoice, according to Jesus.

10. _____ On a single occasion, Jesus healed ten lepers.

11. _____ When Jesus healed ten lepers, only one returned to thank him.

12. _____ Zacchaeus climbed a tree so he could see Jesus.

13. _____ Zacchaeus gave half of his wealth to the poor.

14. _____ Anna and Simeon saw Jesus in the manger.

15. _____ The city of David was Bethlehem.

16. _____ Jesus's parents went to Jerusalem every year for the feast of the Passover.

17. _____ When Jesus was twelve, he referred to the temple in Jerusalem as his Father's house.

18. _____ Jesus's hometown was Nazareth.

19. _____ Jesus was born in a small, cramped cottage.

20. _____ The Lord's Supper was to be a reminder of Christ's body and blood.

Group 24

1. _____ An angel came to strengthen Jesus when he was in Gethsemane.

2. _____ While Jesus prayed in Gethsemane, the disciples were sleeping.

3. _____ Jesus frequently went to the Mount of Olives.

4. _____ After his resurrection, Jesus had his first dinner in the village of Emmaus.

5. _____ Pontius Pilate was a tax collector.

6. _____ A garner is a place to store grain.

7. _____ The tax collector Matthew held a feast for Jesus.

8. _____ Matthew was also known as Levi.

9. _____ Peter said to Jesus, "Depart from me; for I am a sinful man, O Lord."

10. _____ Jesus told his disciples to pray for the people who curse them.

11. _____ Jesus brought the dead son of the widow of Nain back to life.

12. _____ Paul was asleep on a boat during a storm on the Sea of Galilee.

13. _____ Jesus brought Jairus's wife back to life.

14. _____ Jesus sent James and Andrew to prepare the Passover meal.

15. _____ At Jesus's baptism, the Holy Spirit took the form of a swan.

16. _____ John the Baptist baptized people in the Nile River.

17. _____ Moses said he was unworthy to unloosen another man's sandals.

18. _____ Jesus accused the Pharisees of devouring widows' houses.

19. _____ Simon the leper entertained Jesus in his home.

20. _____ The word *Golgotha* is translated "the place of a skull."

94

Group 25

1. _____ Three criminals were crucified with Jesus.

2. _____ Jesus told his followers that they would have the power to safely handle dangerous snakes.

3. _____ Serpents were cast out of Mary Magdalene.

4. _____ Mary Magdalene was healed by Jesus of seven demons.

5. _____ James and John where "the sons of thunder."

6. _____ When Jesus entered a town or village, people placed the sick in the marketplaces.

7. _____ Joseph was told in a dream about the miraculous conception of Jesus.

8. _____ Emmanuel means "the anointed one."

9. _____ Jesus descended from the tribe of Judah.

10. _____ Jesus said you can recognize a tree by its fruit.

11. _____ Jesus used seven loaves of bread to feed five thousand people.

12. _____ James was enabled by Jesus to briefly walk on water.

13. _____ Herodias, the wife of Herod, plotted the death of King David.

14. _____ Jesus sent Matthew to catch a fish with a coin in its mouth.

15. _____ A map led the wise men to the baby Jesus.

16. _____ When the wise men saw a peculiar star, they were in the west.

17. _____ Jesus cursed a fig tree because it did not bear fruit.

18. _____ Matthew is the only Gospel to mention Jesus riding on a donkey.

19. _____ Jesus talked about end times from the Mount of Olives.

20. _____ Jesus delivered his final discourse on the Mount of Olives.

95

Group 26

1. _____ In the Bible, sometimes Christians are referred to as lambs.
2. _____ Judas was given fifty pieces of silver to betray Jesus.
3. _____ The chief priests paid Judas Iscariot to betray Jesus.
4. _____ Peter denied Jesus five times.
5. _____ Peter wept bitterly after denying the Lord.
6. _____ The prisoner Barabbas was released in place of Jesus.
7. _____ The criminals crucified next to Christ were murderers.
8. _____ A huge stone was used to seal the tomb that temporarily held Jesus.
9. _____ The potter's field was also known as "the field of worship."
10. _____ John the Baptist preached in the wilderness in Judea.
11. _____ John the Baptist ate locusts and honey in the wilderness.
12. _____ John the Baptist wore a tunic made of camel hair.
13. _____ After Jesus was tempted in the wilderness, God ministered to him.
14. _____ After leaving Nazareth, Jesus moved to Bethany.
15. _____ Jesus said, "Man shall not live by water alone."
16. _____ God said a foolish man builds his house on mud.

17. _____ Hosea prophesied Assyria's destruction.

18. _____ Moses wrote the first six books of the Bible.

19. _____ Hannah's story takes place in 2 Chronicles.

20. _____ The serpent was cursed by God.

96

Group 27

1. _____ Mary, the mother of Jesus, had no other children.

2. _____ Numbers is the third book of the Old Testament.

3. _____ The book of Jude comes before the book of Revelation in the New Testament.

4. _____ Ruth is the tenth book of the Old Testament.

5. _____ Luke is the shortest book of the New Testament.

6. _____ The story of Samson is found in the book of Acts.

7. _____ Levi (Matthew) was the son of Alphaeus.

8. _____ Idolatry is the worship of false gods.

9. _____ Jesus prophesied the destruction of Jerusalem.

10. _____ The story of Leah is recorded in the book of Genesis.

11. _____ The Jordan River connects the Dead Sea with the Sea of Galilee.

12. _____ James and John were the sons of Zebedee.

13. _____ Hosanna means "thank the Lord."

14. _____ There are twenty-seven books in the New Testament.

15. _____ Amos is the last book of the Old Testament.

16. _____ The first word of the Bible is "in."

17. _____ The longest chapter in the Bible is Psalm 119 with 176 verses.

18. _____ The third book of the Old Testament is Exodus.

19. _____ The fifth book of the New Testament is Romans.

20. _____ The Lord used wind from the sea to bring quail to the Israelites.

97

Group 28

1. _____ Moses sent twelve spies into Canaan.
2. _____ Because Korah and his men were rebellious, the earth swallowed them up.
3. _____ The house of Israel mourned Aaron's death for forty days.
4. _____ The prophet Balaam had a talking donkey.
5. _____ Phinehas killed two people at the same time with a single spear.
6. _____ Aaron was one hundred years old when he died.
7. _____ Aaron died on Mount Hor.
8. _____ When Paul was in Thessalonica, the Philippians sent help to him.
9. _____ Solomon compared a lovely woman who lacks discretion to a jewel of gold in a swine's snout.
10. _____ According to Proverbs, the bread of deceit is sweet to man.
11. _____ The proverbs of Solomon were copied by the men of Hezekiah, the king of Judah.
12. _____ Open rebuke is better than hidden love.
13. _____ There are sixty-six books in the Bible.

14. _____ Genesis has fifty chapters.

15. _____ Noah had a vision of Jesus walking among seven golden lampstands.

16. _____ The book of Genesis says that the divine voice sounds like a waterfall.

17. _____ The seven churches in the book of Revelation were located in Asia.

18. _____ In a vision, John was told to measure the temple in Jerusalem.

19. _____ According to Revelation, the beast will ascend out of the abyss and slay the two witnesses.

20. _____ In heaven, Michael and his angels fought against the dragon.

98

Group 29

1. _____ The book of Revelation mentions a talking altar.

2. _____ In Revelation, the great harlot rode on a scarlet beast.

3. _____ John heard a voice speaking of the fall of Babylon.

4. _____ In the book of Revelation, the fiery lake was composed of burning wood.

5. _____ In the book of Revelation, an angel bound Satan with a chain.

6. _____ Seven angels were at the gates of the new Jerusalem.

7. _____ The new Jerusalem was decorated with twelve precious stones.

8. _____ The church of Laodicea was neither hot nor cold.

9. _____ Moses had a vision of a sea of glass.

10. _____ Daniel saw a creature that resembled a lion near the throne of God.

11. _____ When John saw the four angels standing on the four corners of the earth, they were dancing.

12. _____ In Revelation, sand fell on earth's waters to make them bitter.

13. _____ Faith comes by hearing the Word of God.

14. _____ Jesus Christ will judge all of mankind.

15. _____ Paul said to greet one another with a holy hug.

16. _____ The apostle Paul had the book of Romans written down for him by Tertius.

17. _____ The wages of sin is death.

18. _____ Nothing can separate us from God's love.

19. _____ Joseph was Naomi's husband.

20. _____ Ruth was married to Chilion of Israel.

Group 30

1. _____ Ruth had a sister-in-law named Orpah.

2. _____ Ruth's first husband was Mahlon.

3. _____ One of Jesus's ancestors was a Moabite named Ruth.

4. _____ Solomon had a throne with blue cushions.

5. _____ There are twenty-nine books in the Old Testament.

6. _____ Zenas was a lawyer.

7. _____ Zechariah had a vision of an angel on a red horse.

8. _____ The book of Zechariah describes the Mount of Olives splitting in half.

9. _____ During the time of Zechariah, Saul was the high priest.

10. _____ Obadiah wrote a book against Edom.

100

Did You Know?
(Set 10)

Here are more wonderful mind benders from the Bible.

- Three squared is nine. Those two digits are thirty-nine. There are thirty-nine books in the Old Testament. Three times nine equals twenty-seven. There are twenty-seven books in the New Testament.

- Moses did not cast down the rod that transformed into a snake before Pharaoh. It was his brother, Aaron (Exodus 7:8–12).

- Second Samuel 12:1–14 tells of the prophet Nathan confronting David with a parable about David's sinful, adulterous affair with Bathsheba and her husband's murder. David became angry after hearing the parable and said the sinful man featured in it should die and make a fourfold restitution. Since the sinful man of the parable was David himself, David's "judgment" for the man in the parable came true. David killed one man, Bathsheba's husband, but four of David's sons died, a fourfold restitution (2 Samuel 12:15–19; 13:28–33; 18:14–15; 1 Kings 2:23–25).

- Samson once caught three hundred foxes and tied them tail to tail. Between the knotted tails, Samson inserted lit torches and released the frantic foxes to burn up the fields of the Philistines (Judges 15:4–5).
- In the book of Joshua, there is a woman named Noah (Joshua 17:3).

101

Memory Verses

Every brilliant Bible scholar has memorized a good portion of Scripture. I have carefully selected some of the most important passages in the Bible for the next step in becoming Bible brilliant. In the following exercise, fill in the blanks using the words listed below each Scripture passage. Give yourself 2 points for each passage you complete accurately.

1. Genesis 1:1
   In the _____ God created the _____ and the _____.

   earth   heaven   beginning

2. Genesis 1:26
   And God said, Let us make man in our _____, after our likeness: and let them have _____ over the fish of the sea, and over the fowl of the air, and over the cattle, and over all the earth, and over every creeping thing that creepeth upon the _____.

   image   dominion   earth

3. Genesis 1:27
   So God created man in his own _____, in the image of God created he him; _____ and _____ created he them.

   female   image   male

4. Joshua 1:8

This book of the law shall not depart out of thy _____;
but thou shalt meditate therein day and _____, that thou
mayest observe to do according to all that is written therein:
for then thou shalt make thy way _____, and then thou
shalt have good _____.

prosperous   success   night   mouth

5. Joshua 1:9

Have not I commanded thee? Be strong and of a good _____;
be not afraid, neither be thou _____: for the LORD thy God
is with _____ whithersoever thou goest.

dismayed   thee   courage

6. Psalm 37:4

Delight _____ also in the LORD; and he shall give thee
the _____ of thine _____.

desires   heart   thyself

7. Psalm 133:1–2

Behold, how good and how pleasant it is for _____ to
dwell together in _____! It is like the precious _____
upon the head, that ran down upon the _____, even Aaron's beard: that went down to the skirts of his garments.

beard   ointment   brethren   unity

8. Psalm 139:14

I will praise thee; for I am _____ and _____ made:
marvellous are thy _____; and that my soul knoweth
right well.

wonderfully   works   fearfully

9. Proverbs 3:5–6

_____ in the LORD with all thine _____; and lean not
unto thine own understanding. In all thy ways _____ him,
and he shall direct thy _____.

acknowledge   trust   paths   heart

10. Proverbs 30:5

Every _____ of _____ is pure: he is a shield unto them that put their _____ in him.

God   word   trust

11. Isaiah 26:3

Thou wilt keep him in perfect _____, whose _____ is stayed on thee: because he _____ in thee.

trusteth   peace   mind

12. Isaiah 40:31

But they that wait upon the LORD shall renew their _____; they shall mount up with _____ as _____; they shall run, and not be weary; and they shall walk, and not _____.

eagles   strength   faint   wings

13. Isaiah 41:10

Fear thou not; for I am with thee: be not _____; for I am thy God: I will strengthen thee; yea, I will help thee; yea, I will uphold _____ with the right _____ of my righteousness.

hand   dismayed   thee

14. Isaiah 53:4

Surely he hath borne our _____, and carried our sorrows: yet we did esteem him _____, smitten of God, and _____.

afflicted   griefs   stricken

15. Isaiah 53:5

But he was wounded for our _____, he was bruised for our _____: the _____ of our peace was upon him; and with his _____ we are healed.

chastisement   stripes   transgressions   iniquities

16. Isaiah 53:6

All we like _____ have gone _____; we have turned every one to his own way; and the LORD hath laid on him the _____ of us all.

iniquity   astray   sheep

17. Isaiah 55:8

For my thoughts are not your _____, neither are your
ways my _____, saith the _____.

LORD   thoughts   ways

18. Jeremiah 29:11

For I know the thoughts that I think toward you, saith the
LORD, thoughts of _____, and not of _____, to give
you an expected _____.

evil   peace   end

19. Micah 6:8

He hath shewed _____, O man, what is good; and what
doth the _____ require of thee, but to do justly, and to
love _____, and to walk _____ with thy God?

mercy   humbly   thee   LORD

20. Matthew 3:2

And saying, _____ ye: for the _____ of heaven is at
_____.

hand   kingdom   repent

21. Matthew 5:16

Let your _____ so shine before men, that they may see your
_____ works, and glorify your Father which is in _____.

good   light   heaven

22. Matthew 11:28–30

Come unto me, all ye that labour and are heavy laden, and
I will give you _____. Take my _____ upon you, and
learn of me; for I am _____ and lowly in _____: and ye
shall find rest unto your souls. For my yoke is easy, and my
burden is light.

yoke   rest   heart   meek

23. Matthew 22:37

_____ said unto him, Thou shalt _____ the Lord thy
God with all thy heart, and with all thy _____, and with
all thy _____.

mind   love   Jesus   soul

24. Matthew 28:18

And _____ came and spake unto them, saying, All _____ is given unto me in _____ and in _____.

heaven   Jesus   earth   power

25. Matthew 28:19–20

Go ye therefore, and teach all _____, baptizing them in the name of the Father, and of the Son, and of the Holy _____: Teaching them to _____ all things whatsoever I have _____ you: and, lo, I am with you always, even unto the end of the world. Amen.

commanded   observe   nations   Ghost

26. John 1:1

In the _____ was the _____, and the Word was with God, and the Word was _____.

Word   beginning   God

27. John 1:12

But as many as received him, to them gave he _____ to become the sons of God, even to them that _____ on his _____.

name   power   believe

28. John 3:16

For God so loved the _____, that he gave his only begotten Son, that whosoever believeth in him should not _____, but have everlasting _____.

perish   life   world

29. John 3:17

For God sent not his Son into the _____ to _____ the world; but that the world through him might be _____.

saved   condemn   world

30. John 5:24

Verily, verily, I say unto you, He that heareth my _____, and believeth on him that sent me, hath everlasting _____, and shall not come into condemnation; but is passed from _____ unto life.

death   word   life

31. John 10:10

The _____ cometh not, but for to steal, and to _____, and to _____: I am come that they might have _____, and that they might have it more abundantly.

life   destroy   kill   thief

32. John 11:25

Jesus said unto her, I am the _____, and the life: he that believeth in me, though he were _____, yet shall he _____.

dead   resurrection   live

33. John 13:35

By this shall all _____ know that ye are my _____, if ye have _____ one to another.

disciples   men   love

34. John 14:6

_____ saith unto him, I am the way, the _____, and the _____: no man cometh unto the _____, but by me.

Father   truth   life   Jesus

35. John 14:27

Peace I leave with you, my _____ I give unto you: not as the _____ giveth, give I unto you. Let not your _____ be troubled, neither let it be afraid.

peace   world   heart

36. John 15:13

Greater _____ hath no _____ than this, that a man lay down his _____ for his _____.

life   love   friends   man

37. John 16:33

These things I have spoken unto you, that in me ye might have _____. In the _____ ye shall have _____: but be of good _____; I have overcome the world.

tribulation   peace   world   cheer

38. Acts 1:8

But ye shall receive _____, after that the Holy Ghost is come upon you: and ye shall be _____ unto me both in _____, and in all Judaea, and in _____, and unto the uttermost part of the _____.

Samaria   power   earth   Jerusalem   witnesses

39. Acts 2:38

Then _____ said unto them, Repent, and be _____ every one of you in the name of Jesus Christ for the remission of _____, and ye shall receive the _____ of the Holy Ghost.

sins   baptized   Peter   gift

40. Acts 4:12

Neither is there _____ in any other: for there is none other _____ under heaven given among _____, whereby we must be _____.

men   saved   name   salvation

41. Acts 17:11

These were more noble than those in _____, in that they received the word with all readiness of _____, and searched the _____ daily, whether those _____ were so.

things   Thessalonica   mind   scriptures

42. Romans 3:23

For all have _____, and come short of the _____ of _____.

glory   sinned   God

43. Romans 5:8

But _____ commendeth his _____ toward us, in that, while we were yet sinners, _____ died for us.

Christ   love   God

44. Romans 6:23

For the wages of _____ is _____; but the gift of God is eternal life through Jesus Christ our _____.

Lord   sin   death

45. Romans 8:28

And we know that all things _____ together for good to them that love _____, to them who are the called according to his _____.

purpose   work   God

46. Romans 8:38–39

For I am persuaded, that neither _____, nor life, nor angels, nor principalities, nor _____, nor things present, nor things to come, Nor height, nor depth, nor any other _____, shall be able to separate us from the love of God, which is in Christ Jesus our _____.

creature   death   powers   Lord

47. Romans 10:9–10

That if thou shalt confess with thy _____ the Lord Jesus, and shalt believe in thine _____ that God hath raised him from the _____, thou shalt be saved. For with the heart man believeth unto righteousness; and with the mouth confession is made unto _____.

heart   salvation   mouth   dead

48. Romans 10:17

So then _____ cometh by _____, and hearing by the _____ of God.

hearing   word   faith

49. Romans 12:1

I beseech you therefore, brethren, by the _____ of God, that ye present your _____ a living _____, holy, acceptable unto _____, which is your reasonable service.

sacrifice   God   mercies   bodies

50. Romans 12:2

And be not _____ to this world: but be ye transformed by the renewing of your _____, that ye may prove what is that good, and _____, and perfect, _____ of God.

acceptable   conformed   mind   will

51. Romans 15:13

Now the God of _____ fill you with all joy and _____ in believing, that ye may abound in hope, through the _____ of the Holy Ghost.

hope   peace   power

52. 1 Corinthians 6:19

What? know ye not that your _____ is the temple of the _____ _____ which is in you, which ye have of God, and ye are not your own?

Ghost   body   Holy

53. 1 Corinthians 10:13

There hath no temptation taken you but such as is common to man: but God is _____, who will not _____ you to be tempted above that ye are able; but will with the _____ also make a way to _____, that ye may be able to bear it.

faithful   temptation   escape   suffer

54. 2 Corinthians 5:17

Therefore if any _____ be in Christ, he is a new _____: old _____ are passed away; behold, all things are become new.

creature   man   things

55. 2 Corinthians 5:21

For he hath made him to be sin for us, who knew no _____; that we might be made the _____ of God in _____.

righteousness   him   sin

56. 2 Corinthians 12:9

And he said unto me, My _____ is sufficient for thee: for my _____ is made perfect in _____. Most gladly therefore will I rather glory in my _____, that the power of Christ may rest upon me.

infirmities   weakness   grace   strength

57. 2 Timothy 1:7

For God hath not given us the _____ of _____; but of _____, and of love, and of a sound _____.

power   mind   spirit   fear

58. 2 Timothy 3:16–17
All _____ is given by inspiration of God, and is profitable
for _____, for reproof, for correction, for _____ in righteousness: That the man of God may be perfect, thoroughly
furnished unto all good _____.

works   doctrine   scripture   instruction

59. Hebrews 4:12
For the word of God is quick, and powerful, and sharper than
any twoedged sword, piercing even to the dividing asunder of
_____ and _____, and of the joints and _____, and
is a discerner of the thoughts and intents of the _____.

marrow   spirit   heart   soul

60. Hebrews 4:15
For we have not an high priest which cannot be _____ with
the feeling of our _____; but was in all points _____
like as we are, yet without sin.

infirmities   touched   tempted

61. Hebrews 4:16
Let us therefore come _____ unto the throne of _____,
that we may obtain _____, and find grace to _____
in time of need.

boldly   mercy   help   grace

62. Hebrews 10:24–25
And let us consider one _____ to provoke unto _____
and to good _____: Not forsaking the _____ of ourselves together, as the manner of some is; but exhorting one
another: and so much the more, as ye see the day approaching.

another   assembling   works   love

63. Hebrews 11:1
Now _____ is the _____ of things hoped for, the
_____ of things not seen.

substance   faith   evidence

64. Hebrews 11:6

But without _____ it is impossible to please him: for he that cometh to God must _____ that he is, and that he is a _____ of them that diligently _____ him.

believe   rewarder   faith   seek

65. Hebrews 12:1–2

Wherefore seeing we also are compassed about with so great a cloud of _____, let us lay aside every weight, and the sin which doth so easily beset us, and let us run with patience the race that is set before us, Looking unto Jesus the author and _____ of our faith; who for the joy that was set before him endured the _____, despising the _____, and is set down at the right hand of the throne of God.

finisher   shame   witnesses   cross

66. Hebrews 13:5

Let your _____ be without _____; and be _____ with such things as ye have: for he hath said, I will never leave thee, nor forsake thee.

covetousness   conversation   content

67. James 1:2–3

My _____, count it all joy when ye fall into divers _____; Knowing this, that the trying of your _____ worketh patience.

temptations   faith   brethren

68. James 1:12

_____ is the man that endureth temptation: for when he is tried, he shall receive the crown of _____, which the Lord hath _____ to them that _____ him.

life   blessed   promised   love

69. James 5:16

Confess your faults one to another, and pray one for another, that ye may be _____. The effectual fervent _____ of a righteous _____ _____ much.

prayer   healed   availeth   man

70. 1 Peter 2:24

Who his own self bare our sins in his own body on the
_____, that we, being dead to _____, should live unto
_____: by whose _____ ye were healed.

righteousness   tree   stripes   sins

71. 1 Peter 3:15–16

But sanctify the Lord God in your _____: and be ready
always to give an answer to every man that asketh you a
reason of the hope that is in you with meekness and fear:
Having a good _____; that, whereas they speak evil of
you, as of _____, they may be ashamed that falsely accuse
your good conversation in _____.

Christ   hearts   evildoers   conscience

72. 1 Peter 5:7

_____ all your _____ upon him; for he careth for
_____.

you   casting   care

73. 1 John 1:9

If we confess our _____, he is _____ and just to forgive
us our sins, and to cleanse us from all _____.

faithful   unrighteousness   sins

74. 1 John 3:16

Hereby perceive we the love of _____, because he laid
down his _____ for us: and we ought to lay down our
lives for the _____.

brethren   God   life

75. Revelation 1:10

I was in the _____ on the Lord's _____, and heard
behind me a great _____, as of a _____

trumpet   Spirit   voice   day

102

Did You Know?
(Set 11)

Here are more absolutely amazing facts to ponder.

- Second Samuel 21:20 speaks of a man with twelve fingers and twelve toes.
- As Jesus was being crucified, three of the four women present were named Mary.
- The word *amen* means "so be it."
- Jerusalem at one time was called Jebus (Judges 19:10).
- Samson's incredible head of hair featured only seven separate locks (Judges 16:19).
- The apostle Paul had a sister (Acts 23:16).
- There was a man named Judas who lived on a street named Straight, or Straight Street (Acts 9:11).

103

Scrambled Scriptures

All the words in the following Scripture passages are scrambled. Place the words in the proper order, and give yourself 30 points for each passage you complete correctly.

1. Psalm 46:10
   be will and I the I in exalted exalted that heathen the be still God I among will be know earth am

   _____

   _____

   _____

   _____

   _____

2. Psalm 118:24
   the made rejoice which day hath will LORD the is glad it be this and we in

   _____

   _____

   _____

   _____

3. Psalm 119:11

   against I heart have I word that thee sin hid thy not in mine might

   _____

   _____

   _____

   _____

4. Luke 11:9

   shall and you opened ye unto unto be ask shall given say it and I shall you it you and be seek find and knock

   _____

   _____

   _____

   _____

   _____

5. Luke 11:10

   and findeth one receiveth and asketh opened to that that him shall seeketh every be for he knocketh it that

   _____

   _____

   _____

   _____

   _____

6. John 14:6

   no cometh the the man am me the life him by I unto and the truth Father saith but Jesus unto way

   _____

   _____

   _____

   _____

7. Romans 3:23
   the sinned and for have short glory all of God come of

   _____

   _____

   _____

   _____

8. Romans 5:8
   us toward commendeth were yet love sinners God that in
   died we us his for while Christ but

   _____

   _____

   _____

   _____

9. Romans 10:9
   raised him thy thou shalt with that from believe and heart
   shalt God confess be hath shalt that the in thou the thine if
   Jesus saved mouth Lord dead

   _____

   _____

   _____

   _____

10. Romans 10:13
    be the saved shall shall the name upon call Lord whosoever
    for of

    _____

    _____

    _____

    _____

104

Did You Know?
(Set 12)

This makes an even dozen sets of astonishing Bible facts.

- God cast down boulders from heaven on some of Israel's enemies (Joshua 10:11).
- The Israelites did not circumcise any of their sons during the forty-year exodus in the wilderness after escaping from Egypt (Joshua 5:2–7).
- The prophet Ezekiel wore a tire (turban) on his head (Ezekiel 24:16–17).
- Psalm 78:23–25 indicates that angels eat manna, as God sent the "angels' food" from heaven down to the Israelites in the wilderness.
- The most quoted command in the New Testament is "Love thy neighbour as thyself," appearing in eight places (Matthew 5:43; 19:19; 22:39; Mark 12:31; Luke 10:27; Romans 13:9; Galatians 5:14; James 2:8).
- The word *testament* means "a profession of conviction."

WORD SEARCHES

Word searches are fun. In these puzzles, words are placed horizontally, vertically, and diagonally, both forward and backward. Some words may overlap in the puzzle. Simply circle the words in the list in whatever direction they appear. But here's the Bible brilliant twist. For the first two word searches of a topic, you will have the list of words. For the third puzzle of the series, you will not have the list of words but must still find them all.

Names of God Part 1

Find the Bible words for God in this puzzle. If you find all the words, give yourself 10 points on the score card.

```
Q U E M U N M G R E A T I A M
H H S G N I K F O G N I K Y K
G A W R C B H Y U C L A V G D
V I N N E T S G X U R H Y A Z
H S H W P T D O G F O B M A L
Y S R O I V A S H L A L P H A
A E F V A N F W Y L K J S T Z
S M T E S C S S G K C Y Q S P
H Y V H A E P A C N E M B I G
E Q K Y E I J O U O I I F R R
W V Q M R V R Y E M V V V H E
A Q Z I G E I K V E D Y I C H
T B T H H N Q N P G J G D L G
A B M T G D S F E A T A T O D
G O O D S H E P H E R D D T R
```

ALPHA   KING OF KINGS   SAVIOR
CHRIST   LAMB OF GOD   THE ROCK
GOOD SHEPHERD   LIVING WATER   THE VINE
GREAT I AM   MESSIAH   YASHEWA
HOLY SPIRIT   OMEGA

Names of God Part 2

Here are the same names of God but in a different puzzle. If you find all the words, give yourself 10 points on the score card.

```
P M R O I V A S F K N H J D L
U H E F B R H T R K J R F N F
S F D S T I R I P S Y L O H D
U G O I S Q O O F K I F A Y R
O B N J Z I J W H C I J Y A E
L W V I Y L A J L O P V N S T
A K K H K K L H C R H P O H A
M K Z V P F T A M E L J E E W
B Q G V L S O A M H N V L W G
O U G X I F I G O T I T E A N
F R Y R O T T S N N S Y U W I
G T H M A S H N E I B Z E C V
O C E E J I F I U A K U H X I
D G R A H P L A F V W W H D L
A G O O D S H E P H E R D F A
```

ALPHA
CHRIST
GOOD SHEPHERD
GREAT I AM
HOLY SPIRIT

KING OF KINGS
LAMB OF GOD
LIVING WATER
MESSIAH
OMEGA

SAVIOR
THE ROCK
THE VINE
YASHEWA

107

Names of God Part 3

Try to find the same fourteen names for God as you did in the previous two word searches, but this time you do not have the words. If you are successful, give yourself 25 points.

```
L I V I N G W A T E R O N N J
G O O D S H E P H E R D K D Z
A Z I X V P I V N E R A L T Z
H G J E F J K W F U H U I W E
P F Q N S A V I O R K R U C H
L J S I J M A M Y K I T H M S
A W D V P B E I B P N A Z A S
M Z E E D G N D S V G G M G G
B A D H A K W Y K C O R E H T
O D W T U B L E I C F E S R P
F W G E L O M F H X K A S B Z
G Q O B H I L R U X I T I W W
O H X J X S I W T V N I A H A
D K I F X S A G U K G A H W H
D G Y K T D B Y J E S M K P Y
```

108

People and Angels Part 1

Find the following names of people and angels. If you find all the words, give yourself 10 points.

```
C O R N E L I U S O X Q A T G
I Z A C H A R I A S J E M P U
D S R A B G S E M A N O A H Y
G A A N V F E N Q M W C P L E
S I N I R J R K Q U T H F Q L
G U D I A Z A F Q C X A A J I
L Z K E E H P P L U N P B I J
X O A K O L H E L N H A R V A
M T H J J N I Q A B G Q A R H
I Y A R O R M O B C J D H U E
C I H A B S J C X B A L A A M
H Q A A N A E A B U J I M Y T
A F G H V H S P C U K O A O V
E L A Z A R U S H O Y U H O B
L T R D Z E S P M Y B C I N E
```

ABRAHAM (Genesis 22:11, 15)
BALAAM (Numbers 22:31)
CORNELIUS (Acts 10:3)
DANIEL (Daniel 6:22)
ELIJAH (2 Kings 1:3, 15)
GABRIEL (Luke 1:19, 26)
GIDEON (Judges 6:11, 22)

HAGAR (Genesis 21:17)
ISAIAH (Isaiah 6:2, 6)
JACOB (Genesis 31:11; 32:1)
JESUS (Matthew 4:11)
JOANNA (Luke 24:4-10)
JOHN (Revelation 1:1)
JOSEPH (Matthew 2:13)

LAZARUS (Luke 16:20-22)
MANOAH (Judges 13:13-21)
MICHAEL (Jude 1:9; Revelation 12:7)
SERAPHIM (Isaiah 6:2, 6)
ZACHARIAS (Luke 1:12)

109

People and Angels Part 2

Once again, find the names of people and angels. Give yourself 10 points if you find them all.

```
D L W V N S G B L A Z A R U S
A M H H U P E Z R I F N V H Q
N E O S W R C R U R B V G X R
I J J Z Y J I S A I A H N H V
E Y S P K I T G E P W G N S E
L E B A L A A M A O H R U V J
H L V D Z H Y L A B M I O U O
K Y D J A T E Z J N L N M R S
G J J V C A G I D E O N A B E
A Q E O H I Y X N F N A B Y P
B R G C A Z Q R B E Y S H Y H
R T I K R N O L A B R A H A M
I M H J I C N J E S U S I K I
E U V Q A U U A D H J A C O B
L S I O S N E L I J A H O T R
```

ABRAHAM	HAGAR	LAZARUS
BALAAM	ISAIAH	MANOAH
CORNELIUS	JACOB	MICHAEL
DANIEL	JESUS	SERAPHIM
ELIJAH	JOANNA	ZACHARIAS
GABRIEL	JOHN	
GIDEON	JOSEPH	

People and Angels Part 3

Give yourself 25 points if you find all nineteen hidden names.

```
A K J S R Z A C H A R I A S M
B U T A C T P L P T K S F U I
R W G J C G H D T W B A R N C
A A K G K O B M N J B I E Z H
H J S E E K B M A N O A H T A
A C O Q L A V S V G L H X C E
M U E S D I S O A I I X N O L
U V N I E U J N R D T G Q R U
J R D H R P N A E E G A S N D
H J F A E A H S H O E B B E A
A H Z A O O U K N N J R A L N
H A I J Y S E Q A Q B I L I I
L N W M E W M J Z K L E A U E
V Y H J X L L F E I L L A S L
U K I Z S E R A P H I M M X O
```

Abraham's Progeny Part 1

Find the following names of Abraham's progeny. Give yourself 10 points if you find them all.

```
K Z M I D I A N C T C P N L L
E S I A L E U M M I M V Y H N
D H F M F K S M Q M C O W A I
A N D S R U M O E I D V D M Z
R A S H U A H J A Z B E R O G
O S C F F N N V D Z D A B L U
R S Q G D W Z M U A C E W W H
O H E Z R O N P D H W D W C K
P U E P H R A I M J P I O S Y
B R N A Q G O Y J W H N O H J
R I Z B Y A O W V W A W S A G
R M N E B A J O T H R D H M A
G H E I S H M A E L E R E M T
N A H A T H B H T C Z H B A B
J O K S H A N J S H E L A H R
```

ASSHURIM (Genesis 25:3)   JOKSHAN (Genesis 25:2)   PHAREZ (Genesis 38:29)
CARMI (Genesis 46:9)   KEDAR (Genesis 25:13)   SHAMMAH (Genesis 36:13)
DEDAN (Genesis 10:7)   LEUMMIM (Genesis 25:3)   SHEBA (Genesis 10:7)
EPHRAIM (Genesis 41:52)   MIDIAN (Genesis 25:2)   SHELAH (Genesis 38:5)
HANOCH (Genesis 25:4)   MIZZAH (Genesis 36:13)   SHUAH (Genesis 25:2)
HEZRON (Genesis 46:9)   NAHATH (Genesis 36:13)   ZIMRAN (Genesis 25:2)
ISHMAEL (Genesis 16:11)   NEBAJOTH (Genesis 25:13)

Abraham's Progeny Part 2

Once again, find the following names. Give yourself 10 points if you find them all.

```
A S S H U R I M U C K X R G D
R S D K H M I Z Z A H H U S L
U K V N V S H U A H K A E Y L
P H A R E Z P E W T K N I Y V
G K L T T I C I V O N O G R E
T H Y S H E B A H A A C A K P
J O K S H A N Y I N A H A T H
S H A M M A H D O C H W D R R
I Q Q F Y Z I M R A N E H A A
B X C H Q M J M L N S W D N I
D O K V C S V E Z W R E M J M
E A Y Z S A H E B J K X I E Q
D K O A W S R K L E U M M I M
A K O V H N F M F H E Z R O N
N E B A J O T H I S H M A E L
```

ASSHURIM	JOKSHAN	PHAREZ
CARMI	KEDAR	SHAMMAH
DEDAN	LEUMMIM	SHEBA
EPHRAIM	MIDIAN	SHELAH
HANOCH	MIZZAH	SHUAH
HEZRON	NAHATH	ZIMRAN
ISHMAEL	NEBAJOTH	

Abraham's Progeny Part 3

Give yourself 25 points if you find all twenty names.

```
Q B P K V M B N G J Z Z C N T
Q Z H N W V A L D J Z L J A K
X I A I V D W I E J I Z V Y Z
N M R U E A S S H U R I M Y F
T R E D K T X H D C M X F R S
C A Z T S H A M M A H M A Y H
S N B L K I H A I A S D I P E
H R E G M H S E U Z E U H M L
E V F R T K T L Z K Z C M J A
B E A A E H R N C R O A H O H
A C H A M I D I A N O P H K G
B A N P A G T T A C X N M S M
N E B A J O T H G Q O I Z H C
R Z R Y K E P H R A I M K A R
S H U A H J K E M X O N T N V
```

Cities of Judah Part 1

Find the following names of cities of Judah. If you find them all, give yourself 10 points.

```
G G I O G W I Y X Z D E S M L
M A D M A N N A H H S E H Y M
C U Q J Y H E A A J H A I B G
Z M N Q R Q P D R E E Q L F R
V P V U U X A U A R M P H N B
Z F G Y Z D P H X U A Q I D E
Y A X F A N S H D S A H M C A
J Q P K I E I A X A A D V Z L
N K L Z D T L Y C L O I E I O
P O X E W O M J A E Q M W K T
E H K U T T Z A F M O O K L H
Y A O L E P B W C S L N A A X
V Z E Q L Q X J M E K A M G T
Q O L H E B R O N B T H A F I
K R S G M O B X P Y J B M M U
```

ADADAH	HAZOR	SHEMA
AMAM	HEBRON	SHILHIM
BAALAH	JAGUR	TELEM
BEALOTH	JERUSALEM	ZIKLAG
DIMONAH	KEDESH	
ELTOLAD	MADMANNAH	

Cities of Judah Part 2

Once again, give yourself 10 points if you find all the following names of cities.

```
C W R M L B K E D E S H W H U
K C V C I G C V T E L E M C H
E L T O L A D P L P L L X A E
B J E R U S A L E M J O L N B
E T E N E K O F K B C A M A R
A J C Y R L J E E M A F G K O
L B V H A Z O R S B T J X U N
O Y F Q Z L D K H H U D O E R
T H G Q I R L K I L E I Y T R
H T S A K C I U L Q J M D H A
B S B B L S L W H T G O A A M
B Z K P A W W B I R Q N Z Z A
C I D U G T C R M K U A H R M
A D A D A H R D Y T U H N X V
M A D M A N N A H I Y G O L M
```

ADADAH	HAZOR	SHEMA
AMAM	HEBRON	SHILHIM
BAALAH	JAGUR	TELEM
BEALOTH	JERUSALEM	ZIKLAG
DIMONAH	KEDESH	
ELTOLAD	MADMANNAH	

116

Cities of Judah Part 3

If you find all sixteen names, give yourself 25 points.

```
J E R U S A L E M R X Q X B V
Y D I M O N A H R Y T P O A T
I A Q S K K C Z A V Y A V A E
G R G E G E P A U X K M V L L
H A Z O R K D D D P C L U A E
Q D K T N P P E K D J K V H M
M A F B E F V S S Z I K L A G
A D L B E A L O T H V A Z S W
D A L E Y W C K D X E O M M E
M H W D X P N X F H I I A J L
A X F L N C U V P P H M A Z T
N S B I S H E M A L A B K K O
N P I G U W E I I W Y X N R L
A U U S O N W H V V D J O M A
H E B R O N S O J A G U R S D
```

Women in the Bible Part 1

Find the following names of women in the Bible. Give yourself 10 points if you find them all.

```
R X D I N A H E B E O H P H Q
E H A N N A H I N O A M L M B
H N B S F R M L A P L V H D R
T Q R S M I U D E B O R A H O
S I E P A D B T E B I L H A H
E J H V N R V V H O E L J T Y
Q B T K P S A C R O D Z L J R
H A E Q Q N Y H C Q B E E H J
A T B L Z R A B I G A I L J U
L H A G A R G V E H N Q H K D
I S S M Q A G P K E V L U B I
L H I G X C D A M A R I S S T
E E L H Z H Q L P D Q D K T H
D B E A Q E B R A Y H E I F X
C A R O Q L I B M O T X X C O
```

ABIGAIL (1 Samuel 25:3)
AHINOAM (1 Samuel 14:50)
BATHSHEBA
(2 Samuel 12:24)
BILHAH (Genesis 29:29)
DAMARIS (Acts 17:34)
DEBORAH (Genesis 35:8)
DELILAH (Judges 16:4)

DINAH (Genesis 30:21)
DORCAS (Acts 9:36)
ELISABETH (Luke 1:7)
ESTHER (book of Esther)
HAGAR (Genesis 16:1)
HANNAH (1 Samuel 1:2)
JEZEBEL (1 Kings 16:31)

JUDITH (Genesis 26:34)
LEAH (Genesis 29:16)
MARY (Matthew 1:16)
PHOEBE (Romans 16:1 NKJV)
RACHEL (Genesis 29:6)
RUTH (book of Ruth)
SARAH (Genesis 17:15)

Women in the Bible Part 2

Once again, find the following women's names. If you find them all, give yourself 10 points.

```
K E A J H A N I D T J V Y X C
U B M W O K J W H T I D U J J
M E F A X L E H C A R A G A H
H O E L I S A B E T H Q I Y W
A H W Z I H B L J E Z E B E L
N P X A U A Z F L Y S N H A E
N O C B J H G U F Z U A S S Y
A R G E S L J I P D R I R M T
H E D H A I T O B O R U U A Q
I H E S C B E B B A T R X P H
N T L H R Y G E M H H A E L G
O S I T O U D A X M O N I W Z
A E L A D T D D V A Y U X K A
M C A B S P X U B R Z B F R L
P T H T G E M C J Y X S U N Z
```

ABIGAIL	DINAH	JUDITH
AHINOAM	DORCAS	LEAH
BATHSHEBA	ELISABETH	MARY
BILHAH	ESTHER	PHOEBE
DAMARIS	HAGAR	RACHEL
DEBORAH	HANNAH	RUTH
DELILAH	JEZEBEL	SARAH

Women in the Bible Part 3

If you find all twenty-one names, give yourself 25 points.

```
N S E U V M A O N I H A L H Q
D E B O R A H K F A M I F Q P
D M E I H Y D U N D A T D R N
Q N O P U O H N H G O J T B M
H Z H I E G A K I H G R R Y I
R B P J I H G B K A E Y C M B
A I X Z E D A A U L S G R A B
C L A H C Z R C I I T O W G S
H H P N A U E S B L H E N Z A
E A D Q U N A B C E E O H F H
L H E G L B I O E D R A C J T
R O B L E D P D P L R Z X M I
U B A T H S H E B A W K A X D
T O H V A X R Q S X C R U X U
H W N S I R A M A D Y X H U J
```

120

Paul's Journeys Part 1

If you find the following words concerning the travels of the apostle Paul, give yourself 10 points.

```
A I C Y L E A T H O J P L Z W
G C H M R O V Z A F Z B F C D
Q M O Y R A N R Y M S N A O X
K B T G A L A T I A K L U L P
S E G I S T A P J C D Y X O E
S U D S A W T I A L A S X S Z
E U S P U V Z I N O Y T W S P
D B U R T R N D T O G R N E X
O H O R A O P K I R L A E C S
H F O L D T P Y O S T O A G Y
R A R E K H G U C S I N P V R
S E C A R H T U H Y L Z O P I
J A Y S H H S T X T M P L M A
M K H I V I V N G Y I V I R W
B G S A L A M I S N Y U S S P
```

ANTIOCH
APPOLONIA
ASIA
COLOSSE
CYPRUS
GALATIA
LYCIA

LYSTRA
MACEDONIA
NEAPOLIS
PATARA
RHODES
SALAMIS
SMYRNA

SYRIA
TARSUS
THRACE
TROAS
TYRE

Paul's Journeys Part 2

Once again, find the following words related to Paul's journeys. If you find them all, give yourself 10 points.

```
K Q E F S P A T A R A A I C C
G E N X A Z M B D I I E V O S
A S I L O P A E N R O W L D A
L N M E R N J Y Y R H O D E S
A H S Y T A R S U S S Q W I R
T P O I R O S G S S V A B W J
I I O L Q N R K E U F I A B A
A C S S I M A L A S R M J K I
H K E L A I N O L O P P A Y N
E I C H H D A Y S E L G Y G O
Q Q A D C H C I R Y D U J C D
H R R O S I Z Y S O Q D Y F E
P G H E A U T T S A U I W M C
U X T K L X R E K B P S H X A
V M Q O S A C B Q H P M C S M
```

ANTIOCH	LYSTRA	SYRIA
APPOLONIA	MACEDONIA	TARSUS
ASIA	NEAPOLIS	THRACE
COLOSSE	PATARA	TROAS
CYPRUS	RHODES	TYRE
GALATIA	SALAMIS	
LYCIA	SMYRNA	

Paul's Journeys Part 3

If you find all nineteen words, give yourself 25 points.

```
A P P O L O N I A I R R P F X
E R U J F U L K R N S T O B O
N H K A K R A E A A R T Y R E
A O E D J I K S T C J Y V E C
N D O A C W B S A R C Q M Y Y
T E S Y S I L O P A E N M S P
I S L X L A W L N Z B E D M R
O Y U S X I S O E F G K U Y U
C R Z H M T I C S I M A L A S
H B O C S A W D Z A A K S S D
A R T S Y L S T A P S I X U J
J R V Y L A S X X L A G D S I
A E B Y D G V R E I I B T R E
S Y R I A M A C E D O N I A V
T H R A C E F T S A O R T T N
```

Prisoners and Exiles Part 1

Find the following names of prisoners and exiles. If you find them all, give yourself 10 points.

```
S U S M L I S A I A H D O Q P
D I U V O M A N A S S E H M E
J A U U F R Z E D E K I A H T
G O N T M S D O W V Q N D Y E
I X H I R O H E Q T S B O C R
Y K M N E P R S C R Z E Y A S
J W D Q E L J T O A C A I N H
E S Z S F O T H L Q I Z E F G
R X O Q X A X E K L Q A O E N
E J M J Q Z P R J A C O B E X
M Y Z K D A Q A Z L W Z H S R
I U W Z Q R A R U K O P C I X
A L F E G I M D J L E Z A L A
H H M M V A R Y N T H A G A R
Y C T H C H N Z S W X L M S Z
```

AZARIAH (2 Chronicles 26:20)

CAIN (Genesis 4:16)

DANIEL (Daniel 2:20)

ESTHER (book of Esther)

HAGAR (Genesis 21:17)

ISAIAH (2 Kings 19:5)

JACOB (Genesis 28:5)

JEREMIAH (book of Jeremiah)

JOHN (book of John)

JOSEPH (Genesis 37:28)

MANASSEH (Genesis 46:20)

MORDECAI (Esther 7:10)

NOAH (Genesis 8:1)

PAUL (Acts 16:16)

PETER (John 18:27)

SILAS (Acts 15:22)

STEPHEN (Acts 6:5)

ZEDEKIAH (2 Kings 24:20)

Prisoners and Exiles Part 2

Once again, give yourself 10 points if you find the following names.

```
Z U K X S Q K X S A C U M N C
E L C Z N B A H T X F X I P V
D A N I E L A S E T K A O V S
E L B J A I V I P S C T R X J
K E X X R S H L H H T J P X Q
I U U A A A J A E W B H P T L
A P Z I I E P S N O J O E U N
H A H A G A R R C J B F A R M
G C S A K R H A Q O G P T P O
O I H W S P J P D H L F S A R
T U X H E Y K O E N S W I V D
V Z A S H F G V Y T D P S C E
V O O G E Q G Y U X E M T G C
N J W M A N A S S E H R M K A
V H X C J E R E M I A H G A I
```

AZARIAH	JACOB	NOAH
CAIN	JEREMIAH	PAUL
DANIEL	JOHN	PETER
ESTHER	JOSEPH	SILAS
HAGAR	MANASSEH	STEPHEN
ISAIAH	MORDECAI	ZEDEKIAH

Prisoners and Exiles Part 3

If you find all eighteen names, give yourself 25 points.

```
D J I I S A I A H T N H J B U
O U W K X T E C A P N A R R B
Z C N C R S E H W Z P G Q G I
N O A H A B A P G W Q A M I X
Z O B L R I K H H J T R U T R
Q E I M R Q A D J E E C Q L R
J S D A A I L G P E N P P E D
N A Z E M N J S F P R C T T A
W A C E K A A D Y L Y E H R N
E D R O X I F S C Y P G A W I
Q E P F B K A B S F E D G S E
J F B V X M L H V E J O H N L
O A J M I X U R X E H N E B D
C A I N P I M O R D E C A I W
J O S E P H E S T H E R I M F
```

126

The Book of Genesis

A thorough knowledge of the Bible's first book is essential to being truly Bible brilliant. The following questions follow a precise chapter-by-chapter order, hitting the most important parts of each of the fifty chapters. Give yourself 3 points for each correct answer (there are 257 questions in all).

Chapter 1

1. What was created on the first day?
2. What was created on the second day?
3. What was created on the third day?
4. What was created on the fourth day?
5. What was created on the fifth day?
6. What was created on the sixth day?
7. What happened on the seventh day?

Chapter 2

1. From what substance was Adam formed?
2. From what were the animals and birds formed?
3. From which human body part was Eve formed?
4. What place did God give Adam as a home?

Chapter 3

1. Adam and Eve where forbidden to eat from which tree?
2. Who deceived Eve into eating from the tree?
3. How did God curse the serpent for his trickery?
4. What curse did God put on the man?
5. What curse did God put on the woman?
6. Why did God place the cherubims at the east of the Garden of Eden?
7. Why was a flaming sword placed to guard the tree of life?

Chapter 4

1. Why did God reject Cain's offering?
2. What did Cain do to Abel?
3. What did God do to Cain for committing this heinous crime?
4. Why was Cain so worried about God's judgment on him?
5. What did God do to alleviate Cain's worry?
6. Who was born to Adam and Eve after the loss of their son Abel?

Chapter 5

1. Who were Noah's sons?

Chapter 6

1. What did the sons of God do against God's wishes?
2. How did God view the world he created?
3. How did God feel about his creation?
4. What man did God find righteous?

5. What did God instruct the righteous man to do?

6. What were the dimensions of the ark?

7. How many of each animal were to be taken on the ark?

Chapter 7

1. How many of each unclean animal were taken on the ark?

2. How many of each clean animal were taken on the ark?

3. How many of each bird were taken on the ark?

4. How many days did it rain on the earth?

5. How many people were on the ark?

6. Where were the animals of the seas during the voyage of the ark?

Chapter 8

1. After it stopped raining, how many days did the ark float on water?

2. How many months passed before the water receded enough to make mountains visible?

3. In which month of the year did the earth finally become dry again?

Chapter 9

1. What did God consider justice if a man was killed by another man or a beast?

2. What symbol did God provide to show he would never destroy the earth by flood again?

3. What was Ham's reaction to seeing his father drunk and unclothed?

Chapter 10

1. Nimrod was from the line of which of Noah's sons?
2. Where did Japheth's line live?
3. Where did Shem's line live?
4. Whose lines formed the various nations?

Chapter 11

1. What monstrosity did the people decide to build?
2. Why did they want to build the monstrosity?
3. What did God do to foil them?
4. How many years after the flood was Abram born?
5. Who was Lot?

Chapter 12

1. What did God instruct Abram to do?
2. What promise did God make to Abram?
3. What land did God promise Abram?
4. Why did God send plagues on Pharaoh's house?

Chapter 13

1. What problem was caused because of Abram's and Lot's livestock?
2. How was the problem solved?
3. Where did Abram decide to go?
4. Where did Lot decide to go?

Chapter 14

1. When the kings went to war, who was taken captive?
2. Who rescued him?

3. What did Abram do with some of the spoils of war he won in battle?

4. Who witnessed Abram's tithing?

5. What did the king of Sodom offer to Abram?

6. Why did Abram reject the king's offer?

Chapter 15

1. Who was Eliezer?

2. What did God reveal to Abram about his descendants?

3. What horrible thing would happen to Abram's descendants?

4. How long would this horrible thing last?

5. What place would be God's gift to Abram's descendants?

Chapter 16

1. Sarai advised her husband, Abram, to have children with whom?

2. How did Sarai feel toward Hagar after Hagar gave birth?

3. What promise did God make to Hagar?

4. What was the name of Hagar's son?

Chapter 17

1. When Abram was ninety-nine years old, to what did God change his name?

2. What did Abram's new name mean?

3. What was the sign of the covenant between God and Abraham?

4. To what was Sarai's name changed?

5. What did God promise Abraham through Sarah?

Chapter 18

1. While sitting in his tent, what did Abraham see?

2. Whom did Abraham realize his visitors were?

3. What did the visitors tell Abraham about Sarah?

4. What was Sarah's response?

5. What place was considered very evil and was about to be destroyed?

6. What worried Abraham about Lot?

Chapter 19

1. How many of the angels went to Sodom?

2. Who met the angels when they arrived in Sodom?

3. Who gathered outside of Lot's house?

4. What did the people outside of Lot's house want?

5. What did the angels do to the men?

6. Who had sent the men to Sodom?

7. What were they commanded to do to Sodom?

8. What did Lot's sons-in-law think of Lot's dire warning about Sodom's demise?

9. Where did Lot and his family flee to?

10. Who looked back at the burning city of Sodom despite warnings not to?

11. What happened to her?

12. What did Lot's daughters plot to do to him?

13. Why did they make this plot?

14. What two groups are the descendants of Lot?

Chapter 20

1. Why did Abraham call Sarah his sister in Gerar?
2. Who prevented King Abimelech from touching Sarah?
3. After Sarah was returned to Abraham, what happened to Abimelech's household?

Chapter 21

1. What did Abraham and Sarah name their son?
2. What does the name of their son mean?
3. What did Sarah tell Abraham to do with Hagar and her son?
4. What did God tell Hagar he would do for her son?
5. What was the covenant between Abraham and Abimelech?

Chapter 22

1. Why did God command Abraham to sacrifice his son?
2. Who carried the wood for the sacrifice?
3. How did God know that Abraham really did fear him?
4. What did God provide for Abraham to sacrifice instead of his son?
5. In whom would the nations be blessed?
6. Who was Rebekah's father?

Chapter 23

1. Where did Sarah die?
2. Where was Sarah buried?

Chapter 24

1. Whom did Abraham send to find a wife for Isaac?
2. Who met Abraham's servant at the well?
3. How was the servant to distinguish which woman the Lord sent for Isaac?
4. What did Rebekah do when she saw Isaac?
5. Did Isaac approve of Rebekah?

Chapter 25

1. Where was Abraham buried?
2. What did God tell Rebekah about the babies she carried in her womb?
3. What were her children's names?
4. What do the names of her children mean?
5. Who was Isaac's favorite son?
6. Why was Isaac's favorite son his favorite?
7. What did Jacob take from Esau by trickery?

Chapter 26

1. Isaac and Rebekah were in which town?
2. Isaac tried to pass off Rebekah as which of his relatives?
3. Who spotted Isaac and Rebekah while looking through his window?
4. When Isaac became very rich, what did King Abimelech advise him to do?
5. In what town did the Lord bless Isaac?

Chapter 27

1. What was Isaac's blessing for his son Jacob?
2. What was Isaac's blessing for his son Esau?

3. What did Esau swear to do to Jacob after Isaac's death?

4. Where did Rebekah send Jacob?

5. Why did she send Jacob away?

Chapter 28

1. Isaac sent Jacob to marry one of the daughters of whom?

2. What did Jacob dream about on the way to Haran?

3. What was Jacob promised in his dream?

4. What was the name Jacob gave this place?

5. What does the name of the place mean?

Chapter 29

1. How was Rachel related to Jacob?

2. What was Rachel's profession?

3. What did Jacob ask from Laban as payment for his hard labor?

4. Whom did Laban give to Jacob as a wife?

5. How much longer did Jacob serve Laban before he could marry Rachel?

6. What were the names of Leah's first four sons?

Chapter 30

1. Before Rachel conceived, what three people had children for Jacob?

2. What were the names of Leah's next two sons?

3. What was the name of Leah's daughter?

4. What was the name of Rachel's son?

5. Why did Laban want Jacob to stay in the land and not leave?

6. After marriage, what did Jacob want as wages?

7. What did Jacob use to help his livestock multiply?

Chapter 31

1. Who told Jacob to leave Laban's household?
2. What did Rachel take from Laban's house?
3. Where did Rachel hide the stolen goods?
4. How many years in all had Jacob stayed with Laban?

Chapter 32

1. Why did Jacob divide his possessions and people into two groups?
2. Why did Jacob send gifts to Esau?
3. With whom did Jacob think he had wrestled?
4. What happened to the sinew in Jacob's hip as a result of the wrestling?

Chapter 33

1. When Esau saw Jacob, what was his reaction to Jacob?
2. Why didn't Jacob travel to Seir at the same pace as Esau?
3. Where did Jacob finally pitch his tent?
4. From whom did Jacob buy land?

Chapter 34

1. What did Shechem do to Dinah, Jacob's daughter?
2. How did Jacob's sons react upon learning of what had happened to Dinah?
3. Who was Shechem's father?
4. What did Shechem's father suggest they do to remedy the situation?
5. What did Jacob's sons demand be done to all the men in the city?
6. What did Jacob's sons do to the men of the city of Shechem?

Chapter 35

1. Where did God instruct Jacob to go?

2. To what did God change Jacob's name?

3. What does the name Israel mean?

4. Rachel died while doing what?

5. Who was the last child born of Rachel?

6. With whom did Reuben lie, which was immoral?

7. How old was Isaac when he died?

8. What two people buried Isaac?

Chapter 36

1. From what land did Esau choose his wives?

2. What other name did Esau have?

3. From what son of Isaac did the Amalekites originate?

Chapter 37

1. Why did Jacob love Joseph more than his other children?

2. What special garment did Jacob make for Joseph?

3. Why did Joseph's brothers despise him?

4. What did the brothers do in Joseph's dream that was demeaning to them?

5. What did Joseph's brothers plot to do to him?

6. What brother did not want to take part in the plot against Joseph?

7. What did the brothers do to Joseph?

8. Where did the Ishmaelites take Joseph?

9. What did the brothers tell their father, Jacob, about Joseph?

Chapter 38

1. Who killed Judah's sons Er and Onan?
2. Whom did Judah promise to Tamar as a husband?
3. How many children did Tamar have?

Chapter 39

1. Where was Joseph taken as a slave?
2. Who became Joseph's master?
3. What position did Joseph hold in his master's house?
4. What did the master's wife want from Joseph?
5. How did Joseph respond to the advances?
6. What false accusation did the master's wife bring against Joseph?
7. Where was Joseph sent because of the accusation?
8. What position did Joseph have while in prison?

Chapter 40

1. What two people were thrown into prison with Joseph?
2. What was the meaning of the chief butler's dream?
3. What was the meaning of the chief baker's dream?
4. What did Joseph ask of the chief butler?

Chapter 41

1. When Pharaoh had his dream, how many years had passed since the chief butler had gotten out of prison?
2. What did Joseph say Pharaoh's dream meant?

3. What did Joseph recommend Pharaoh do as a result of the dream?

4. Who was the only person ranked higher than Joseph in the land?

5. How old was Joseph when he was placed over Egypt?

Chapter 42

1. Who was left behind when Joseph's ten brothers went to Egypt?

2. Why did they leave the brother behind?

3. What was Joseph's official title in the land of Egypt?

4. What did Joseph accuse his brothers of being?

5. What did Joseph do to his brothers?

6. How long were Joseph's brothers in prison?

7. Why did Joseph's brothers think that prison was retribution against them?

8. When the brothers were released and went back home, who did Joseph keep back?

Chapter 43

1. When did Jacob decide to let his sons go back to Egypt?

2. What did he give his sons to take to Egypt?

3. Why were the brothers frightened of Joseph's dinner invitation?

4. What did Joseph do when he saw Benjamin?

5. What was the seating order for Joseph's brothers?

6. How did Joseph treat Benjamin?

Chapter 44

1. What did Joseph command his steward put in Benjamin's sack?
2. What did Joseph request Benjamin become to him?
3. What did Joseph's brothers do when they became aware of Joseph's wishes for Benjamin?
4. What did Judah tell Joseph his father would do if he found out about Joseph's request for Benjamin?

Chapter 45

1. When Joseph revealed to his brothers who he was, how did they react?
2. Whom did Joseph tell his brothers had elevated him to such a status?
3. Who approved of Joseph's family moving to Egypt?

Chapter 46

1. After his sons returned from Egypt, who spoke to Jacob in a dream?
2. Who was Joseph's Egyptian wife?
3. Where was Jacob told to go in the dream?
4. To what land did Jacob and his family go?

Chapter 47

1. When their money was exhausted, how did the people pay Joseph for grain?
2. What was the next method of payment for people to buy grain?

3. How long did Jacob get to be with Joseph before Jacob died?

4. What did Jacob ask Joseph to promise him upon his death?

Chapter 48

1. What were the names of Joseph's two sons?

2. Which of Joseph's sons did Jacob bless first?

3. What was Jacob's blessing for Joseph?

Chapter 49

1. What was Reuben's harsh blessing?

2. Why did Reuben receive such a harsh blessing?

3. What did Jacob say would happen to Simeon and Levi?

4. What was Judah's blessing?

5. From which son would the stone of Israel come?

6. Where did Jacob wish to be buried?

7. What other five notable people were buried in the same place?

Chapter 50

1. What did Joseph's brothers fear after their father died?

2. Why did Joseph sob when the messengers came from the brothers?

3. What did Joseph ask his people to do on his behalf when he died?

Did You Know?
(Set 13)

A Bible brilliant–worthy set of facts follows.

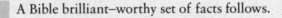

- There was a man named Dodo in the Bible (Judges 10:1).
- According to the book of Revelation, God's new earth will not have any seas (Revelation 21:1).
- King Ahab built a house made entirely of ivory (1 Kings 22:39).
- The Gadites, the tribe of Gad, had faces like lions (1 Chronicles 12:8).
- King Solomon had black, bushy hair (Song of Solomon 5:11).
- The Sea of Galilee was also known as the Sea of Tiberias (John 21:1).

128

The Miracles of Jesus

The miracles of Jesus are well documented in the four Gospels of Matthew, Mark, Luke, and John. Answer the following questions correctly for 10 points each, and enter your well-earned points on the score card.

1. Matthew 8:1–4—Jesus cleansed a man who had _____.
2. Matthew 8:5–13—Jesus healed a centurion's _____.
3. Matthew 8:14–15—Jesus healed Peter's _____.
4. Matthew 8:16–17—One evening, Jesus healed many who were _____.
5. Matthew 8:23–27—Jesus created calm during a _____.
6. Matthew 8:28–33—Jesus cast demons into a herd of _____.
7. Matthew 9:1–2—After crossing over on a boat, Jesus healed a man who was _____.
8. Matthew 9:20–22—While in a crowd, Jesus felt someone touch his cloak. He then healed a woman who had been bleeding for _____.
9. Matthew 9:23–26—Jesus raised from the dead Jairus's _____.

10. Matthew 9:27–31—Jesus healed two blind men when he
    _____.

11. Matthew 9:32–34—Jesus healed a man unable to _____.

12. Matthew 12:9–14—Jesus healed a man with a withered
    _____.

13. Matthew 12:22–23—Jesus healed a demon-possessed man
    who was also _____.

14. Matthew 14:13–21—Jesus used five loaves of bread and two
    fish to feed _____.

15. Matthew 14:25–27—Jesus walked on _____.

16. Matthew 14:34–36—At Gennesaret, Jesus healed all the sick
    who touched his _____.

17. Matthew 15:21–28—Jesus healed a Gentile woman's demon-
    possessed _____.

18. Matthew 15:32–39—When a crowd following Jesus had not
    eaten in three days, Jesus used seven loaves of bread and a
    few fish to feed _____.

19. Matthew 17:14–20—Jesus freed a boy from a _____.

20. Matthew 17:24–27—Jesus paid a temple tax with a coin
    from the mouth of a _____.

21. Matthew 20:29–34—As Jesus and his disciples were leav-
    ing Jericho, Jesus encountered two men and restored their
    _____.

22. Matthew 21:18–22—Jesus caused a fig tree to _____.

23. Mark 1:21–27—In Capernaum, Jesus cured a man of an
    _____.

24. Mark 7:31–37—When Jesus touched a man's ears and tongue,
    the man could _____.

25. Mark 8:22–26—At Bethsaida, Jesus healed a _____.

26. Luke 5:1–11—When fishermen were coming up empty and Jesus instructed them to cast their nets, yielding an abundance of fish, they were on the boat of _____.

27. Luke 7:11–17—In Nain, Jesus brought back to life the son of _____.

28. Luke 13:10–17—In a synagogue, Jesus healed a woman who had been bent over for _____.

29. Luke 14:1–6—Jesus healed a man with dropsy (excessive accumulation of fluid in body tissues) on _____.

30. Luke 17:11–19—Jesus cleansed a group of ten _____.

31. Luke 22:50–51—Jesus healed a servant's severed _____.

32. John 2:1–11—Jesus turned water into _____.

33. John 4:49–54—Jesus healed an official's _____.

34. John 5:1–15—Jesus healed an invalid in the town of _____.

35. John 9:1–11—Jesus healed a man who had been born _____.

36. John 11:1–45—Jesus famously raised from the dead _____.

37. John 21:4–11—Jesus repeated one of his most famous miracles, the catching of _____.

129

Who Is?

Identify the following people in this brief but vital test. Correct answers are worth 10 points each.

1. Who is "perfect and upright, and one that feared God"?
2. Who is "the bright and morning star"?
3. Who is "the voice of one crying in the wilderness"?
4. Who is "a rod out of the stem of Jesse"?
5. Who is "my own son in the faith," according to Paul?
6. Who is the "son of the morning"?
7. Who is "the last Adam"?
8. Who is "the salt of the earth," according to Jesus?
9. Who is "a mighty hunter before the LORD"?
10. Who is the "generation of vipers" according to Jesus?

THE BIBLE BRILLIANT SECTION

This final large section is the Bible scholar section. It has the most difficult challenges but offers the greatest rewards. Expect nothing easy here, but your sense of satisfaction at answering these questions will be the highest of at any point during your Bible brilliant experience. (Answers to section 3 begin on page 618.)

I wish to see the Bible study as much a matter of course in the secular colleges as in the seminary. No educated man can afford to be ignorant of the Bible, and no uneducated man can afford to be ignorant of the Bible.

> Theodore Roosevelt, twenty-sixth president
> of the United States

There is nothing in this world that can compare with the Christian fellowship; nothing that can satisfy but Christ.

> John D. Rockefeller, American business
> magnate and philanthropist

The New Testament is the greatest Book the world has ever known or ever will know.

> Charles Dickens, renowned author

130

Crossword Puzzle 2

Give yourself 25 bonus points if you solve this crossword puzzle
with three or fewer mistakes.

The Bible Brilliant Section

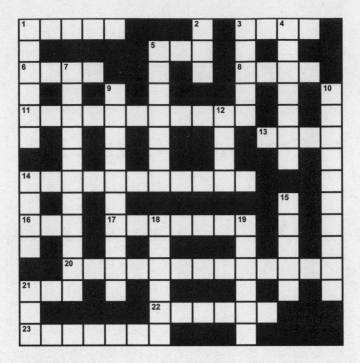

Across

1. What Jesus died on
3. Revelation 9:1, And the fifth angel sounded, and I saw a ___ fall from heaven
5. The Almighty
6. Zephaniah 3:19, Behold, at that time I will ___ all that afflict thee
8. One of the four books of the Gospels
11. What Jesus suffered
13. Delivery of Moses
14. What the repentant seek
16. Jesus died for ours
17. Savior of the world
20. She traveled with Jesus
21. Genesis 12:1, Therefore it shall come to pass, when the Egyptians shall see thee, that they shall ___
22. Resurrection Sunday
23. Bad event in the Garden of Eden (2 words)

Down

1. Place to find a choir
2. Genesis 30:24, And she called his name Joseph; and said, The LORD shall ___ to me another son
3. Mark 6:3, Is not this the carpenter, the son of Mary, the brother of James, and of Joses, and of Juda, and ___
4. Isaac's father
5. Sea of ___
7. Old Testament book
9. Mother of Jesus (2 words)
10. Event in which Jesus knew His betrayal (2 words)
12. 1 Chronicles 16:13, O ye seed of Israel his servant, ye children of Jacob, his chosen ___
14. Go without meals
15. Book after Hebrews
18. He chose Saul as Israel's first king
19. Angel's abode
21. ___ on the throne

Crossword Puzzle 3

Give yourself 25 bonus points if you solve this crossword puzzle with three or fewer mistakes.

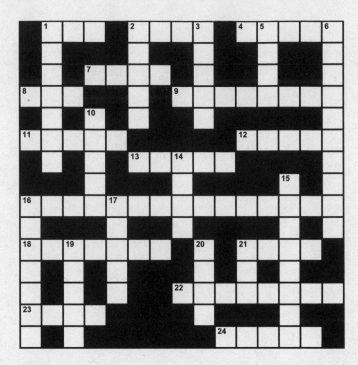

Across

1. "___ is greatly to be feared . . ." (Psalm 89:7)
2. "I have coveted no man's silver, or___" (Acts 20:33)
4. Son of Isaac
7. Eve's husband
8. Genesis 7:3, Of fowls also of the ___ by sevens
9. From 13-Down
11. Savior of the world
12. The "tree" 11-Across hung on
13. "Kingly" version of the Bible
16. The act of having a meal together
18. It should follow a sin
21. ". . . deliver us from ___" (Matthew 6:13)
22. What God has given to all humans
23. It guided the wise men
24. Peter, for one

Down

1. Christ lived there
2. ". . . the ___ of God was upon him" (Luke 2:40)
3. King who was "the sweet psalmist of Israel"
5. Genesis 3:10, And he said, I heard thy voice in the garden, ___ was afraid, because I was naked; and I hid myself.
6. Good thing to do with a church group
10. Herod's kingdom
14. Bethlehem visitors
15. Faith
16. Immersion in water
17. 1 or 2 of the Old Testament
19. Nehemiah 2:1, And it came to pass in the month ___
20. Second book of the New Testament
21. Mother of Cain

THIRTEEN GROUPS
OF TRIVIA

Each of the following groups of trivia contains fifty questions. Do one group at a time and give yourself 5 points for each correct answer. You may do any or all of the groups as many times as necessary to achieve your goal. Record your score for each group on the score card.

132

Group 1

1. How long was Solomon the king over Israel?
2. In the Sermon on the Mount, what did Jesus say would happen to the meek?
3. Into what did Jesus say the merchants had turned his house of prayer?
4. What relation was Annas to Caiaphas?
5. What was the first plague God inflicted on Egypt?
6. "He leadeth me beside the still waters" is a part of what psalm?
7. Who, full of good works and acts of charity, was raised from the dead by Peter?
8. According to James, what is pure and undefiled religion?
9. How many churches were there in Asia Minor in Revelation?
10. In the new Jerusalem, where are the names of the twelve tribes written?
11. In the parable of the ten virgins, what were they waiting for?
12. What did Daniel do for Nebuchadnezzar that no one else could do?
13. When people brought their young children to Jesus, what did the disciples do?

14. Where did Moses meet his future wife for the very first time?

15. Who wrote the majority of the book of Psalms?

16. Of the ten lepers Jesus healed, what nationality was the one who returned to give thanks?

17. What occurred to facilitate the release of Paul and Silas from prison?

18. What did Gideon place on the floor in order to receive a sign from God?

19. In Revelation, what was on the head of the woman clothed with the sun?

20. At what time during their prison stay did Paul and Silas pray and sing to God?

21. What prophet anointed David as king?

22. Who did Jesus say are the two most important people to love?

23. Who was compared to the lilies of the field?

24. What was Jesus's final command to his disciples?

25. What does a soft answer turn away?

26. How did Bathsheba's husband Uriah die?

27. At the temple gate called Beautiful, Peter and John healed a man of what?

28. What did Daniel and his three companions eat and drink instead of the king's meat and drink?

29. What happened to Jesus the eighth day after his birth?

30. What prisoner did the crowd want to be released instead of Jesus?

31. What tribe of Israel looked after the religious aspects of life?

32. Why did Moses's hand become leprous?

33. When Jacob and Esau were in the womb, what did God say they were?

34. What did God do on the seventh day?

35. According to James, how should we treat the rich and the poor?

36. In which city in Judah did Cyrus tell the Israelites to build the temple?

37. What did Jesus say is the first commandment in the law?

38. What did Saul see on his way to Damascus?

39. What job did the prodigal son resort to after spending his inheritance?

40. When Paul was shipwrecked on Malta, how many people from the ship drowned?

41. Where was Paul when he wrote the letter to Philemon?

42. Which region was specially noted for its balm?

43. Who watched over the coats of the men who stoned Stephen?

44. When a man asked Jesus, "Who is my neighbor?" with what parable did Jesus reply?

45. When speaking to the woman at the well, how did Jesus say true worshipers should worship God?

46. How long did Jonah say it would be before Nineveh would be overthrown?

47. How many plagues did God send on Egypt?

48. What was the profession of Zebedee, the father of James and John?

49. What missionary was said to have known the Holy Scriptures from an early age?

50. Who admonished, "Repent ye: for the kingdom of heaven is at hand"?

133

Group 2

1. What is the root of all evil?
2. Who was Joseph's master in Egypt?
3. The Ethiopian eunuch was reading from which book of prophecy?
4. Who laid hands on Saul of Tarsus and cured him of the blindness he received on the road to Damascus?
5. Whom did Jesus raise from the dead with a prayer of thanks to God?
6. After Aaron turned his rod into a serpent before Pharaoh, what happened to the serpents conjured up by Pharoah's magicians?
7. What did Elisha do for the Shunammite's son?
8. What did Joseph want to do when he discovered Mary was pregnant?
9. What does the law say to do when you see a bird in its nest?
10. Where was Paul from?
11. Where was Jesus crucified?
12. Who said, "When I was a child, I spake as a child"?
13. Whom was Paul with when he wrote the letter to Philemon?
14. The king's wrath is as the roaring of what?

15. When Herod killed all the babies in Bethlehem, to which country did Mary and Joseph escape?

16. What did Boaz claim that Naomi was selling?

17. What did Joseph send to his father from Egypt?

18. How does Psalm 1 start?

19. What object was featured in Jacob's dream at Bethel?

20. What book of the Bible comes before Philemon?

21. What judge was betrayed to the Philistines by a woman?

22. What tribe of Israel did not receive an inheritance of land?

23. Who spotted the baby Moses in the Nile River?

24. What was the name of Ruth's son?

25. In addition to gold and silver, what was Abram rich in?

26. In Nebuchadnezzar's dream, what destroyed the statue of different metals?

27. Martha and Mary lived in what town?

28. Who were Joseph's parents?

29. What happened to forty-two children who made fun of Elisha's baldness?

30. With what ailment was Peter's mother-in-law sick?

31. What were the names of Elimelech's two sons?

32. Who was Bathsheba's first husband?

33. What happens if you break one commandment of the law, according to James?

34. How much of Elijah's spirit did Elisha receive?

35. The baby Jesus remained in Egypt with his parents until what event happened?

36. What animal did Samson kill on his way to Timnah?

37. What came out of a fire and attacked Paul on Malta?

38. What king took possession of Naboth's vineyard?

39. What land did the Lord promise to Abram?

40. Who told her daughter to ask for the head of John the Baptist?

41. Who stole her father's household gods?

42. Why were Shadrach, Meshach, and Abednego thrown into the fiery furnace?

43. For how many days did Jesus appear to his disciples after his resurrection?

44. In the parable of the sower, what was the seed?

45. Out of the ten lepers healed by Jesus, how many came back to thank him?

46. What happened to the man who had no wedding robe in the parable of the marriage feast?

47. What was the name of Ruth's second husband?

48. What unusual trait was common among the seven hundred soldiers who could sling a stone and hit their target every time?

49. Who said that a census of the entire Roman world should be taken at the time of Jesus's birth?

50. How did the wise men know that Jesus had been born?

134

Group 3

1. The fear of the Lord is the beginning of knowledge, but what do fools despise?

2. What was the source of Samson's strength?

3. What sea did the Israelites cross to escape from the Egyptians?

4. What is more difficult than a camel going through the eye of a needle?

5. How many years did the Israelites wander in the wilderness?

6. What does a good tree bring forth?

7. What small body part has the ability to boast of great things?

8. How were sins forgiven in the Old Testament?

9. How does James say we should wait for the coming of the Lord?

10. How is man tempted?

11. Bethlehem is referred to as "little" among the thousands of what place?

12. John was on what island when he was given the vision of Revelation?

13. What type of animal spoke to Balaam?

14. Naaman was told to wash in what river to rid himself of leprosy?

15. To whom did Pilate send Jesus after he finished interrogating him?

16. Why did Jacob and his family seek a new life in Egypt?

17. The blessed man will be like a tree planted by what?

18. Daniel had a dream about what four great things?

19. How were the Thessalonians told to pray?

20. What bizarre things happened to King Nebuchadnezzar before he was restored as king?

21. What is the last book of the Old Testament?

22. What miracle had Jesus just performed when he said, "It is I; be not afraid"?

23. What horrific disaster occurred when Abram and Sarai arrived in the land of Canaan?

24. What was Peter doing when he denied Jesus for the second of three times?

25. Why were the Pharisees upset when Jesus forgave the sins of the sick man lowered through a roof?

26. How was Isaac's wife chosen for him?

27. How old was Abraham when his son Isaac was born?

28. In the parable of the sower, what did the seed that fell among thorns represent?

29. What did Jonah do while he waited to see what would happen to Nineveh?

30. What happened to Daniel after he loudly gave thanks to God by his open window?

31. After the priests blew their trumpets, what happened to the city of Jericho?

32. What was the name of Abraham's nephew?

33. Where did Jonah attempt to flee to instead of going to Nineveh as God had commanded?

34. What disciple did Paul commend for having the same faith his mother, Eunice, had?

35. Why did Solomon turn away from God when he became old?

36. Whose father was so delighted to see him that he gave him his best robe and killed a fatted calf?

37. What did the Pharisee thank God for in the parable of the Pharisee and the publican?

38. After Israel split into two kingdoms after the reign of King Solomon, what kingdom was in the south?

39. What did the shepherds do after they visited the baby Jesus?

40. What chorus in Psalm 136 is repeated in every verse?

41. How did Jonah react to the way the people of Nineveh responded to God's message?

42. To what garden did Jesus go to pray before his arrest?

43. Who carried the cross part of the way for Christ?

44. What woman did Paul send to Rome, requesting that she be given a welcome worthy of the saints?

45. Who was Jonah's father?

46. Which son of Solomon succeeded him as king?

47. How many times did Jesus say you should forgive your brother when he sins against you?

48. In what city did Jesus spend his childhood?

49. On what mountains did Noah's ark finally come to rest?

50. What did the mother of James and John ask of Jesus?

135

Group 4

1. What was Lot in relation to Abram?
2. Who was instructed by God to leave his home and family to travel to a strange land?
3. Who traveled back to Jerusalem after the captivity to urge the people to rebuild the walls of the city?
4. Whose mother made him a coat year after year?
5. What did an angel tell Zacharias and Elisabeth their son would be called?
6. In what manner did the people listening to the Sermon on the Mount think that Jesus taught?
7. How did Jesus say we should receive the kingdom of God?
8. What did the dove bring back to Noah on the ark?
9. What question concerning marriage did the Pharisees use to try to trap Jesus?
10. What was Jesus teaching about when he said, "What therefore God hath joined together, let not man put asunder"?
11. What female judge described herself as a mother in Israel?
12. What judge killed Eglon, the king of Moab?
13. What two tribes of Israel were not named after sons of Jacob?

14. Who was the first apostle to perform a miracle in the name of Jesus?

15. What person will the "least person in the kingdom of God" be greater than?

16. What does faith require to make it a living faith?

17. How did Korah and his family die?

18. How does Paul tell us to work out our own salvation?

19. How many books are there in the New Testament?

20. In a parable told by Jesus, what did the rich man do after he had a plentiful harvest?

21. In the Lord's Prayer, what follows "hallowed be thy name"?

22. Gabriel, an angel of the Lord, appeared to Mary during what month of Elisabeth's pregnancy?

23. What valuable things did the queen of Sheba give to Solomon?

24. What happened to anyone whose name was not written in the book of life?

25. What did Jesus advise to do if someone asks you to go with them for a mile?

26. According to Peter, what covers a multitude of sins?

27. What did Jesus say about tomorrow in his Sermon on the Mount?

28. In Jesus's parable, why does a man not put new wine into old bottles?

29. In the parable of the leaven, what was the leaven?

30. What was Philemon to do if his slave owed him anything?

31. What was Jonah doing on a ship while a storm was raging?

32. Who was Isaac's wife?

33. Who replaced Judas Iscariot as a disciple?

34. In the parable of the grain of mustard seed, what did birds do when it became a tree?

35. What does "hope deferred" make sick?

36. Five of the ten virgins did not take enough of what?

37. In what direction was the location of the Garden of Eden?

38. How many books are there in the Old Testament?

39. For whom did Joseph interpret dreams while he was in prison?

40. King Herod was living in what city at the time of Jesus's birth?

41. What birds could the poor use for sacrifices if they could not afford lambs?

42. What did Abraham's son carry for his own sacrifice?

43. What did Joseph command to be placed in Benjamin's sack?

44. Aceldama, the field that Judas Iscariot purchased with his betrayal money, was also known as what?

45. What was the name of Abraham's first wife?

46. According to Old Testament law, in what shouldn't a young goat be cooked?

47. In John's vision of Jesus in Revelation, what came out of Jesus's mouth?

48. In what Bible book do we find Haman, the son of Hammedatha?

49. To what condiment did Jesus compare his disciples?

50. What did Paul do to the soothsayer that angered her masters?

136

Group 5

1. Who was afflicted with leprosy for speaking out against Moses's marriage?

2. Why shouldn't we give the title of Father to anyone?

3. What happens to the man who puts his hand to the plough and looks back?

4. After the Babylonian exile, the Jews sought wealth instead of doing what?

5. Elymas the sorcerer was struck with what affliction by Paul?

6. What unique type of water did Jesus speak of with the Samaritan woman at the well?

7. What was the name of Samson's father?

8. When Jesus asked, "Who do you say that I am," what did Peter say in response?

9. What profession did Jesus compare himself to spiritually?

10. What two sisters married Jacob?

11. Why should a father not provoke a child to anger?

12. After discovering his bride had been given to another, what did Samson do to the Philistines' crops?

13. How did Jesus heal the blind man?

14. In what land did God send Abraham to sacrifice Isaac?

15. Under the law, what was the punishment for someone who struck their father?

16. What bird did God provide to the Israelites for meat in the wilderness?

17. What did God count Abram's faith as?

18. What did God rain down on the Amorite army as they passed through Bethhoron?

19. When God appeared to him in a dream, what did King Solomon ask of the Lord?

20. What woman did Amnon hate more than he had loved?

21. In Revelation, in what is the wife of the Lamb arrayed?

22. What animals were carved on Solomon's throne?

23. When Joseph was given charge over Egypt, what presents did Pharaoh give him?

24. What sin prevented Moses from leading the children of Israel into the Promised Land?

25. Where were the Jews taken captive when Jerusalem was destroyed?

26. While John was conducting baptisms, what did he call the Pharisees and Sadducees?

27. Who closed the door of Noah's ark?

28. Who spoke the words, "Whosoever shall not receive the kingdom of God as a little child shall in no wise enter therein"?

29. Hate stirs up strife, but what does love cover?

30. How did the angel of the Lord appear to Moses?

31. To the beauty of what flower did Jesus compare King Solomon?

32. After the resurrection, what did Jesus and the disciples have for breakfast by the Sea of Tiberias?

33. What was the name of Jesus's cousin who was born six months before him?

34. What was taken off and given to signify the agreement between Boaz and the guardian-redeemer?

35. The Passover was established because of what horrific event?

36. What Israelite woman had two Moabite daughters-in-law?

37. Whose son did Elijah raise from the dead?

38. What king of Israel imported peacocks?

39. What sinful problem did Noah have after disembarking the ark?

40. What was on top of the ark of the covenant?

41. When Peter was asked if Jesus paid temple taxes, what animal was produced with the tax money in its mouth?

42. Which of David's descendants will reign forever?

43. What woman sold purple goods?

44. Who was the first child born of a woman?

45. "The LORD is my shepherd; I shall not want" is in which psalm?

46. In the dream of Nebuchadnezzar, what did the different metals of the statue represent?

47. On what mountain did Moses receive God's law?

48. What marriage restrictions were enacted for the daughters of Zelophehad?

49. Which "full of grace" apostle was stoned to death?

50. Who killed a lion with his bare hands?

Group 6

1. What was the new name given to Daniel while he was in captivity?
2. According to Jesus in the Sermon on the Mount, what can a city that is on a hill not be?
3. For how long had the infirm man lain at the pool of Bethesda?
4. How many people were saved in the ark?
5. How many times did Samson lie to Delilah about his source of strength?
6. In the Sermon on the Mount, what did Jesus say should be done while fasting?
7. Where is the best place to pray?
8. What wise man wrote the majority of the book of Proverbs?
9. What does good like a medicine?
10. What does James say happens if we draw nigh to God?
11. What happened to Shechem, the prince who fell in love with Jacob's daughter Dinah?
12. What Bible book starts, "The book of the generation of Jesus Christ, the son of David, the son of Abraham"?
13. What church did Jesus accuse of being lukewarm?
14. Whom did Abram marry?

15. What king asked for the foreskins of one hundred Philistines?

16. The name of the Lord is like what place of safety?

17. What did God promise to give Abraham as an everlasting possession?

18. Where was Jesus baptized?

19. Who rolled away the stone covering Jesus's tomb?

20. Why were the Thessalonians told not to worry about Christians who had died?

21. During Jacob's wrestling match with an angel, which part of Jacob's body was touched and knocked out of joint?

22. In the parable of the sower, what happened to the seed that fell on the path?

23. What did Paul ask Philemon to have ready for him?

24. What was the covenant God made with Noah?

25. What plant is "the least of all seeds: but when it is grown, it is the greatest among herbs"?

26. Who did Mary think Jesus was when she first saw him after the resurrection?

27. What was used to pierce the side of Jesus as he hung on the cross?

28. What did Samson find in the carcass of the animal he had killed?

29. In Egypt, what did Joseph accuse his brothers of being?

30. Who requested Jesus's body for burial?

31. What aspect of the afterlife did the Sadducees reject?

32. What city came down from heaven prepared as a bride?

33. What prophet said, "Behold, a virgin shall conceive, and bear a son"?

34. The Sadducees did not believe in what type of supernatural beings?

35. Who wrote the book of Acts?

36. How did Jesus reveal which of his disciples would betray him?

37. How many Philistines did Samson kill with the jawbone of a donkey?

38. James compared the tongue to what object?

39. What was Jesus's reply when the Pharisees asked why he ate with publicans and sinners?

40. Where did Jesus first see Nathanael?

41. Caleb gave the hand of his daughter Achsah in marriage to what man?

42. What two Old Testament men appeared with Jesus at the transfiguration?

43. How did Moses command the Red Sea to divide to allow passage for the Israelites?

44. What did God breathe into Adam's nostrils?

45. What is the light of the body?

46. What was Bartimaeus's affliction?

47. What book of the Bible comes just before Jonah?

48. What disciple was a tax collector?

49. Which of David's sons rebelled against him?

50. What is the next to last book of the Bible?

138

Group 7

1. What did Pharaoh's dream of good and bad ears of grain represent?

2. What did Paul say about a woman's long hair?

3. What color robe was placed on Jesus by soldiers in the common hall?

4. Whom did Samuel think was speaking to him when he was called by the Lord as a child?

5. Where was Jonah when he prayed to God with a voice of thanksgiving?

6. From where was the letter to Philemon written?

7. With whom was Jesus speaking when he said, "Verily, verily, I say unto thee, Except a man be born again, he cannot see the kingdom of God"?

8. What horrific things did women do to their own children during the Babylonian siege of Jerusalem?

9. Noah's ark was made from what material?

10. You will be healed if you pray for one another and do what else?

11. Who convinced Delilah to betray Samson?

12. What sea did the Israelites cross to escape from the Egyptians?

13. How long was Jonah inside the great fish?

14. In the Sermon on the Mount, what did Jesus say the earth was?

15. What does the name Abraham mean?

16. What is in the eye of a hypocrite?

17. What was the first bird released from the ark?

18. When Jesus advised his disciples to beware of the "leaven of the Pharisees and of the Sadducees," to what was he referring?

19. Who brought Elijah bread and meat during a severe drought?

20. Who did Paul say is head of the woman?

21. When Jesus died, darkness fell over the land for how long?

22. What happened to the lions in the den with Daniel?

23. What nationality was Timothy's father?

24. What position did Nehemiah hold for King Artaxerxes?

25. Jesus walked on the water of what sea?

26. Paul refers to Jesus as the "head of the body." In this reference, what is "the body"?

27. What two people sang a celebratory song about the downfall of Sisera?

28. Whose mother-in-law did Jesus heal?

29. "Every man that is proud in heart" is what to the Lord?

30. In the book of Revelation, what is the number of a man?

31. What happens to treasure laid up on earth?

32. What inscription was on the altar in Athens?

33. Where was Abram born?

34. Jesus said we are more valuable than what bird?

35. Who told Joseph that Jesus would save his people from their sins?

36. When Philip and the Ethiopian eunuch neared some water, what did the eunuch ask?

37. How many elders sat around the throne of God in John's vision in Revelation?

38. What Bible book features the valley of dry bones?

39. From what city did David rule over Israel?

40. What did Abigail prevent David from doing to Nabal?

41. What did John the Baptist say when he first laid eyes on Jesus?

42. Where did the man who received one talent from his master hide the talent?

43. Although accused by a priest of being drunk, who was given a son after praying to God in the temple?

44. Whose mother was told to drink no wine during her pregnancy?

45. Who told Mary, "Blessed art thou among women, and blessed is the fruit of thy womb"?

46. How old was Moses when he died?

47. To whom did Jesus say, "Why are ye fearful, O ye of little faith"?

48. What strange request did Joshua make to God while fighting the Amorites?

49. Who asked for an understanding heart to judge God's people?

50. Who was the nurse for Ruth's son?

139

Group 8

1. Who was the successor to Moses?
2. Seven fat and seven thin of what type of animal appeared to Pharaoh in a dream?
3. For what reason, according to the law, could the Israelites not eat blood?
4. What was the occupation of Demetrius of Ephesus?
5. In healing Hezekiah of his illness, how many years did God add to his life?
6. According to 1 John 3:4, what is the transgression of the law?
7. What should you not cast before swine?
8. What was the name of Hagar's son?
9. Who asked Jesus to remember him when he came into his kingdom?
10. How old was Sarah when her son, Isaac, was born?
11. How many years did David reign as king?
12. What were Adam and Eve forbidden to eat from in the Garden of Eden?
13. On what day of the year could the high priest enter the most holy part of the temple?

14. What relation was Jacob to Abraham?

15. What was the name of the woman who hid the spies in Jericho?

16. What apostle was once a Pharisee?

17. How old was Jesus when he was baptized?

18. How many psalms are there in the Bible?

19. In his letter to the Corinthians, whom did Paul state was a new creature?

20. What was Jesus wrapped in when he was born?

21. What did Solomon build for the Lord?

22. What was the temple gate called at which the lame man was laid daily?

23. What disciple looked after Mary after the crucifixion of Christ?

24. How many horsemen are there in Revelation 6?

25. What did Jesus ask about the blind?

26. Nicodemus belonged to what Jewish sect?

27. What did the Israelites make while Moses was receiving the Ten Commandments from God?

28. What prophet's prayer for no rain was answered when it did not rain for three and a half years?

29. What will happen at the return of Christ to believers who are alive?

30. What was the first dream of Joseph?

31. Who told Peter to "watch and pray, that ye enter not into temptation"?

32. According to Jesus, why should we not judge people?

33. What is more difficult than a camel going through the eye of a needle?

34. What happened to the prison keeper and his family after Paul and Silas were freed from their chains?

35. What was Paul's command to husbands in his letter to the Colossians?

36. Who was Noah's father?

37. What was the name of Ruth's great-grandson?

38. What does a good tree bring forth?

39. During the temptation of Jesus in the wilderness, what was he tempted to turn into loaves of bread?

40. What religious leaders continually tried to trap Jesus with their questions?

41. Who was Solomon's father?

42. What was the profession of Joseph, the father of Jesus?

43. How did Judas betray Christ?

44. Solomon judged which mother should be the rightful owner of a child by threatening to do what?

45. Whose father was stopped at the last moment from sacrificing his son on an altar?

46. At the age of twelve, Jesus went missing in Jerusalem but was found where?

47. Whom did the disciples think Jesus was at first when they saw him walking on water?

48. What gift did Salome, the daughter of Herodias, ask for after she danced for Herod?

49. How did Samson kill the people in the temple?

50. What musical instrument did David play for Saul?

140

Group 9

1. What was Esau doing when Jacob stole his blessing?
2. Why did Jacob first send Joseph's brothers into Egypt?
3. Who was David's great friend?
4. Who said, "Thy people shall be my people, and thy God my God"?
5. Which of Christ's belongings did the soldiers cast lots for during his crucifixion?
6. What does the name Emmanuel mean?
7. What disciple attempted to walk on water?
8. With whom did David commit adultery?
9. After reaching dry land, where did Jonah go?
10. What king was saved from death by the prayers of Abraham?
11. What course of action did Abram take when he heard that Lot was made a prisoner of war?
12. When God appeared to Jacob in a vision on the way to Egypt, what assuring words did God offer him?
13. After the flood, what did God tell the people to avoid eating?
14. What punishment was given to Gehazi for his greed?
15. How did Rahab help the invading Israelites identify her house?

16. What angel told Daniel the meaning of his vision of the ram and the goat?

17. What king helped King Solomon with his various building projects?

18. How many missionary journeys did Paul go on before his journey to Rome?

19. What was Timothy urged to take to help with his illnesses?

20. Who was the goddess of the Ephesians?

21. Gideon commanded how many volunteer soldiers?

22. What will Jesus drink new in the kingdom of God?

23. Who owned a slave named Onesimus?

24. What psalm is the shortest?

25. How did citizens regard Ruth?

26. How many people from each tribe were sealed, according to the book of Revelation?

27. Who slept under a juniper tree after fleeing for his life?

28. Who thought that the gift of God could be purchased with mere money?

29. What did Daniel spot by the river Hiddekel?

30. What did the chief priest and Pharisees supply to Judas to help arrest Jesus?

31. What type of seed did manna resemble?

32. After leaving Berea, where did Silas and Timothy meet up with Paul?

33. At what young age did Josiah become king of Judah?

34. Whose mother found him a wife from Egypt?

35. What disciple brought to Jesus the boy with five loaves and two fish?

36. Of what was Noah a preacher?

37. Paul thanked God that he did not baptize any Corinthians except for whom?

38. What was the name of Abigail's first husband?

39. Who told his wife not to worry that she was barren and asked her, "Am not I better to thee than ten sons"?

40. According to James, what should we do when we fall into temptation?

41. What did Job say was poured out like the waters?

42. Which of the twelve sons of Jacob had a name that means praise?

43. What Pharisee claimed that if the gospel truly came from God, no one could stop it from spreading?

44. Why did Jephthah flee to the land of Tob?

45. According to David, whose days are like grass?

46. Where did the hypocrites love to pray?

47. In Revelation, unclean spirits came out of the mouth of the dragon in what form?

48. How many people were in the temple watching Samson entertain them?

49. Melchizedek was not only a high priest but also the king of what city?

50. Where did Samson kill thirty men?

141

Group 10

1. What creature did the ten spies compare themselves to when comparing themselves to the inhabitants of the land of Canaan?

2. Who was the father of Abraham?

3. What animal skins that were dyed red were used as offerings to help make the tabernacle?

4. After Pilate could find no guilt in Jesus, why did the Jews say that Jesus should die?

5. How were Joseph and Mary warned that someone wanted to kill the baby Jesus?

6. To whom was Paul writing when he wrote, "I will receive you. And will be a Father unto you, and ye shall be my sons and daughters, saith the Lord Almighty"?

7. How did the sailors learn that Jonah was responsible for the storm?

8. In a parable told by Jesus, what two men went up to the temple to pray?

9. What part of King Asa's body was diseased?

10. What servant had his ear cut off during Jesus's arrest?

11. In what Jewish month is the Passover?

12. Paul and Silas were imprisoned in what city during their second missionary journey?

13. What did Samson carry to the top of the hill overlooking Hebron?

14. What priest anointed Solomon?

15. Whom did Daniel see sitting on a throne in his vision of the four beasts?

16. How many sons did Gideon have?

17. What is the shortest book in the Old Testament?

18. Whose house did Paul enter in Caesarea?

19. The Ethiopian eunuch held what office under Candace, the queen of the Ethiopians?

20. According to Matthew, what was the first of the Beatitudes of the Sermon on the Mount?

21. On what day of creation did God create trees and vegetation?

22. What disciple asked Jesus to show him the Father?

23. Who dozed off during one of Paul's sermons and fell out of a window?

24. Psalm 100 states that we should come before the Lord's presence with what?

25. After his resurrection, Jesus appeared to his disciples at what sea?

26. Paul preached during his first missionary journey on what island?

27. When Athaliah saw her son Ahaziah was dead, what did she do?

28. What prophet told Naaman to wash in the Jordan River to cure his leprosy?

29. How many concubines did Solomon have?

30. How many wise men does the Bible say came to visit Jesus?

31. What was Priscilla's occupation?

32. Who had a bed 9 cubits (13.5 feet) long by 4 cubits (6 feet) wide?

33. How did Moses make the acrid waters of Marah drinkable?

34. What does El Shaddai, a name for God, mean?

35. What did Samson offer as a reward to the Philistines if they could solve his riddle?

36. Where did Philip preach about the kingdom of God, leading many to become baptized?

37. Whose handkerchiefs could heal the sick?

38. Were Adam and Eve ashamed about their nakedness at first?

39. How many of Nineveh's inhabitants weren't able to discern between their right hand and their left hand?

40. When Paul got his sight back, what did he do next?

41. What is the seventh commandment?

42. How many cities of refuge were on the east side of Jordan?

43. What did an angel throw into the sea representing the throwing down of Babylon?

44. In what city did Elijah raise a widow's son from the dead?

45. What Old Testament prophet was given a book to eat by God?

46. As God calls us to a life of holiness, what are we doing if we ignore this advice?

47. Who was the centurion who watched over Paul on his journey to Rome?

48. Who said, "To obey is better than sacrifice"?

49. What sort of man was Noah, according to the Bible?

50. How did Paul escape from Damascus?

142

Group 11

1. Who was given the Spirit of God, enabling him to become a competent craftsman and help with the building of the tabernacle?

2. Bread of deceit is sweet to a man, but what will his mouth be filled with afterward?

3. What is bound in the heart of a child?

4. How old was Abraham's first wife, Sarah, when she died?

5. What prophet told Jeroboam he would rule over ten tribes?

6. What did Melchizedek supply to Abram?

7. In a vision, what did Zechariah see destroying the houses of thieves and liars?

8. How was Lois related to Timothy?

9. The prophecy involving seventy weeks refers to what awaited event?

10. How many years did it take for Solomon to build his own house?

11. What were the disciples arguing about when Jesus told them he would judge the twelve tribes in the kingdom?

12. What occurred when the third vial of wrath was poured on the earth?

13. Anna the prophetess belonged to what tribe?

14. At what battle were the Israelites defeated because Joshua did not first seek the Lord's guidance?

15. As part of the high priest's garments, on what type of stone were the twelve tribes of Israel to have their names engraved?

16. In what city was Lydia converted?

17. Jephthah led Israel against what enemy army?

18. In the parable of the debtors, while one owed five hundred denarii, the other owed how much?

19. The fifth trumpet plague in the book of Revelation is like what plague that was also delivered on Egypt?

20. What prophet prophesied that Paul would be bound in Jerusalem?

21. Who was the father-in-law of Caiaphas, the high priest at the time of Jesus's crucifixion?

22. For how long did the son of Hillel, Abdon, judge Israel?

23. What four beasts did Daniel see in a vision?

24. Whom did Paul take along with him on his first missionary journey?

25. When Jesus sent out the disciples to preach for the first time, to whom did he send them?

26. How many palm trees were in Elim when the Israelites arrived?

27. Wisdom is more precious than which valuable gems?

28. How many rivers did the river in Eden split into outside of the garden?

29. What did the Israelites borrow from their neighbors, the Egyptians?

30. Where will the believers reign in the kingdom of God?

31. Who went into labor and had a child after hearing that the ark of God had been captured and her father-in-law and husband were both dead?

32. What sorcerer did Paul meet on the island of Cyprus?

33. Who arrived in Galilee preaching about the kingdom of God?

34. Joseph's brothers sold him to what kind of people?

35. Who does the prayer of faith save?

36. Pharaoh gave the Egyptian name Zaphnathpaaneah to what person?

37. Where did Delilah live?

38. Who thanked King David for allowing David's son Absalom to return to Jerusalem?

39. Who was Paul speaking about when he said, "The Lord give mercy unto the house of Onesiphorus; for he oft refreshed me, and was not ashamed of my chain"?

40. According to Jesus, what would the twelve apostles receive for forsaking everything and following him?

41. According to the book of Job, what is the hope of a tree that is cut down?

42. Initially, how was the earth watered before rain?

43. What group of many said, "Worthy is the Lamb that was slain"?

44. What feast came into existence when Queen Esther saved the Jews from destruction?

45. What fraction of his goods did Zacchaeus give away to the poor?

46. In answering his prayers, who gave water to the camels of Abraham's servant?

47. How old was Anna the prophetess when she first saw Jesus?

48. What book states that Jesus is the bread of life?

49. What offering did Gideon present to the Lord under an oak tree?

50. Abraham buried his wife in what field?

143

Group 12

1. What did Rachel steal from her father when she left home with Jacob?
2. An excellent wife is what to her husband?
3. What psalm mentions a snail?
4. Samson belonged to what tribe?
5. Why did Pharaoh give Joseph's family land in Goshen?
6. Who was the first man to pass by the wounded man in the parable of the good Samaritan?
7. Balaam and his donkey are in what book of the Bible?
8. Why should children listen to the instruction of a father?
9. What did Jesus eat to convince the disciples that he really had been raised from the dead?
10. How old was Joseph when he died?
11. Jesus said not to swear by your head because you cannot do what?
12. What is acceptable to God because of the Word of God and prayer?
13. According to Proverbs, how shall a man's belly be satisfied?
14. What did God make on the fourth day?
15. Where was King David born?

16. In the good father parable, if a son asks for an egg, what does the good father not give him?

17. How were the Thessalonians told to keep their own bodies?

18. How many companions did the Philistines give to Samson at the feast in Timnah?

19. Psalm 90:1 is a prayer of what famous person?

20. How long did Noah live after the flood?

21. What musical instruments were played to praise God when the temple foundation was rebuilt?

22. How many years did Jacob live?

23. What brother did Joseph send to prison while his other brothers returned home to Jacob?

24. Whom did the Lord command to walk barefoot and naked for three years?

25. How many silver shekels did Jeremiah pay to Hanameel to purchase a field in Anathoth?

26. In the Song of Solomon, the woman's hair is described as a flock of what animal?

27. What was the first offering made to the Lord in the book of Genesis?

28. In the fig tree parable, what was near when one saw a tree putting forth leaves?

29. Who has the right to the tree of life, according to the book of Revelation?

30. The book of Proverbs says that those seeking death acquire their wealth by doing what?

31. What was the color of the high priest's robe?

32. What does the name Israel mean?

33. When building a new house, what was an Israelite to do?

34. What prophet said, "I loved him, and called my son out of Egypt"?

35. What killed twenty-seven thousand Syrians in the city of Aphek?

36. What was the weight of the gold that Solomon acquired in a single year?

37. Who was killed by a thick cloth dipped in water?

38. According to Ezekiel's prophecy, who was the mother of Jerusalem?

39. According to James, what should we do after confessing our faults to one another?

40. The disciple Tabitha was also known by what name?

41. What book of the Bible contains the story of David and Goliath?

42. It is better to obtain wisdom than what?

43. What did the Holy Spirit appear as when the disciples received him?

44. What water creatures were deemed unclean?

45. Which of Leah's sons brought her mandrakes?

46. Why was David forbidden to build God's house?

47. Zipporah was married to what man?

48. Who dreamed of a tree that grew all the way to heaven?

49. Who was King Jehu's father?

50. The inscription "Jesus of Nazareth, King of the Jews" on the cross of Jesus was written in what three languages?

144

Group 13

1. Who had his sight restored by Ananias in Damascus?
2. In Numbers, what two men had an army of 603,554 for war in Israel?
3. Who leapt inside his mother's womb when Mary paid a visit?
4. When David was anointed the king of Israel, how old was he?
5. Who said, "But as for me and my house, we will serve the LORD"?
6. To receive the crown of life, what does one need to do, according to the book of Revelation?
7. Both the longest and the shortest chapter in the Bible can be found in what book?
8. How old was Abraham when his son Isaac was born?
9. How many rivers were formed from the river that flowed out of Eden?
10. How tall was Goliath?
11. When Jesus said, "Get thee behind me, Satan," to whom was he talking?
12. The disciples were called Christians for the first time in what city?

13. According to Paul, what is the fulfillment of the law?

14. Who helped the battered Jesus carry his cross?

15. Moses belonged to what tribe of Israel?

16. In Revelation, what was the name of the city of God?

17. To what king did Isaac claim that Rebekah was his sister, not his wife?

18. After he killed an Egyptian, to what land did Moses flee?

19. Who was Abraham's second wife?

20. What three women, along with other unnamed women, discovered the empty tomb of Jesus?

21. Of the two brothers, Moses and Aaron, which one was older?

22. What two books of the Bible are named after women?

23. The first two disciples chosen by Jesus were what two brothers?

24. Who ate honey out of the carcass of a lion?

25. Of the twelve tribes of Israel, which was forbidden to own land in Canaan?

26. What historical relics did Moses take from Egypt during the time of the exodus?

27. What was the sign of the covenant between Abraham and God?

28. Who, according to the book of Judges, was a good old age when he died?

29. What was the city of David?

30. Who was Manasseh's and Ephraim's father?

31. Who adopted the baby Moses?

32. Who was chosen to be Moses's spokesperson?

33. What two creatures in the Bible spoke to humans?

34. Moses was taking care of the flock of what man when he came across the burning bush?

35. After Jesus's miracle in which he fed five thousand with five loaves of bread and two fish, how much food was left over?

36. Who was described by God as a blameless and upright man?

37. How many demons were cast out of Mary Magdalene?

38. How old was Abraham when he was circumcised?

39. Who replaced Judas as the twelfth apostle?

40. When Cain was forced to leave Eden, where did he go?

41. When Jesus said, "Man shall not live by bread alone," to whom was he speaking?

42. How long had Lazarus been dead before being raised by Jesus?

43. How many hours did Jesus suffer on the cross before saying, "My God, my God, why hast thou forsaken me?"

44. According to the book of John, it was not Jesus but whom who baptized?

45. Where was Moses buried?

46. Who was the third son of Adam and Eve?

47. The twelve gates of the new Jerusalem were made from what gems?

48. Cain was the founder of what city?

49. How many righteous people exist, according to Paul?

50. How long did Adam live?

145

Fulfilled Prophecies about Jesus

In the following exercise, an Old Testament prophecy about Jesus is listed. You must name the New Testament book(s) in which the prophecy was fulfilled. In some cases, more than one New Testament book mentions the same prophecy. Give yourself 20 points for each prophecy for which you correctly identify the New Testament book or books.

You do not need to provide the verse to get a correct answer in this section, only the book(s), although it is an excellent idea to try to memorize as many verses as you can.

You may do this section as many times as you wish and record only your highest score on the score card.

1. The Messiah would be born of a virgin. Old Testament: Isaiah 7:14, New Testament (2 books): _____ and _____
2. A messenger would prepare the way for the Messiah. Old Testament: Isaiah 40:3–5, New Testament: _____
3. The Messiah would be born of a woman. Old Testament: Genesis 3:15, New Testament (2 books): _____ and _____

4. Jesus would be declared the Son of God. Old Testament: Psalm 2:7, New Testament: _____

5. The Messiah would be born in Bethlehem. Old Testament: Micah 5:2, New Testament (2 books): _____ and _____

6. Jesus would be called King. Old Testament: Psalm 2:6, New Testament (2 books): _____ and _____

7. Jesus's throne will be eternal. Old Testament: Psalm 45:6–7 and Daniel 2:44, New Testament (2 books): _____ and _____

8. The Messiah would come from the tribe of Judah. Old Testament: Genesis 49:10, New Testament (2 books): _____ and _____

9. The Savior would come from the line of Abraham. Old Testament: Genesis 12:3 and Genesis 22:18, New Testament (2 books): _____ and _____

10. The Messiah would come to heal the brokenhearted. Old Testament: Isaiah 61:1–2, New Testament: _____

11. The Messiah would spend a season in Egypt. Old Testament: Hosea 11:1, New Testament: _____

12. The Savior would be crucified with criminals. Old Testament: Isaiah 53:12, New Testament: _____

13. The Messiah would be heir to King David's throne. Old Testament: 2 Samuel 7:12–13 and Isaiah 9:7, New Testament (2 books): _____ and _____

14. Jesus would be rejected by his own people. Old Testament: Psalm 69:8 and Isaiah 53:3, New Testament (1 book, 2 chapters): _____ and _____

15. The Messiah would be called Immanuel. Old Testament: Isaiah 7:14, New Testament: _____

16. The Savior would be given vinegar to drink. Old Testament: Psalm 69:21, New Testament (2 books): _____ and _____

17. The Messiah would be a prophet. Old Testament: Deuteronomy 18:15, New Testament: _____

18. The Messiah would be called a Nazarene. Old Testament: Isaiah 11:1, New Testament: _____

19. The Messiah would be praised by little children. Old Testament: Psalm 8:2, New Testament: _____

20. Jesus would be spat upon and struck. Old Testament: Isaiah 50:6, New Testament: _____

21. The Savior would be hated without cause. Old Testament: Psalm 35:19 and Psalm 69:4, New Testament: _____

22. The Messiah would be mocked, teased, and ridiculed. Old Testament: Psalm 22:7–8, New Testament: _____

23. The Messiah would come from the line of Isaac. Old Testament: Genesis 17:19 and Genesis 21:12, New Testament: _____

24. Jesus would be a sacrifice for sin. Old Testament: Isaiah 53:5–12, New Testament: _____

25. The Messiah would speak in parables. Old Testament: Psalm 78:2–4 and Isaiah 6:9–10, New Testament: _____

26. The Savior would be betrayed. Old Testament: Psalm 41:9 and Zechariah 11:12–13, New Testament (2 books): _____ and _____

27. Jesus's bones would not be broken during his crucifixion. Exodus 12:46 and Psalm 34:20, New Testament: _____

28. Jesus's hands and feet would be pierced. Old Testament: Psalm 22:16 and Zechariah 12:10, New Testament: _____

29. The Messiah would be falsely accused. Old Testament: Psalm 35:11, New Testament: _____

30. Jesus would be silent before his accusers. Old Testament: Isaiah 53:7, New Testament: _____

31. Soldiers would gamble for the Messiah's garments. Old Testament: Psalm 22:18, New Testament (2 books): _____ and _____

32. The Messiah would be forsaken by God. Old Testament: Psalm 22:1, New Testament: _____

33. Soldiers would pierce Jesus in his side. Old Testament: Zechariah 12:10, New Testament: _____

34. The Messiah would be resurrected from the dead. Old Testament: Psalm 16:10 and Psalm 49:15, New Testament (2 books): _____ and _____

35. The Savior would ascend to heaven. Old Testament: Psalm 24:7–10, New Testament (2 books): _____ and _____

36. The Messiah would be seated at the right hand of the Father. Old Testament: Psalm 68:18 and Psalm 110:1, New Testament (2 books): _____ and _____

146

100 Common Phrases
That Originated in the Bible

This fascinating section lists Scripture verses that have spawned common, everyday phrases. Many people are not aware that many phrases in use today were lifted directly from the Bible. Read and study the Scripture passage or passages provided and reward yourself 10 points if you provide the correct phrase. Some of the answers will be self-evident, but some will take a bit of thought. How much fun will it be to tell someone using one of these common phrases that it originated in the Bible?

1. Isaiah 40:15
   Behold, the nations are as a drop of a bucket, and are counted as the small dust of the balance: behold, he taketh up the isles as a very little thing.

2. Ecclesiastes 10:1
   Dead flies cause the ointment of the apothecary to send forth a stinking savour: so doth a little folly him that is in reputation for wisdom and honour.

3. Deuteronomy 5:8
   Thou shalt not make thee any graven image, or any likeness of any thing that is in heaven above, or that is in the earth beneath, or that is in the waters beneath the earth.

4. Matthew 12:25
   And Jesus knew their thoughts, and said unto them, Every kingdom divided against itself is brought to desolation; and every city or house divided against itself shall not stand.

5. 1 Thessalonians 1:2–3
   We give thanks to God always for you all, making mention of you in our prayers; remembering without ceasing your work of faith, and labour of love, and patience of hope in our Lord Jesus Christ, in the sight of God and our Father.

   Hebrews 6:10
   For God is not unrighteous to forget your work and labour of love, which ye have shewed toward his name, in that ye have ministered to the saints, and do minister.

6. Romans 2:14
   For when the Gentiles, which have not the law, do by nature the things contained in the law, these, having not the law, are a law unto themselves.

7. Jeremiah 13:23
   Can the Ethiopian change his skin, or the leopard his spots? then may ye also do good, that are accustomed to do evil.

8. 1 Samuel 13:14
   But now thy kingdom shall not continue: the LORD hath sought him a man after his own heart, and the LORD hath commanded him to be captain over his people, because thou hast not kept that which the LORD commanded thee.

   Acts 13:22
   And when he had removed him, he raised up unto them David to be their king; to whom also he gave their testimony, and said, I have found David the son of Jesse, a man after mine own heart, which shall fulfil all my will.

9. James 5:20
   Let him know, that he which converteth the sinner from the error of his way shall save a soul from death, and shall hide a multitude of sins.

1 Peter 4:8
And above all things have fervent charity among yourselves: for charity shall cover the multitude of sins.

10. Leviticus 3:6
And if his offering for a sacrifice of peace offering unto the LORD be of the flock; male or female, he shall offer it without blemish.

11. Matthew 16:3
And in the morning, It will be foul weather to day: for the sky is red and lowering. O ye hypocrites, ye can discern the face of the sky; but can ye not discern the signs of the times?

12. Proverbs 15:1
A soft answer turneth away wrath: but grievous words stir up anger.

13. 2 Corinthians 12:7
And lest I should be exalted above measure through the abundance of the revelations, there was given to me a thorn in the flesh, the messenger of Satan to buffet me, lest I should be exalted above measure.

14. Proverbs 5:4
But her end is bitter as wormwood, sharp as a two-edged sword.

15. John 1:23
He said, I am the voice of one crying in the wilderness, Make straight the way of the Lord, as said the prophet Esaias.

16. Matthew 7:15
Beware of false prophets, which come to you in sheep's clothing, but inwardly they are ravening wolves.

17. Matthew 24:6–8
And ye shall hear of wars and rumours of wars: see that ye be not troubled: for all these things must come to pass, but the end is not yet. For nation shall rise against nation, and kingdom against kingdom: and there shall be famines, and pestilences, and earthquakes, in divers places. All these are the beginning of sorrows.

18. 1 Corinthians 9:22

    To the weak became I as weak, that I might gain the weak: I am made all things to all men, that I might by all means save some.

19. Genesis 4:9

    And the LORD said unto Cain, Where is Abel thy brother? And he said, I know not: Am I my brother's keeper?

20. Matthew 5:38

    Ye have heard that it hath been said, An eye for an eye, and a tooth for a tooth.

21. Genesis 5:27

    And all the days of Methuselah were nine hundred sixty and nine years: and he died.

22. Job 15:7

    Art thou the first man that was born? or wast thou made before the hills?

23. Daniel 7:9

    I beheld till the thrones were cast down, and the Ancient of days did sit, whose garment was white as snow, and the hair of his head like the pure wool: his throne was like the fiery flame, and his wheels as burning fire.

24. Galatians 6:7

    Be not deceived; God is not mocked: for whatsoever a man soweth, that shall he also reap.

25. Genesis 3:19

    In the sweat of thy face shalt thou eat bread, till thou return unto the ground; for out of it wast thou taken: for dust thou art, and unto dust shalt thou return.

26. Psalm 107:27

    They reel to and fro, and stagger like a drunken man, and are at their wit's end.

27. Matthew 3:11

    I indeed baptize you with water unto repentance: but he that cometh after me is mightier than I, whose shoes I am not worthy to bear: he shall baptize you with the Holy Ghost, and with fire.

28. Genesis 1:22

    And God blessed them, saying, Be fruitful, and multiply, and fill the waters in the seas, and let fowl multiply in the earth.

29. Isaiah 2:4

    And he shall judge among the nations, and shall rebuke many people: and they shall beat their swords into plowshares, and their spears into pruninghooks: nation shall not lift up sword against nation, neither shall they learn war any more.

30. Psalm 72:9

    They that dwell in the wilderness shall bow before him; and his enemies shall lick the dust.

31. John 3:3

    Jesus answered and said unto him, Verily, verily, I say unto thee, Except a man be born again, he cannot see the kingdom of God.

32. Genesis 2:7

    And the LORD God formed man of the dust of the ground, and breathed into his nostrils the breath of life; and man became a living soul.

33. Job 19:20

    My bone cleaveth to my skin and to my flesh, and I am escaped with the skin of my teeth.

34. Genesis 3:19

    In the sweat of thy face shalt thou eat bread.

35. Ecclesiastes 11:1

    Cast thy bread upon the waters: for thou shalt find it after many days.

36. John 8:7

    So when they continued asking him, he lifted up himself, and said unto them, He that is without sin among you, let him first cast a stone at her.

37. 1 Timothy 5:8
But if any provide not for his own, and specially for those of his own house, he hath denied the faith, and is worse than an infidel.

38. Genesis 37:23
And it came to pass, when Joseph was come unto his brethren, that they stript Joseph out of his coat, his coat of many colours that was on him.

Genesis 37:32
And they sent the coat of many colours, and they brought it to their father; and said, This have we found: know now whether it be thy son's coat or no.

39. Matthew 7:6
Give not that which is holy unto the dogs, neither cast ye your pearls before swine, lest they trample them under their feet, and turn again and rend you.

40. Luke 14:27
And whosoever doth not bear his cross, and come after me, cannot be my disciple.

41. Ecclesiastes 8:15
Then I commended mirth, because a man hath no better thing under the sun, than to eat, and to drink, and to be merry: for that shall abide with him of his labour the days of his life, which God giveth him under the sun.

42. Isaiah 52:8
Thy watchmen shall lift up the voice; with the voice together shall they sing: for they shall see eye to eye, when the LORD shall bring again Zion.

43. Matthew 21:21
Jesus answered and said unto them, Verily I say unto you, If ye have faith, and doubt not, ye shall not only do this which is done to the fig tree, but also if ye shall say unto this mountain, Be thou removed, and be thou cast into the sea; it shall be done.

44. Galatians 5:4

   Christ is become of no effect unto you, whosoever of you are
   justified by the law; you are fallen from grace.

45. Daniel 2:33

   His legs of iron, his feet part of iron and part of clay.

46. 1 Timothy 6:12

   Fight the good fight of faith, lay hold on eternal life, where-
   unto thou art also called, and hast professed a good profession before many witnesses.

47. Genesis 19:24

   Then the LORD rained upon Sodom and upon Gomorrah
   brimstone and fire from the LORD out of heaven.

48. Matthew 16:17

   And Jesus answered and said unto him, Blessed art thou,
   Simon Barjona: for flesh and blood hath not revealed it unto
   thee, but my Father which is in heaven.

49. Ecclesiastes 3:1–8

   To every thing there is a season, and a time to every purpose
   under the heaven: A time to be born, and a time to die; a
   time to plant, and a time to pluck up that which is planted; A
   time to kill, and a time to heal; a time to break down, and a
   time to build up; A time to weep, and a time to laugh; a time
   to mourn, and a time to dance; A time to cast away stones,
   and a time to gather stones together; a time to embrace, and
   a time to refrain from embracing; A time to get, and a time
   to lose; a time to keep, and a time to cast away; A time to
   rend, and a time to sew; a time to keep silence, and a time
   to speak; A time to love, and a time to hate; a time of war,
   and a time of peace.

50. Genesis 3:3

   But of the fruit of the tree which is in the midst of the garden, God hath said, Ye shall not eat of it, neither shall ye
   touch it, lest ye die.

51. Psalm 84:7

    They go from strength to strength, every one of them in Zion appeareth before God.

52. Luke 4:8

    And Jesus answered and said unto him, Get thee behind me, Satan: for it is written, Thou shalt worship the Lord thy God, and him only shalt thou serve.

53. 1 Kings 18:46

    And the hand of the LORD was on Elijah; and he girded up his loins, and ran before Ahab to the entrance of Jezreel.

54. Acts 12:23

    And immediately the angel of the Lord smote him, because he gave not God the glory: and he was eaten of worms, and gave up the ghost.

55. Matthew 5:41

    And whosoever shall compel thee to go a mile, go with him twain.

56. Luke 10:30–33

    And Jesus answering said, A certain man went down from Jerusalem to Jericho, and fell among thieves, which stripped him of his raiment, and wounded him, and departed, leaving him half dead. And by chance there came down a certain priest that way: and when he saw him, he passed by on the other side. And likewise a Levite, when he was at the place, came and looked on him, and passed by on the other side. But a certain Samaritan, as he journeyed, came where he was: and when he saw him, he had compassion on him.

57. Exodus 4:21

    And the LORD said unto Moses, When thou goest to return into Egypt, see that thou do all those wonders before Pharaoh, which I have put in thine hand: but I will harden his heart, that he shall not let the people go.

58. Matthew 26:52

    Then said Jesus unto him, Put up again thy sword into his place: for all they that take the sword shall perish with the sword.

59. Psalm 21:2

    Thou hast given him his heart's desire, and hast not withholden the request of his lips.

60. Isaiah 65:5

    Which say, Stand by thyself, come not near to me; for I am holier than thou. These are a smoke in my nose, a fire that burneth all the day.

61. 2 Samuel 1:19

    The beauty of Israel is slain upon thy high places: how are the mighty fallen!

62. 1 Corinthians 15:52

    In a moment, in the twinkling of an eye, at the last trump: for the trumpet shall sound, and the dead shall be raised incorruptible, and we shall be changed.

63. Acts 20:35

    I have shewed you all things, how that so labouring ye ought to support the weak, and to remember the words of the Lord Jesus, how he said, It is more blessed to give than to receive.

64. Jeremiah 11:19

    But I was like a lamb or an ox that is brought to the slaughter; and I knew not that they had devised devices against me, saying, Let us destroy the tree with the fruit thereof, and let us cut him off from the land of the living, that his name may be no more remembered.

65. 2 Corinthians 3:6

    Who also hath made us able ministers of the new testament; not of the letter, but of the spirit: for the letter killeth, but the spirit giveth life.

66. Genesis 45:17–18

And Pharaoh said unto Joseph, Say unto thy brethren, This do ye; lade your beasts, and go, get you unto the land of Canaan; And take your father and your households, and come unto me: and I will give you the good of the land of Egypt, and ye shall eat the fat of the land.

67. 1 Timothy 6:10

For the love of money is the root of all evil: which while some coveted after, they have erred from the faith, and pierced themselves through with many sorrows.

68. Romans 13:9

For this, Thou shalt not commit adultery, Thou shalt not kill, Thou shalt not steal, Thou shalt not bear false witness, Thou shalt not covet; and if there be any other commandment, it is briefly comprehended in this saying, namely, Thou shalt love thy neighbour as thyself.

69. Deuteronomy 8:2–3

And thou shalt remember all the way which the LORD thy God led thee these forty years in the wilderness, to humble thee, and to prove thee, to know what was in thine heart, whether thou wouldest keep his commandments, or no. And he humbled thee, and suffered thee to hunger, and fed thee with manna, which thou knewest not, neither did thy fathers know; that he might make thee know that man doth not live by bread only, but by every word that proceedeth out of the mouth of the LORD doth man live.

70. Exodus 16:15

And when the children of Israel saw it, they said one to another, It is manna: for they wist not what it was. And Moses said unto them, This is the bread which the LORD hath given you to eat.

71. Matthew 22:11–14

And when the king came in to see the guests, he saw there a man which had not on a wedding garment: And he saith unto him, Friend, how camest thou in hither not having a wedding garment? And he was speechless. Then said the king to the servants, Bind him hand and foot, and take him away, and cast him into outer darkness, there shall be weeping and gnashing of teeth. For many are called, but few are chosen.

72. Psalm 23:5

Thou preparest a table before me in the presence of mine enemies: thou anointest my head with oil; my cup runneth over.

73. Isaiah 57:20–21

But the wicked are like the troubled sea, when it cannot rest, whose waters cast up mire and dirt. There is no peace, saith my God, to the wicked.

74. Ecclesiastes 1:9

The thing that hath been, it is that which shall be; and that which is done is that which shall be done: and there is no new thing under the sun.

75. Luke 12:27–28

Consider the lilies how they grow: they toil not, they spin not; and yet I say unto you, that Solomon in all his glory was not arrayed like one of these. If then God so clothe the grass, which is to day in the field, and to morrow is cast into the oven; how much more will he clothe you, O ye of little faith?

76. Psalm 8:2

Out of the mouth of babes and sucklings hast thou ordained strength because of thine enemies, that thou mightest still the enemy and the avenger.

Matthew 21:16

And said unto him, Hearest thou what these say? And Jesus saith unto them, Yea; have ye never read, Out of the mouth of babes and sucklings thou hast perfected praise?

77. James 5:11

Behold, we count them happy which endure. Ye have heard of the patience of Job, and have seen the end of the Lord; that the Lord is very pitiful, and of tender mercy.

78. Luke 4:23

    And he said unto them, Ye will surely say unto me this proverb, Physician, heal thyself: whatsoever we have heard done in Capernaum, do also here in thy country.

79. Proverbs 16:18

    Pride goeth before destruction, and an haughty spirit before a fall.

80. 2 Samuel 14:3

    And come to the king, and speak on this manner unto him. So Joab put the words in her mouth.

81. 2 Kings 20:1

    In those days was Hezekiah sick unto death. And the prophet Isaiah the son of Amoz came to him, and said unto him, Thus saith the Lord, Set thine house in order; for thou shalt die, and not live.

82. Hosea 8:7

    For they have sown the wind, and they shall reap the whirlwind: it hath no stalk; the bud shall yield no meal: if so be it yield, the strangers shall swallow it up.

83. Jeremiah 31:30

    But every one shall die for his own iniquity: every man that eateth the sour grape, his teeth shall be set on edge.

84. Proverbs 13:24

    He that spareth his rod hateth his son: but he that loveth him chasteneth him betimes.

85. Matthew 7:13–14

    Enter ye in at the strait gate: for wide is the gate, and broad is the way, that leadeth to destruction, and many there be which go in thereat: Because strait is the gate, and narrow is the way, which leadeth unto life, and few there be that find it.

86. Matthew 6:34

    Take therefore no thought for the morrow: for the morrow shall take thought for the things of itself. Sufficient unto the day is the evil thereof.

87. Psalm 25:6

    Remember, O LORD, thy tender mercies and thy lovingkind-
    nesses; for they have been ever of old.

88. Deuteronomy 32:10

    He found him in a desert land, and in the waste howling
    wilderness; he led him about, he instructed him, he kept him
    as the apple of his eye.

89. Matthew 15:14

    Let them alone: they be blind leaders of the blind. And if the
    blind lead the blind, both shall fall into the ditch.

90. Zechariah 9:10

    And I will cut off the chariot from Ephraim, and the horse
    from Jerusalem, and the battle bow shall be cut off: and he
    shall speak peace unto the heathen: and his dominion shall
    be from sea even to sea, and from the river even to the ends
    of the earth.

91. Genesis 35:11

    And God said unto him, I am God Almighty: be fruitful and
    multiply; a nation and a company of nations shall be of thee,
    and kings shall come out of thy loins.

92. Job 19:28

    But ye should say, Why persecute we him, seeing the root of
    the matter is found in me?

93. Matthew 5:13

    Ye are the salt of the earth: but if the salt have lost his savour,
    wherewith shall it be salted? it is thenceforth good for noth-
    ing, but to be cast out, and to be trodden under foot of men.

94. Matthew 26:41

    Watch and pray, that ye enter not into temptation: the spirit
    indeed is willing, but the flesh is weak.

95. Romans 6:23

    For the wages of sin is death; but the gift of God is eternal
    life through Jesus Christ our Lord.

96. Genesis 6:12

   And God looked upon the earth, and, behold, it was corrupt; for all flesh had corrupted his way upon the earth.

97. Luke 11:31

   The queen of the south shall rise up in the judgment with the men of this generation, and condemn them: for she came from the utmost parts of the earth to hear the wisdom of Solomon; and, behold, a greater than Solomon is here.

98. Matthew 27:24

   When Pilate saw that he could prevail nothing, but that rather a tumult was made, he took water, and washed his hands before the multitude, saying, I am innocent of the blood of this just person: see ye to it.

99. Job 31:6

   Let me be weighed in an even balance that God may know mine integrity.

100. Job 10:15

   If I be wicked, woe unto me; and if I be righteous, yet will I not lift up my head. I am full of confusion; therefore see thou mine affliction.

147

Imprisoned

In this twelve-question quiz, give yourself 5 points for each correct answer.

1. Who experienced a great, rumbling earthquake while in prison?
   A. The butler and the baker
   B. Paul and Silas
   C. Peter
   D. John the Baptist

2. What apostle was imprisoned in Jerusalem for preaching the gospel?
   A. Paul and Barnabas
   B. Matthew and Luke
   C. Peter
   D. Paul and James

3. What relative of Jesus was jailed for daring to criticize King Herod's marriage to Herodias?
   A. Joseph
   B. James
   C. David
   D. John the Baptist

4. Who was sent to prison after being falsely accused of trying to seduce Potiphar's wife?

    A. Joseph

    B. David

    C. Joshua

    D. Absalom

5. Whose brothers were imprisoned after being falsely accused of being spies in Egypt?

    A. Jacob's

    B. David's

    C. Samson's

    D. Joseph's

6. Who was jailed for prophesying that the kingdom of Judah would be destroyed?

    A. Nathan

    B. Jeremiah

    C. Elisha

    D. Hanani

7. What king of Judah was put in jail and blinded for resisting Babylonian authority?

    A. Rehoboam

    B. Manasseh

    C. Zedekiah

    D. Amaziah

8. Who was jailed for prophesying King Asa's demise?

    A. Jeremiah

    B. Hanani

    C. Isaiah

    D. Elijah

9. Who was imprisoned and declared an enemy of the Philistines?

    A. Samson

    B. Simeon

    C. Daniel

    D. Barabbas

10. What king of Judah was exiled and jailed in Babylon?
    A. Joash
    B. Jehoiachin
    C. Uzziah
    D. Hezekiah

11. Who was imprisoned after he prophesied that King Ahab would face a bitter defeat?
    A. Micah
    B. Obadiah
    C. Jeremiah
    D. Micaiah

12. What king of Israel was jailed for refusing to recognize Assyrian authority?
    A. Jehu
    B. Jehoash
    C. Hoshea
    D. Shallum

148

The Fast 100

Here are one hundred trivia questions called the "fast" 100 because the answers should pop into your mind relatively quickly. Give yourself 1 point for each correct answer.

1. What garden did Jesus go to before being falsely arrested?
2. While a storm raged, what was Jonah doing on board a ship at the time?
3. When Joseph was in Egypt, who was his master?
4. When Herod was killing babies in Bethlehem, where did Mary and Joseph go?
5. When the priests blew their trumpets, what happened to the city of Jericho?
6. What land was promised to Abram by the Lord?
7. What event aided in the release of Paul and Silas from prison?
8. How many plagues did God inflict on Egypt?
9. What did King Solomon request when God appeared to him in a dream?
10. In the Old Testament, how were sins forgiven?
11. In what form did the Lord appear to Moses?
12. According to the Bible, what should we seek first?

13. Which of Jacob's wives does the Bible say he loved the most?

14. In what manner were the Thessalonians told to pray?

15. What were the commandments given to Moses kept in?

16. According to the Bible, what is the best place to pray?

17. What did God breathe into Adam's nostrils?

18. Who wrote the book of Revelation?

19. How long was Jonah stuck inside a great fish?

20. Who was Hagar's son?

21. When Moses was receiving the Ten Commandments from God, what were the Israelites doing?

22. Whom did God tell to leave his home and family and travel to an unknown country?

23. What two things guided the Israelites in the wilderness?

24. How old was Jesus when he began his ministry?

25. The sinful man Balaam was spoken to by what creature?

26. Who was the first woman Jacob married?

27. Who, through the power of God, parted the Red Sea?

28. When Pilate asked the unruly crowd what prisoner should be released, whom did they choose?

29. Who married Abram?

30. Who baptized Jesus?

31. What angel appeared to Mary?

32. When Abraham's servant went looking for a wife for Isaac, whom did he find?

33. To whom was Jesus talking when he said, "Why are ye fearful, O ye of little faith?"

34. Where did the man who received one talent hide it?

35. Jacob agreed to work seven years of hard labor to win the hand in marriage of what woman?

36. What woman promised the Lord that if she were blessed with a son she would dedicate the boy to him?

37. When Jesus was born, in what was he wrapped?

38. What was the name of David's first wife?

39. When Jesus asked the disciples, "But whom say ye that I am?" what was Peter's reply?

40. In the parable of the ten virgins, for what were the virgins waiting?

41. Who could be considered the stepfather of Jesus?

42. After the death of Naomi's husband and sons, who stayed with her?

43. Who lied and claimed that Joseph had tried to commit adultery with her?

44. How did God curse the serpent that deceived Eve?

45. What was the name of Moses's wife?

46. Who betrayed Jesus with a kiss?

47. In the book of Genesis, in what way did God say mankind was similar to him?

48. When Jesus gave his Sermon on the Mount, what did he say about tomorrow?

49. Whose name did God change to Israel?

50. How should we treat the rich and the poor, according to James?

51. Where was Jesus baptized?

52. After Jesus was crucified, who led the church?

53. According to James, what happens when we draw nigh (near) to God?

54. Who was taken captive into Egypt but later saved the entire country from famine?

55. What holiday is referred to as resurrection day?

56. When an adulteress was accused by a crowd, what was Jesus's response?

57. What woman betrayed Samson to the Philistines by persuading him to reveal the secret of his incredible strength?

58. Who spoke the words, "My soul doth magnify the Lord"?

59. Who tried to tempt Jesus by saying, "If thou be the Son of God, command that these stones be made bread"?

60. Who was converted to Christianity on the road to Damascus?

61. What does Eve's name mean?

62. What Israelite became the queen of Persia?

63. What evil queen wanted to kill the prophet Elijah?

64. How did the height-challenged Zacchaeus manage to see Jesus in a crowd?

65. Who sold his birthright to his brother for a hot meal?

66. Who gave birth to Moses?

67. Who could interpret King Nebuchadnezzar's dream?

68. Who was turned into a pillar of salt after being warned not to look back at Sodom and Gomorrah?

69. Who was the sister-in-law of Ruth?

70. Why did Adam hide himself from the Lord?

71. After refusing to eat the food of the king, who gained the ability to interpret visions and dreams?

72. What does Emmanuel mean?

73. What kind of wood did Noah use to build the ark?

74. Who advised Joseph that Jesus would be the Savior who would save his people from their sins?

75. Why was David so confident that he could defeat Goliath?

76. In what sermon did Jesus deliver the Beatitudes?

77. After Aaron put his staff into the tabernacle, what was produced on it?

78. What form did the Holy Spirit take during Jesus's baptism?

79. Who said, "This is my beloved Son, in whom I am well pleased"?

80. What happened to those whose names were not written in the book of life?

81. Where did Jesus miraculously walk on water?

82. Before he exiled them from the Garden of Eden, what did God do to Adam and Eve?

83. The prophet Hosea was commanded to marry what harlot?

84. What was the name of Sarah's handmaiden?

85. How did Jonah feel about the way the people of Nineveh responded to his message about God?

86. After Moses died, who became the leader of the children of Israel?

87. According to Jesus, how should we receive the kingdom of God?

88. What happened to Daniel after he gave thanks to the Lord by an open window?

89. Who was jealous of the prodigal son?

90. Who could be heard from heaven after the baptism of Jesus Christ?

91. What position did Zacchaeus hold?

92. When Joseph was in prison, for what trait did he become known?

93. Why did Jesus choose to use parables in his teaching?

94. In the book of Genesis, people traveled from many countries to Egypt to buy what food item?

95. Who told Jesus, "All these things will I give thee, if thou wilt fall down and worship me"?

96. How did a man inflicted with palsy at Capernaum gain access to the house in which Jesus preached?

97. Who refused to believe that Jesus was resurrected until he saw him with his own eyes?

98. Which one of Joseph's brothers did Jacob not allow to travel to Egypt?

99. What did God place in the Garden of Eden to protect the tree of life?

100. According to the Bible, what is "the least of all the seeds: but when it is grown, it is the greatest among herbs"?

149

Did You Know?
(Set 14)

Here is the final set of astounding Bible facts.

- The longest word in the Bible is also the longest name. Isaiah 8:1 states, "Moreover the LORD said unto me, Take thee a great roll, and write in it with a man's pen concerning Mahershalalhashbaz."
- King Ahasuerus once had a single feast that lasted for 180 days (Esther 1:3–4).
- The only woman the Bible *commands* us to remember is Lot's wife (Luke 17:32).
- Paul was guarded by 470 soldiers when he was taken to see Governor Felix (Acts 23:23).
- The writings of 2 Kings 19 and Isaiah 37 are so similar that they are almost identical.
- The only time the Bible mentions snow is in reference to Benaiah being killed by a lion on a snowy day (2 Samuel 23:20; 1 Chronicles 11:22).
- Hebrews 11 is known as the "faith hall of fame," as it contains within its pages the following biblical heroes: Abel, Enoch, Noah, Abraham, Sarah, Isaac, Jacob, Joseph, Moses, and Joshua.

TRIVIA BY TOPIC

In the following section, complete each multiple-choice quiz and give yourself 2 points for each correct answer.

150

Fasting

1. After being baptized, who fasted for forty days?
   A. John the Baptist
   B. Peter
   C. John
   D. Jesus

2. Who fasted for forty days while on Mount Sinai?
   A. Jeremiah
   B. Jacob
   C. Moses
   D. Joshua

3. Who was saved from starvation by birds that brought him food?
   A. Elisha
   B. Elijah
   C. Jonah
   D. Joel

4. Who tried to save the life of his and Bathsheba's son by fasting?
   A. Saul
   B. David
   C. Uriah
   D. Esau

5. How many men took an oath to fast until Paul was assassinated?
   A. 3
   B. 12
   C. More than 40
   D. 100

6. Who fasted for 14 days on a ship with 276 passengers?
   A. Paul
   B. Stephen
   C. Peter
   D. John

7. What king fasted after Daniel was thrown into the lions' den?
   A. Darius
   B. Zedekiah
   C. Amon
   D. Uzziah

8. What two apostles prayed and fasted when selecting elders for churches?
   A. Peter and John
   B. Paul and Barnabas
   C. Timothy and Titus
   D. Mark and Luke

9. What Persian court official fasted before approaching the king with a case?
   A. Nehemiah
   B. Obadiah
   C. Jeremiah
   D. Elijah

10. When the people of Jerusalem gathered for a fast, who read the prophecy of Jeremiah?
    A. Baruch
    B. Deborah
    C. Samson
    D. Josiah

Wine

1. Whom does the Bible call gluttonous and a winebibber?
   A. Peter
   B. Paul
   C. John the Baptist
   D. Jesus

2. Paul recommended wine for what part of the body?
   A. Head
   B. Leg
   C. Stomach
   D. Back

3. What church official must be "not given to wine," according to Paul?
   A. A bishop
   B. A deacon
   C. A widow
   D. A layman

4. What kind of person should be given wine, according to Proverbs?
   A. A sad or afflicted person
   B. A sick person
   C. A healthy person
   D. A happy person

5. Whose army murdered Zeeb the Midianite at his winepress?
   A. Joshua's
   B. Gideon's
   C. David's
   D. Saul's

6. To whom did the Lord say that if a man or woman wanted to make a special vow of dedication to the Lord as a Nazirite, they must abstain from wine?
   A. Moses
   B. Aaron
   C. Noah
   D. Abraham

7. What was mixed with the wine Jesus was offered on the cross?
   A. Myrrh
   B. Vinegar or gall
   C. Water
   D. Nutmeg

8. According to Jesus, people prefer what type of wine?
   A. Fresh wine
   B. Chilled wine
   C. Old wine
   D. Pressed wine

The Apostles

1. Who was the first apostle to be martyred?
   A. James
   B. John
   C. Matthew
   D. Peter

2. Who succeeded Judas Iscariot as an apostle?
   A. Jude
   B. Timothy
   C. Matthias
   D. Joseph

3. What apostle was a tax collector from Capernaum?
   A. Matthew
   B. Matthias
   C. Mattathah
   D. Matthan

4. Who was called the beloved disciple?
   A. Matthew
   B. Mark
   C. Luke
   D. John

153

Kings

1. In Israel, what king called Elijah a troublemaker?
   A. Abimelech
   B. Joash
   C. Zebah
   D. Ahab

2. What king had nine hundred iron chariots?
   A. Og
   B. Jabin
   C. Joash
   D. Agag

3. Who was the last king to reign in Israel?
   A. Saul
   B. David
   C. Hoshea
   D. Abijah

4. What king permitted his daughter to marry Ahab?
   A. Ethbaal
   B. Arad
   C. Zedikiah
   D. Agag

5. What king was later destroyed after attacking the Israelites as they made their way to Canaan?
   A. The king of Arad
   B. Agag
   C. King David
   D. King Solomon

6. What ruler of Hazor formed an alliance against Joshua?
   A. Og
   B. Jabin
   C. Joash
   D. Agag

7. What king infamously owned an enormous iron bed?
   A. Ethbaal
   B. Arad
   C. Agag
   D. Og

8. Although he anointed the first two kings, who rebelled against having a king over himself?
   A. Elijah
   B. Elisha
   C. Samuel
   D. Daniel

9. What meager shepherd boy did Samuel make king in front of the boy's brothers?
   A. Joseph
   B. David
   C. Josiah
   D. Joash

10. Nathan was angered by the adulterous activities of what king?
    A. Saul
    B. David
    C. Josiah
    D. Joash

154

Heaven Awaits

1. Who is preparing heaven for all the saints?
   A. Jesus Christ
   B. Angels
   C. The prophets of old
   D. Everyone

2. Who is heaven designed for?
   A. Angels
   B. The devil
   C. Born-again believers
   D. Everyone

3. What describes heaven?
   A. Sunny and bright
   B. The same as earth
   C. A glorious city
   D. None of the above

4. What is the name of the city of God?
   A. The new Jerusalem
   B. The golden city
   C. The city of gold
   D. New Hope City

5. How many foundation stones does the city of God rest upon?
   A. 5
   B. 7
   C. 10
   D. 12

6. What is the wall that surrounds the city made of?
   A. Pure silver
   B. Pure jasper
   C. Pure gold
   D. Pure joy

7. What are gates around the city made of?
   A. Solid brass
   B. Solid jasper
   C. Solid pearl
   D. Solid gold

8. How many varieties of fruit does the tree of life bear?
   A. 12
   B. 2
   C. 7
   D. 5

9. How many thrones (seats) surround the throne of God?
   A. 3
   B. 5
   C. 7
   D. 24

10. How many creatures who worship God continually are beside the throne of God?
   A. 3
   B. 4
   C. 5
   D. 7

11. Of what is the main street of the city of God composed?
    A. Clear glass
    B. Silver
    C. Pearls
    D. Pure gold

12. In heaven, there will be no more what?
    A. Night
    B. Sin
    C. Sickness, pain, or death
    D. All of the above

Hairy and Hairless

1. What type of people were forbidden to shave their heads or grow their hair long?
   A. Pharisees
   B. Prophets
   C. Priests
   D. Scribes

2. What Israelite judge never shaved or cut his hair until his mistress did it for him?
   A. Othniel
   B. Barak
   C. Samson
   D. Joseph

3. Who was purified by cutting his hair?
   A. Joseph
   B. Paul
   C. Jonathan
   D. James

4. What king of Babylon once lived in the wilderness and let his hair grow wild?
   A. Daniel
   B. Nebuchadnezzar
   C. Elijah
   D. Naaman

5. Who was the first person in the Bible said to be hairy?
   A. Noah
   B. Abraham
   C. Esau
   D. Joseph

6. Who shaved his head after learning his children had been destroyed?
   A. Noah
   B. Naaman
   C. David
   D. Job

7. Which of David's sons cut his hair once a year, yielding two hundred shekels' worth of hair (nearly six pounds)?
   A. Samson
   B. Solomon
   C. Jonathan
   D. Absalom

8. Who had to shave all his hair twice, six days apart?
   A. An epileptic
   B. A blind person
   C. A leper
   D. A paralytic

9. Who was forbidden to "round the corners of your heads"?
   A. Greeks
   B. Chaldeans
   C. The children of Israel
   D. Egyptians

10. Who is the only man mentioned in the Bible as being naturally bald?
   A. Elijah
   B. Jacob
   C. Elisha
   D. Esau

11. God told what prophet to shave his head and beard?
    A. Isaiah
    B. Jeremiah
    C. Ezekiel
    D. Daniel

12. What prophet was described as a very hairy man?
    A. Elisha
    B. Hosea
    C. Elijah
    D. Amos

156

Citified

1. Where was the home of Apollos?
   A. Alexandria
   B. Anathoth
   C. Antioch
   D. Arad

2. According to Acts 21:17, how was Paul received on his final trip to Jerusalem?
   A. Angrily
   B. Gladly
   C. Sadly
   D. With repentance

3. Anathoth was the home of what prophet?
   A. Jeremiah
   B. Obadiah
   C. Daniel
   D. Ezekiel

4. In what city were the disciples first called Christians?
   A. Acre
   B. Arad
   C. Antioch
   D. Alexandria

5. Joseph, who requested the body of Jesus, was from what city?
   A. Acre
   B. Athens
   C. Arimathea
   D. Antioch

6. Besides Ashdod, what was another key Philistine city?
   A. Antioch
   B. Ashkelon
   C. Athens
   D. Acre

7. Where did Daniel and Ezekiel live while writing their Old Testament books?
   A. Babylon
   B. Berea
   C. Bethany
   D. Bethel

8. Where did Paul preach his Mars Hill sermon?
   A. Acre
   B. Ashdod
   C. Athens
   D. Alexandria

9. Just before Jesus rode into Jerusalem, where did he mount a donkey?
   A. Beth-peor
   B. Bethphage
   C. Bethsaida
   D. Bethlehem

10. Where did Paul witness to Felix and Agrippa?
    A. Cana
    B. Caesarea
    C. Capernaum
    D. Bethel

11. During Paul's first missionary journey, where was his stopping point?
    A. Derbe
    B. Gath
    C. Cana
    D. Dothan

157

Are You Speaking to Me?

1. According to Deuteronomy 4:33, where did God's voice come from?
   A. The fire
   B. The cloud
   C. The burning bush
   D. The desert

2. Who was the "voice crying in the wilderness"?
   A. Jesus
   B. Moses
   C. John the Baptist
   D. Aaron

3. What book describes the divine voice as "the sound of many waters"?
   A. Psalms
   B. Revelation
   C. Job
   D. Genesis

4. From where did Moses hear God's voice when he was in the tabernacle?
   A. Above the tabernacle
   B. Above the table of showbread
   C. Above the ark of the covenant
   D. Through the inner veil

5. Who moved her lips in prayer but made no sound?
   A. Hannah
   B. Rebekah
   C. Mary
   D. Sarah

6. Where does it say that the voice of Rachel wept for her children?
   A. John
   B. Luke
   C. Matthew
   D. Mark

7. Who heard the voice of an angel commanding that a large tree be cut down to the ground?
   A. Joseph
   B. David
   C. Dinah
   D. Daniel

8. Who said, "Is this your voice, David my son"?
   A. Jesse
   B. Solomon
   C. Saul
   D. Pharaoh

9. Who informed Saul that obeying God's voice was more critical than sacrificing animals?
   A. Nathan
   B. Samuel
   C. Jonathan
   D. David

158

Jesus

1. Where was Jesus born?
   A. Nazareth
   B. Jerusalem
   C. Bethlehem
   D. Egypt

2. Where did the wise men come from?
   A. The north
   B. The east
   C. The south
   D. The west

3. What does Emmanuel mean?
   A. God our Father
   B. God is love
   C. God with us
   D. God loves us

4. Who was the legal father of Jesus?
   A. God
   B. David
   C. Joseph of Arimathaea
   D. Joseph of the line of David

5. Which of the following was not presented to the baby Jesus?
   A. Gold
   B. Myrrh
   C. Silver
   D. Frankincense

6. Who presented gifts to Jesus?
   A. The shepherds
   B. The scribes
   C. The wise men
   D. The astrologers

7. Who told Mary, "Blessed art thou among women"?
   A. Angel Michael
   B. Angel Gabriel
   C. Elisabeth
   D. Zacharias

8. Who said, "My soul doth magnify the Lord"?
   A. Mary
   B. Joseph
   C. Elisabeth
   D. Zacharias

9. How old was Jesus when he was circumcised?
   A. 12 years old
   B. 8 days old
   C. 12 days old
   D. 8 years old

10. When Herod died, who reigned in Judaea?
    A. Pharaoh
    B. John the Baptist
    C. Archelaus
    D. Pilate

11. Who prophesied that Jesus would be born in Bethlehem?
    A. Micah
    B. Nahum
    C. Isaiah
    D. Amos

12. Who prophesied, "Behold, a virgin shall conceive, and bear a son"?
    A. Jeremiah
    B. Daniel
    C. Zechariah
    D. Isaiah

159

Firsts

1. Who was the first Christian martyr?
   A. Peter
   B. James
   C. Stephen
   D. Paul

2. Who was the first hunter mentioned in the Bible?
   A. Nimrod
   B. Abel
   C. Cain
   D. Lamech

3. Who was the first daughter mentioned by name in the Bible?
   A. Naamah
   B. Adah
   C. Zillah
   D. Sarai

4. Who hosted the first mention of a beauty contest in the Bible?
   A. The court of Ahasuerus
   B. The court of David
   C. The court of Xerxes
   D. The court of Saul

5. Who was the first prophet mentioned in the Bible?
   A. Isaiah
   B. Jeremiah
   C. Enoch
   D. Noah

6. Who was the first king of Israel?
   A. Adam
   B. Pharaoh
   C. Saul
   D. David

7. Who built the first city?
   A. Adam
   B. Abel
   C. Noah
   D. Cain

8. Who was the first metal craftsman?
   A. Adam
   B. Ham
   C. Tubalcain
   D. Shem

9. Who were the first foreign missionaries?
   A. Paul and Silas
   B. Peter and John
   C. Paul and Barnabas
   D. Peter and James

10. Who celebrated the first birthday party mentioned in the Bible?
    A. Joseph
    B. Herod
    C. Adam
    D. Pharaoh

Costly

1. What king of Persia ordered a decree to allow the people of Judah to rebuild their temple?
   A. Elah
   B. Omri
   C. Jeroboam
   D. Cyrus

2. Who, in John's Gospel, was the "son of perdition"?
   A. The prodigal son
   B. Jesus
   C. Judas
   D. Thomas

3. Whom did the Sanhedrin jail with the crime of disturbing the peace?
   A. Paul and Barnabas
   B. Timothy and Titus
   C. Peter and John
   D. Stephen and Silas

4. What man wanted letters of commendation from a high priest that would allow him to arrest Christians?
   A. Peter
   B. Saul
   C. John the Baptist
   D. Cornelius

5. Who lived in a cave with his daughters after Sodom and Gomorrah were destroyed?
   A. Abraham
   B. Caleb
   C. Elijah
   D. Lot

6. As five Canaanite kings hid in a cave, who trapped them inside? ·
   A. Jeremiah
   B. Joshua
   C. Elisha
   D. Aholiab

7. What king of Gezer had his entire army destroyed by Joshua's army?
   A. Menahem
   B. Horam
   C. Joram
   D. Pekah

8. When the Babylonian king's forces first attacked Judah, who was reigning?
   A. Jesaiah
   B. Jehoiakim
   C. Berechiah
   D. Hilkiah

9. After the Israelites had been taken away, what Assyrian king sent foreigners to settle in Israel?
   A. Elimelech
   B. Togarmah
   C. Esarhaddon
   D. Rechab

10. Who said, "Let me die with the Philistines"?
    A. Samson
    B. David
    C. Saul
    D. Judas

161

Women

1. Who was one of the women who brought spices to anoint Jesus's body after his death?
   A. Salome
   B. Priscilla
   C. Anna
   D. Dorcas

2. What woman sought to know the secret of Samson's strength?
   A. Dinah
   B. Diane
   C. Delilah
   D. Deborah

3. What woman of the Old Testament is mentioned in Hebrews in the roll of the faithful?
   A. Rahab
   B. Rebekah
   C. Rachel
   D. Hannah

4. What woman of the Old Testament was ninety years old when she bore a child?
   A. Sarah
   B. Rebekah
   C. Deborah
   D. Mary

5. What woman encouraged the execution of John the Baptist?
    A. Euodias
    B. Eunice
    C. Herodias
    D. Hannah

6. Rizpah was a concubine of what king of Israel?
    A. David
    B. Saul
    C. Solomon
    D. Jeroboam

7. Who was ousted as queen mother for making an idol?
    A. Maachah
    B. Herodias
    C. Asenath
    D. Cleopatra

8. What widowed eighty-four-year-old prophetess saw Jesus in the temple?
    A. Miriam
    B. Anna
    C. Hulda
    D. Phoebe

9. What courageous Jewish girl saved her exiled people from annihilation?
    A. Ruth
    B. Naomi
    C. Esther
    D. Deborah

10. Which of David's wives was the mother of their sabotaging son Adonijah?
    A. Abigail
    B. Bathsheba
    C. Michal
    D. Haggith

11. Who was the sister of Moses?
    A. Sarah
    B. Miriam
    C. Deborah
    D. Rebekah

12. Which of Mary's cousins was the mother of John the Baptist?
    A. Elisabeth
    B. Anna
    C. Bernice
    D. Herodias

13. Philip witnessed to an Ethiopian eunuch who was the servant of what queen?
    A. Queen Herodias
    B. Queen Candace
    C. Queen Nitocris
    D. Queen Esther

14. Bernice was associated with what ruler?
    A. Pilate
    B. King Herod
    C. Caiaphas
    D. King Agrippa

15. Who was the only female judge of Israel?
    A. Deborah
    B. Sarah
    C. Rebekah
    D. Ruth

16. What queen traveled a great distance for a face-to-face meeting with Solomon?
    A. Queen Vashti
    B. Queen Esther
    C. The queen of Sheba
    D. Queen Maachah

17. What woman died giving birth to Benjamin?
    A. Rachel
    B. Rebekah
    C. Rahab
    D. Hannah

18. Who complained about Moses marrying an Ethiopian woman?
    A. Rahab
    B. Miriam
    C. Deborah
    D. Ruth

19. Which of David's wives was designated "very beautiful to look upon"?
    A. Michal
    B. Abigail
    C. Bathsheba
    D. Anna

20. What woman requested water from Jesus that would quench her thirst forever?
    A. The Samaritan woman
    B. The Phoenician woman
    C. Rhoda
    D. Anna

21. Who was accepted by a man who would soon be her husband by lying at his feet?
    A. Hannah
    B. Esther
    C. Rahab
    D. Ruth

22. What royal figure was the mother of Nathan, Shimea, and Shobab?
    A. Bathsheba (Bathshua)
    B. Esther
    C. Vashti
    D. Michal

23. What shepherd's wife complained that her husband was a complete fool?
   A. Hannah
   B. Esther
   C. Abigail
   D. Ruth

24. Who protected the corpses of her children from birds and animals?
   A. Rizpah
   B. Baara
   C. Bathsheba
   D. Reumah

25. Who was married to the soldier Uriah but later became the wife of King David?
   A. Jezebel
   B. Abigail
   C. Bathsheba
   D. Delilah

26. What princess, a worshiper of the false god Baal, influenced Ahab into idolatry?
   A. Salome
   B. Jezebel
   C. Bithiah
   D. Serah

27. Who went against her royal husband, was removed, and was replaced by a foreign woman?
   A. Esther
   B. Deborah
   C. Vashti
   D. Claudia

28. What daughter of Ahab tried to destroy the entire line of Judah?
   A. Jemima
   B. Myrrina
   C. Huldah
   D. Athaliah

29. What prophetess during Josiah's reign comforted the king while reprimanding the people of Judah?

A. Deborah

B. Naomi

C. Huldah

D. Miriam

30. What calculating princess of Tyre married and negatively influenced Ahab?

A. Ruth

B. Bathsheba

C. Esther

D. Jezebel

162

Who Asked?

1. Who asked, "Am I my brother's keeper?"
   A. Joseph
   B. Jacob
   C. Cain
   D. Esau

2. Who wanted to know, "What wilt thou give me, seeing I go childless?"
   A. Sarah
   B. Abram
   C. Leah
   D. Jacob

3. Who inquired, "Shall not the Judge of all the earth do right?"
   A. Joshua
   B. Nahum
   C. Abraham
   D. Micah

4. Who asked, "Why is it that thou hast sent me?"
   A. Moses
   B. Joshua
   C. Matthew
   D. Joseph

5. Who asked the Lord, "LORD God, whereby shall I know that I shall inherit it?"

    A. Thomas

    B. Jacob

    C. Peter

    D. Abram

6. Who inquired, "Why is my pain perpetual, and my wound incurable?"

    A. Jeremiah

    B. Isaiah

    C. Jehoshaphat

    D. Isaac

7. Who said, "Why dost thou shew me iniquity, and cause me to behold grievance?"

    A. Solomon

    B. Habakkuk

    C. Amos

    D. Pharaoh

8. What men asked, "Shall one man sin, and wilt thou be wroth with all the congregation?"

    A. Moses and Aaron

    B. Cain and Abel

    C. Paul and Timothy

    D. Peter and John

9. Who wanted to know, "Ah, LORD God! wilt thou make a full end of the remnant of Israel?"

    A. Jeremiah

    B. Hezekiah

    C. Ezekiel

    D. Zephaniah

10. Who asked, "Behold, when I come unto the children of Israel, and shall say unto them, The God of your fathers hath sent me unto you; and they shall say to me, What is his name? what shall I say unto them?"
    A. Aaron
    B. Jacob
    C. Moses
    D. Abraham

11. Who inquired, "Behold, I am vile; what shall I answer thee?"
    A. Paul
    B. Job
    C. Nathan
    D. Simon

12. Who asked, "Shall I go and smite these Philistines?"
    A. Moses
    B. Elijah
    C. Samson
    D. David

163

Hearing from God

1. Who was called to build a ship?
   A. Jonah
   B. Esau
   C. Noah
   D. Abram

2. Who was called to leave his home for a strange land?
   A. Jonah
   B. Esau
   C. Noah
   D. Abram

3. Who was Israel's first high priest?
   A. Joshua
   B. Moses
   C. Caleb
   D. Aaron

4. What man was called by God to be king over the ten tribes of Israel?
   A. Solomon
   B. David
   C. Saul
   D. Jeroboam

5. What prophet raised a widow's son from the dead?
   A. Jonah
   B. Daniel
   C. Elijah
   D. Elisha

6. Who freed the Israelites from Egyptian bondage?
   A. Joshua
   B. Moses
   C. Caleb
   D. Aaron

7. Who was called to receive God's covenant of peace for his family?
   A. Eleazar
   B. Phinehas
   C. Joshua
   D. Moses

8. Who dreamed he would have authority over his brothers?
   A. Esau
   B. Jacob
   C. Joseph
   D. Isaac

164

Bible Brilliant Level

1. What is the shortest verse in the Bible?
   A. 1 John 1:35
   B. Luke 11:35
   C. John 11:35
   D. 1 Chronicles 1:1

2. Who washed his steps with butter?
   A. John
   B. Job
   C. Jonah
   D. Joshua

3. What person with the occupation of dressmaker was raised from the dead?
   A. Dinah
   B. Diane
   C. Dorcas
   D. Deborah

4. How many households did Joshua leave undisturbed in Jericho?
   A. 1
   B. 2
   C. 3
   D. 4

5. Who in Genesis wept when he kissed his sweetheart?
   A. Jacob
   B. Esau
   C. Laban
   D. Abraham

6. What man infamously killed sixty-nine of his brothers?
   A. Gideon
   B. Abimelech
   C. Joshua
   D. Absalom

7. What was the common thing shared by Samson, David, and Benaiah the son of Jehoiada?
   A. They all had eight wives
   B. They all killed a lion
   C. They were all rugged and handsome
   D. None of the above

8. Who killed six hundred men with an ox goad?
   A. Sisera
   B. Shamgar
   C. Shimshai
   D. Shishak

9. Who possessed hair like eagle feathers and fingernails similar to bird claws?
   A. Nebushazban
   B. Onesiphorus
   C. Melchishua
   D. Nebuchadnezzar

10. From what material was the covering for the tent over the tabernacle made?
   A. Ram skins
   B. Shittim wood
   C. Wheat and barley sacks
   D. Fig leaves

11. What did Elisha do when he learned that Jericho had bad water?

    A. He prayed

    B. He fasted and prayed

    C. He threw salt into it

    D. He poured a bowl of sugar in it

12. What two books of the Bible were written for Theophilus?

    A. Matthew and Mark

    B. Mark and Luke

    C. Luke and John

    D. Luke and Acts

13. What was the name of King Saul's wife?

    A. Salome

    B. Anna

    C. Ahinoam

    D. Sarah

14. Who stopped the Israelites from burning incense to the bronze snake that Moses made?

    A. Samuel

    B. Hezekiah

    C. Aaron

    D. Jeremiah

15. What book of the Bible mentions a synagogue of Satan?

    A. Daniel

    B. John

    C. Revelation

    D. Joel

16. What biblical character claimed that laughter is mad?

    A. David

    B. Saul

    C. Solomon

    D. Jonathan

17. How many years were the Israelites in Egypt?

   A. 40

   B. 365

   C. 400

   D. 430

18. How many angels will be stationed at the gates of the new Jerusalem?

   A. 10

   B. 12

   C. 15

   D. 20

19. How many years did God add to Hezekiah's life?

   A. 10

   B. 12

   C. 15

   D. 20

20. How many men mentioned in the Bible had the name Judas?

   A. 1

   B. 3

   C. 6

   D. 11

Anything Goes

1. How many people were saved in Noah's ark?
   A. 5
   B. 6
   C. 7
   D. 8

2. What was the name of the first woman judge in Israel?
   A. Dorcas
   B. Salome
   C. Priscilla
   D. Deborah

3. What was the name of the angel who revealed to Mary that she would be the mother of Jesus?
   A. Michael
   B. Gabriel
   C. John
   D. Joelah

4. How many stories or levels were in Noah's ark?
   A. 2
   B. 3
   C. 4
   D. 5

5. Who escaped from Damascus in a basket?
   A. Paul
   B. Peter
   C. John
   D. Thomas

6. Who interpreted Pharaoh's dream as seven good years and seven lean years in Egypt?
   A. Joseph
   B. Paul
   C. Daniel
   D. John

7. Who was killed when they lied to the Holy Spirit?
   A. Aquila and Priscilla
   B. Boaz and Ruth
   C. Ananias and Sapphira
   D. Abraham and Sarah

8. What was the name of the queen who was devoured by dogs?
   A. Esther
   B. Vashti
   C. Jezebel
   D. Sheba

9. What does the word *Ichabod* mean?
   A. The glory is departed
   B. The glory is revealed
   C. The glory is prepared
   D. The glory is recognized

10. Who asked God to put his tears in a bottle?
   A. Saul
   B. Jonathan
   C. David
   D. Samuel

11. What was the name of Ruth's father-in-law?

A. Elhanan

B. Eliakim

C. Eliezer

D. Elimelech

12. What king in the Bible had the longest reign?

A. Saul

B. David

C. Manasseh

D. Josiah

13. What queen came from a far land to experience the wisdom of King Solomon?

A. Queen Esther

B. Queen Vashti

C. The queen of Sheba

D. Queen Jezebel

14. Who wore clothes made out of camel's hair?

A. John the Baptist

B. Paul

C. Peter

D. Jesus

15. Paul was blind for how many days while in Damascus?

A. 0

B. 3

C. 12

D. 40

16. Who said, "Divide the living child in two, give half to one, and half to the other"?

A. King David

B. King Josiah

C. King Solomon

D. King Saul

17. Who came to Jesus by night to talk with him?
    A. Simon
    B. Lazarus
    C. Nicodemus
    D. John

18. Who was released from prison by an angel?
    A. Peter
    B. John
    C. Paul
    D. Silas

19. According to 1 Peter 3:20, referring to the ark, how many souls were saved by water?
    A. None
    B. 8
    C. Every soul forever
    D. 144,000

20. What woman was the wife of both Nabal and King David?
    A. Bathsheba
    B. Michal
    C. Rebekah
    D. Abigail

21. Who was Nebuchadnezzar's son?
    A. Belshazzar
    B. Sheshbazzar
    C. Meshezabel
    D. Hammolecheth

22. What runaway slave eventually returned to his master?
    A. Belshazzar
    B. Onesimus
    C. Meshezabel
    D. Hammolecheth

23. What king stayed in his bed and pouted because he could not purchase another person's vineyard?
   A. King David
   B. King Saul
   C. King Ahab
   D. King Solomon

24. In a dream, what did Abimelech learn about Sarah?
   A. She was married
   B. She was single
   C. She was divorced
   D. She was a widow

25. How many times did Noah send a dove out of the ark to try to find land?
   A. 1
   B. 2
   C. 3
   D. 4

26. Whose ten sons were hung on the same gallows as he?
   A. Achin's
   B. Haman's
   C. Absalom's
   D. Bigthan's

27. What member of Pharaoh's staff was hung for theft?
   A. The cook
   B. The chief baker
   C. The cup bearer
   D. The musician

28. What king did Bigthan and Teresh plan to assassinate?
   A. King Ahasuerus
   B. King Elah
   C. King Saul
   D. King David

29. What was not in Solomon's house because Solomon considered it to be of little value?
    A. Brass
    B. Garnet
    C. Silver
    D. Pearls

30. What did Solomon do when he got older?
    A. Divorced his seven hundred wives
    B. Became closer to the Lord
    C. Started worshiping false gods
    D. Enjoyed fasting and praying more

31. How many times was Paul stoned?
    A. Once
    B. Twice
    C. Three times
    D. None

32. What group of people believed in the resurrection and in angels?
    A. Sadducees
    B. Pharisees
    C. Jews
    D. Romans

33. Who was Solomon's son?
    A. Rehoboam
    B. Rehob
    C. Regem-Melech
    D. Rehabiah

34. How many sons and daughters did Solomon's son have?
    A. 21 sons and 50 daughters
    B. 28 sons and 60 daughters
    C. 22 sons and 40 daughters
    D. 25 sons and 75 daughters

35. From what material was the covering for the tent over the tabernacle made?

    A. Ram skins

    B. Shittim wood

    C. Wheat and barley sacks

    D. Fig leaves

36. What did Elisha do when he learned of the bad water in Jericho?

    A. He prayed

    B. He left the city

    C. He threw salt into it

    D. He made a mud mixture

37. People weren't given permission to do what until after the flood?

    A. Take baths

    B. Eat meat

    C. Make fires

    D. Comb their hair

38. What two books of the Bible were written for Theophilus?

    A. Matthew and Mark

    B. Mark and Luke

    C. Luke and John

    D. Luke and Acts

39. What was the name of King Saul's wife?

    A. Salome

    B. Anna

    C. Ahinoam

    D. Sarah

40. Who stopped the Israelites from burning incense to the bronze snake that Moses made?

    A. Samuel

    B. Hezekiah

    C. Aaron

    D. Jeremiah

41. What book of the Bible mentions a synagogue of Satan?
    A. Daniel
    B. John
    C. Revelation
    D. Joel

42. What person in the Bible claimed that laughter is mad?
    A. David
    B. Saul
    C. Solomon
    D. Jonathan

43. How many years were the Israelites in Egypt?
    A. 40
    B. 365
    C. 400
    D. 430

44. How many angels will stand at the gates of the new Jerusalem?
    A. 10
    B. 12
    C. 15
    D. 20

45. How many years did God add to Hezekiah's life?
    A. 10
    B. 12
    C. 15
    D. 20

46. How many men in the Bible had the name Judas?
    A. 4
    B. 5
    C. 6
    D. 7

166

Royalty

1. How many wives did Solomon have?
   - A. 500
   - B. 600
   - C. 700
   - D. 800

2. What future king of Israel was anointed by Samuel?
   - A. Saul
   - B. Solomon
   - C. Uzziah
   - D. Joash

3. To please his foreign wives, who built pagan temples?
   - A. Saul
   - B. Darius
   - C. David
   - D. Solomon

4. Of what was Paul a maker?
   - A. Ships
   - B. Tents
   - C. Idols
   - D. Gallows

5. Who infamously created a golden calf?
   A. Gilead
   B. Demetrius
   C. Moses
   D. Aaron

6. When Jesus was arrested, what king demanded that Jesus prove himself by performing miracles?
   A. Hiram
   B. Herod
   C. Agag
   D. Ahab

7. Who was the last king of Judah?
   A. Zedekiah
   B. Hezekiah
   C. Tirhakah
   D. Hazael

8. Who was in charge of all the bronze work in the temple?
   A. Haramn
   B. Hiram
   C. Hunram
   D. Haran

9. What king held a banquet in which a hand left a message on the palace wall?
   A. Jabin
   B. Achish
   C. Herod
   D. Belshazzar

10. What leader of his people created a brass snake?
    A. Joshua
    B. Gideon
    C. Moses
    D. Abimelech

167

More Firsts

1. Whom did Jesus choose to be his first disciple(s)?
   A. Simon Peter and Andrew
   B. Matthew
   C. James
   D. John

2. Who was the first judge of Israel?
   A. Deborah
   B. Othniel
   C. Ruth
   D. Aaron

3. Who was the first man to be exiled alone, without a mate?
   A. Esau
   B. Ishmael
   C. Cain
   D. Joseph

4. Who constructed the first altar?
   A. Noah
   B. Solomon
   C. Abraham
   D. Abel

5. Who wore the first bridal veil?
   A. Michal
   B. Sarah
   C. Rebekah
   D. Rachel

6. Who was the wearer of the first ring mentioned in the Bible?
   A. Abraham
   B. Abimelech
   C. Jacob
   D. Pharaoh

7. Who was the Bible's first crop farmer?
   A. Abel
   B. Cain
   C. Noah
   D. Shem

8. Who was the first priest mentioned in Scripture?
   A. Jethro
   B. Zecharias
   C. Aaron
   D. Melchizedek

9. Who was the Bible's first shepherdess?
   A. Rachel
   B. Abigail
   C. Anna
   D. Eve

10. Who were the first foreign missionaries revealed in Scripture?
    A. Peter and John
    B. Paul and Silas
    C. Aquila and Priscilla
    D. Paul and Barnabas

168

More Random Bible Trivia

1. Who preached at Pentecost?
   A. Paul
   B. Peter
   C. Barnabas
   D. Philip

2. In Revelation, what church was described as neither hot nor cold?
   A. The church of Laodicea
   B. The church of Sardis
   C. The church of Philadelphia
   D. The church of Thyatira

3. By what other name was the disciple Matthew known?
   A. James
   B. Simon
   C. Levi
   D. John

4. Who reluctantly denied he knew Christ?
   A. John
   B. Paul
   C. Peter
   D. James

5. How many times did Moses strike the rock at Kadesh before water gushed forth?
   A. 1
   B. 2
   C. 7
   D. 13

6. Who had a vision of the Ancient of days seated on a throne?
   A. David
   B. Joshua
   C. Daniel
   D. Jonah

7. A multitude of what bird appeared miraculously and became food for the Israelites during the exodus?
   A. Quail
   B. Raven
   C. Eagle
   D. Duck

8. The words of what prophet caused the Syrian soldiers to be struck blind?
   A. Elisha
   B. Jeremiah
   C. Isaiah
   D. Elijah

9. What man said, "For in him we live, and move, and have our being"?
   A. Jacob
   B. Paul
   C. David
   D. Ruth

10. What Bible book includes a passage that advises sleepers to rise from the dead?
    A. 1 Corinthians
    B. Romans
    C. Ephesians
    D. Acts

11. Who hurled a javelin at David?
    A. Absalom
    B. Saul
    C. Uzziah
    D. Abner

12. How many angels were sent to save Lot and his family from the wicked city of Sodom?
    A. 2
    B. 3
    C. 4
    D. 5

13. Where was Jesus when he was strengthened by an angel sent by the Father?
    A. The wilderness
    B. Garden of Gethsemane
    C. Mount Carmel
    D. Lystra

14. What river was turned into blood?
    A. Gihon
    B. Jordan
    C. Nile
    D. Euphrates

15. In what Gospel is Satan called Beelzebub?
    A. Matthew
    B. Mark
    C. Luke
    D. John

16. What prophet was exiled to Babylon?
    A. Isaiah
    B. Jonah
    C. Jeremiah
    D. Ezekiel

17. When Jesus called in a loud voice, who came forth?
    A. John Mark
    B. John the Baptist
    C. Mary
    D. Lazarus

18. What was Sarai's name changed to?
    A. Rachel
    B. Miriam
    C. Sarah
    D. Elisheba

19. Who slept during a raging storm on the Sea of Galilee?
    A. Paul
    B. Timothy
    C. Jesus
    D. Jonah

20. Who had a wife named Judith?
    A. Esau
    B. Abner
    C. Jairus
    D. Jethro

21. What just and good king of Judah was assassinated by two of his own court officials?
    A. King Jehu
    B. King Joash
    C. King Jehoash
    D. King Josiah

22. What Egyptian woman married Joseph, according to the book of Genesis?
    A. Asenath
    B. Chloe
    C. Abigail
    D. Vashti

23. In one of his many miracles, how many pots of water did Jesus turn into wine?

    A. 2

    B. 6

    C. 77

    D. 144

24. Who referred to Mary as "the mother of my Lord"?

    A. Herod's daughter

    B. John the Baptist

    C. Elisabeth

    D. Zacharias

25. Who was a widow for approximately eighty-four years?

    A. Mary

    B. Lois

    C. Eunice

    D. Anna

WORD FILL

In the following section, divided by topic, simply fill in all the blanks to complete the Scripture passage. Give yourself 5 points for each passage you complete correctly.

169

Encouragement

1. Proverbs 18:10
   The name of the LORD is a strong _____; the righteous runneth into it, and is _____.

2. _____ 3:5–6
   _____ in the LORD with all thine _____; and lean not unto thine own understanding. In all thy ways acknowledge him, and he shall direct thy paths.

3. Isaiah 41:10
   _____ thou not; for I am with thee: be not _____; for I am thy God: I will strengthen thee; yea, I will help thee; yea, I will uphold thee with the right _____ of my righteousness.

4. _____ 14:27
   _____ I leave with you, my peace I give unto you: not as the _____ giveth, give I unto you. Let not your heart be troubled, neither let it be afraid.

5. _____ 16:33
   These things I have spoken unto you, that in _____ ye might have peace. In the _____ ye shall have tribulation: but be of good cheer; I have overcome the world.

6. Psalm 46:1–2
   _____ is our _____ and strength, a very present help in trouble. Therefore will not we fear, though the earth be removed, and though the _____ be carried into the midst of the _____.

7. 2 _____ 1:7
   For God hath not given us the _____ of fear; but of
   _____, and of _____, and of a sound mind.

8. _____ 16:8
   I have set the _____ always before me: because he is at
   my right hand, I shall not be moved.

9. Psalm 55:22
   _____ thy burden upon the _____, and he shall sustain
   thee: he shall never suffer the righteous to be moved.

10. 1 _____ 5:7
    Casting all your _____ upon him; for he careth for you.

11. Isaiah 26:3
    Thou wilt keep him in _____ peace, whose _____ is
    stayed on thee: because he trusteth in thee.

12. _____ 118:14
    The _____ is my strength and _____, and is become
    my salvation.

13. _____ 119:114
    Thou art my _____ place and my _____: I hope in
    thy word.

14. Psalm 119:25
    My soul cleaveth unto the _____: quicken thou me ac-
    cording to thy _____.

15. _____ 119:50
    This is my comfort in my affliction: for thy _____ hath
    quickened me.

16. Psalm 119:71
    It is good for me that I have been _____; that I might
    _____ thy statutes.

17. _____ 120:1
    In my _____ I cried unto the _____, and he heard me.

170

Friendship

1. Proverbs 18:24
   A man that hath friends must shew himself friendly: and there is a _____ that sticketh closer than a _____.

2. _____ 22:24–25
   Make no friendship with an _____ man; and with a furious man thou shalt not go: Lest thou learn his ways, and get a snare to thy _____.

3. Proverbs 13:20
   He that walketh with _____ men shall be wise: but a companion of _____ shall be destroyed.

4. Proverbs 27:5–6
   Open rebuke is _____ than secret love. Faithful are the wounds of a friend; but the _____ of an enemy are deceitful.

5. Ecclesiastes 4:9–10
   _____ are better than one; because they have a good reward for their labour. For if they fall, the one will lift up his fellow: but woe to him that is alone when he falleth; for he hath not another to _____ him up.

6. _____ 15:12
   This is my commandment, That ye _____ one another, as I have loved you.

7. Proverbs 17:17

A _____ loveth at all times, and a _____ is born for adversity.

8. Proverbs 27:17

_____ sharpeneth iron; so a _____ sharpeneth the countenance of his friend.

9. Proverbs 12:26

The _____ is more excellent than his neighbour: but the way of the _____ seduceth them.

10. James 4:4

Ye _____ and adulteresses, know ye not that the friendship of the _____ is enmity with God? whosoever therefore will be a friend of the world is the _____ of God.

11. Job 16:20–21

My _____ scorn me: but mine eye poureth out _____ unto God. O that one might plead for a man with God, as a man pleadeth for his neighbour!

Forgiveness

1. Matthew 6:14–15

   For if ye _____ men their trespasses, your _____ _____ will also forgive you: But if ye forgive not men their trespasses, neither will your Father forgive your trespasses.

2. 1 _____ 1:9

   If we confess our sins, he is _____ and just to _____ us our sins, and to cleanse us from all unrighteousness.

3. Isaiah 43:25

   I, even I, am he that blotteth out thy _____ for mine own sake, and will not remember thy _____.

4. _____ 3:19

   _____ ye therefore, and be converted, that your _____ may be blotted out, when the times of refreshing shall come from the presence of the Lord.

5. _____ 1:18

   Come now, and let us _____ together, saith the LORD: though your sins be as _____, they shall be as white as _____; though they be red like crimson, they shall be as wool.

6. 2 Corinthians 5:17

   Therefore if any man be in _____, he is a new _____: old things are passed away; behold, all things are become new.

7. Ephesians 1:7
   In whom we have _____ through his _____, the for-
   giveness of sins, according to the riches of his _____.

8. Hebrews 10:17
   And their _____ and iniquities will I _____ no more.

9. Daniel 9:9
   To the Lord our God belong mercies and forgivenesses,
   though we have _____ against him.

10. Colossians 1:13–14
    Who hath _____ us from the power of _____, and hath
    translated us into the kingdom of his dear Son: In whom we
    have redemption through his blood, even the forgiveness of
    _____.

11. _____ 103:12
    As far as the _____ is from the west, so far hath he re-
    moved our _____ from us.

12. Micah 7:18–19
    Who is a _____ like unto thee, that pardoneth iniquity, and
    passeth by the transgression of the remnant of his heritage?
    he retaineth not his anger for ever, because he delighteth in
    mercy. He will turn again, he will have compassion upon
    us; he will subdue our iniquities; and thou wilt cast all their
    _____ into the depths of the _____.

13. _____ 6:9–15
    After this manner therefore _____ ye: Our Father which
    art in heaven, _____ be thy name. Thy kingdom come,
    Thy will be done in earth, as it is in _____. Give us this
    day our daily bread. And forgive us our debts, as we forgive
    our debtors. And lead us not into temptation, but deliver
    us from _____: For thine is the kingdom, and the power,
    and the glory, for ever. Amen. For if ye forgive men their
    trespasses, your heavenly Father will also forgive you: But if
    ye forgive not men their trespasses, neither will your Father
    forgive your trespasses.

14. Mark 11:25

And when ye stand _____, _____, if ye have ought against any: that your Father also which is in heaven may forgive you your _____.

15. Matthew 26:28

For this is my _____ of the new testament, which is shed for many for the remission of _____.

172

Inspiration

1. _____ 29:11
   For I know the _____ that I think toward you, saith the LORD, thoughts of peace, and not of _____, to give you an expected end.

2. _____ 27:4
   One thing have I desired of the LORD, that will I seek after; that I may _____ in the _____ of the LORD all the days of my life, to behold the beauty of the LORD, and to enquire in his temple.

3. _____ 34:8
   O _____ and see that the LORD is _____: blessed is the man that trusteth in him.

4. _____ 17:17
   A _____ loveth at all times, and a brother is born for adversity.

5. Isaiah 40:28
   Hast thou not known? hast thou not _____, that the everlasting God, the LORD, the _____ of the ends of the _____, fainteth not, neither is weary? there is no searching of his understanding.

6. _____ 15:13
   _____ _____ hath no man than this, that a man lay down his life for his friends.

7. Romans 8:28

And we know that all _____ work together for good to them that _____ God, to them who are the called according to his _____.

8. _____ 8:31

What shall we then _____ to these things? If God be for us, who can be _____ us?

9. Romans 15:13

Now the _____ of hope fill you with all joy and _____ in believing, that ye may abound in hope, through the _____ of the Holy Ghost.

10. _____ 8:38–39

For I am persuaded, that neither _____, nor life, nor _____, nor principalities, nor powers, nor things present, nor things to come, Nor height, nor depth, nor any other creature, shall be able to _____ us from the love of God, which is in Christ Jesus our Lord.

11. Lamentations 3:22–23

It is of the LORD's mercies that we are not consumed, because his compassions fail _____. They are new every _____: great is thy faithfulness.

12. 2 Corinthians 4:16

For which cause we faint not; but though our outward _____ perish, yet the inward man is _____ day by day.

13. 1 Corinthians 16:13

Watch ye, stand fast in the _____, quit you like men, be _____.

14. Philippians 3:7–9

But what things were gain to me, those I counted _____ for Christ. Yea doubtless, and I count all things but loss for the excellency of the knowledge of Christ Jesus my Lord: for whom I have suffered the loss of all things, and do count them but _____, that I may win Christ, And be found in him, not having mine own righteousness, which is of the law, but that which is through the _____ of Christ, the righteousness which is of God by faith.

15. 1 John 3:1
Behold, what manner of love the _____ hath bestowed upon us, that we should be called the sons of God: therefore the _____ knoweth us not, because it knew him not.

16. Hebrews 10:22
Let us draw near with a true _____ in full assurance of _____, having our hearts sprinkled from an evil conscience, and our bodies _____ with pure water.

17. 1 Peter 2:9
But ye are a _____ generation, a royal priesthood, an holy _____, a peculiar people; that ye should shew forth the praises of him who hath called you out of darkness into his marvellous _____.

18. _____ 1:2–3
My brethren, count it all _____ when ye fall into divers temptations; Knowing this, that the trying of your _____ worketh patience.

19. _____ 1:17
For therein is the righteousness of God revealed from faith to faith: as it is written, The just shall live by _____.

20. _____ 31:6
Be strong and of a good _____, fear not, nor be afraid of them: for the LORD thy God, he it is that doth go with thee; he will not fail thee, nor _____ thee.

21. 1 Corinthians 15:58
Therefore, my beloved brethren, be ye stedfast, unmoveable, always abounding in the _____ of the _____, forasmuch as ye know that your labour is not in _____ in the Lord.

22. Hebrews 12:1

Wherefore seeing we also are compassed about with so great a cloud of _____, let us lay aside every weight, and the sin which doth so easily beset us, and let us run with _____ the race that is set before us.

173

Anger

1 Ephesians 4:26
   Be ye angry, and _____ not: let not the sun go down upon your wrath.

2. _____ 1:19–20
   Wherefore, my beloved _____, let every man be swift to hear, slow to speak, slow to wrath: For the _____ of man worketh not the righteousness of God.

3. _____ 29:11
   A _____ uttereth all his mind: but a wise man keepeth it in till afterwards.

4. Proverbs 19:11
   The discretion of a man deferreth his _____; and it is his glory to pass over a _____.

5. Ecclesiastes 7:9
   Be not hasty in thy _____ to be angry: for anger resteth in the bosom of _____.

6. Proverbs 15:1
   A soft _____ turneth away _____: but grievous words stir up anger.

7. _____ 15:18
   A wrathful man stirreth up strife: but he that is slow to _____ appeaseth strife.

8. Colossians 3:8

But now ye also put off all these; _____, wrath, malice, blasphemy, filthy communication out of your _____.

9. Proverbs 16:32

He that is slow to _____ is better than the mighty; and he that ruleth his spirit than he that taketh a _____.

10. _____ 22:24

Make no _____ with an angry man; and with a furious man thou shalt not go.

11. _____ 37:8–9

Cease from _____, and forsake wrath: fret not thyself in any wise to do evil. For evildoers shall be cut off: but those that wait upon the LORD, they shall inherit the _____.

12. _____ 14:29

He that is slow to _____ is of great understanding: but he that is hasty of _____ exalteth folly.

174

Who Is God?

Twenty descriptions of God are scattered throughout the Bible in fifty-two places. In this challenging exercise, try to name the book of the Bible that mentions each description.

Give yourself 10 points for each book you name correctly out of fifty-two possible answers. If you can name twenty, you've done extremely well. More than half correct, or a score of 260 or better, is truly outstanding.

1. Omnipotent or all-powerful is mentioned in what three Bible books?
2. Eternal or lasting without end is mentioned in what three Bible books?
3. Infinite or having no boundaries or limits is mentioned in what four Bible books?
4. Self-sufficient or self-existent is mentioned in what three Bible books?
5. Omnipresent or present everywhere is mentioned in what Bible book?
6. Light is mentioned in what two Bible books?
7. Sovereign or exercising supreme, permanent authority is mentioned in what two Bible books?

8. Omniscient or all-knowing is mentioned in what two Bible books?

9. Unchanging is mentioned in what two Bible books?

10. Holy is mentioned in what two Bible books?

11. Wise is mentioned in what three Bible books?

12. Righteous or just is mentioned in what three Bible books?

13. True or the truth is mentioned in what four Bible books?

14. Faithful is mentioned in what two Bible books?

15. Gracious is mentioned in what three Bible books?

16. Good is mentioned in what three Bible books?

17. Merciful is mentioned in what four Bible books?

18. Spirit is mentioned in what Bible book?

19. Love is mentioned in what three Bible books?

20. Trinity or three in one is mentioned in what two Bible books?

THE BONUS SECTION

The nearer I approach to the end of my pilgrimage, the clearer is the evidence of the divine origin of the Bible, and the grandeur and sublimity of God's remedy for fallen man are more appreciated, and the future is illumined with hope and joy.

Francis Bacon, English philosopher, scientist, lawyer, and father of the scientific method

175

The Book of Revelation

Just as a thorough knowledge of the Bible's first book is essential to becoming Bible brilliant, knowing the final book well is equally essential. Give yourself 10 bonus points for each question you answer correctly as you move through many key points of the book of Revelation chapter by chapter.

Chapter 1

1. Who received this book's revelation from Jesus by way of an angel?
2. Who was called the Alpha and Omega?
3. The book was written to what group of seven?
4. What did the seven stars and seven candlesticks represent?

Chapter 2

1. What was the problem with the church of Ephesus?
2. What was wrong with the church of Smyrna?
3. What church allowed idolatry and immorality?
4. What church was led into uncleanness and immorality by a prophetess?

Chapter 3

1. What church had become a dead church?
2. What church was the faith church that served God well?
3. What type of church was the church of the Laodiceans?

Chapter 4

1. Whom did John see sitting on a throne?
2. What did the seven lamps before the throne represent?
3. What did each of the four living creatures look like?
4. What twenty-four things/people were around the throne?

Chapter 5

1. What was in God's hand?
2. Who was the only one worthy to loose the seals and open the book?

Chapter 6

1. What was the color of the horse of the first seal?
2. What did the red horse of the second seal bring to earth?
3. What did the black horse of the third seal bring to earth?
4. What horse of the fourth seal brought death to a fourth of the earth?
5. Whose souls were revealed because of the fifth seal?
6. What great thing did the sixth seal bring?

Chapter 7

1. What was the number of people sealed?
2. What group was the great multitude before the throne?

Chapter 8

1. What began following the prayers of the saints?
2. What did the first trumpet release?
3. What did the second trumpet bring?
4. The third trumpet initiated the falling of what item from heaven?
5. The fourth trumpet prevented what portion of the sun from giving light?

Chapter 9

1. What did the locusts do to mankind?
2. What did the sixth trumpet release on earth?
3. How large was the army of destruction?
4. Did the rest of mankind repent from their evil?

Chapter 10

1. What did the mighty angel proclaim?
2. After the sounding of the seventh trumpet, what would happen to the mystery of God?

Chapter 11

1. How long was the holy city of Jerusalem to be overrun by the Gentiles?
2. What did the two witnesses do for 1,260 days?
3. Who killed the two witnesses?
4. What happened to the two witnesses after three and a half days?
5. What did the seventh trumpet proclaim?

Chapter 12

1. What did the woman with the twelve stars represent?
2. What was the fiery red dragon?
3. What did John see come down to the earth and sea?
4. Who was the child born to the woman?
5. Who was the woman's other offspring?

Chapter 13

1. The beast John saw was like what animal?
2. What was the beast permitted to do?
3. What rose from out of the earth?
4. What two places did people wear the mark of the beast?

Chapter 14

1. Who stood victorious with Jesus on Mount Zion?
2. What did the first angel proclaim?
3. What angel proclaimed the fall of Babylon?
4. The third angel warned against accepting what?
5. On what did Jesus come?

Chapter 15

1. Who was standing, equipped with harps of God?
2. Seven angels had vials that represented what?

Chapter 16

1. What did the first angel pour out on the earth?
2. What did the second angel cause the sea to turn into?

3. What did the third angel cause the rivers and springs to turn into?

4. What did the fourth angel cause people to be scorched from?

5. What did the fifth angel cause the beast and its kingdom to become full of?

6. What river did the sixth angel cause to dry up?

7. What calamity did the seventh angel cause?

Chapter 17

1. What did the seven heads of the beast represent?

2. What did the ten horns represent?

Chapter 18

1. How long did the judgment of Babylon take?

2. What did one strong angel throw into the sea?

Chapter 19

1. What was completely destroyed as this chapter begins?

2. Who rode the white horse?

3. What was the fate of the beast and the false prophet?

Chapter 20

1. Where was Satan cast and for how long?

2. What first thing did all believers become part of?

3. What was Satan's final fate?

4. Who was judged at the great white throne?

Chapter 21

1. What two new things were created?
2. What came down to earth?
3. Whose names were on the twelve gates of the new Jerusalem?
4. How large was the city?
5. What gem were the walls constructed of in the new Jerusalem?
6. From what were the gates of the new Jerusalem constructed?
7. What lit up the city?

Chapter 22

1. What proceeded from the throne?
2. What sat in the middle of the main street?
3. What does anyone who reads the book of Revelation receive?
4. What is the final word of the Bible?

176

Food by the Book

In this admittedly difficult exercise fit for the truly Bible brilliant, give yourself 20 bonus points for each correct answer. This is an open-book exercise. Use of your Bible is permitted.

Dairy Products

1. What dairy product is mentioned in Proverbs 30:33?
2. What dairy product is mentioned in 1 Samuel 17:18; 2 Samuel 17:29; and Job 10:10?
3. What dairy product is mentioned in Isaiah 7:15?
4. What dairy product is mentioned in Job 6:6 and Luke 11:12?
5. What dairy product is mentioned in Exodus 33:3; Judges 5:25; and Job 10:10?

Fruits

1. What fruit is mentioned in Song of Solomon 2:5?
2. What fruit is mentioned in 2 Samuel 6:19 and 1 Chronicles 16:3?
3. What fruit is mentioned in Nehemiah 13:15 and Jeremiah 24:1–3?

4. What fruit is mentioned in Leviticus 19:10 and Deuteronomy 23:24?

5. What fruit is mentioned in Numbers 11:5 and Isaiah 1:8?

6. What fruit is mentioned in Isaiah 17:6 and Micah 6:15?

7. What fruit is mentioned in Numbers 20:5 and Deuteronomy 8:8?

8. What fruit is mentioned in Numbers 6:3 and 2 Samuel 6:19?

9. What fruit is mentioned in Psalm 78:47 and Amos 7:14?

Vegetables

1. What vegetables are mentioned in Numbers 11:5?

2. What vegetables are mentioned in 2 Kings 4:39?

Nuts

1. What nuts are mentioned in Numbers 17:8?

2. What nuts are mentioned in Genesis 43:11?

Legumes

1. What two types of legumes are mentioned in Ezekiel 4:9?

2. What legumes are mentioned in Genesis 25:34 and 2 Samuel 17:28?

Spices and Herbs

1. What spice or herb is mentioned in Matthew 23:23?

2. What spice or herb is mentioned in Exodus 16:31 and Numbers 11:7?

3. What spice or herb is mentioned in Exodus 30:23 and Revelation 18:13?

4. What spice or herb is mentioned in Isaiah 28:25 and Matthew 23:23?

5. What spice or herb is mentioned in Matthew 23:23?

6. What spice or herb is mentioned in Numbers 11:5?

7. What spice or herb is mentioned in Matthew 23:23 and Luke 11:42?

8. What spice or herb is mentioned in Matthew 13:31?

9. What spice or herb is mentioned in Luke 11:42?

10. What spice or herb is mentioned in Ezra 6:9 and Job 6:6?

Fish

1. Along with fish, how many loaves of bread did Jesus give to his disciples in Matthew 15:36?

2. In John 21:11, who pulled up a net full of 153 fish?

Various Grains

1. What grain is mentioned in Deuteronomy 8:8 and Ezekiel 4:9?

2. What grain is mentioned in Genesis 25:34; 2 Samuel 6:19; 16:1; and Mark 8:14?

3. What grain is mentioned in Matthew 12:1?

4. What grain is mentioned in 2 Samuel 17:28 and 1 Kings 17:12?

5. What grain is mentioned in Ezekiel 4:9?

6. What grain is mentioned in Ezekiel 4:9?

7. What grain is mentioned in Genesis 19:3 and Exodus 12:20?

8. What grain is mentioned in Deuteronomy 8:8 and Ezra 6:9?

Various Meats

1. What type of meat is mentioned in Proverbs 15:17 and Luke 15:23?
2. What type of meat is mentioned in Genesis 27:9?
3. What type of meat is mentioned in 2 Samuel 12:4?
4. What type of meat is mentioned in 1 Kings 19:21?
5. What type of meat is mentioned in Deuteronomy 14:4?
6. What type of meat is mentioned in Genesis 27:7?

Various Fowl

1. What type of fowl/bird is mentioned in 1 Samuel 26:20 and Jeremiah 17:11?
2. What type of fowl/bird is mentioned in Genesis 15:9 and Leviticus 12:8?
3. What type of fowl/bird is mentioned in Psalm 105:40?
4. What type of fowl/bird is mentioned in Leviticus 12:8?

Miscellaneous

1. What drink, suitable for children or adults, is mentioned in Numbers 6:3?
2. What healthy food is mentioned in Exodus 33:3; Deuteronomy 8:8; and Judges 14:8–9?
3. What type of oil is mentioned in Deuteronomy 8:8 and Ezra 6:9?
4. What type of liquid is mentioned in Ruth 2:14 and John 19:29?
5. What drink is mentioned in Ezra 6:9 and John 2:1–10?

177

The Sixty Hardest Questions

Give yourself 20 bonus points for each answer you get correct.

1. Name five of the seven people who lived to be over nine hundred years old.
2. Who was the first left-handed person mentioned in the Bible?
3. What man of the Old Testament captured thirty-one kings?
4. Who was the only woman to have her age of death listed in the Bible?
5. What man in Genesis lived to be less than 111 years old?
6. Name either of the two kings who were burned to death?
7. Name the three times God the Father spoke audibly while Jesus was on earth.
8. How many years older was Aaron than his brother Moses?
9. Who was the first man mentioned in the Bible as shaving?
10. Whose head was put on display in the temple of Dagon after his death?
11. What type of animal was the first used for an animal sacrifice?
12. Who was Ruth's first husband?

13. Sarah died how many years after giving birth to Isaac?

14. How old was Jairus's daughter when Jesus brought her back to life?

15. Although Cain was the Bible's first murderer, who was the second?

16. While leading the Israelites out of Egypt, Moses took along the bones of what man?

17. What man was responsible for building the first altar mentioned in the Bible?

18. Who became the first person to convert to Christianity in Europe?

19. Name one of the three books of the New Testament that does not include the word *amen*.

20. Who was the only man that the Bible states was placed in a coffin?

21. The wives of what three men were found at a well?

22. Although lawyers are mentioned in the Bible eight times, who was the only one mentioned by name?

23. Who reigned for fifty-five years, the longest reigning king in the Bible?

24. Who was the first person God killed for being wicked?

25. Name six of the eight weapons mentioned in the Bible that people used to fight each other.

26. Who was the first Christian martyr?

27. What king had the shortest reign at only seven days?

28. Who was the first woman the Bible mentions as singing?

29. Who was Paul's teacher?

30. What was the name of Jacob's daughter?

31. Who was the first judge of Israel?

32. Who was Herod's brother?

33. Before becoming a disciple of Jesus, Andrew was a disciple of what other man?

34. What group of people did not believe in angels or resurrection from the dead?

35. Who was Goliath's brother?

36. What was the first question God asked in the entire Bible?

37. In the list of unclean birds in the book of Leviticus, what is the largest bird listed?

38. Who was the first person to be called a Hebrew in the Bible?

39. The mother of John the Baptist, Elisabeth, was a direct descendent of what Genesis man?

40. What two women of the Bible died during childbirth?

41. What was the first color mentioned in the Bible?

42. Who was the first man in the Bible to prophesy?

43. Name the three people in the entire Bible whose names begin with the letter F.

44. God speaks for the vast majority of what Bible book?

45. After Eden, what is the second region mentioned in the Bible?

46. Who broke his neck falling backward off a chair after hearing bad news?

47. Name either of David's two sisters.

48. Levites could not serve in the tabernacle until they reached what age?

49. What king, when calling his people to repent, even had animals fast?

50. What book of the Bible references people riding on white donkeys?

51. Who was the first apostle to be martyred?

52. Who became the youngest biblical king at age seven?

53. King David was the great-grandson of what famous woman?

54. Who was told by God to select his men for battle by the way they drank water?

55. Name five of the six cities that had only two letters in their names.

56. What is the only miracle of Jesus that is mentioned in all four Gospels?

57. According to Luke 2:1, Jesus was born during the reign of what man who ordered a census?

58. Besides Jesus, what two men fasted for forty days?

59. Name eight of the ten instances in the Bible in which someone was raised from the dead.

60. Name the four times that Jesus used fish in his miracles.

Crossword Puzzle 4

This crossword puzzle is supersized. Give yourself 50 bonus points if you solve it with five or fewer mistakes.

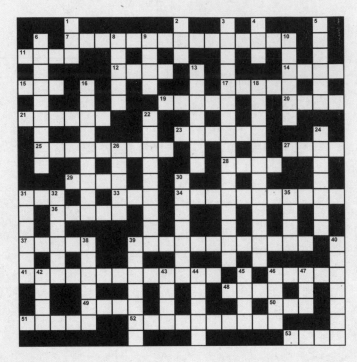

Across

7. With what Jesus fed 5,000 (3 words)
11. 1 Kings 16:30, And ___ the son of Omri did evil
12. ___ the Bible every day
14. 1 Samuel 14:1, And that first slaughter, which Jonathan and his armourbearer made, was about twenty men, within as it were an half ___ of land
15. Genesis 1:27, So God created man in his own image, in the image of God created he ___
17. Abraham's grandson
19. Jerusalem's region
20. Exodus 16:28, And the LORD said unto Moses, How long refuse ye to keep my commandments and my ___?
21. Jeremiah 2:32, Can a maid forget her ornaments, or a bride her ___?
23. Atone for something, with "oneself"
25. Event in Luke, with "the"
27. Apostle to the Gentiles
28. Psalm 128:3, Thy wife shall be as a fruitful ___ by the sides of thine house
29. Leviticus 19:5, And if ye offer a sacrifice of peace offerings unto the LORD, ye shall offer ___ your own will (2 words)
31. Adam's mate
33. Genesis 17:5, Neither shall thy name ___ more be called Abram
34. What those who believe in Jesus Christ shall have (2 words)
36. Brother of Moses
37. Opposite of loves
39. First paradise (3 words)
41. A female follower of Jesus during his time on earth (2 words)
46. "The evidence of things not seen": Hebrews 11:1
48. Genesis 24:29, And Rebekah ___ brother, and his name was Laban (2 words)
49. ". . . Lord is against them that do ___" (Psalm 34:16)
50. Greed, envy, or pride
51. Exodus 9:9, And it shall become ___ dust in all the land of Egypt
52. 1 John 2:18, Little children, it is the last time: and as ye have heard that ___ shall come
53. 2 Samuel 22, The sorrows of ___ compassed me about; the snares of death prevented me

Down

1. Priest's gown
2. Man ___ wife
3. Standard Holy Bible (3 words)
4. Opposite of he
5. Abraham, Isaac, or Jacob
6. December holiday
8. "Jesus wept" in the Bible
9. Matthew 2:2, ". . . for we have seen his ___ in the east"
10. 1 Chronicles 16:30, Fear before him, all the earth: the world also shall be ___, that it be not moved
13. Term referring to the Almighty
16. Jesus's early profession
18. Features of some modern Bibles
22. What Jesus calmed (2 words)
24. Beelzebub
20. See 24-Down
30. Father of James and John
31. God, in Hebrew texts
32. Holiday when the hymn "Rise Again" is sung
35. Third book of the New Testament
38. Prophet who anointed Saul and David as kings
39. What was written on the commandments (2 words)
40. Genesis 16:16, And Abram was fourscore and six years old, when Hagar bare ___ to Abram
42. First human
43. 40-day period before Easter
44. Member of the family
45. Three came from the East
46. Go without food purposely
47. Genesis 43:21, And it came to pass, when we came to the ___, that we opened our sacks

179

Crossword Puzzle 5

Award yourself 50 bonus points if you complete this puzzle with five or fewer mistakes.

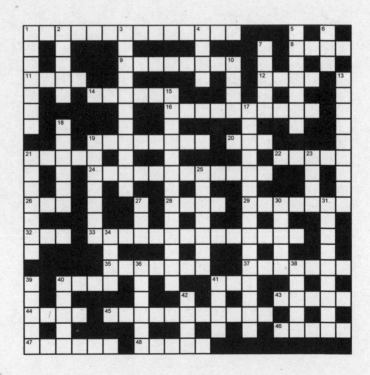

Across

1. Ceremony in which something is made holy
8. Biblical birthright seller
9. Christianity is one
11. Prophet Elisha cursed a bunch of youths for making fun of a ___ man
12. Lazurus was raised from the ___
14. Matthew 10:3, ____, and Bartholomew; Thomas, and Matthew the publican
16. Prayer topic, often
19. A name for Jesus (3 words)
20. Genesis 6:13, And God said unto Noah, The ___ of all flesh is come
21. ". . . the ___ of God was upon him" (Luke 2:40)
22. ___ of Cyrene
24. What Easter celebrates
26. Go against God
28. First gardener
29. Name for Jesus
32. Roman 3:23, For ____ have sinned, and come short of the glory of God
33. Whom we worship (3 words)
35. The devil
37. Human-made rules that can contradict 21-Down (2 words)
40. Apostle to the Gentiles
41. Adam's mate
43. Old Testament books labeled I and II
44. ". . . for we have seen his ___ in the east"
45. Jesus was born via it (2 words)
46. Genesis 12:9, And Abram journeyed, going on ___ toward the south
47. Prophet who anointed Saul and David as kings
48. Salome danced for him

Down

1. Day of rest
2. 2 Chronicles 3:9, And the weight of the ___ was fifty shekels of gold
3. What Jesus recommends one offer to his brothers
4. Matthew 4:4, But he answered and said, ___ written, Man shall not live by bread alone (2 words)
5. Atonement for sins
6. Genesis 1:4, And God ___ the light, that it was good
7. What 48-Across was king of
10. Psalm 55:17, Evening, and morning, and at ___, will I pray, and cry aloud
13. Book before Haggai
15. Belief that each individual human soul existed before conception (2 words)
17. What God gave Moses on Mount Sinai (2 words)
18. Where there will be no more crying
19. Aaron's rod, at one point
21. It is greater than 37-Across (2 words)
23. Three came from the East
25. Part of a Bible book
27. Remains of a burnt offering?
30. See 35-Across
31. Michael or Gabriel
34. Opposite of 18-Down
36. Body of Christians, especially on Sundays?
38. Mark, for one
39. The Christ
40. One of 150 in the Bible
41. ". . . Lord is against them that do ___" (Psalm 34:16)
42. Do ___ others as . . .

Reading the Bible in One Year

Here is a precise schedule for reading the Bible in one year that offers easily digested chunks of God's Word for consistent study. You may start on any date.

Day 1—Genesis 1–3

Day 2—Genesis 4–8

Day 3—Genesis 9–13

Day 4—Genesis 14–17

Day 5—Genesis 18–20

Day 6—Genesis 21–23

Day 7—Genesis 24–26

Day 8—Genesis 27–29

Day 9—Genesis 30–32

Day 10—Genesis 33–35

Day 11—Genesis 36–38

Day 12—Genesis 39–41

Day 13—Genesis 42–44

Day 14—Genesis 45–47

Day 15—Genesis 48–50

Day 16—Exodus 1–3

Day 17—Exodus 4–6

Day 18—Exodus 7–9

Day 19—Exodus 10–12

Day 20—Exodus 13–16

Day 21—Exodus 17–20

Day 22—Exodus 21–23

Day 23—Exodus 24–27

Day 24—Exodus 28–31

Day 25—Exodus 32–34

Day 26—Exodus 35–37

Day 27—Exodus 38–40

Day 28—Leviticus 1–4

Day 29—Leviticus 5–7

Day 30—Leviticus 8–10

Day 31—Leviticus 11–13

Day 32—Leviticus 14–16

Day 33—Leviticus 17–19

Day 34—Leviticus 20–21

Day 35—Leviticus 22–23

Day 36—Leviticus 24–25

Day 37—Leviticus 26–27

Day 38—Numbers 1–2

Day 39—Numbers 3–4

Day 40—Numbers 5–6

Day 41—Numbers 7

Day 42—Numbers 8–10

Day 43—Numbers 11–13

Day 44—Numbers 14–15

Day 45—Numbers 16–18

Day 46—Numbers 19–22

Day 47—Numbers 23–25

Day 48—Numbers 26–28

Day 49—Numbers 29–31

Day 50—Numbers 32–34

Day 51—Numbers 35–36

Day 52—Deuteronomy 1–2

Day 53—Deuteronomy 3–4

Day 54—Deuteronomy 5–8

Day 55—Deuteronomy 9–11

Day 56—Deuteronomy 12–15

Day 57—Deuteronomy 16–19

Day 58—Deuteronomy 20–22

Day 59—Deuteronomy 23–25

Day 60—Deuteronomy 26–27

Day 61—Deuteronomy 28–29

Day 62—Deuteronomy 30–32

Day 63—Deuteronomy 33–34

Day 64—Joshua 1–3

Day 65—Joshua 4–7

Day 66—Joshua 8–10

Day 67—Joshua 11–13

Day 68—Joshua 14–17

Day 69—Joshua 18–20

Day 70—Joshua 21–22

Day 71—Joshua 23–24

Day 72—Judges 1–3

Day 73—Judges 4–5

Day 74—Judges 6–8

Day 75—Judges 9–10

Day 76—Judges 11–13

Day 77—Judges 14–16

Day 78—Judges 17–19

Day 79—Judges 20–21

Day 80—Ruth 1–4

Day 81—1 Samuel 1–3

Day 82—1 Samuel 4–7

Day 83—1 Samuel 8–11

Day 84—1 Samuel 12–14

Day 85—1 Samuel 15–17

Day 86—1 Samuel 18–19

Day 87—1 Samuel 20–22

Day 88—1 Samuel 23–25

Day 89—1 Samuel 26–28

Day 90—1 Samuel 29–31

Day 91—2 Samuel 1–3

Day 92—2 Samuel 4–7

Day 93—2 Samuel 8–10

Day 94—2 Samuel 11–12

Day 95—2 Samuel 13–16

Day 96—2 Samuel 17–19

Day 97—2 Samuel 20–22

Day 98—2 Samuel 23–24

Special References

Alphabetical List of Names of God

Advocate—1 John 2:1

Almighty—Revelation 1:8

Alpha and Omega—Revelation 1:8

Amen—Revelation 3:14

Anointed One—Psalm 2:2

Apostle—Hebrews 3:1

Author and finisher of our faith—Hebrews 12:2

Beginning and end—Revelation 21:6

Beginning of the creation of God—Revelation 3:14

Bishop of your souls—1 Peter 2:25

Branch—Zechariah 3:8

Bread of life—John 6:35, 48

Bridegroom—Matthew 9:15

Carpenter—Mark 6:3

Chief shepherd—1 Peter 5:4

The Christ—Matthew 1:16

Comforter—Jeremiah 8:18

Consolation of Israel—Luke 2:25

Corner stone—Ephesians 2:20

Dayspring—Luke 1:78

Day star—2 Peter 1:19

Deliverer—Romans 11:26

Desire of all nations—Haggai 2:7

Door of the sheep—John 10:7

Emmanuel—Matthew 1:23

Everlasting Father—Isaiah 9:6

Faithful and true witness—Revelation 3:14

Firstfruits—1 Corinthians 15:23

Foundation—Isaiah 28:16

Fountain—Zechariah 13:1

Friend of publicans and sinners—Matthew 11:19

God—John 1:1

Good shepherd—John 10:11

Governor—Matthew 2:6

Great shepherd—Hebrews 13:20

Guide—Psalm 48:14

Head of the body (church)—Colossians 1:18

High priest—Hebrews 3:1; 4:15

Holy One of Israel—Isaiah 41:14

Horn of salvation—Luke 1:69

I Am—Exodus 3:14

Jehovah—Psalm 83:18

Jesus—Matthew 1:21

King of Israel—Matthew 27:42

King of Kings—1 Timothy 6:15; Revelation 19:16

Lamb of God—John 1:29

Last Adam—1 Corinthians 15:45

Life—John 11:25

Light of the world—John 8:12; 9:5

Lion of the tribe of Judah—Revelation 5:5

Lord of Lords—1 Timothy 6:15; Revelation 19:16

Master—Matthew 23:8

Mediator—1 Timothy 2:5

Messiah—John 1:41

Mighty God—Isaiah 9:6

Morning star—Revelation 22:16

Nazarene—Matthew 2:23

Our passover—1 Corinthians 5:7

Potentate—1 Timothy 6:15

Prince of Peace—Isaiah 9:6

Prophet—Acts 3:22

Propitiation—1 John 2:2

Purifier—Malachi 3:3

Rabbi—John 1:49

Ransom—1 Timothy 2:6

Redeemer—Isaiah 41:14

Refiner—Malachi 3:3

Refuge—Isaiah 25:4

Resurrection—John 11:25

Righteousness—Jeremiah 23:6

Rock—Deuteronomy 32:4; 2 Samuel 22:47

Root and the offspring of David—Revelation 22:16

Rose of Sharon—Song of Solomon 2:1

Sacrifice—Ephesians 5:2

Saviour—Luke 1:47

Seed of David—2 Timothy 2:8

Seed of the woman—Genesis 3:15

Servant—Isaiah 42:1

Shepherd—1 Peter 2:25

Shiloh—Genesis 49:10

Son of David—Matthew 15:22

Son of God—Luke 1:35

Son of man—Matthew 18:11

Son of Mary—Mark 6:3

Son of the Most High—Luke 1:32

Stone—Isaiah 28:16

Sun of righteousness—Malachi 4:2

Teacher—Matthew 26:18

Truth—John 14:6

Vine—John 15:1

Way—John 14:6

Wonderful Counselor—Isaiah 9:6

Word—John 1:1

The Ten Commandments

1. Thou shalt have no other gods before me. (Exodus 20:3)
2. Thou shalt not make unto thee any graven image, or any likeness of any thing that is in heaven above, or that is in the earth beneath, or that is in the water under the earth. (Exodus 20:4)
3. Thou shalt not take the name of the LORD thy God in vain; for the LORD will not hold him guiltless that taketh his name in vain. (Exodus 20:7)
4. Remember the sabbath day, to keep it holy. (Exodus 20:8)
5. Honour thy father and thy mother: that thy days may be long upon the land which the LORD thy God giveth thee. (Exodus 20:12)

6. Thou shalt not kill. (Exodus 20:13)

7. Thou shalt not commit adultery. (Exodus 20:14)

8. Thou shalt not steal. (Exodus 20:15)

9. Thou shalt not bear false witness against thy neighbour. (Exodus 20:16)

10. Thou shalt not covet thy neighbour's house, thou shalt not covet thy neighbour's wife, nor his manservant, nor his maidservant, nor his ox, nor his ass, nor any thing that is thy neighbour's. (Exodus 20:17)

The Seven "I Am" Statements of Jesus

1. And Jesus said unto them, I am the bread of life. (John 6:35)

2. Then spake Jesus again unto them, saying, I am the light of the world. (John 8:12)

3. Then said Jesus unto them again, Verily, verily, I say unto you, I am the door of the sheep. (John 10:7).

4. I am the good shepherd: the good shepherd giveth his life for the sheep. (John 10:11)

5. Jesus said unto her, I am the resurrection, and the life. (John 11:25)

6. Jesus saith unto him, I am the way, the truth, and the life: no man cometh unto the Father, but by me. (John 14:6)

7. I am the true vine, and my Father is the husbandman. (John 15:1)

The Eight Beatitudes

1. Blessed are the poor in spirit: for theirs is the kingdom of heaven. (Matthew 5:3)

2. Blessed are they that mourn: for they shall be comforted. (Matthew 5:4)

3. Blessed are the meek: for they shall inherit the earth. (Matthew 5:5)

4. Blessed are they which do hunger and thirst after righteousness: for they shall be filled. (Matthew 5:6)

5. Blessed are the merciful: for they shall obtain mercy. (Matthew 5:7)

6. Blessed are the pure in heart: for they shall see God. (Matthew 5:8)

7. Blessed are the peacemakers: for they shall be called the children of God. (Matthew 5:9)

8. Blessed are they which are persecuted for righteousness' sake: for theirs is the kingdom of heaven. (Matthew 5:10)

Scripture Is Inspired by God

1. All Scripture is given by inspiration of God, and is profitable for doctrine, for reproof, for correction, for instruction in righteousness, that the man of God may be perfect, thoroughly furnished unto all good works. (2 Timothy 3:16–17)

2. Knowing this first, that no prophecy of Scripture is of any private interpretation. For the prophecy came not in old time by the will of man: but holy men of God spake as they were moved by the Holy Ghost. (2 Peter 1:20–21)

The Twenty-Four Titles of Christ

1. Adam, last Adam (1 Corinthians 15:45)

2. Alpha and Omega (Revelation 21:6)

3. Bread of life (John 6:35)

4. Chief corner stone (Ephesians 2:20)

5. Chief shepherd (1 Peter 5:4)

6. Emmanuel, God with us (Matthew 1:23)

7. Firstborn from the dead (Colossians 1:18)

8. Good shepherd (John 10:11)

9. Great shepherd of the sheep (Hebrews 13:20)

10. High Priest (Hebrews 3:1)

11. Holy One of God (Mark 1:24)

12. King of Kings, Lord of Lords (Revelation 19:16)

13. Lamb of God (John 1:29)

14. Light of the world (John 9:5)

15. Lion of Judah (Revelation 5:5)

16. Lord of glory (1 Corinthians 2:8)

17. Mediator between God and men (1 Timothy 2.5)

18. Only begotten of the Father (John 1:14)

19. Prophet (Acts 3:22)

20. Saviour (Luke 1:47)

21. Seed of Abraham (Galatians 3:16)

22. Son of God (Mark 1:1)

23. Son of man (Matthew 18:11)

24. The Word (John 1:1)

The Twelve Apostles

1. Simon Peter

2. Andrew (Peter's brother)

3. James (son of Zebedee)

4. John (James's brother)

5. Philip

6. Bartholomew

7. Thomas

8. Matthew

9. James (son of Alphaeus)

10. Thaddaeus

11. Simon

12. Judas Iscariot (After Judas betrayed the Lord Jesus Christ, Matthias was chosen by the other disciples as his replacement.)

Seven Women Who Had Miraculous Births

1. Sarah, Abraham's wife (Genesis 11:30)

2. Rebekah, Isaac's wife (Genesis 25:21)

3. Rachel, Jacob's wife (Genesis 29:31)

4. Samson's mother (Judges 13:2)

5. Hannah, Samuel's mother (1 Samuel 1:5)

6. Elisabeth, the mother of John the Baptist (Luke 1:7)

7. Mary, the virgin mother of Jesus (Luke 1:26–2:20)

Ten People Who Were Raised from the Dead

1. Widow of Zarephath's son, by Elijah (1 Kings 17:22)

2. Shunammite woman's son, by Elisha (2 Kings 4:34–35)

3. The man who came in contact with Elisha's bones (2 Kings 13:20–21)

4. Widow of Nain's son, raised by Jesus (Luke 7:14–15)

5. Jairus's daughter, raised by Jesus (Luke 8:52–56)

6. Lazarus, raised by Jesus (John 11)

7. Jesus (Matthew 28:6; Acts 2:24)

8. The mass of holy people in tombs when Jesus gave up his spirit (Matthew 27:52–53)

9. Dorcas, by Peter (Acts 9:40)

10. Eutychus, by Paul (Acts 20:9–12)

Witnesses Who Saw Jesus Christ after His Resurrection

1. Mary Magdalene (Mark 16:9)
2. The other women (Matthew 28:9)
3. The two disciples (Luke 24:15)
4. The eleven disciples (Luke 24:36)
5. Peter (1 Corinthians 15:5)
6. Five hundred brethren (1 Corinthians 15:6)
7. Ten disciples (John 20:19)
8. James (1 Corinthians 15:7)
9. Witnesses at his ascension (Luke 24:50)
10. Paul (Acts 9:5; 1 Corinthians 15:8)

Score Card

	Possible Scores	Bonus Points	Your Scores
	12,909	2,475	
Section 1: The Must-Know Section			
1 Do Not Be Fooled	150		
2 The Essentials	100		
3 Books of the Bible	186		
5 The Ultimate Books of the Bible Test	150		
6 Facts about the King James Bible	80		
8 450 Key Verses	900		
10 The Ten Plagues Inflicted on Egypt	280		
All about Money			
11 Maintaining Budgets	20		
12 Debt	18		
13 Wealth	16		
15 Being Happy with What You Have	20		
16 Giving and Being Generous	44		
17 Receiving	10		
18 Running a Business	32		
19 Investing	12		

		Possible Scores	Bonus Points	Your Scores
20	God's Provisions	18		
21	Lending	24		
22	Planning for the Future	34		
23	The Love of Money	6		
24	Being Truly Prosperous	28		
25	Being a Good Steward over One's Money	12		
26	Saving	10		
27	Tithing	34		
28	Ultimate Success	24		
	Specialized Multiple-Choice Trivia			
30	All about Food	12		
31	From Sweet to Bitter	10		
32	Residential Area	12		
33	Kiddie Land	10		
35	Window Display	10		
36	That Makes Scents	10		
37	Nighty-Night	11		
38	Wedding Bells	8		
39	Farming	10		
40	Rulers	13		
41	The Apostles	4		
42	Doorway	11		
43	In the Military	9		
44	Women and Rulers	10		
45	Hair Apparent	11		
46	Anointment	9		
47	The Swift	9		
48	Special Women	10		
49	Funny Money	10		
50	Fly High	6		
51	What's That I Hear?	9		
53	The Story of Joseph	12		
54	Have a Laugh	10		

		Possible Scores	Bonus Points	Your Scores
55	Anything Goes	50		
56	Priests	8		
57	Lions' Den	8		
58	More of Anything Goes	70		
	Scripture Fill in the Blanks			
60	Fill in the Blanks	30		
61	Scriptures on Salvation	12		
62	Scriptures on Security	50		
63	Scriptures on Prayer	44		
64	Scriptures on Temptation	16		
65	Scriptures on Never Losing Faith	50		
66	Scriptures on Hope	16		
67	Scriptures on Love	92		
68	Crossword Puzzle 1		25	
Section 2: The Advanced Section				
	Specialized True or False Trivia			
70	Group 1	20		
71	Group 2	20		
72	Group 3	20		
73	Group 4	20		
74	Group 5	20		
75	Group 6	20		
76	Group 7	20		
77	Group 8	20		
78	Group 9	20		
79	Group 10	20		
80	Group 11	20		
81	Group 12	20		
82	Group 13	20		
83	Group 14	20		
84	Group 15	20		

		Possible Scores	Bonus Points	Your Scores
85	Group 16	20		
86	Group 17	20		
87	Group 18	20		
88	Group 19	20		
89	Group 20	20		
90	Group 21	20		
91	Group 22	20		
92	Group 23	20		
93	Group 24	20		
94	Group 25	20		
95	Group 26	20		
96	Group 27	20		
97	Group 28	20		
98	Group 29	20		
99	Group 30	10		
	Scripture Trivia			
101	Memory Verses	150		
103	Scrambled Scriptures	300		
	Word Searches			
105	Names of God Part 1	10		
106	Names of God Part 2	10		
107	Names of God Part 3	25		
108	People and Angels Part 1	10		
109	People and Angels Part 2	10		
110	People and Angels Part 3	25		
111	Abraham's Progeny Part 1	10		
112	Abraham's Progeny Part 2	10		
113	Abraham's Progeny Part 3	25		
114	Cities of Judah Part 1	10		
115	Cities of Judah Part 2	10		
116	Cities of Judah Part 3	25		
117	Women in the Bible Part 1	10		
118	Women in the Bible Part 2	10		

		Possible Scores	Bonus Points	Your Scores
119	Women in the Bible Part 3	25		
120	Paul's Journeys Part 1	10		
121	Paul's Journeys Part 2	10		
122	Paul's Journeys Part 3	25		
123	Prisoners and Exiles Part 1	10		
124	Prisoners and Exiles Part 2	10		
125	Prisoners and Exiles Part 3	25		
126	The Book of Genesis	771		
128	The Miracles of Jesus	370		
129	Who Is?	100		

Section 3: The Bible Brilliant Section

		Possible Scores	Bonus Points	Your Scores
130	Crossword Puzzle 2		25	
131	Crossword Puzzle 3		25	

Thirteen Groups of Trivia

		Possible Scores	Bonus Points	Your Scores
132	Group 1	250		
133	Group 2	250		
134	Group 3	250		
135	Group 4	250		
136	Group 5	250		
137	Group 6	250		
138	Group 7	250		
139	Group 8	250		
140	Group 9	250		
141	Group 10	250		
142	Group 11	250		
143	Group 12	250		
144	Group 13	250		
145	Fulfilled Prophecies about Jesus	720		
146	100 Common Phrases That Originated in the Bible	1000		
147	Imprisoned	60		
148	The Fast 100	100		

		Possible Scores	Bonus Points	Your Scores
	Trivia by Topic			
150	Fasting	20		
151	Wine	16		
152	The Apostles	8		
153	Kings	20		
154	Heaven Awaits	24		
155	Hairy and Hairless	24		
156	Citified	22		
157	Are You Speaking to Me?	18		
158	Jesus	24		
159	Firsts	20		
160	Costly	20		
161	Women	60		
162	Who Asked?	24		
163	Hearing from God	16		
164	Bible Brilliant Level	40		
165	Anything Goes	92		
166	Royalty	20		
167	More Firsts	20		
168	More Random Bible Trivia	50		
	Word Fill			
169	Encouragement	85		
170	Friendship	55		
171	Forgiveness	75		
172	Inspiration	110		
173	Anger	60		
174	Who Is God?	520		
Section 4: The Bonus Section				
175	The Book of Revelation		860	
176	Food by the Book		1,100	
177	The Sixty Hardest Questions		1,200	
178	Crossword Puzzle 4		50	
179	Crossword Puzzle 5		50	

Answers

Section 1: The Must-Know Section

1. Do Not Be Fooled

1. False, that phrase does not appear in the Bible at all.
2. False, the Bible does not mention an "apple," only "fruit."
3. False, that phrase is from a seventeenth-century poem by Samuel Butler.
4. False, that phrase is from a poem by English poet William Cowper, who was born in 1731.
5. False, that phrase is not written in any book of the Bible.
6. False, the Bible does not give a specific number of wise men.
7. False, "The Little Drummer Boy" is a Christmas carol and is not based on any biblical character.
8. False, according to Jonah 1:17, Jonah was in the belly of "a great fish."
9. False, the Bible never mentions Satan taking the form of or entering into the serpent in the Garden of Eden.
10. False, this phrase does not appear anywhere in the Bible.
11. False, 1 Timothy 6:10 says, "For *the love of* money is the root of all evil."
12. False, "To thine own self be true" was written by Shakespeare in act 1 of *Hamlet*.
13. False, "Love the sinner, hate the sin" does not appear in the Bible. St. Augustine wrote it in a letter in the fifth century AD.
14. False, according to Matthew 2:11, by the time the wise men visited Jesus, he was in a "house."
15. False, there were two sets. Moses broke one set in anger when he saw the false idol, the golden calf (Exodus 32:19; 34:1).

I hope you scored well on your first test. Simply knowing that these fifteen "facts" are all false puts you ahead of the vast majority of the public. You are well on your way to becoming Bible brilliant.

2. The Essentials

1. "In the beginning God created the heaven and the earth" (Genesis 1:1)
2. Mary (Matthew 1:18)
3. Garden of Eden (Genesis 2:8)
4. Serpent (Genesis 3:1–6)
5. Crucifixion (Mark 15:24–25)
6. Death (Romans 6:23)
7. Aaron (Exodus 7:1)
8. Murder (Genesis 4:8)
9. Daniel (Daniel 6:16)
10. God (Genesis 1:27)
11. "Our Father which art in heaven" (Matthew 6:9)
12. Loaves of bread and fishes (Matthew 14:15–20)
13. Rib (Genesis 2.21–22)
14. Blasphemy against the Holy Ghost (Matthew 12:31; Mark 3:29)
15. Dust (Genesis 2:7)
16. Flood (Genesis 7:7)
17. Peter (Matthew 26:69–74)
18. Crown of thorns (Matthew 27:29)
19. Cain (Genesis 4:9)
20. Stone (Exodus 34:1; Deuteronomy 5:22)
21. Twelve (Luke 6:13)
22. Shepherds (Luke 2:8–17)
23. Exodus
24. Shepherd (1 Samuel 17:12–15)
25. Genesis
26. Matthew
27. He struck him with a stone from his sling (1 Samuel 17:48–50)
28. Judaea (Matthew 3:1)
29. This is Jesus the King of the Jews (Matthew 27:37)
30. Manger (Luke 2:7)
31. Abraham (James 2:21–22)
32. She was a virgin (Matthew 1:22–25)
33. Forty (Genesis 7:12)
34. Moses (Exodus 2:3)
35. He was swallowed by a great fish (Jonah 1:17)
36. She was Naomi's daughter-in-law (Ruth 1:4)
37. Joseph (Matthew 1:18–19)
38. Psalms
39. Swine (Matthew 8:32)
40. Psalm 23 (Psalm 23:1)
41. Paul (Romans 1:1–Jude 1:25)
42. They tossed him into a pit and eventually sold him to strangers (Genesis 37:23–28)
43. Jesse (1 Samuel 17:12; Ruth 4:17, 22)
44. David (Matthew 1:6)
45. Revelation
46. Amen (Revelation 22:21)
47. Sixty-six
48. He washed their feet (John 13:1–5)
49. Cain (Genesis 4:1)
50. Six days (Exodus 20:11)

3. Books of the Bible

1.
  2. Exodus
  4. Numbers
2.
  1. Genesis
  5. Deuteronomy
3.
  3. Leviticus
  5. Deuteronomy
4.
  2. Exodus
  3. Leviticus

5.
  4. Numbers
  6. Joshua
6.
  5. Deuteronomy
  7. Judges
  8. Ruth
7.
  7. Judges
  9. 1 Samuel
8.
  5. Deuteronomy
  8. Ruth
  10. 2 Samuel

9.
  6. Joshua
  8. Ruth
10.
  8. Ruth
  10. 2 Samuel
  12. 2 Kings
11.
  9. 1 Samuel
  11. 1 Kings
  13. 1 Chronicles
12.
  10. 2 Samuel
  12. 2 Kings

13.
- 8. Ruth
- 11. 1 Kings
- 13. 1 Chronicles

14.
- 12. 2 Kings
- 15. Ezra
- 18. Job

15.
- 15. Ezra
- 17. Esther
- 19. Psalms

16.
- 16. Nehemiah
- 20. Proverbs

17.
- 15. Ezra
- 18. Job
- 20. Proverbs

18.
- 12. 2 Kings
- 15. Ezra
- 17. Esther
- 20. Proverbs

19.
- 11. 1 Kings
- 16. Nehemiah
- 19. Psalms

20.
- 17. Esther
- 20. Proverbs
- 22. Song of Solomon

21.
- 19. Psalms
- 21. Ecclesiastes
- 23. Isaiah

22.
- 17. Esther
- 21. Ecclesiastes
- 24. Jeremiah

23.
- 18. Job
- 22. Song of Solomon
- 25. Lamentations

24.
- 20. Proverbs
- 22. Song of Solomon
- 26. Ezekiel
- 29. Joel

25.
- 22. Song of Solomon
- 25. Lamentations
- 30. Amos

26.
- 23. Isaiah
- 26. Ezekiel
- 28. Hosea

27.
- 20. Proverbs
- 24. Jeremiah
- 27. Daniel
- 30. Amos

28.
- 22. Song of Solomon
- 25. Lamentations
- 29. Joel

29.
- 23. Isaiah
- 26. Ezekiel
- 27. Daniel
- 29. Joel

30.
- 20. Proverbs
- 24. Jeremiah
- 27. Daniel
- 30. Amos

31.
- 26. Ezekiel
- 29. Joel
- 32. Jonah
- 34. Nahum

32.
- 28. Hosea
- 31. Obadiah
- 33. Micah

33.
- 26. Ezekiel
- 31. Obadiah
- 34. Nahum

34.
- 27. Daniel
- 32. Jonah
- 35. Habakkuk

35.
- 32. Jonah
- 35. Habakkuk
- 37. Haggai

36.
- 33. Micah
- 36. Zephaniah
- 39. Malachi

37.
- 31. Obadiah
- 34. Nahum
- 37. Haggai
- 39. Malachi

38.
- 32. Jonah
- 35. Habakkuk
- 37. Haggai

39.
- 30. Amos
- 33. Micah
- 36. Zephaniah
- 38. Zechariah

40.
- 42. Luke

41.
- 40. Matthew
- 43. John

42.
- 41. Mark
- 44. Acts

43.
- 41. Mark
- 43. John
- 45. Romans
- 46. 1 Corinthians
- 47. 2 Corinthians
- 49. Ephesians

44.
- 44. Acts
- 47. 2 Corinthians
- 50. Philippians

45.
- 43. John
- 44. Acts
- 46. 1 Corinthians
- 48. Galatians

46.
- 45. Romans
- 48. Galatians
- 51. Colossians
- 53. 2 Thessalonians

47.
- 47. 2 Corinthians
- 49. Ephesians
- 51. Colossians
- 55. 2 Timothy

48.
- 50. Philippians
- 52. 1 Thessalonians

49.
- 49. Ephesians
- 51. Colossians
- 56. Titus
- 58. Hebrews

50.
- 50. Philippians
- 53. 2 Thessalonians
- 57. Philemon
- 59. James

51.
- 49. Ephesians
- 54. 1 Timothy
- 55. 2 Timothy
- 57. Philemon
- 59. James

52.
- 50. Philippians
- 51. Colossians
- 56. Titus
- 59. James

53.
- 53. 2 Thessalonians
- 57. Philemon
- 60. 1 Peter

54.
- 53. 2 Thessalonians
- 55. 2 Timothy
- 58. Hebrews

55.
- 59. James
- 62. 1 John

56.
- 55. 2 Timothy
- 56. Titus
- 60. 1 Peter
- 62. 1 John

57.
- 61. 2 Peter
- 64. 3 John

58.
- 58. Hebrews
- 60. 1 Peter
- 62. 1 John
- 64. 3 John

59.
- 59. James
- 65. Jude

60.
- 56. Titus
- 58. Hebrews
- 61. 2 Peter
- 64. 3 John
- 66. Revelation

5. The Ultimate Books of the Bible Test

1. Genesis
2. Leviticus
3. Deuteronomy
4. Ruth
5. 1 Samuel
6. 2 Kings
7. Ezra
8. Job
9. Ecclesiastes
10. Song of Solomon
11. Lamentations
12. Hosea
13. Amos
14. Obadiah
15. Micah
16. Habakkuk
17. Zechariah
18. Malachi
19. Matthew
20. Luke
21. Acts
22. 1 Corinthians
23. Ephesians
24. Colossians
25. 2 Thessalonians
26. 2 Timothy
27. James
28. 2 Peter
29. 3 John
30. Revelation

6. Facts about the King James Bible

1. C. 1,600 years
2. B. 40
3. C. 66
4. B. 39
5. C. 27
6. C. 5
7. A. Psalm 119
8. C. 176
9. B. Psalms
10. B. 150
11. B. 3 John
12. A. Esther 8:9
13. A. 90
14. B. Jesus wept (John 11:35)
15. C. 876 times
16. C. Over 1,200

8. 450 Key Verses

1. believeth
2. Word
3. Father
4. nations
5. sinned
6. grace
7. beginning
8. power
9. All
10. Jesus
11. death
12. Repent
13. believe
14. good
15. Light
16. image
17. bodies
18. sinners
19. power
20. born
21. gospel
22. thief
23. Word
24. salvation
25. prayers
26. Spirit
27. Trust
28. evil
29. saved
30. world
31. troubled
32. baptized
33. evangelists
34. sin
35. rest
36. faith
37. created
38. gospel
39. cleanse
40. Pentecost
41. Christ
42. faith
43. approved
44. condemnation
45. saved
46. free
47. government
48. love
49. one
50. commandment
51. truth
52. Christ
53. sins
54. Father

55. darkness
56. spirit
57. Confess
58. virgin
59. believe
60. water
61. mind
62. sin
63. wrath
64. nothing
65. witnesses
66. made
67. rock
68. crucified
69. throne
70. fulfil
71. faith
72. righteousness
73. Spirit
74. truth
75. blood
76. salvation
77. truth
78. power
79. God
80. tables
81. baptized
82. righteous
83. woman
84. faith
85. Father
86. death
87. spirit
88. kind
89. joy
90. firstborn
91. mind
92. hope
93. praise
94. cloud
95. Samaria
96. humbly
97. Sanctify
98. Paul
99. house
100. resurrection
101. Abraham
102. tongues
103. branches

104. baptized
105. child
106. serpent
107. wisdom
108. prophets
109. truth's
110. eternal
111. water
112. disciples
113. instructed
114. voice
115. tasted
116. Father
117. hope
118. will
119. begotten
120. Abram
121. Spirit
122. vine
123. life
124. Let
125. light
126. chosen
127. sixth
128. judgment
129. Rabbi
130. light
131. Moses
132. deceived
133. life
134. Ask
135. Blessed
136. birth
137. excuse
138. Jesus
139. light
140. hope
141. forsake
142. spirit
143. gift
144. treasures
145. preach
146. one
147. promise
148. Jesus
149. sick
150. Son
151. principalities
152. pray

153. Repent
154. faith
155. Lord
156. saved
157. angel
158. fruitful
159. workmanship
160. sin
161. grace
162. salvation
163. death
164. brother
165. world
166. widows
167. overcome
168. graves
169. scriptures
170. women
171. worshippers
172. Judge
173. mediator
174. wilderness
175. God
176. prisoner
177. Spirit
178. submit
179. sea
180. coming
181. Father
182. disciples
183. lamp
184. man
185. fellowship
186. sins
187. wounded
188. redemption
189. church
190. flesh
191. love
192. Spirit
193. Moses
194. born
195. gate
196. deceiving
197. wife
198. sheep
199. created
200. Christ
201. repent

202. Comforter
203. sins
204. assembling
205. marriage
206. opened
207. earth
208. Submit
209. life
210. stripes
211. world
212. Father
213. elders
214. infirmities
215. Magdalene
216. little
217. sabbath
218. image
219. Father
220. deceitful
221. God
222. Jacob
223. Father
224. scripture
225. mind
226. testify
227. pray
228. love
229. Peter
230. Herod
231. elders
232. Silas
233. cross
234. faith
235. righteous
236. sober
237. peace
238. priest
239. word
240. free
241. gift
242. sin
243. Lucifer
244. forever
245. vain
246. songs
247. thirst
248. serve
249. light
250. led

251. Solomon
252. John
253. Martha
254. against
255. passover
256. light
257. fear
258. words
259. judgment
260. prophecy
261. sin
262. pray
263. footstool
264. work
265. prophets
266. temple
267. sabbath
268. love
269. house
270. mocked
271. life
272. merciful
273. Adultery
274. Jews
275. mercy
276. puffed
277. bread
278. disciples
279. multiplied
280. world
281. Jesus
282. Jesus
283. unbelievers
284. life
285. called
286. sorrows
287. feet
288. people
289. beginning
290. think
291. law
292. Jesus
293. Father
294. walk
295. wilderness
296. miracles
297. many
298. glory
299. nations

300. Peace	331. covenant	362. Rejoice	392. Christ	423. ask
301. spirit	332. condemned	363. judge	393. Peter	424. seven
302. darkness	333. riches	364. bosom	394. repent	425. Mary
303. seventy	334. name	365. law	395. fire	426. Father
304. Pharisees	335. sins	366. love	396. David	427. five
305. Elisabeth	336. proud	367. scriptures	397. world	428. ransom
306. Uzziah	337. tongues	368. love	398. pray	429. masters
307. throne	338. heaven	369. world	399. Blessed	430. Ananias
308. nature	339. firmament	370. enemy	400. ungodly	431. Andrew
309. repent	340. John	371. trump	401. prophet	432. grudge
310. abomination	341. temptation	372. cross	402. fear	433. ghost
311. God	342. enemies	373. commandment	403. servants	434. Salome
312. temple	343. end	374. Timothy	404. God	435. light
313. save	344. written	375. tongues	405. Israel	436. perfect
314. Teaching	345. wise	376. Satan	406. righteous	437. heaven
315. sepulchre	346. Satan	377. tempted	407. sabbath	438. flesh
316. priest	347. tooth	378. Spirit	408. unclean	439. sword
317. name	348. him	379. household	409. sabbath	440. knowledge
318. God	349. world	380. Antioch	410. sixth	441. iniquity
319. gospel	350. tempted	381. perish	411. possessed	442. rich
320. Father	351. received	382. wrath	412. Jesus	443. offspring
321. prison	352. peace	383. Christ	413. Moses	444. stewards
322. times	353. light	384. power	414. fear	445. women
323. fruit	354. soul	385. godliness	415. unbelieving	446. deceit
324. gods	355. abominations	386. dead	416. prophets	447. mind
325. Peter	356. season	387. Philip	417. receive	448. parents
326. forgive	357. prophesy	388. bread	418. save	449. beginning
327. men	358. Jerusalem	389. word	419. Israel	450. thoughts
328. masters	359. incense	390. church	420. kingdom	
329. heaven	360. equal	391. mother	421. Blessed	
330. Son	361. virgin		422. faith	

10. The Ten Plagues Inflicted on Egypt

1.
  1. Water turned into blood

2.
  5. Death of livestock

3.
  9. Darkness

4.
  1. Water turned into blood
  4. Flies
  5. Death of livestock
  8. Locusts
  9. Darkness

5.
  2. Frogs
  3. Lice
  6. Boils
  7. Hailstorm

6.
  2. Frogs
  3. Lice
  4. Flies
  6. Boils
  7. Hailstorm
  9. Darkness

7.
  1. Water turned into blood
  2. Frogs
  3. Lice
  4. Flies
  5. Death of livestock
  6. Boils
  7. Hailstorm
  8. Locusts
  9. Darkness
  10. Death of all firstborn

11. Maintaining Budgets

1. Proverbs 6:6–8
   Go to the ant, thou <u>sluggard</u>; consider her ways, and be wise: Which having no <u>guide</u>, overseer, or ruler, Provideth her meat in the summer, and gathereth her food in the <u>harvest</u>.

2. Proverbs 21:5
   The <u>thoughts</u> of the <u>diligent</u> tend only to plenteousness; but of every one that is <u>hasty</u> only to want.

3. Proverbs 22:3
   A prudent man <u>foreseeth</u> the evil, and <u>hideth</u> himself: but the <u>simple</u> pass on, and are <u>punished</u>.

4. Proverbs 24:3–4
   Through <u>wisdom</u> is an house builded; and by understanding it is established: And by <u>knowledge</u> shall the <u>chambers</u> be <u>filled</u> with all precious and <u>pleasant</u> riches.

5. Proverbs 25:28
   He that hath no <u>rule</u> over his own <u>spirit</u> is like a <u>city</u> that is broken down, and without <u>walls</u>.

6. Proverbs 27:12
   A <u>prudent</u> man foreseeth the <u>evil</u>, and hideth <u>himself</u>; but the simple <u>pass</u> on, and are punished.

7. Proverbs 27:23
   Be thou <u>diligent</u> to know the state of thy <u>flocks</u>, and <u>look</u> well to thy <u>herds</u>.

8. Proverbs 27:26
   The <u>lambs</u> are for thy <u>clothing</u>, and the goats are the <u>price</u> of the <u>field</u>.

9. Luke 14:28–30
   For which of you, intending to <u>build</u> a <u>tower</u>, sitteth not down first, and counteth the cost, whether he have sufficient to <u>finish</u> it? Lest haply, after he hath laid the <u>foundation</u>, and is not able to finish it, all that behold it begin to <u>mock</u> him, Saying, This man began to build, and was not able to finish.

10. 1 Corinthians 16:2
    Upon the first day of the <u>week</u> let every one of you <u>lay</u> by him in store, as God hath <u>prospered</u> him, that there be no <u>gatherings</u> when I come.

12. Debt

1. Exodus 22:14
   And if a man <u>borrow</u> ought of his neighbour, and it be <u>hurt</u>, or <u>die</u>, the owner thereof being not with it, he shall surely make it <u>good</u>.

2. Deuteronomy 15:6
   For the Lord thy God blesseth thee, as he <u>promised</u> thee: and thou shalt lend unto many <u>nations</u>, but thou shalt not <u>borrow</u>; and thou shalt <u>reign</u> over many nations, but they shall not reign over thee.

3. Deuteronomy 28:12
   The Lord shall open unto thee his good <u>treasure</u>, the <u>heaven</u> to give the rain unto thy land in his <u>season</u>, and to bless all the work of thine <u>hand</u>: and thou shalt lend unto many nations, and thou shalt not borrow.

4. 2 Kings 4:7
   Then she came and told the man of <u>God</u>. And he said, Go, sell the <u>oil</u>, and pay thy <u>debt</u>, and live thou and thy <u>children</u> of the rest.

5. Psalm 37:21
   The wicked borroweth, and <u>payeth</u> not again: but the <u>righteous</u> sheweth <u>mercy</u>, and giveth.

6. Proverbs 22:7
   The <u>rich</u> ruleth over the <u>poor</u>, and the bor<u>rower</u> is servant to the <u>lender</u>.

7. Proverbs 22:26–27
   Be not thou one of them that strike <u>hands</u>, or of them that are <u>sureties</u> for <u>debts</u>. If thou hast <u>nothing</u> to pay, why should he take away thy <u>bed</u> from under thee?

8. Ecclesiastes 5:5
   <u>Better</u> is it that thou shouldest not <u>vow</u>, than that thou shouldest vow and not <u>pay</u>.

9. Romans 13:8
   Owe no <u>man</u> any thing, but to love one an<u>other</u>: for he that loveth another hath fulfilled the <u>law</u>.

13. Wealth

1. Exodus 23:12
   Six days thou shalt do thy work, and on the <u>seventh</u> day thou shalt rest: that thine <u>ox</u> and thine ass may rest, and the son of thy <u>handmaid</u>, and the <u>stranger</u>, may be <u>refreshed</u>.

2. Proverbs 12:11
   He that tilleth his <u>land</u> shall be satisfied with <u>bread</u>: but he that followeth <u>vain</u> persons is <u>void</u> of understanding.

3. Proverbs 13:11
   <u>Wealth</u> gotten by <u>vanity</u> shall be <u>diminished</u>: but he that gathereth by labour shall <u>increase</u>.

4. Proverbs 14:15
   The <u>simple</u> believeth every <u>word</u>: but the prudent <u>man</u> looketh <u>well</u> to his going.

5. Proverbs 19:2
   Also, that the soul be without <u>knowledge</u>, it is not <u>good</u>; and he that hasteth with his <u>feet</u> <u>sinneth</u>.

6. Proverbs 21:5
   The <u>thoughts</u> of the <u>diligent</u> <u>tend</u> only to plenteousness; but of <u>every</u> one that is <u>hasty</u> only to want.

7. Proverbs 23:4
   <u>Labour</u> not to be <u>rich</u>: cease from <u>thine</u> own <u>wisdom</u>.

8. Proverbs 28:19–20
   He that tilleth his land shall have plenty of <u>bread</u>: but he that followeth after <u>vain</u> persons shall have <u>poverty</u> enough. A faithful man shall abound with blessings: but he that maketh haste to be <u>rich</u> shall not be <u>innocent</u>.

15. Being Happy with What You Have

1. Psalm 23:1
   The L<small>ORD</small> is my <u>shepherd</u>; I shall not <u>want</u>.

2. Ecclesiastes 5:10
   He that loveth <u>silver</u> shall not be satisfied with silver; nor he that loveth <u>abundance</u> with <u>increase</u>: this is also <u>vanity</u>.

3. Matthew 6:31–33
   Therefore take no <u>thought</u>, saying, What shall we eat? or, What shall we <u>drink</u>? or, Wherewithal shall we be <u>clothed</u>? (For after all these things do the <u>Gentiles</u> seek:) for your heavenly Father knoweth that ye have need of all these things. But seek ye first the kingdom of God, and his <u>righteousness</u>, and all these things shall be added unto you.

4. Luke 3:14
   And the <u>soldiers</u> likewise demanded of him, saying, And what shall we do? And he said unto them, Do <u>violence</u> to no man, neither accuse any <u>falsely</u>; and be content with your <u>wages</u>.

5. Philippians 4:11–13
   Not that I speak in respect of want: for I have learned, in whatsoever <u>state</u> I am, therewith to be <u>content</u>. I know both how to be abased, and I know how to abound: every where and in all things I am <u>instructed</u> both to be full and to be <u>hungry</u>, both to abound and to suffer need. I can do all things through <u>Christ</u> which strengtheneth me.

6. 1 Thessalonians 4:11
   And that ye study to be <u>quiet</u>, and to do your own <u>business</u>, and to work with your own <u>hands</u>, as we <u>commanded</u> you.

7. 1 Timothy 6:6
   But <u>godliness</u> with <u>contentment</u> is great <u>gain</u>.

8. 1 Timothy 6:7–10
   For we brought nothing into this world, and it is certain we can carry nothing out. And having food and <u>raiment</u> let us be therewith content. But they that will be rich fall into temptation and a snare, and into many <u>foolish</u> and hurtful <u>lusts</u>, which drown men in <u>destruction</u> and perdition. For the love of money is the root of all evil: which while some coveted after, they have erred from the <u>faith</u>, and pierced themselves through with many <u>sorrows</u>.

9. Hebrews 13:5
   Let your <u>conversation</u> be without covetousness; and be content with such things as ye have: for he hath said, I will <u>never</u> leave thee, nor <u>forsake</u> thee.

10. James 4:1–3
    From whence come <u>wars</u> and fightings among you? come they not hence, even of your lusts that <u>war</u> in your <u>members</u>? Ye lust, and have not: ye kill, and desire to have, and cannot obtain: ye fight and war, yet ye have not, because ye ask not. Ye <u>ask</u>, and receive not, because ye ask amiss, that ye may <u>consume</u> it upon your lusts.

16. Giving and Being Generous

1. Deuteronomy 15:10
   Thou shalt surely give him, and thine <u>heart</u> shall not be grieved when thou givest unto him: because that for this thing the Lord thy God shall <u>bless</u> thee in all thy <u>works</u>, and in all that thou puttest thine <u>hand</u> unto.

2. Deuteronomy 16:17
   Every <u>man</u> shall give as he is able, according to the <u>blessing</u> of the Lord thy <u>God</u> which he hath given <u>thee</u>.

3. 1 Chronicles 29:9
   Then the <u>people</u> rejoiced, for that they offered willingly, because with perfect <u>heart</u> they offered willingly to the Lord: and David the <u>king</u> also rejoiced with great joy.

4. Proverbs 3:9–10
   Honour the Lord with thy <u>substance</u>, and with the <u>firstfruits</u> of all thine increase: So shall thy <u>barns</u> be filled with plenty, and thy <u>presses</u> shall burst out with new <u>wine</u>.

5. Proverbs 3:27
   Withhold not <u>good</u> from them to whom it is <u>due</u>, when it is in the <u>power</u> of thine <u>hand</u> to do it.

6. Proverbs 11:24–25
   There is that <u>scattereth</u>, and yet <u>increaseth</u>; and there is that withholdeth more than is meet, but it tendeth to poverty. The liberal <u>soul</u> shall be made <u>fat</u>: and he that watereth shall be <u>watered</u> also himself.

7. Proverbs 21:26
   He <u>coveteth</u> <u>greedily</u> all the <u>day</u> long: but the righteous giveth and <u>spareth</u> not.

8. Proverbs 22:9
   He that hath a bountiful <u>eye</u> shall be <u>blessed</u>; for he giveth of his <u>bread</u> to the <u>poor</u>.

9. Proverbs 28:27
   He that giveth unto the <u>poor</u> shall not <u>lack</u>: but he that hideth his <u>eyes</u> shall have many a <u>curse</u>.

10. Malachi 3:10
    Bring ye all the tithes into the <u>storehouse</u>, that there may be meat in mine house, and prove me now herewith, saith the Lord of <u>hosts</u>, if I will not open you the windows of heaven, and pour you out a <u>blessing</u>, that there shall not be <u>room</u> enough to receive it.

11. Matthew 6:3–4
    But when thou doest <u>alms</u>, let not thy left <u>hand</u> know what thy right hand doeth: That thine alms may be in <u>secret</u>: and thy <u>Father</u> which seeth in secret himself shall reward <u>thee</u> openly.

12. Mark 12:41–44
    And Jesus sat over against the <u>treasury</u>, and beheld how the people <u>cast</u> money into the treasury: and many that were rich cast in much. And there came a certain poor widow, and she threw in two mites, which make a farthing. And he called unto him his disciples, and saith unto them, Verily I say unto you, That this poor widow hath cast more in, than all they which have cast into the treasury: For all they did cast in of their <u>abundance</u>; but she of her want did cast in all that she had, even all her <u>living</u>.

13. Luke 3:11
    He <u>answereth</u> and saith unto them, He that hath two <u>coats</u>, let him <u>impart</u> to him that hath <u>none</u>; and he that hath <u>meat</u>, let him do likewise.

14. Luke 6:30
    Give to every <u>man</u> that asketh of <u>thee</u>; and of him that taketh away thy <u>goods</u> ask them not again.

15. Luke 6:38
    Give, and it shall be given unto you; good measure, pressed down, and <u>shaken</u> together, and <u>running</u> over, shall men give into your <u>bosom</u>. For with the same measure that ye mete withal it shall be <u>measured</u> to you again.

16. Acts 20:35
    I have shewed you all <u>things</u>, how that so <u>labouring</u> ye ought to support the weak, and to remember the words of the Lord <u>Jesus</u>, how he said, It is more <u>blessed</u> to give than to receive.

17. Romans 12:8
    Or he that exhorteth, on <u>exhortation</u>: he that giveth, let him do it with <u>simplicity</u>; he that ruleth, with <u>diligence</u>; he that sheweth mercy, with <u>cheerfulness</u>.

18. 2 Corinthians 9:6–8
    But this I say, He which <u>soweth</u> sparingly shall reap also sparingly; and he which soweth bountifully shall reap also bountifully. Every man according as he purposeth in his <u>heart</u>, so let him give; not <u>grudgingly</u>, or of necessity: for God loveth a cheerful giver. And God is able to make all grace <u>abound</u> toward you; that ye, always having all <u>sufficiency</u> in all things, may abound to every good <u>work</u>.

19. 2 Corinthians 9:10
    Now he that ministereth <u>seed</u> to the sower both minister <u>bread</u> for your <u>food</u>, and multiply your seed sown, and increase the <u>fruits</u> of your righteousness.
20. Galatians 6:7
    Be not deceived; <u>God</u> is not <u>mocked</u>: for whatsoever a man <u>soweth</u>, that shall he also <u>reap</u>.
21. Philippians 4:15–17
    Now ye Philippians know also, that in the beginning of the <u>gospel</u>, when I departed from Macedonia, no <u>church</u> communicated with me as concerning giving and receiving, but ye only. For even in Thessalonica ye sent once and again unto my <u>necessity</u>. Not because I desire a gift: but I desire <u>fruit</u> that may <u>abound</u> to your <u>account</u>.
22. James 2:15–16
    If a brother or <u>sister</u> be naked, and destitute of daily <u>food</u>, And one of you say unto them, Depart in peace, be ye warmed and <u>filled</u>; notwithstanding ye give them not those things which are needful to the body; what doth it <u>profit</u>?

17. Receiving

1. Ecclesiastes 5:19
   Every man also to whom <u>God</u> hath given riches and wealth, and hath given him power to eat thereof, and to take his <u>portion</u>, and to rejoice in his <u>labour</u>; this is the <u>gift</u> of God.
2. John 3:27
   <u>John</u> answered and said, A <u>man</u> can receive <u>nothing</u>, except it be given him from <u>heaven</u>.
3. Acts 20:35
   I have shewed you all things, how that so <u>labouring</u> ye ought to support the <u>weak</u>, and to remember the <u>words</u> of the Lord Jesus, how he said, It is more <u>blessed</u> to give than to receive.
4. 1 Corinthians 9:10–11
   Or saith he it altogether for our sakes? For our sakes, no doubt, this is <u>written</u>: that he that <u>ploweth</u> should plow in hope; and that he that <u>thresheth</u> in hope should be partaker of his hope. If we have sown unto you spiritual <u>things</u>, is it a great thing if we shall reap your <u>carnal</u> things?
5. 1 Timothy 5:18
   For the <u>scripture</u> saith, thou shalt not <u>muzzle</u> the <u>ox</u> that treadeth out the corn. And, The <u>labourer</u> is worthy of his <u>reward</u>.

18. Running a Business

1. Leviticus 19:13
   <u>Thou</u> shalt not defraud thy <u>neighbour</u>, neither rob him: the <u>wages</u> of him that is hired shall not abide with <u>thee</u> all night until the <u>morning</u>.
2. Deuteronomy 25:13–15
   Thou shalt not have in thy <u>bag</u> divers weights, a great and a small. Thou shalt not have in thine house divers measures, a great and a small. But thou shalt have a <u>perfect</u> and just <u>weight</u>, a perfect and just <u>measure</u> shalt thou have: that thy days may be lengthened in the land which the LORD thy <u>God</u> giveth thee.
3. Job 31:13–14
   If I did despise the cause of my <u>manservant</u> or of my maidservant, when they contended with me; What then shall I do when God <u>riseth</u> up? and when he <u>visiteth</u>, what shall I answer him?
4. Psalm 112:5
   A good man sheweth <u>favour</u>, and <u>lendeth</u>: he will guide his <u>affairs</u> with <u>discretion</u>.
5. Proverbs 10:4
   He becometh <u>poor</u> that <u>dealeth</u> with a slack <u>hand</u>: but the hand of the <u>diligent</u> maketh rich.
6. Proverbs 11:1
   A false <u>balance</u> is <u>abomination</u> to the LORD: but a just weight is his <u>delight</u>.
7. Proverbs 13:4
   The <u>soul</u> of the <u>sluggard</u> desireth, and hath <u>nothing</u>: but the soul of the diligent shall be made <u>fat</u>.
8. Proverbs 13:11
   <u>Wealth</u> gotten by <u>vanity</u> shall be diminished: but he that gathereth by <u>labour</u> shall <u>increase</u>.
9. Proverbs 16:8
   <u>Better</u> is a little with <u>righteousness</u> than great <u>revenues</u> without <u>right</u>.
10. Proverbs 22:16
    He that <u>oppresseth</u> the <u>poor</u> to increase his <u>riches</u>, and he that giveth to the <u>rich</u>, shall surely come to want.

11. Jeremiah 22:13
Woe unto him that <u>buildeth</u> his house by un-righteousness, and his chambers by wrong; that useth his neighbour's <u>service</u> without <u>wages</u>, and giveth him not for his <u>work</u>.

12. Malachi 3:5
And I will come near to you to judgment; and I will be a swift witness against the sorcerers, and against the <u>adulterers</u>, and against false <u>swearers</u>, and against those that oppress the <u>hireling</u> in his wages, the widow, and the fatherless, and that turn aside the stranger from his right, and <u>fear</u> not me, saith the LORD of <u>hosts</u>.

13. Luke 16:10
He that is faithful in that which is <u>least</u> is <u>faithful</u> also in much: and he that is <u>unjust</u> in the least is unjust also in <u>much</u>.

14. Ephesians 6:9
And, ye masters, do the same <u>things</u> unto them, forbearing threatening: knowing that your <u>Master</u> also is in <u>heaven</u>; neither is there respect of <u>persons</u> with him.

15. Colossians 4:1
<u>Masters</u>, give unto your <u>servants</u> that which is just and equal; knowing that ye also have a <u>Master</u> in <u>heaven</u>.

16. James 5:4
Behold, the hire of the <u>labourers</u> who have reaped down your <u>fields</u>, which is of you kept back by <u>fraud</u>, crieth: and the <u>cries</u> of them which have reaped are entered into the ears of the <u>Lord</u> of sabaoth.

19. Investing

1. Proverbs 13:11
<u>Wealth</u> gotten by <u>vanity</u> shall be <u>diminished</u>: but he that gathereth by <u>labour</u> shall increase.

2. Proverbs 15:22
Without <u>counsel</u> <u>purposes</u> are disappointed: but in the <u>multitude</u> of counsellors they are <u>established</u>.

3. Proverbs 19:2
Also, that the <u>soul</u> be without <u>knowledge</u>, it is not <u>good</u>; and he that hasteth with his feet <u>sinneth</u>.

4. Proverbs 24:27
Prepare thy <u>work</u> without, and make it fit for thyself in the <u>field</u>; and afterwards <u>build</u> thine <u>house</u>.

5. Proverbs 28:20
A faithful <u>man</u> shall abound with <u>blessings</u>: but he that maketh <u>haste</u> to be <u>rich</u> shall not be <u>innocent</u>.

6. Ecclesiastes 11:2
Give a portion to <u>seven</u>, and also to eight; for <u>thou</u> knowest not what <u>evil</u> shall be upon the <u>earth</u>.

20. God's Provisions

1. 1 Kings 17:13–16
And Elijah said unto her, Fear not; go and do as thou hast said: but make me thereof a little cake first, and bring it unto me, and after make for thee and for thy <u>son</u>. For thus saith the LORD God of <u>Israel</u>, The barrel of meal shall not waste, neither shall the cruse of oil fail, until the day that the LORD sendeth rain upon the earth. And she went and did according to the saying of <u>Elijah</u>: and she, and he, and her <u>house</u>, did eat many days. And the barrel of <u>meal</u> wasted not, neither did the cruse of oil fail, according to the word of the LORD, which he spake by Elijah.

2. Nehemiah 6:9
For they all made us <u>afraid</u>, saying, Their <u>hands</u> shall be <u>weakened</u> from the work, that it be not done. Now <u>therefore</u>, O God, strengthen my hands.

3. Psalm 37:25
I have been <u>young</u>, and now am <u>old</u>; yet have I not seen the righteous forsaken, nor his <u>seed</u> begging <u>bread</u>.

4. Matthew 6:31–32
Therefore take no thought, saying, What shall we eat? or, What shall we drink? or, Wherewithal shall we be <u>clothed</u>? (For after all these things do the <u>Gentiles</u> seek:) for your heavenly <u>Father</u> knoweth that ye have need of all these <u>things</u>.

5. Matthew 7:11
If ye then, being <u>evil</u>, know how to give good gifts unto your <u>children</u>, how much more shall your <u>Father</u> which is in <u>heaven</u> give good things to them that ask him?

6. Luke 12:7
   But even the very <u>hairs</u> of your <u>head</u> are all <u>numbered</u>. Fear not therefore: ye are of more <u>value</u> than many <u>sparrows</u>.
7. John 21:6
   And he said unto them, <u>cast</u> the <u>net</u> on the <u>right</u> side of the <u>ship</u>, and ye shall find. They cast therefore, and now they were not able to draw it for the multitude of <u>fishes</u>.

8. 2 Corinthians 9:8
   And God is able to make all <u>grace</u> abound toward you; that ye, always having <u>all</u> <u>suf</u>-<u>ficiency</u> in all things, may <u>abound</u> to every good <u>work</u>.
9. Philippians 4:19
   But my <u>God</u> shall supply all your need according to his <u>riches</u> in <u>glory</u> by Christ <u>Jesus</u>.

21. Lending

1. Exodus 22:25
   If thou lend <u>money</u> to any of my <u>people</u> that is poor by thee, <u>thou</u> shalt not be to him as an usurer, neither shalt thou lay upon him <u>usury</u>.
2. Leviticus 25:35–37
   And if thy brother be <u>waxen</u> poor, and fallen in <u>decay</u> with thee; then thou shalt relieve him: yea, though he be a stranger, or a <u>sojourner</u>; that he may live with thee. Take thou no usury of him, or increase: but fear thy God; that thy <u>brother</u> may live with thee. Thou shalt not give him thy <u>money</u> upon usury, nor lend him thy <u>victuals</u> for increase.
3. Deuteronomy 15:8
   But thou shalt open thine <u>hand</u> wide unto him, and shalt surely lend him <u>sufficient</u> for his <u>need</u>, in that which he <u>wanteth</u>.
4. Deuteronomy 23:19–20
   Thou shalt not <u>lend</u> upon usury to thy <u>brother</u>; usury of money, usury of victuals, usury of any thing that is lent upon usury: Unto a <u>stranger</u> thou mayest lend upon usury; but unto thy brother thou shalt not lend upon usury: that the LORD thy <u>God</u> may <u>bless</u> thee in all that thou settest thine <u>hand</u> to in the land whither thou goest to possess it.
5. Deuteronomy 24:10
   When thou dost <u>lend</u> thy <u>brother</u> any thing, thou shalt not go into his <u>house</u> to fetch his <u>pledge</u>.

6. Psalm 15:5
   He that putteth not out his <u>money</u> to <u>usury</u>, nor taketh reward against the <u>innocent</u>. He that doeth these <u>things</u> shall never be <u>moved</u>.
7. Psalm 37:26
   <u>He</u> is ever <u>merciful</u>, and lendeth; and his <u>seed</u> is <u>blessed</u>.
8. Psalm 112:5
   A good <u>man</u> <u>sheweth</u> favour, and <u>lendeth</u>: he will guide his affairs with <u>discretion</u>.
9. Proverbs 3:27–28
   Withhold not good from them to whom it is due, when it is in the <u>power</u> of thine <u>hand</u> to do it. Say not unto thy <u>neighbour</u>, Go, and come again, and to morrow I will give; when thou hast it by <u>thee</u>.
10. Proverbs 28:8
    He that by <u>usury</u> and unjust gain <u>increaseth</u> his <u>substance</u>, he shall gather it for him that will pity the <u>poor</u>.
11. Matthew 5:42
    Give to him that <u>asketh</u> <u>thee</u>, and from him that would <u>borrow</u> of thee turn not <u>thou</u> away.
12. Luke 6:35
    But love ye your <u>enemies</u>, and do good, and lend, hoping for <u>nothing</u> again; and your reward shall be <u>great</u>, and ye shall be the <u>children</u> of the <u>Highest</u>: for he is kind unto the unthankful and to the <u>evil</u>.

22. Planning for the Future

1. Genesis 41:34–36
   Let <u>Pharaoh</u> do this, and let him appoint officers over the land, and take up the fifth part of the land of <u>Egypt</u> in the seven plenteous <u>years</u>. And let them gather all the food of those good years that come, and lay up corn under the <u>hand</u> of Pharaoh, and let them keep food in the <u>cities</u>. And that food shall be for store to the land against the seven years of <u>famine</u>, which shall be in the land of Egypt; that the land perish not through the famine.
2. Proverbs 1:1
   The <u>proverbs</u> of <u>Solomon</u> the son of David, king of <u>Israel</u>.

3. Proverbs 13:16

Every prudent man dealeth with knowledge: but a fool layeth open his folly.

4. Proverbs 13:19

The desire accomplished is sweet to the soul: but it is abomination to fools to depart from evil.

5. Proverbs 15:22

Without counsel purposes are disappointed: but in the multitude of counsellors they are established.

6. Proverbs 16:1

The preparations of the heart in man, and the answer of the tongue, is from the LORD.

7. Proverbs 16:9

A man's heart deviseth his way: but the LORD directeth his steps.

8. Proverbs 20:18

Every purpose is established by counsel: and with good advice make war.

9. Proverbs 22:3

A prudent man foreseeth the evil, and hideth himself: but the simple pass on, and are punished.

10. Proverbs 24:3–4

Through wisdom is an house builded; and by understanding it is established: And by knowledge shall the chambers be filled with all precious and pleasant riches.

11. Proverbs 24:27

Prepare thy work without, and make it fit for thyself in the field; and afterwards build thine house.

12. Proverbs 27:23

Be thou diligent to know the state of thy flocks, and look well to thy herds.

13. Ecclesiastes 10:2

A wise man's heart is at his right hand; but a fool's heart at his left.

14. Luke 12:16–21

And he spake a parable unto them, saying, The ground of a certain rich man brought forth plentifully: And he thought within himself, saying, What shall I do, because I have no room where to bestow my fruits? And he said, This will I do: I will pull down my barns, and build greater; and there will I bestow all my fruits and my goods. And I will say to my soul, Soul, thou hast much goods laid up for many years; take thine ease, eat, drink, and be merry. But God said unto him, Thou fool, this night thy soul shall be required of thee: then whose shall those things be, which thou hast provided? So is he that layeth up treasure for himself, and is not rich toward God.

15. Luke 14:28–30

For which of you, intending to build a tower, sitteth not down first, and counteth the cost, whether he have sufficient to finish it? Lest haply, after he hath laid the foundation, and is not able to finish it, all that behold it begin to mock him, Saying, This man began to build, and was not able to finish.

16. 1 Corinthians 16:1–2

Now concerning the collection for the saints, as I have given order to the churches of Galatia, even so do ye. Upon the first day of the week let every one of you lay by him in store, as God hath prospered him, that there be no gatherings when I come.

17. 1 Timothy 6:7

For we brought nothing into this world, and it is certain we can carry nothing out.

23. The Love of Money

1. Mark 4:19

And the cares of this world, and the deceitfulness of riches, and the lusts of other things entering in, choke the word, and it becometh unfruitful.

2. Mark 8:36

For what shall it profit a man, if he shall gain the whole world, and lose his own soul?

3. 1 Timothy 6:9–11

But they that will be rich fall into temptation and a snare, and into many foolish and hurtful lusts, which drown men in destruction and perdition. For the love of money is the root of all evil: which while some coveted after, they have erred from the faith, and pierced themselves through with many sorrows. But thou, O man of God, flee these things; and follow after righteousness, godliness, faith, love, patience, meekness.

24. Being Truly Prosperous

1. Genesis 26:12
   Then Isaac sowed in that <u>land</u>, and received in the same <u>year</u> an <u>hundredfold</u>: and the Lᴏʀᴅ <u>blessed</u> him.

2. Genesis 39:3
   And his <u>master</u> saw that the Lᴏʀᴅ was with him, and that the Lᴏʀᴅ made all that he did to <u>prosper</u> in his <u>hand</u>.

3. Deuteronomy 8:18
   But thou shalt <u>remember</u> the Lᴏʀᴅ thy God: for it is he that giveth thee <u>power</u> to get <u>wealth</u>, that he may establish his <u>covenant</u> which he sware unto thy <u>fathers</u>, as it is this day.

4. Deuteronomy 15:10
   <u>Thou</u> shalt surely give him, and thine heart shall not be grieved when thou givest unto him: because that for this thing the Lᴏʀᴅ thy God shall <u>bless</u> thee in all thy <u>works</u>, and in all that thou puttest thine <u>hand</u> unto.

5. Deuteronomy 24:19
   When thou cuttest down thine <u>harvest</u> in thy field, and hast forgot a <u>sheaf</u> in the field, thou shalt not go again to <u>fetch</u> it: it shall be for the stranger, for the fatherless, and for the widow: that the Lᴏʀᴅ thy God may bless thee in all the <u>work</u> of thine hands.

6. Deuteronomy 30:8–10
   And thou shalt return and obey the voice of the Lᴏʀᴅ, and do all his commandments which I command thee this day. And the Lᴏʀᴅ thy God will make thee plenteous in every <u>work</u> of thine hand, in the fruit of thy body, and in the fruit of thy <u>cattle</u>, and in the fruit of thy land, for good: for the Lᴏʀᴅ will again rejoice over thee for good, as he rejoiced over thy <u>fathers</u>: If thou shalt hearken unto the <u>voice</u> of the Lᴏʀᴅ thy God, to keep his <u>commandments</u> and his statutes which are written in this book of the law, and if thou turn unto the Lᴏʀᴅ thy God with all thine heart, and with all thy <u>soul</u>.

7. Joshua 1:8
   This book of the law shall not depart out of thy <u>mouth</u>; but thou shalt meditate therein day and <u>night</u>, that thou mayest observe to do according to all that is <u>written</u> therein: for then thou shalt make thy way prosperous, and then thou shalt have good <u>success</u>.

8. 1 Chronicles 22:12
   Only the Lᴏʀᴅ give thee wisdom and understanding, and give thee <u>charge</u> concerning Israel, that thou mayest keep the <u>law</u> of the Lᴏʀᴅ thy <u>God</u>.

9. 2 Chronicles 31:20
   And thus did <u>Hezekiah</u> throughout all <u>Judah</u>, and wrought that which was good and right and truth before the Lᴏʀᴅ his <u>God</u>.

10. Psalm 1:1–3
    Blessed is the man that walketh not in the counsel of the <u>ungodly</u>, nor standeth in the way of sinners, nor sitteth in the seat of the <u>scornful</u>. But his delight is in the law of the Lᴏʀᴅ; and in his law doth he meditate day and night. And he shall be like a <u>tree</u> planted by the rivers of <u>water</u>, that bringeth forth his fruit in his season; his leaf also shall not wither; and whatsoever he doeth shall <u>prosper</u>.

11. Psalm 35:27
    Let them shout for joy, and be glad, that favour my <u>righteous</u> cause: yea, let them say continually, Let the Lᴏʀᴅ be <u>magnified</u>, which hath pleasure in the <u>prosperity</u> of his <u>servant</u>.

12. Jeremiah 17:8
    For he shall be as a <u>tree</u> planted by the <u>waters</u>, and that spreadeth out her roots by the <u>river</u>, and shall not see when heat cometh, but her leaf shall be <u>green</u>; and shall not be careful in the year of <u>drought</u>, neither shall cease from yielding fruit.

13. Malachi 3:10
    Bring ye all the <u>tithes</u> into the storehouse, that there may be meat in mine <u>house</u>, and prove me now herewith, saith the Lᴏʀᴅ of <u>hosts</u>, if I will not open you the windows of <u>heaven</u>, and pour you out a <u>blessing</u>, that there shall not be room enough to receive it.

14. 3 John 1:2
    <u>Beloved</u>, I wish above all things that thou mayest <u>prosper</u> and be in <u>health</u>, even as thy <u>soul</u> prospereth.

25. Being a Good Steward over One's Money

1. Genesis 2:15
   And the LORD God took the man, and put him into the garden of Eden to dress it and to keep it.

2. Deuteronomy 10:14
   Behold, the heaven and the heaven of heavens is the LORD's thy God, the earth also, with all that therein is.

3. Luke 12:42–44
   And the Lord said, Who then is that faithful and wise steward, whom his lord shall make ruler over his household, to give them their portion of meat in due season? Blessed is that servant, whom his lord when he cometh shall find so doing. Of a truth I say unto you, that he will make him ruler over all that he hath.

4. Luke 12:47–48
   And that servant, which knew his lord's will, and prepared not himself, neither did according to his will, shall be beaten with many stripes. But he that knew not, and did commit things worthy of stripes, shall be beaten with few stripes. For unto whomsoever much is given, of him shall be much required: and to whom men have committed much, of him they will ask the more.

5. Luke 16:9–11
   And I say unto you, Make to yourselves friends of the mammon of unrighteousness; that, when ye fail, they may receive you into everlasting habitations. He that is faithful in that which is least is faithful also in much: and he that is unjust in the least is unjust also in much. If therefore ye have not been faithful in the unrighteous mammon, who will commit to your trust the true riches?

6. Romans 14:8
   For whether we live, we live unto the Lord; and whether we die, we die unto the Lord: whether we live therefore, or die, we are the Lord's.

26. Saving

1. Proverbs 21:5
   The thoughts of the diligent tend only to plenteousness; but of every one that is hasty only to want.

2. Proverbs 21:20
   There is treasure to be desired and oil in the dwelling of the wise; but a foolish man spendeth it up.

3. Proverbs 27:12
   A prudent man foreseeth the evil, and hideth himself; but the simple pass on, and are punished.

4. Proverbs 30:25
   The ants are a people not strong, yet they prepare their meat in the summer.

5. 1 Corinthians 16:2
   Upon the first day of the week let every one of you lay by him in store, as God hath prospered him, that there be no gatherings when I come.

27. Tithing

1. Genesis 14:20
   And blessed be the most high God, which hath delivered thine enemies into thy hand. And he gave him tithes of all.

2. Genesis 28:20–22
   And Jacob vowed a vow, saying, If God will be with me, and will keep me in this way that I go, and will give me bread to eat, and raiment to put on, So that I come again to my father's house in peace; then shall the LORD be my God: And this stone, which I have set for a pillar, shall be God's house: and of all that thou shalt give me I will surely give the tenth unto thee.

3. Exodus 23:19
   The first of the firstfruits of thy land thou shalt bring into the house of the LORD thy God. Thou shalt not seethe a kid in his mother's milk.

4. Leviticus 27:30
   And all the tithe of the land, whether of the seed of the land, or of the fruit of the tree, is the LORD's: it is holy unto the LORD.

5. Numbers 18:26
   Thus speak unto the Levites, and say unto them, When ye take of the children of Israel the tithes which I have given you from them for your inheritance, then ye shall offer up

an heave offering of it for the LORD, even a tenth part of the tithe.

6. Deuteronomy 14:22–23
Thou shalt truly tithe all the increase of thy seed, that the field bringeth forth year by year. And thou shalt eat before the LORD thy God, in the place which he shall choose to place his name there, the tithe of thy corn, of thy wine, and of thine oil, and the firstlings of thy herds and of thy flocks; that thou mayest learn to fear the LORD thy God always.

7. Deuteronomy 14:28
At the end of three years thou shalt bring forth all the tithe of thine increase the same year, and shalt lay it up within thy gates.

8. Deuteronomy 26:12
When thou hast made an end of tithing all the tithes of thine increase the third year, which is the year of tithing, and hast given it unto the Levite, the stranger, the fatherless, and the widow, that they may eat within thy gates, and be filled.

9. 2 Chronicles 31:5
And as soon as the commandment came abroad, the children of Israel brought in abundance the firstfruits of corn, wine, and oil, and honey, and of all the increase of the field; and the tithe of all things brought they in abundantly.

10. Nehemiah 10:38
And the priest the son of Aaron shall be with the Levites, when the Levites take tithes: and the Levites shall bring up the tithe of the tithes unto the house of our God, to the chambers, into the treasure house.

11. Proverbs 3:9–10
Honour the LORD with thy substance, and with the firstfruits of all thine increase: So

shall thy barns be filled with plenty, and thy presses shall burst out with new wine.

12. Ezekiel 44:30
And the first of all the firstfruits of all things, and every oblation of all, of every sort of your oblations, shall be the priest's: ye shall also give unto the priest the first of your dough, that he may cause the blessing to rest in thine house.

13. Amos 4:4
Come to Bethel, and transgress; at Gilgal multiply transgression; and bring your sacrifices every morning, and your tithes after three years.

14. Malachi 3:8
Will a man rob God? Yet ye have robbed me. But ye say, Wherein have we robbed thee? In tithes and offerings.

15. Matthew 23:23
Woe unto you, scribes and Pharisees, hypocrites! for ye pay tithe of mint and anise and cummin, and have omitted the weightier matters of the law, judgment, mercy, and faith: these ought ye to have done, and not to leave the other undone.

16. 1 Corinthians 16:1–2
Now concerning the collection for the saints, as I have given order to the churches of Galatia, even so do ye. Upon the first day of the week let every one of you lay by him in store, as God hath prospered him, that there be no gatherings when I come.

17. Hebrews 7:4
Now consider how great this man was, unto whom even the patriarch Abraham gave the tenth of the spoils.

28. Ultimate Success

1. Deuteronomy 30:9
And the LORD thy God will make thee plenteous in every work of thine hand, in the fruit of thy body, and in the fruit of thy cattle, and in the fruit of thy land, for good: for the LORD will again rejoice over thee for good, as he rejoiced over thy fathers.

2. Joshua 1:8
This book of the law shall not depart out of thy mouth; but thou shalt meditate therein

day and night, that thou mayest observe to do according to all that is written therein: for then thou shalt make thy way prosperous, and then thou shalt have good success.

3. Nehemiah 2:20
Then answered I them, and said unto them, The God of heaven, he will prosper us; therefore we his servants will arise and build: but ye have no portion, nor right, nor memorial, in Jerusalem.

4. Psalm 1:1–3
Blessed is the man that <u>walketh</u> not in the counsel of the ungodly, nor standeth in the way of sinners, nor sitteth in the seat of the scornful. But his <u>delight</u> is in the law of the LORD; and in his law doth he <u>meditate</u> day and night. And he shall be like a tree planted by the <u>rivers</u> of water, that bringeth forth his fruit in his season; his leaf also shall not <u>wither</u>; and whatsoever he doeth shall <u>prosper</u>.

5. Psalm 37:4
Delight <u>thyself</u> also in the LORD: and he shall give thee the <u>desires</u> of thine <u>heart</u>.

6. Proverbs 22:29
Seest thou a <u>man</u> diligent in his <u>business</u>? he shall stand before <u>kings</u>; he shall not stand before mean <u>men</u>.

7. Proverbs 22:4
By <u>humility</u> and the <u>fear</u> of the LORD are <u>riches</u>, and honour, and <u>life</u>.

8. Isaiah 1:19
If ye be <u>willing</u> and <u>obedient</u>, ye shall eat the <u>good</u> of the <u>land</u>.

9. Matthew 6:24
No man can <u>serve</u> two <u>masters</u>: for either he will hate the one, and <u>love</u> the other; or else he will hold to the one, and <u>despise</u> the other. Ye cannot serve God and <u>mammon</u>.

10. Matthew 23:12
And <u>whosoever</u> shall exalt himself shall be <u>abased</u>; and he that shall <u>humble</u> himself shall be <u>exalted</u>.

11. Luke 9:48
And said unto them, <u>Whosoever</u> shall receive this child in my <u>name</u> receiveth me: and whosoever shall receive me receiveth him that sent me: for he that is least among <u>you</u> all, the same shall be <u>great</u>.

12. Ephesians 3:20
Now unto him that is able to do exceeding abundantly above all that we <u>ask</u> or <u>think</u>, according to the <u>power</u> that <u>worketh</u> in us.

30. All about Food

1. C (Matthew 3:4)
2. D (Genesis 25:34)
3. B (Genesis 40)
4. C (Genesis 27)
5. B (Ezekiel 3:3)
6. A (Judges 6:19)
7. B (Exodus 3:17)
8. D (Luke 15:22–24)
9. C (Numbers 11:4–5)
10. D (Judges 14:8–10)
11. B (2 Kings 4:38–41)
12. B (Exodus 16:31)

31. From Sweet to Bitter

1. D (Revelation 10:8–10)
2. C (Judges 14:12–14)
3. A (Proverbs 20:16–18)
4. C (Jeremiah 31:28–30)
5. C (Exodus 12:8)
6. D (Proverbs 9:17)
7. A (Exodus 15:23–25)
8. D (Mark 16:18)
9. D (Exodus 32:20)
10. C (Proverbs 27:7)

32. Residential Area

1. C (Genesis 9:21)
2. D (1 Samuel 17:54)
3. A (Genesis 9:27)
4. B (Joshua 7:20–21)
5. B (Genesis 24:67)
6. A (Genesis 4:20)
7. A (Song of Solomon 1:5)
8. C (Zechariah 12:7)
9. A (Numbers 25:1–8)
10. B (Jeremiah 35:5–7)
11. A (2 Kings 7:3–16)
12. C (Habakkuk 3:7)

33. Kiddie Land

1. A (Genesis 4:1)
2. C (Genesis 9:22–24)
3. B (1 Samuel 16:6–13)
4. B (Genesis 48:13–14)
5. D (1 Kings 16:28–30)
6. B (Genesis 35:16–19)
7. B (Judges 8:30)
8. A (2 Chronicles 11:21)
9. B (1 Corinthians 14:20)
10. C (2 Samuel 17:14–17; 18:33)

35. Window Display

1. A (Acts 20:9)
2. C (Genesis 8:6–8)
3. B (2 Samuel 6:16, 20–21)
4. A (1 Samuel 19:11–12)
5. A (2 Kings 13:16–17)
6. A (Acts 9:1–25)
7. C (Genesis 26:8)
8. D (2 Kings 9:30–37)
9. A (Proverbs 7:6–23)
10. B (Malachi 3:10)

36. That Makes Scents

1. B (Matthew 2:11)
2. D (Esther 2:12–14)
3. C (John 12:3)
4. A (Luke 7:36)
5. C (Song of Solomon 4:13–15)
6. B (Proverbs 7:17)
7. A (Song of Solomon 3:6–7)
8. B (Daniel 10:2–3)
9. B (Proverbs 27:9)
10. D (Jeremiah 4:30; Ezekiel 23:40)

37. Nighty-Night

1. A (Genesis 32:24–32)
2. B (Exodus 12:12)
3. B (1 Samuel 3:1–18)
4. C (Acts 12:5–10)
5. D (Acts 27:1–44)
6. D (John 3:1–2)
7. B (Mark 6:45–51)
8. D (John 18:2–5)
9. B (1 Samuel 26:7–12)
10. C (1 Samuel 28:7–8)
11. B (Judges 7:15–20)

38. Wedding Bells

1. B (Genesis 4:19)
2. D (Genesis 29:1–35)
3. B (1 Samuel 1:1–2)
4. B (1 Samuel 14:50)
5. B (Ruth 4:8–10)
6. D (Genesis 38:1–30)
7. A (2 Chronicles 13:21)
8. A (Judges 14:20)

39. Farming

1. D (Genesis 2:8)
2. B (Job 1:1–22)
3. D (Ecclesiastes 2:4–5)
4. A (Judges 6:11)
5. D (Genesis 9:20)
6. C (Ruth 1:22–2:3; 4:13–17)
7. B (Genesis 26:12)
8. A (2 Chronicles 26:9–10)
9. B (1 Kings 21:1–4)
10. C (2 Samuel 9:1–13)

40. Rulers

1. C (1 Kings 3:16–28)
2. B (1 Kings 2:11)
3. D (Matthew 2:16–18)
4. C (Daniel 6:1–16)
5. A (1 Kings 15:23)
6. B (1 Samuel 16:11–13)
7. C (Genesis 41:1–40)
8. B (1 Kings 3:1)
9. C (Joshua 12:7–24)
10. A (Numbers 22:2–7)
11. C (Judges 9:1–6)
12. B (1 Samuel 15:1–35)
13. A (1 Samuel 21:10)

41. The Apostles

1. C (Matthew 10:2)
2. B (Matthew 17:1–3)
3. C (Acts 9:32–34)
4. A (John 12:20–22)

42. Doorway

1. D (Genesis 7:16)
2. B (Psalm 24:7)
3. C (Acts 3:1–11)
4. A (Exodus 12:1–7)
5. C (Job 38:1, 16–18)
6. A (2 Samuel 11:8–11)
7. A (Deuteronomy 6:9)
8. C (Judges 16:3)
9. B (Nehemiah 3:1)
10. C (2 Kings 18:16)
11. C (Revelation 21:10–12)

43. In the Military

1. C (Acts 12:5–8)
2. D (2 Kings 5:1)
3. B (Luke 7:1–5)
4. B (Acts 27:1–3)
5. C (Joshua 14:6–13)
6. C (2 Samuel 11:3, 14–15)
7. B (2 Samuel 15:14–22)
8. C (1 Kings 16:8–10)
9. B (2 Samuel 17:25)

44. Women and Rulers

1. C (2 Samuel 11:27; 12:24)
2. B (2 Samuel 21:11)
3. C (Matthew 14:3–8)
4. B (1 Kings 16:31)
5. C (1 Kings 10:1–2)
6. C (Esther 1:11–12; 2:17)
7. B (1 Samuel 25:39–42)
8. A (2 Chronicles 15:16)
9. B (Acts 8:27)
10. D (2 Chronicles 22:10)

45. Hair Apparent

1. C (Judges 16:17–19)
2. B (Acts 21:23–26)
3. B (Daniel 4:33)
4. C (Genesis 25:24–26)
5. C (2 Kings 1:8)
6. D (Job 1:20)
7. C (Leviticus 19:27)
8. C (2 Kings 2:22–23)
9. C (Leviticus 14:7–9)
10. C (Ezekiel 44:15–20)
11. C (Ezekiel 1:1–3; 5:1–4)

46. Anointment

1. D (Acts 10:38)
2. C (Exodus 40:1–9)
3. B (Genesis 28:18)
4. D (2 Corinthians 1:22)
5. C (Leviticus 8:23–24)
6. D (1 Samuel 9:15–16; 10:1)
7. C (James 5:14)
8. B (Isaiah 45:1)
9. B (1 Kings 1:39)

47. The Swift

1. C (1 Samuel 17:48–49)
2. C (Luke 19:2–4)
3. A (Genesis 33:4)
4. C (1 Kings 18:44–46)
5. B (Genesis 17:1; 18:1–3)
6. C (Genesis 24:27–29)
7. A (2 Samuel 18:21)
8. A (1 Kings 1:5)
9. D (2 Kings 4:8–37)

48. Special Women

1. A (Judges 4:3–5)
2. A (Luke 1:34–36, 57–60)
3. B (Exodus 15:20)
4. C (Esther 1–10)
5. D (1 Kings 16:31–34)
6. C (1 Samuel 25:1–42)
7. D (Joshua 6:25)
8. D (2 Samuel 3:2–5)
9. A (2 Samuel 21:8–10)
10. C (2 Kings 22:14–20)

49. Funny Money

1. A (Matthew 26:14–15)
2. A (Matthew 22:17–22)
3. A (Luke 19:2–5)
4. C (Luke 5:29)
5. C (Genesis 41:25–36)
6. A (Acts 24:24–27)
7. A (Esther 10:1)
8. B (2 Kings 15:19–20)
9. D (2 Kings 17:1–3)
10. C (Ezra 7:1–24)

50. Fly High

1. B (James 3:7–8)
2. C (Matthew 3:16)
3. D (Genesis 7:2–3)
4. A (Revelation 1:1–2; 12:14)
5. B (Exodus 16:13)
6. C (Mark 4:1–4)

51. What's That I Hear?

1. A (Acts 2:1–14)
2. A (Revelation 1:1–2; 18:1–3)
3. B (Matthew 3:16–17)
4. C (Revelation 1:1–2, 6:10)
5. C (1 Kings 19:1–21)
6. D (1 Samuel 3:2–4)
7. C (Psalm 29:5)
8. D (2 Kings 19:14–22)
9. C (1 Samuel 28:7–12)

53. The Story of Joseph

1. B (Genesis 42:3)
2. B (Genesis 42:4)
3. A (Genesis 42:17)
4. D (Genesis 42:18–24)
5. A (Genesis 42:25)
6. B (Genesis 44:2)
7. C (Genesis 44:17)
8. B (Genesis 47:1–6)
9. B (Genesis 45:18)
10. C (Genesis 50:26)
11. D (Genesis 41:51)
12. C (Genesis 45:22)

54. Have a Laugh

1. B (Matthew 9:23–24)
2. C (Genesis 17:17)
3. A (2 Samuel 6:12–14)
4. D (Genesis 18:12)
5. A (Exodus 32:4, 19)
6. D (Genesis 21:6)
7. C (Luke 6:21)
8. D (Judges 11:34)
9. C (1 Samuel 30:16–19)
10. A (Nehemiah 2:19)

55. Anything Goes

1. C (Matthew 4:7)
2. D (Matthew 2:14)
3. C (Matthew 8:14)
4. B (Numbers 11:28)
5. D (Proverbs 31:10)
6. B (Matthew 26:65)
7. A (Esther 8:2)
8. C (1 Samuel 17:26–28)
9. A (2 Kings 11:2–3)
10. A (Ruth 1:20)
11. B (Revelation 1:9)
12. D (Acts 18:1–3)
13. B (Jonah 1:15)
14. C (Job 42:12–14)
15. C (Acts 6:8–9; 7:59–60; 8:1)
16. B (Genesis 41:50–52)
17. C (2 Kings 15:29)
18. B (John 9:6)
19. B (Genesis 42:29–32; 48:10)
20. D (Mark 10:46–52)
21. B (Jonah 3:1–10)
22. C (Acts 18:24–26)
23. C (2 Chronicles 30:1–10)
24. A (1 Kings 15:17)
25. B (2 Kings 21:18–19, 23)
26. A (1 Samuel 22:1–2; 23:14–29)
27. D (John 13:6–8)
28. B (Galatians 1:19)
29. B (Exodus 7:1; 32:15–24)
30. D (2 Samuel 4:4)
31. A (2 Kings 6:24–30)
32. C (Luke 2:36–38)
33. C (John 4:7–15)
34. B (Genesis 12:14–19)
35. A (Deuteronomy 3:11)
36. D (Joshua 9:7–27)
37. C (2 Corinthians 11:13–14)

Answers

38. D (1 Samuel 22:13–17)
39. B (John 20:1–2)
40. D (1 Samuel 18:1–30)
41. B (Habakkuk 1:1; 2:6)
42. D (Mark 12:1–12)

43. C (2 Chronicles 21:1–6)
44. B (Matthew 25:14–30)
45. D (Joshua 6:22–25)
46. B (2 Samuel 13:1–36)

47. A (2 Kings 11:21; 12:1–3)
48. C (Zechariah 1:1–2; 2:1–3)
49. D (2 Kings 3:4)
50. C 27

56. Priests

1. C (Deuteronomy 17:12)
2. B (Exodus 28:15–21)
3. B (Hebrews 7:1–3)

4. B (Hebrews 7:1–3)
5. A (1 Samuel 1:12–14)
6. D (2 Kings 23:1–30)

7. C (1 Samuel 2:12–17, 34)
8. B (Exodus 18:13–27)

57. Lions' Den

1. C (Revelation 1:1–2; 4:6–7)
2. D (Daniel 7:2–4)

3. C (1 Samuel 17:34–35)
4. A (1 Peter 5:8)
5. B (Judges 14:5–6)

6. B (2 Samuel 1:23)
7. C (Ezekiel 1:1–10)
8. D (2 Samuel 23:20)

58. More of Anything Goes

1. B (Numbers 8:5–7)
2. D (Judges 7:13)
3. A (Genesis 20:2)
4. B (2 Kings 9:22)
5. D (Matthew 26:6)
6. B (Song of Solomon 1:1)
7. A (Daniel 5:31)
8. B (Ezekiel 23:2–4)
9. A (2 Kings 17:27)
10. A (John 20:2–4)
11. C (Isaiah 8:1–4)
12. B (1 Kings 16:8–10)
13. B (1 Kings 2:20)
14. B (Judges 21:20–21)
15. C (Job 8:1, 20–21)
16. A (Numbers 21:1)
17. C (Isaiah 1:1; 24:21–22)
18. B (Acts 9:36, 39)
19. A (Numbers 12:15)
20. A (1 Samuel 28:7–25)
21. B (1 Kings 17:9–15)
22. C (2 Kings 4:8–37; 8:1)
23. B (John 8:3–11)

24. A (Genesis 6:2)
25. B (John 11:1)
26. D (Matthew 26:3)
27. C (Deuteronomy 18:1–2)
28. D (Genesis 4:22)
29. C (Genesis 4:17)
30. B (Genesis 17:9–10)
31. D (John 4:46–54)
32. B (Acts 15:40)
33. A (Genesis 29:33)
34. C (2 Samuel 2:9–11)
35. B (Genesis 5:20)
36. D (Ezra 3:8–9; 5:2; 6:14–16)
37. D (Job 38:1)
38. C (2 Samuel 4:4)
39. A (2 Samuel 17:14, 23)
40. A (1 Samuel 17:5)
41. C (Malachi 3:8)
42. D (Jeremiah 39:1)
43. A (2 Kings 11:15–18)
44. D (Nehemiah 3:1)
45. C (Acts 2:14–17)
46. B (Romans 16:6)

47. C (Mark 6:22)
48. D (Hosea 1:1–2, 9)
49. B (1 Kings 1:5–11)
50. B (Judges 4:1–3)
51. A (1 Kings 11:19)
52. C (Luke 17:11–19)
53. C (John 11:41–51)
54. C (Judges 3:17–22)
55. D (John 4:7, 17–18)
56. C (Acts 16:14)
57. D (Revelation 2:18–20)
58. B (1 Kings 14:2)
59. B (Acts 3:1; 4:3)
60. A (Genesis 31:24)
61. B (1 Kings 16:29–33)
62. A (Esther 2:1–18)
63. D (Matthew 24:1–2)
64. C (Exodus 17:15)
65. D (Amos 3:14)
66. B (2 Kings 15:13–15)
67. C (Acts 3:1; 4:1–4)
68. A (Acts 17:15–22)
69. D (Genesis 19:30)
70. D (Matthew)

60. Fill in the Blanks

1. Genesis 1:1
   In the <u>beginning</u> God created the <u>heaven</u> and the <u>earth</u>.

2. Psalm 37:4
   Delight <u>thyself</u> also in the L<small>ORD</small>: and he shall give thee the <u>desires</u> of thine <u>heart</u>.

3. Isaiah 9:6
   For unto us a <u>child</u> is born, unto us a son is given: and the <u>government</u> shall be upon his shoulder: and his name shall be called <u>Wonderful</u>, Counsellor, The mighty God, The everlasting Father, The Prince of Peace.

4. Isaiah 40:28
   Hast thou not <u>known</u>? hast thou not heard, that the <u>everlasting</u> God, the L<small>ORD</small>, the Creator of the ends of the earth, fainteth not, neither is <u>weary</u>? there is no searching of his understanding.

5. Jeremiah 29:11
   For I know the <u>thoughts</u> that I think toward you, saith the L<small>ORD</small>, thoughts of peace, and not of <u>evil</u>, to give you an expected end.

6. John 3:16
   For God so <u>loved</u> the <u>world</u>, that he gave his only begotten <u>Son</u>, that whosoever believeth in him should not perish, but have everlasting <u>life</u>.

7. John 15:7
   If ye <u>abide</u> in me, and my words abide in you, ye shall ask what ye <u>will</u>, and it shall be done unto <u>you</u>.

8. Romans 4:21
   And being <u>fully</u> persuaded that, what he had <u>promised</u>, he was able also to <u>perform</u>.

9. Romans 8:1
   There is therefore now no <u>condemnation</u> to them which are in Christ <u>Jesus</u>, who walk not after the flesh, but after the <u>Spirit</u>.

10. Romans 8:28
    And we know that all things <u>work</u> together for <u>good</u> to them that <u>love</u> God, to them who are the called according to his <u>purpose</u>.

11. 2 Corinthians 1:20
    For all the <u>promises</u> of God in him are yea, and in him <u>Amen</u>, unto the <u>glory</u> of God by us.

12. Ephesians 2:10
    For we are his workmanship, created in Christ Jesus unto good <u>works</u>, which God hath before <u>ordained</u> that we should walk in them.

13. Philippians 4:6–7
    Be careful for <u>nothing</u>; but in every thing by <u>prayer</u> and supplication with <u>thanksgiving</u> let your requests be made known unto God. And the peace of God, which passeth all understanding, shall keep your hearts and <u>minds</u> through Christ Jesus.

14. Philippians 4:19
    But my God shall <u>supply</u> all your need according to his <u>riches</u> in <u>glory</u> by Christ Jesus.

15. 2 Peter 1:4
    Whereby are given unto us exceeding <u>great</u> and precious <u>promises</u>: that by these ye might be partakers of the divine <u>nature</u>, having escaped the corruption that is in the world through lust.

61. Scriptures on Salvation

1. John 14:6
   Jesus saith unto him, I am the <u>way</u>, the truth, and the <u>life</u>: no man cometh unto the <u>Father</u>, but by me.

2. Romans 3:23
   For all have <u>sinned</u>, and come short of the <u>glory</u> of God.

3. Romans 6:23
   For the wages of <u>sin</u> is <u>death</u>; but the gift of God is eternal <u>life</u> through Jesus Christ our Lord.

4. 2 Corinthians 5:17
   Therefore if any man be in <u>Christ</u>, he is a new <u>creature</u>: old things are passed away; behold, all things are become <u>new</u>.

5. Ephesians 2:8–9
   For by <u>grace</u> are ye saved through <u>faith</u>; and that not of yourselves: it is the gift of God: Not of works, lest any man should <u>boast</u>.

6. Revelation 3:20
   Behold, I stand at the <u>door</u>, and <u>knock</u>: if any man hear my <u>voice</u>, and open the door, I will come in to him, and will sup with him, and he with me.

62. Scriptures on Security

1. Psalm 27:1
   The Lord is my light and my salvation; whom shall I fear? the Lord is the strength of my life; of whom shall I be afraid?

2. Psalm 37:4
   Delight thyself also in the Lord: and he shall give thee the desires of thine heart.

3. Proverbs 3:5–6
   Trust in the Lord with all thine heart; and lean not unto thine own understanding. In all thy ways acknowledge him, and he shall direct thy paths.

4. Isaiah 40:31
   But they that wait upon the Lord shall renew their strength; they shall mount up with wings as eagles; they shall run, and not be weary; and they shall walk, and not faint.

5. Jeremiah 29:11
   For I know the thoughts that I think toward you, saith the Lord, thoughts of peace, and not of evil, to give you an expected end.

6. Lamentations 3:22–23
   It is of the Lord's mercies that we are not consumed, because his compassions fail not. They are new every morning: great is thy faithfulness.

7. Matthew 11:28–30
   Come unto me, all ye that labour and are heavy laden, and I will give you rest. Take my yoke upon you, and learn of me; for I am meek and lowly in heart: and ye shall find rest unto your souls. For my yoke is easy, and my burden is light.

8. Luke 16:13
   No servant can serve two masters: for either he will hate the one, and love the other; or else he will hold to the one, and despise the other. Ye cannot serve God and mammon.

9. Acts 1:8
   But ye shall receive power, after that the Holy Ghost is come upon you: and ye shall be witnesses unto me both in Jerusalem, and in all Judaea, and in Samaria, and unto the uttermost part of the earth.

10. Romans 8:28
    And we know that all things work together for good to them that love God, to them who are the called according to his purpose.

11. Romans 8:38–39
    For I am persuaded, that neither death, nor life, nor angels, nor principalities, nor powers, nor things present, nor things to come, Nor height, nor depth, nor any other creature, shall be able to separate us from the love of God, which is in Christ Jesus our Lord.

12. Romans 12:1
    I beseech you therefore, brethren, by the mercies of God, that ye present your bodies a living sacrifice, holy, acceptable unto God, which is your reasonable service.

13. 1 Corinthians 15:58
    Therefore, my beloved brethren, be ye stedfast, unmoveable, always abounding in the work of the Lord, forasmuch as ye know that your labour is not in vain in the Lord.

14. 2 Corinthians 4:18
    While we look not at the things which are seen, but at the things which are not seen: for the things which are seen are temporal; but the things which are not seen are eternal.

15. 2 Corinthians 12:9
    And he said unto me, My grace is sufficient for thee: for my strength is made perfect in weakness. Most gladly therefore will I rather glory in my infirmities, that the power of Christ may rest upon me.

16. Galatians 2:20
    I am crucified with Christ: nevertheless I live; yet not I, but Christ liveth in me: and the life which I now live in the flesh I live by the faith of the Son of God, who loved me, and gave himself for me.

17. Galatians 5:22–23
    But the fruit of the Spirit is love, joy, peace, longsuffering, gentleness, goodness, faith, Meekness, temperance: against such there is no law.

18. Philippians 4:13
    I can do all things through Christ which strengtheneth me.

19. Colossians 3:23
    And whatsoever ye do, do it heartily, as to the Lord, and not unto men.

20. Hebrews 12:1–2
    Wherefore seeing we also are compassed about with so great a cloud of witnesses, let us lay aside every weight, and the sin which doth so easily beset us, and let us run with patience the race that is set before us, looking unto Jesus the author and finisher of our faith; who for the joy that was set before him endured the cross, despising the

shame, and is set down at the right hand of the throne of God.

21. Hebrews 13:8
Jesus Christ the same <u>yesterday</u>, and to day, and for <u>ever</u>.

22. James 1:22
But be ye <u>doers</u> of the <u>word</u>, and not hearers only, deceiving your own <u>selves</u>.

23. James 4:7
<u>Submit</u> yourselves therefore to <u>God</u>. Resist the devil, and he will <u>flee</u> from you.

24. 2 Peter 3:9
The <u>Lord</u> is not slack concerning his <u>prom-ise</u>, as some men count slackness; but is longsuffering to us-ward, not willing that any should <u>perish</u>, but that all should come to repentance.

25. 1 John 4:7–8
Beloved, let us <u>love</u> one another: for love is of God; and every one that loveth is born of God, and knoweth <u>God</u>. He that loveth not knoweth not God; for God is love.

63. Scriptures on Prayer

1. Psalm 19:14
Let the words of my <u>mouth</u>, and the medita-tion of my <u>heart</u>, be acceptable in thy sight, O Lord, my <u>strength</u>, and my redeemer.

2. Psalm 50:14–15
Offer unto God <u>thanksgiving</u>; and pay thy vows unto the most <u>High</u>: And call upon me in the day of trouble: I will deliver thee, and thou shalt <u>glorify</u> me.

3. Psalm 66:17
I cried unto him with my mouth, and he was extolled with my <u>tongue</u>.

4. Psalm 95:2
Let us come before his presence with <u>thanksgiving</u>, and make a joyful <u>noise</u> unto him with psalms.

5. Psalm 118:25
Save now, I beseech thee, O Lord: O Lord, I beseech thee, send now <u>prosperity</u>.

6. Psalm 119:11
Thy <u>word</u> have I hid in mine <u>heart</u>, that I might not <u>sin</u> against thee.

7. Psalm 119:105
Thy word is a <u>lamp</u> unto my <u>feet</u>, and a light unto my <u>path</u>.

8. Psalm 122:6
<u>Pray</u> for the <u>peace</u> of Jerusalem: they shall prosper that <u>love</u> thee.

9. Romans 10:1
Brethren, my heart's <u>desire</u> and <u>prayer</u> to God for Israel is, that they might be <u>saved</u>.

10. Romans 10:13
For <u>whosoever</u> shall call upon the <u>name</u> of the Lord shall be <u>saved</u>.

11. Romans 15:30
Now I beseech you, <u>brethren</u>, for the Lord Jesus Christ's sake, and for the <u>love</u> of the Spirit, that ye strive together with me in your <u>prayers</u> to God for me.

12. 1 Corinthians 1:4
I thank my God always on your <u>behalf</u>, for the <u>grace</u> of God which is given you by Jesus Christ.

13. 1 Corinthians 14:15
What is it then? I will pray with the <u>spirit</u>, and I will pray with the understanding also: I will sing with the spirit, and I will <u>sing</u> with the understanding also.

14. 2 Corinthians 1:11
Ye also helping together by <u>prayer</u> for us, that for the <u>gift</u> bestowed upon us by the means of many persons thanks may be given by many on our <u>behalf</u>.

15. Ephesians 6:18
<u>Praying</u> always with all prayer and <u>supplica-tion</u> in the <u>Spirit</u>, and watching thereunto with all perseverance and supplication for all saints.

16. Philippians 1:3–4
I thank my <u>God</u> upon every <u>remembrance</u> of you, always in every <u>prayer</u> of mine for you all making request with joy.

17. Colossians 1:3
We give thanks to God and the Father of our Lord Jesus Christ, <u>praying</u> always for you.

18. 1 Thessalonians 5:17
<u>Pray</u> without ceasing.

19. 1 Thessalonians 5:18
In every thing give <u>thanks</u>: for this is the will of God in Christ Jesus concerning <u>you</u>.

20. James 1:6
But let him ask in <u>faith</u>, nothing wavering. For he that wavereth is like a wave of the <u>sea</u> driven with the wind and <u>tossed</u>.

21. James 5:13–14
Is any among you <u>afflicted</u>? let him <u>pray</u>. Is any merry? let him sing psalms. Is any sick among you? let him call for the elders of the

church; and let them pray over him, anointing him with oil in the name of the Lord.

22. James 5:16
Confess your faults one to another, and pray one for another, that ye may be healed. The effectual fervent prayer of a righteous man availeth much.

64. Scriptures on Temptation

1. Matthew 6:13
And lead us not into temptation, but deliver us from evil: For thine is the kingdom, and the power, and the glory, for ever. Amen.

2. Matthew 26:41
Watch and pray, that ye enter not into temptation: the spirit indeed is willing, but the flesh is weak.

3. Luke 4:13
And when the devil had ended all the temptation, he departed from him for a season.

4. Luke 11:4
And forgive us our sins; for we also forgive every one that is indebted to us. And lead us not into temptation; but deliver us from evil.

5. Luke 22:40
And when he was at the place, he said unto them, Pray that ye enter not into temptation.

6. 1 Corinthians 7:2
Nevertheless, to avoid fornication, let every man have his own wife, and let every woman have her own husband.

7. 1 Corinthians 10:13
There hath no temptation taken you but such as is common to man: but God is faithful, who will not suffer you to be tempted above that ye are able; but will with the temptation also make a way to escape, that ye may be able to bear it.

8. 1 Timothy 6:9
But they that will be rich fall into temptation and a snare, and into many foolish and hurtful lusts, which drown men in destruction and perdition.

65. Scriptures on Never Losing Faith

1. Joshua 1:9
Have not I commanded thee? Be strong and of a good courage; be not afraid, neither be thou dismayed: for the LORD thy God is with thee whithersoever thou goest.

2. 2 Chronicles 15:7
Be ye strong therefore, and let not your hands be weak: for your work shall be rewarded.

3. Job 19:25
For I know that my redeemer liveth, and that he shall stand at the latter day upon the earth.

4. Job 23:10
But he knoweth the way that I take: when he hath tried me, I shall come forth as gold.

5. Psalm 16:11
Thou wilt shew me the path of life: in thy presence is fulness of joy; at thy right hand there are pleasures for evermore.

6. Proverbs 14:12
There is a way which seemeth right unto a man, but the end thereof are the ways of death.

7. Proverbs 16:7
When a man's ways please the LORD, he maketh even his enemies to be at peace with him.

8. Proverbs 21:1
The king's heart is in the hand of the LORD, as the rivers of water: he turneth it whithersoever he will.

9. Proverbs 27:17
Iron sharpeneth iron; so a man sharpeneth the countenance of his friend.

10. Isaiah 41:10
Fear thou not; for I am with thee: be not dismayed; for I am thy God: I will strengthen thee; yea, I will help thee; yea, I will uphold thee with the right hand of my righteousness.

11. Isaiah 58:1
Cry aloud, spare not, lift up thy voice like a trumpet, and shew my people their transgression, and the house of Jacob their sins.

12. Matthew 18:18
Verily I say unto you, Whatsoever ye shall bind on earth shall be bound in heaven: and

whatsoever ye shall loose on earth shall be loosed in <u>heaven</u>.

13. Matthew 19:26
But <u>Jesus</u> beheld them, and said unto them, With men this is <u>impossible</u>; but with God all <u>things</u> are possible.

14. Luke 1:37
For with God <u>nothing</u> shall be <u>impossible</u>.

15. John 8:12
Then spake <u>Jesus</u> again unto them, saying, I am the <u>light</u> of the world: he that followeth me shall not walk in darkness, but shall have the light of <u>life</u>.

16. 1 Corinthians 2:14
But the natural <u>man</u> receiveth not the things of the <u>Spirit</u> of God: for they are foolishness unto him: neither can he know them, because they are spiritually <u>discerned</u>.

17. 2 Corinthians 4:1
Therefore seeing we have this <u>ministry</u>, as we have received <u>mercy</u>, we faint not.

18. 2 Corinthians 11:3
But I fear, lest by any means, as the <u>serpent</u> beguiled Eve through his subtilty, so your <u>minds</u> should be corrupted from the simplicity that is in <u>Christ</u>.

19. Galatians 6:9
And let us not be weary in well <u>doing</u>: for in due season we shall <u>reap</u>, if we faint not.

20. Ephesians 4:26
Be ye <u>angry</u>, and <u>sin</u> not: let not the sun go down upon your <u>wrath</u>.

21. Hebrews 4:12
For the word of <u>God</u> is quick, and powerful, and sharper than any twoedged <u>sword</u>, piercing even to the dividing asunder of soul and <u>spirit</u>, and of the joints and marrow, and is a discerner of the thoughts and intents of the <u>heart</u>.

22. Hebrews 11:6
But without faith it is <u>impossible</u> to please <u>him</u>: for he that cometh to God must believe that he is, and that he is a rewarder of them that diligently seek <u>him</u>.

23. Hebrews 12:3
For consider <u>him</u> that endured such contradiction of <u>sinners</u> against himself, lest ye be wearied and faint in your <u>minds</u>.

24. Revelation 7:1
And after these things I saw four <u>angels</u> standing on the four corners of the <u>earth</u>, holding the four winds of the <u>earth</u>, that the wind should not blow on the earth, nor on the sea, nor on any tree.

25. Revelation 12:11
And they overcame him by the blood of the <u>Lamb</u>, and by the word of their <u>testimony</u>; and they loved not their lives unto the <u>death</u>.

66. Scriptures on Hope

1. Numbers 23:19
God is not a <u>man</u>, that he should <u>lie</u>; neither the son of man, that he should repent: hath he said, and shall he not do it? or hath he spoken, and shall he not make it <u>good</u>?

2. Job 13:15
Though he <u>slay</u> me, yet will I <u>trust</u> in him: but I will maintain mine own <u>ways</u> before him.

3. Proverbs 24:14
So shall the knowledge of <u>wisdom</u> be unto thy <u>soul</u>: when thou hast found it, then there shall be a reward, and thy <u>expectation</u> shall not be cut off.

4. Proverbs 24:20
For there shall be no reward to the <u>evil</u> man; the candle of the <u>wicked</u> shall be put out.

5. Romans 8:24–25
For we are saved by <u>hope</u>: but hope that is seen is not <u>hope</u>: for what a man seeth, why doth he yet hope for? But if we hope for that we see not, then do we with <u>patience</u> wait for it.

6. 1 Corinthians 15:19
If in this <u>life</u> only we have hope in <u>Christ</u>, we are of all men most <u>miserable</u>.

7. Hebrews 11:1
Now <u>faith</u> is the substance of things <u>hoped</u> for, the evidence of <u>things</u> not seen.

8. 1 Peter 1:3
Blessed be the <u>God</u> and Father of our Lord Jesus <u>Christ</u>, which according to his abundant mercy hath begotten us again unto a lively hope by the <u>resurrection</u> of Jesus Christ from the <u>dead</u>.

67. Scriptures on Love

1. Leviticus 19:17–18
   Thou shalt not hate thy <u>brother</u> in thine heart: thou shalt in any wise rebuke thy neighbour, and not suffer <u>sin</u> upon him. Thou shalt not avenge, nor bear any grudge against the <u>chil-dren</u> of thy people, but thou shalt <u>love</u> thy neighbour as thyself: I am the Lord.

2. Psalm 30:5
   For his <u>anger</u> endureth but a moment; in his favour is <u>life</u>: weeping may endure for a <u>night</u>, but joy cometh in the morning.

3. Psalm 103:8
   The Lord is merciful and <u>gracious</u>, slow to anger, and plenteous in <u>mercy</u>.

4. Psalm 103:13
   Like as a <u>father</u> pitieth his <u>children</u>, so the Lord pitieth them that fear <u>him</u>.

5. Psalm 143:8
   Cause me to hear thy lovingkindness in the <u>morning</u>; for in thee do I trust: cause me to know the way wherein I should <u>walk</u>; for I lift up my soul unto thee.

6. Proverbs 10:12
   <u>Hatred</u> stirreth up strifes: but <u>love</u> covereth all sins.

7. Proverbs 21:21
   He that followeth after <u>righteousness</u> and mercy findeth <u>life</u>, righteousness, and honour.

8. Isaiah 43:4
   Since thou wast precious in my <u>sight</u>, thou hast been honourable, and I have loved <u>thee</u>: therefore will I give <u>men</u> for thee, and people for thy <u>life</u>.

9. Matthew 5:44
   But I say unto you, <u>Love</u> your <u>enemies</u>, bless them that curse you, do good to them that hate you, and pray for them which despitefully use you, and persecute <u>you</u>.

10. Mark 12:30
    And thou shalt <u>love</u> the Lord thy God with all thy <u>heart</u>, and with all thy soul, and with all thy mind, and with all thy strength: this is the first <u>commandment</u>.

11. Mark 12:31
    And the second is like, namely this, Thou shalt <u>love</u> thy neighbour as thyself. There is none other <u>commandment</u> greater than these.

12. Luke 10:27
    And he answering said, <u>Thou</u> shalt love the Lord thy God with all thy <u>heart</u>, and with all thy <u>soul</u>, and with all thy strength, and with all thy mind; and thy neighbour as thyself.

13. John 14:21
    He that hath my <u>commandments</u>, and keepeth them, he it is that <u>loveth</u> me: and he that loveth me shall be loved of my <u>Father</u>, and I will love him, and will manifest myself to him.

14. John 15:12
    This is my <u>commandment</u>, That ye <u>love</u> one another, as I have <u>loved</u> you.

15. John 15:13
    Greater love hath no <u>man</u> than this, that a man lay down his <u>life</u> for his <u>friends</u>.

16. Romans 8:38–39
    For I am <u>persuaded</u>, that neither death, nor life, nor angels, nor principalities, nor <u>pow-ers</u>, nor things present, nor things to come, nor <u>height</u>, nor depth, nor any other creature, shall be able to separate us from the love of <u>God</u>, which is in Christ Jesus our Lord.

17. Romans 12:9
    Let <u>love</u> be without dissimulation. Abhor that which is <u>evil</u>; cleave to that which is good.

18. Romans 12:10
    Be kindly affectioned one to another with brotherly <u>love</u>; in honour preferring one another.

19. Romans 13:8
    Owe no man any thing, but to <u>love</u> one another: for he that loveth another hath fulfilled the <u>law</u>.

20. Romans 13:10
    <u>Love</u> worketh no <u>ill</u> to his neighbour: therefore love is the fulfilling of the law.

21. 1 Corinthians 2:9
    But as it is <u>written</u>, Eye hath not seen, nor ear <u>heard</u>, neither have entered into the heart of man, the things which God hath prepared for them that <u>love</u> him.

22. 1 Corinthians 10:24
    Let no <u>man</u> seek his own, but every man another's <u>wealth</u>.

23. 1 Corinthians 13:1
    Though I speak with the <u>tongues</u> of men and of <u>angels</u>, and have not charity, I am become as sounding brass, or a tinkling <u>cymbal</u>.

24. 1 Corinthians 13:2
And though I have the gift of <u>prophecy</u>, and understand all <u>mysteries</u>, and all knowledge; and though I have all faith, so that I could remove <u>mountains</u>, and have not charity, I am nothing.

25. 1 Corinthians 13:3
And though I bestow all my <u>goods</u> to feed the poor, and though I give my <u>body</u> to be burned, and have not charity, it profiteth me <u>nothing</u>.

26. 1 Corinthians 13:4–5
<u>Charity</u> suffereth long, and is kind; charity envieth not; charity vaunteth not itself, is not puffed up, doth not <u>behave</u> itself unseemly, seeketh not her own, is not easily provoked, thinketh no <u>evil</u>.

27. 1 Corinthians 16:14
Let all your <u>things</u> be done with <u>charity</u>.

28. Ephesians 3:16–17
That he would grant you, according to the <u>riches</u> of his <u>glory</u>, to be strengthened with might by his <u>Spirit</u> in the inner man; that Christ may dwell in your hearts by faith; that ye, being rooted and grounded in <u>love</u>.

29. Ephesians 4:2
With all lowliness and <u>meekness</u>, with long-suffering, forbearing one another in <u>love</u>.

30. Ephesians 4:15
But speaking the truth in <u>love</u>, may grow up into him in all <u>things</u>, which is the head, even <u>Christ</u>.

31. Ephesians 5:2
And walk in love, as Christ also hath <u>loved</u> us, and hath given <u>himself</u> for us an offering and a sacrifice to <u>God</u> for a sweetsmelling savour.

32. Ephesians 5:25–26
<u>Husbands</u>, love your <u>wives</u>, even as Christ also loved the church, and gave himself for it; That he might sanctify and cleanse it with the washing of water by the word.

33. Colossians 3:14
And above all these things put on <u>charity</u>, which is the bond of <u>perfectness</u>.

34. 1 Thessalonians 3:12
And the Lord make you to increase and abound in <u>love</u> one toward another, and toward all <u>men</u>, even as we do toward you.

35. 2 Thessalonians 3:5
And the Lord direct your <u>hearts</u> into the love of God, and into the <u>patient</u> waiting for Christ.

36. 2 Timothy 1:7
For God hath not given us the spirit of <u>fear</u>; but of power, and of love, and of a sound <u>mind</u>.

37. 1 Peter 4:8
And above all things have fervent <u>charity</u> among yourselves: for charity shall cover the multitude of <u>sins</u>.

38. 1 John 3:1
Behold, what manner of love the <u>Father</u> hath bestowed upon <u>us</u>, that we should be called the sons of God: therefore the world knoweth us not, because it knew him not.

39. 1 John 3:11
For this is the message that ye heard from the <u>beginning</u>, that we should <u>love</u> one another.

40. 1 John 4:9
In this was manifested the <u>love</u> of God toward us, because that God sent his only begotten Son into the <u>world</u>, that we might live through him.

41. 1 John 4:10
Herein is <u>love</u>, not that we loved God, but that he loved us, and sent his <u>Son</u> to be the propitiation for our <u>sins</u>.

42. 1 John 4:12
No man hath seen <u>God</u> at any time. If we love one another, God dwelleth in us, and his love is perfected in <u>us</u>.

43. 1 John 4:16
And we have known and believed the <u>love</u> that God hath to us. God is <u>love</u>; and he that dwelleth in love dwelleth in God, and God in him.

44. 1 John 4:18
There is no fear in love; but perfect <u>love</u> casteth out <u>fear</u>: because fear hath torment. He that feareth is not made perfect in <u>love</u>.

45. 1 John 4:20
If a man say, I love God, and hateth his brother, he is a <u>liar</u>: for he that loveth not his <u>brother</u> whom he hath seen, how can he love God whom he hath not seen?

46. Revelation 3:19
As many as I <u>love</u>, I rebuke and <u>chasten</u>: be zealous therefore, and repent.

68. Crossword Puzzle 1

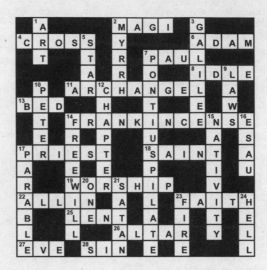

Section 2: The Advanced Section

70. Group 1

1. True—(1 Chronicles 1:34)
2. False—Amnon was David's firstborn son (1 Chronicles 3:1)
3. False—Rehoboam was king after him (1 Chronicles 3:10)
4. False—Her hair is her glory (1 Corinthians 11:15)
5. True—(1 Corinthians 15:50)
6. True—(1 Corinthians 15:56)
7. True—(1 Corinthians 6:19)
8. False—He refers to himself as an apostle (1 Corinthians 9:1)
9. False—Solomon would be king (1 Kings 1:13)
10. False—He ruled for seventeen years (1 Kings 14:21)
11. True—(1 Kings 16:30–31)
12. True—(1 Kings 16:32)
13. False—Elijah performed the miracle (1 Kings 17:19–22)
14. True—(1 Kings 17:2–7)
15. False—He met the prophets of Baal on Mount Carmel (1 Kings 18:19)
16. True—(1 Kings 18:46)
17. False—He was fed two meals (1 Kings 19:5–8)
18. True—(1 Kings 19:8)
19. True—(1 Kings 19:8)
20. True—(1 Kings 4:26)

71. Group 2

1. False—Benaiah was the commander (1 Kings 4:4)
2. False—He was not allowed to build it (1 Kings 5:3)
3. False—He began to build in the fourth year of his reign (1 Kings 6:1)
4. True—(Ephesians 2:20)
5. True—(1 Peter 5:8)

6. True—(1 Samuel 1:9–20)
7. True—(1 Samuel 9:27; 10:1)
8. False—The head is usually anointed (1 Samuel 10:1)
9. True—(1 Samuel 13:8–14)
10. True—(1 Samuel 16:1, 13)
11. True—(1 Samuel 16:15–19)
12. False—He killed a bear and a lion (1 Samuel 17:34–36)
13. True—(Mark 10:46–52)
14. False—He was from Gath (1 Samuel 17:4)
15. True—(1 Samuel 17:4)
16. False—He took five stones (1 Samuel 17:40)
17. False—He used a slingshot and one stone (1 Samuel 17:49–50)
18. True—(1 Samuel 17:54)
19. True—(1 Samuel 18:11)
20. True—(1 Samuel 18:27)

72. Group 3

1. True—(1 Samuel 18:6–7)
2. True—(1 Samuel 2:18–21)
3. True—(1 Samuel 20:16–17)
4. False—He gave David Goliath's sword (1 Samuel 21:8–9)
5. False—He massacred eighty-five priests in the town of Nod (1 Samuel 22:18)
6. True—(1 Samuel 25:3)
7. True—(1 Samuel 28:8)
8. True—(1 Samuel 3:2–10)
9. False—His bones were buried under a tree (1 Samuel 31:12–13)
10. True—(1 Samuel 31:2)
11. True—(1 Samuel 31:3)
12. False—Three of his sons were killed (1 Samuel 31:8)
13. True—(1 Samuel 4:11)
14. True—(1 Samuel 4:4–5)
15. True—(1 Samuel 5:2)
16. True—(1 Samuel 7:17)
17. True—(1 Samuel 7:17)
18. True—(1 Samuel 9:1–2)
19. True—(1 Timothy 2:5)
20. False—Christians should lift up holy hands (1 Timothy 2:8)

73. Group 4

1. True—(2 Chronicles 13:21)
2. True—(2 Chronicles 17:11)
3. False—He saw the Lord sitting upon his throne (2 Chronicles 18:8–18)
4. True—(2 Chronicles 2:8)
5. True—(2 Chronicles 26:9–10)
6. True—(2 Chronicles 26:21)
7. False—Josiah disguised himself (2 Chronicles 35:20–22)
8. False—He was Hebrew by birth (Philippians 3:5)
9. True—(2 Corinthians 11:25)
10. False—Her name appears twice (2 Corinthians 11:3; 1 Timothy 2:13)
11. True—(2 Corinthians 1:1–2; 11:32–33)
12. True—(2 Corinthians 1:1–2; 12:2)
13. False—His bones brought a dead man back to life (2 Kings 13:20–21)
14. True—(2 Kings 2:11)
15. False—It divided (2 Kings 2:12–14)
16. False—He healed the waters of Jericho (2 Kings 2:18–22)
17. True—(Joshua 10:12–13; 2 Kings 20:8–11)
18. True—(2 Kings 22:1)
19. True—(2 Kings 23:29)
20. True—(2 Kings 25:1)

74. Group 5

1. False—Zedekiah was the last king (2 Kings 25:1–7)
2. True—(2 Kings 4:1–12)
3. False—He supplied oil (2 Kings 4:1–7)
4. True—(2 Kings 5:20–27)
5. True—(2 Kings 6:17)
6. True—(2 Kings 8:7–15)
7. True—(Jeremiah 26:20–23)
8. True—(2 Kings 9:31–33)

9. False—Dogs ate her body (2 Kings 9:35–37)
10. True—(2 Samuel 11:2–4)
11. True—(2 Samuel 12:1–15)
12. False—Solomon was their second son (2 Samuel 12:24)
13. True—(2 Samuel 12:24–25)
14. True—(2 Samuel 13:37–38)
15. False—He was handsome (2 Samuel 14:25)
16. True—(2 Samuel 15:30)
17. True—(2 Samuel 18:14–17)
18. True—(2 Samuel 2:4)
19. True—(2 Samuel 2:8–9)
20. False—He was also known as Eshbaal (1 Chronicles 9:39)

75. Group 6

1. True—(2 Samuel 20:15–22)
2. True—(2 Samuel 20:9–10)
3. True—(2 Samuel 21:12–14)
4. True—(2 Samuel 4:4)
5. True—(2 Samuel 4:6)
6. False—Jebusites inhabited Jerusalem (2 Samuel 5:6)
7. True—(2 Samuel 6:16)
8. False—Joab was the commander (2 Samuel 8:16)
9. False—His grandmother was Lois (2 Timothy 1:5)
10. False—His mother was Eunice (2 Timothy 1:5)
11. True—(2 Timothy 4:12)
12. False—There were only two soldiers (Acts 12:6)
13. True—(Acts 1:15–26)
14. True—(Acts 10:1–45)
15. True—(Acts 10:24–48)
16. False—They were first called Christians at the church of Antioch (Acts 11:26)
17. True—(Acts 11:27–28)
18. False—James the brother of John was the first (Acts 12:1–2)
19. True—(Acts 12:1–2)
20. True—(Acts 12:18–19)

76. Group 7

1. True—(Acts 12:23)
2. True—(Acts 12:6–17)
3. True—(Acts 13:13–14)
4. True—(Acts 13:9)
5. True—(Acts 14:8–19)
6. True—(Acts 15:32)
7. False—He was accompanied by Silas (Acts 15:40–41)
8. True—(Acts 16:14)
9. True—(Acts 16:14)
10. True—(Acts 16:14–15)
11. False—They were famous for searching the Scriptures (Acts 17:10–11)
12. True—(Acts 18:2)
13. True—(Acts 18:8)
14. True—(Acts 19:19)
15. False—It was in Ephesus (Acts 19:1–9)
16. False—Peter preached at Pentecost (Acts 2)
17. False—He was in Troas (Acts 20:6–9)
18. True—(Acts 9:36–43; 20:9–12)
19. True—(Acts 21:39)
20. True—(Acts 22:3)

77. Group 8

1. True—(Acts 22:3)
2. False—He came to report a conspiracy (Acts 23:16)
3. True—(Acts 23:20–21)
4. True—(Acts 24:1)
5. True—(Acts 24:27)
6. False—He left Paul bound in prison (Acts 24:27)
7. False—It was the name of a storm (Acts 27:14)
8. True—(Acts 28:3–6)
9. False—John and Peter healed a crippled man (Acts 3:1–10)
10. True—(Acts 4:36)
11. False—It means "the son of consolation" (Acts 4:36)

12. False—Joses was his original name (Acts 4:36)
13. False—About five thousand men believed (Acts 4:4)
14. False—A Pharisee was a doctor of the law (Acts 5:34)
15. True—(Acts 5:34)
16. True—(Acts 6:7–8:2)
17. True—(Acts 7:59)
18. False—The Spirit of the Lord carried him (Acts 8:39–40)
19. False—Simon the sorcerer tried to buy the gifts (Acts 8:9, 18–19)
20. False—Saul was headed to Damascus (Acts 9:1)

78. Group 9

1. False—He was healed by Peter (Acts 9:32–34)
2. False—Peter raised her from the dead (Acts 9:36–41)
3. True—(Acts 9:8)
4. False—He was a herdsman (Amos 1:1)
5. False—He spoke about justice rolling down like a river (Amos 5:24)
6. False—He told believers to set their affections on things above (Colossians 3:2)
7. False—He described him as a beloved physician (Colossians 4:14)
8. False—He was king of Babylon (Daniel 1:1)
9. False—It was Mishael (Daniel 1:7)
10. True—(Daniel 2:1)
11. True—(Daniel 2:6)
12. True—(Daniel 5)
13. False—King Darius was "the Mede" (Daniel 5:31)
14. True—(Daniel 6)
15. False—He prayed three times a day (Daniel 6:10)
16. True—(Daniel 6:18)
17. False—He had a vision of a lion with eagle's wings (Daniel 7:4)
18. True—(Daniel 8:15–26; 9:21–27)
19. False—He visited Daniel (Daniel 9:20)
20. False—He was 120 years old (Deuteronomy 34:7)

79. Group 10

1. True—(Deuteronomy 10:6)
2. True—(Deuteronomy 12:6)
3. True—(Deuteronomy 3:11)
4. True—(Deuteronomy 32:48–49)
5. True—(Deuteronomy 34:3)
6. True—(Deuteronomy 34:5–6)
7. False—They mourned for thirty days (Deuteronomy 34:8)
8. True—(Exodus 20:12; Deuteronomy 5:16)
9. True—(Deuteronomy 9:13)
10. True—(Ecclesiastes 2:2)
11. True—(Ephesians 5:14)
12. False—He recommended the Holy Spirit as a substitute for wine (Ephesians 5:18)
13. False—Hadassah was her Hebrew name (Esther 2:7)
14. True—(Esther 2:7)
15. False—He was angry because Mordecai wouldn't bow down to him (Esther 3:5)
16. True—(Esther 3:8–9)
17. False—Zeresh was his wife (Esther 5:10)
18. True—(Exodus 1:13)
19. True—(Exodus 10:16)
20. True—(Exodus 10:19)

80. Group 11

1. False—They suffered ten plagues (Exodus 10:2)
2. False—It lasted three days (Exodus 10:23)
3. True—(Exodus 12:11–13)
4. True—(Exodus 12:1–20)
5. False—They were in Egypt for 430 years (Exodus 12:40)
6. True—(Exodus 14:13–31)
7. False—A cloud hid them (Exodus 14:19–20)
8. True—(Exodus 14:21)
9. True—(Exodus 15:25)
10. False—Joshua was the commander (Exodus 17:10)
11. True—(Exodus 17:6)

12. False—God appeared as a cloud (Exodus 19:9)
13. True—(Exodus 2:1–2)
14. False—He fled to Midian (Exodus 2:15)
15. True—(Exodus 2:21)
16. False—Zipporah was his first wife (Exodus 2:21)

17. False—The basket was made of bulrushes (Exodus 2:3)
18. False—Pharaoh's daughter found him (Exodus 2:5–6)
19. True—(Exodus 20:2)
20. True—(Exodus 24:12)

81. Group 12

1. True—(Exodus 25:10)
2. True—(Exodus 26:1, 7)
3. False—A canopy separated them (Exodus 26:33)
4. True—(Exodus 3:1)
5. False—He saw it on Mount Horeb (Exodus 3:1)
6. True—(Exodus 31:13)
7. True—(Exodus 31:13)
8. True—(Exodus 31:18)
9. False—Moses rebuked him (Exodus 32:19–22)
10. True—(Exodus 33:11)
11. True—(Exodus 33:21–23)

12. False—Moses fasted for forty days (Exodus 34:27–28)
13. False—It turned into a serpent (Exodus 4:2–4)
14. True—(Exodus 40:9)
15. True—(Exodus 6:20)
16. True—(Exodus 7:14–24)
17. False—It turned into blood (Exodus 7:19–25)
18. True—(Exodus 8:16–17)
19. False—Frogs came out of the Nile River (Exodus 8:5–7)
20. False—He tossed ashes into the air (Exodus 9:9–10)

82. Group 13

1. True—(Ezekiel 1:15)
2. False—Ezekiel ate the book (Ezekiel 2:9–3:3)
3. False—He was forbidden to mourn (Ezekiel 24:16–18)
4. False—His wife died suddenly (Ezekiel 24:18)
5. True—(Ezekiel 25:13)
6. False—It dwelt in Egypt (Ezekiel 29:14)
7. True—(Ezekiel 35:1–7)
8. True—(Ezekiel 47:5)
9. False—It means "the Lord is there" (Ezekiel 48:35)
10. True—(Ezekiel 8:8)

11. True—(Ezra 3:8)
12. True—(Ezra 8:21–23)
13. True—(Galatians 4:25)
14. False—There are nine (Galatians 5:22–23)
15. False—Abraham found a ram (Genesis 22:13)
16. True—(Genesis 5:32)
17. False—He was a priest but also a king (Genesis 14:18)
18. True—(Genesis 15:15)
19. True—(Genesis 1:29)
20. False—He created the world in six days; on the seventh day, he rested (Genesis 1:31–2:1)

83. Group 14

1. True—(Genesis 11:4, 8–9)
2. False—He went to Egypt (Genesis 12:10)
3. True—(Genesis 14:18)
4. False—He was the first priest mentioned (Genesis 14:18)
5. True—(Genesis 15:12–16)

6. False—He pleaded to spare the city of Sodom (Genesis 18:1–33)
7. False—She was the mother of his brother Ishmael (Genesis 16:1)
8. False—The angel of the Lord named him (Genesis 16:11)
9. True—(Genesis 16:13)

10. False—She was approached by an angel (Genesis 16:7–14)
11. True—(Genesis 17:15)
12. False—Abraham met with the Lord there (Genesis 18:1)
13. True—(Genesis 19:1–3)
14. True—(Genesis 19:24–25)
15. True—(Genesis 19:30–36)
16. True—(Genesis 19:26)
17. True—(Genesis 2:19–20)
18. False—He removed Adam's rib (Genesis 2:21–22)
19. True—(Genesis 2:8)
20. False—He became an archer (Genesis 21:14, 20)

84. Group 15

1. False—She gave birth to a son (Genesis 21:1–5)
2. False—His name means "laughter" (Genesis 21:3–6)
3. False—He was one hundred years old (Genesis 21:5)
4. True—(Genesis 22:2)
5. False—Their mother was Milcah (Genesis 22:20–22)
6. True—(Genesis 23:19)
7. False—Bethuel was her father (Genesis 24:24)
8. True—(Genesis 24:29)
9. True—(Genesis 24:52–53)
10. False—She was his wife (Genesis 24:67)
11. True—(Genesis 25:1)
12. False—They were the twin sons of Isaac and Rebekah (Genesis 25:21–26)
13. True—(Genesis 25:28)
14. True—(Genesis 25:29–34)
15. True—(Genesis 25:9)
16. True—(Genesis 29:15–25)
17. False—He had to serve fourteen years (Genesis 29:16–30)
18. True—(Genesis 29:21–25)
19. True—(Genesis 29:32)
20. False—Simeon was his second son (Genesis 29:33)

85. Group 16

1. False—She was tempted by a serpent (Genesis 3:1)
2. False—He blamed Eve (Genesis 3:12)
3. True—(Genesis 5:18)
4. False—It brought forth thorns and thistles (Genesis 3:17–18)
5. False—God cursed the ground (Genesis 3:17–18)
6. True—(Genesis 3:17–18)
7. False—It appears only twice (Genesis 3:20; 4:1)
8. True—(Genesis 3:24)
9. True—(Genesis 3:24)
10. True—(Genesis 30:19)
11. True—(Genesis 31:43–54)
12. False—They parted in Mizpah (Genesis 31:49)
13. True—(Genesis 32:13–18)
14. False—He changed it to Israel (Genesis 32:38)
15. False—Esau and Jacob buried Isaac (Genesis 35:29)
16. True—(Genesis 37:18–28)
17. False—He was taken to Egypt (Genesis 37:28)
18. False—His father made him the coat (Genesis 37:3)
19. True—(Genesis 38:27–30)
20. True—(Genesis 39:7)

86. Group 17

1. True—(Genesis 39:7–20)
2. True—(Genesis 4:11)
3. True—(Genesis 4:16)
4. False—Cain built the first city (Genesis 4:17)
5. False—It was called Enoch (Genesis 4:17)
6. False—Cain invented farming (Genesis 4:2)
7. True—(Genesis 4:25)
8. False—Seth replaced Abel (Genesis 4:25)
9. False—He killed him in the fields (Genesis 4:8)

Answers

10. True—(Genesis 4:8)
11. True—(Genesis 41:41, 43)
12. False—He put a golden chain on his neck (Genesis 41:42)
13. True—(Genesis 41:45)
14. True—(Genesis 41:45)
15. True—(Genesis 42:1–2)
16. True—(Genesis 42:6)
17. False—He accused them of stealing his silver cup (Genesis 44:1–17)
18. False—He lived there for seventeen years (Genesis 47:28)
19. True—(Genesis 47:29)
20. False—Enoch was his father (Genesis 5:21)

87. Group 18

1. False—He was 930 years old (Genesis 5:5)
2. True—(Genesis 6:14)
3. False—It had one window (Genesis 6:16)
4. False—It had three stories (Genesis 6:16)
5. False—He was six hundred years old (Genesis 7:11)
6. False—It was carrying an olive leaf (Genesis 8:11)
7. True—(Genesis 8:4)
8. False—He released a raven and a dove (Genesis 8:7–8)
9. False—The rainbow is a reminder (Genesis 9:13–16)
10. True—(Genesis 9:18)
11. True—(Hebrews 13:4)
12. True—(Hebrews 4:12)
13. False—It means "rest" (Hebrews 4:9)
14. True—(Hebrews 9:15)
15. False—He was told to name her Loruhamah (Hosea 1:6)
16. True—(1 Samuel 22:1–2; 23:14)
17. True—(Isaiah 10:5)
18. True—(Isaiah 20:3)
19. False—He mentioned a voice crying in the wilderness (Isaiah 40:3)
20. True—(Isaiah 47:8)

88. Group 19

1. True—(Isaiah 9:6)
2. False—He is like the waves in the sea (James 1:6–8)
3. True—(James 2:23)
4. False—Jeremiah was ordained (Jeremiah 1:5)
5. True—(Jeremiah 26:18)
6. True—(Jeremiah 31:9)
7. True—(Job 1:1)
8. True—(Job 1:14)
9. True—(Job 1:19)
10. False—They wept when they saw him suffering (Job 2:11–12)
11. True—(Job 2:7)
12. True—(Job 2:8)
13. True—(Job 2:9)
14. True—(Job 20:17)
15. True—(Job 30:29)
16. False—He lived another 140 years (Job 42:16)
17. True—(Joel 1:2–4)
18. True—(John 1:43–51)
19. False—He saw Nathanael sitting under a fig tree (John 1:48)
20. False—He said, "I am the good shepherd" (John 10:14)

89. Group 20

1. True—(John 11:1)
2. True—(John 11:38)
3. True—(John 11:38–44)
4. False—Andrew and Philip brought Greeks to Jesus (John 12:20–28)
5. True—(John 12:3)
6. True—(John 12:3–5)
7. True—(John 13:6–9)
8. True—(John 14:8)
9. False—He cut off Malchus's ear (John 18:10)
10. False—They divided them into four shares (John 19:23)
11. True—(John 2:1–10)
12. False—He turned six jars of water into wine (John 2:1–10)

13. False—He worked his first miracle in Cana (John 2:1–11)
14. False—He told the servants to fill them with water (John 2:7)
15. False—She started to cry (John 20:1, 11)
16. False—Mary Magdalene called Jesus Rabboni (John 20:16)
17. True—(John 21:25)
18. False—Peter jumped into the water (John 21:7)
19. True—(John 3:16)
20. False—He told her he was the Messiah (John 4:25–26)

90. Group 21

1. True—(John 4:6–19)
2. False—He asked for a drink of water (John 4:7)
3. True—(John 6:1)
4. False—Judas Iscariot betrayed him with a kiss (Mark 14:43–45; John 6:70–71)
5. True—(John 8:44)
6. False—Jonah asked to be cast into the sea (Jonah 1:12)
7. False—He was in the fish for three days and three nights (Jonah 1:17)
8. True—(Jonah 1:3)
9. False—He prayed (Jonah 2:1)
10. False—It would be overturned in forty days (Jonah 3:4)
11. False—He was Joshua's father (Joshua 1:1)
12. True—(Joshua 1:4)
13. True—(Joshua 2:1)
14. False—He was 110 years old when he died (Joshua 24:29)
15. True—(Joshua 24:32)
16. True—(Joshua 3:1–6)
17. True—(Joshua 6:20)
18. True—(Judges 11:3)
19. False—He had forty sons (Judges 12:13–14)
20. False—Manoah was his father (Judges 13:22–24)

91. Group 22

1. True—(Judges 14:5–9)
2. True—(Judges 16:15–20)
3. False—Samson was buried with his father, Manoah (Judges 16:31)
4. False—Micah stole the silver (Judges 17:1–2)
5. True—(Judges 17:5)
6. False—He was a very overweight man (Judges 3:17)
7. True—(Judges 3:17–21)
8. False—He gave the captain milk (Judges 4:19–21)
9. False—He was the king of Canaan (Judges 4:2)
10. False—Sisera was killed (Judges 4:21)
11. False—Israel was judged by Deborah (Judges 4:4)
12. False—Gideon was commissioned by an angel (Judges 6:11–23)
13. False—They attacked a Midianite camp late at night (Judges 7:19)
14. False—He was murdered by Gideon's army (Judges 7:25)
15. False—He defeated them with only three hundred men (Judges 7:7)
16. True—(Judges 8:26)
17. False—They experienced forty years of peace (Judges 8:28)
18. True—(Judges 8:30)
19. False—Camels were forbidden as food (Leviticus 11:4)
20. False—They had to cover the lower part of their face (Leviticus 13:45)

92. Group 23

1. False—A goat was released (Leviticus 16:22)
2. False—He anointed Aaron and his sons (Leviticus 8:23–30)
3. False—They were the sons of Aaron (Leviticus 10:1)
4. True—(Luke 1:22)
5. False—She was engaged (Luke 1:27)

6. True—(Luke 1:30–31)
7. True—(Luke 10:17–18)
8. True—(Luke 11:34)
9. False—A repentant sinner causes them to rejoice (Luke 15:10)
10. True—(Luke 17:12–16)
11. True—(Luke 17:18)
12. True—(Luke 19:2–4)
13. True—(Luke 19:8)
14. False—They saw him in Jerusalem at the temple (Luke 2:25, 27, 36–37)
15. True—(Luke 2:4)
16. True—(Luke 2:41)
17. True—(Luke 2:49)
18. True—(Luke 2:51)
19. False—He was born in a stable (Luke 2:7)
20. True—(Luke 22:19)

93. Group 24

1. True—(Luke 22:43)
2. True—(Luke 22:45)
3. True—(Luke 22–39)
4. True—(Luke 24:30)
5. False—He was governor of Judea (Luke 3:1)
6. True—(Luke 3:17)
7. False—The tax collector Levi held a feast for Jesus (Luke 5:29)
8. True—(Luke 5:29–32)
9. True—(Luke 5:8)
10. False—He said to bless them (Luke 6:20, 28)
11. True—(Luke 7:11–15)
12. False—Jesus was asleep on the boat (Luke 8:23–24)
13. False—He brought Jairus's daughter back to life (Luke 8:41–42, 49–55)
14. False—He sent Peter and John to prepare the meal (Luke 22:8)
15. False—He took the form of a dove (Mark 1:10)
16. False—He baptized them in the Jordan River (Mark 1:5)
17. False—John said he was unworthy (Mark 1:7)
18. True—(Mark 12:40)
19. True—(Mark 14:3)
20. True—(Mark 15:22)

94. Group 25

1. False—Two criminals were crucified with Jesus (Mark 15:22, 27)
2. True—(Mark 16:18)
3. False—Seven demons were cast out (Mark 16:9)
4. True—(Mark 16:9)
5. True—(Mark 3:17)
6. True—(Mark 6:56)
7. True—(Matthew 1:18–21)
8. False—It means "God with us" (Matthew 1:23)
9. True—(Matthew 1:3–17)
10. True—(Matthew 12:33)
11. False—He used five loaves of bread (Matthew 14:15–21)
12. False—Peter walked on water (Matthew 14:28–31)
13. False—She plotted the death of John the Baptist (Matthew 14:3–8)
14. False—He sent Peter (Matthew 17:24–27)
15. False—A star led them (Matthew 2:1–9)
16. False—They were in the east (Matthew 2:7–9)
17. True—(Matthew 21:14)
18. True—(Matthew 21:1–9)
19. True—(Matthew 24:3)
20. True—(Matthew 24–25)

95. Group 26

1. False—They are referred to as sheep (Matthew 25:31–34)
2. False—He was given thirty pieces of silver (Matthew 26:14–16)
3. True—(Matthew 26:14–16)
4. False—He denied Jesus three times (Matthew 26:34)
5. True—(Matthew 26:75)
6. True—(Matthew 27:26)
7. False—They were thieves (Matthew 27:44)

8. True—(Matthew 27:60)
9. False—It was known as "the field of blood" (Matthew 27:7–8)
10. True—(Matthew 3:1)
11. True—(Matthew 3:4)
12. True—(Matthew 3:4)
13. False—Angels ministered to him (Matthew 4:1, 11)
14. False—He moved to Capernaum (Matthew 4:13)
15. False—He said, "Man shall not live by bread alone" (Matthew 4:4)
16. False—He builds it on sand (Matthew 7:26)
17. False—Nahum prophesied Assyria's destruction (Nahum 3:18)
18. False—He wrote the first five books
19. False—Her story takes place in 1 Samuel
20. True—(Genesis 3:14)

96. Group 27

1. False—She had other children (Mark 6:3)
2. False—It is the fourth book
3. True
4. False—It is the eighth book
5. False—It is the longest book of the New Testament
6. False—It is found in the book of Judges
7. True—(Mark 2:14)
8. True
9. True
10. True—(Genesis 29)
11. True
12. True—(Mark 3:17)
13. False—It means "praise the Lord"
14. True
15. False—Malachi is the last book of the Old Testament
16. True—(Genesis 1:1)
17. True
18. False—Leviticus is the third book
19. False—Acts is the fifth book
20. True—(Numbers 11:31)

97. Group 28

1. True—(Numbers 13:1–16)
2. True—(Numbers 16:28–33)
3. False—They mourned for thirty days (Numbers 20:27–29)
4. True—(Numbers 22:21–33)
5. True—(Numbers 25:7–8)
6. False—He was 123 years old when he died (Numbers 33:39)
7. True—(Numbers 33:39)
8. True—(Philippians 4:16)
9. True—(Proverbs 11:22)
10. True—(Proverbs 20:17)
11. True—(Proverbs 25:1)
12. True—(Proverbs 27:5)
13. True
14. True
15. False—John had the vision (Revelation 1:12)
16. False—The book of Revelation says this (Revelation 1:15)
17. True—(Revelation 1:4)
18. True—(Revelation 11:1–2)
19. True—(Revelation 11:7)
20. True—(Revelation 12:7)

98. Group 29

1. True—(Revelation 16:7)
2. True—(Revelation 17:3)
3. True—(Revelation 18:2)
4. False—It was composed of burning sulfur (Revelation 19:20)
5. True—(Revelation 20:2)
6. False—Twelve angels were at the gates (Revelation 21:12)
7. True—(Revelation 21:19–20)
8. True—(Revelation 3:15–16)
9. False—John had the vision (Revelation 4:6)
10. False—John saw the creature (Revelation 4:7)
11. False—They were holding the four winds (Revelation 7:1)
12. False—A star fell on earth's waters (Revelation 8:10)

13. True—(Romans 10:17)
14. True—(Romans 14:10)
15. False—He says to greet one another with a holy kiss (Romans 16:16)
16. True—(Romans 16:22)
17. True—(Romans 6:23)
18. True—(Romans 8:35–39)
19. False—Elimelech was her husband (Ruth 1:2)
20. False—She was married to Mahlon (Ruth 4:10)

99. Group 30

1. True—(Ruth 1:4)
2. True—(Ruth 4:10)
3. True—(Ruth 4:17)
4. False—He had a throne with purple cushions (Song of Solomon 3:10)
5. False—There are thirty-nine books
6. True—(Titus 3:13)
7. True—(Zechariah 1:8)
8. True—(Zechariah 14:1–4)
9. False—Joshua was the high priest (Zechariah 6:10–11)
10. True

101. Memory Verses

1. Genesis 1:1
   In the <u>beginning</u> God created the <u>heaven</u> and the <u>earth</u>.

2. Genesis 1:26
   And God said, Let us make man in our <u>image</u>, after our likeness: and let them have <u>domin-ion</u> over the fish of the sea, and over the fowl of the air, and over the cattle, and over all the earth, and over every creeping thing that creepeth upon the <u>earth</u>.

3. Genesis 1:27
   So God created man in his own <u>image</u>, in the image of God created he him; <u>male</u> and <u>female</u> created he them.

4. Joshua 1:8
   This book of the law shall not depart out of thy <u>mouth</u>; but thou shalt meditate therein day and <u>night</u>, that thou mayest observe to do according to all that is written therein: for then thou shalt make thy way <u>prosperous</u>, and then thou shalt have good <u>success</u>.

5. Joshua 1:9
   Have not I commanded thee? Be strong and of a good <u>courage</u>; be not afraid, neither be thou <u>dismayed</u>: for the Lord thy God is with <u>thee</u> whithersoever thou goest.

6. Psalm 37:4
   Delight <u>thyself</u> also in the Lord; and he shall give thee the <u>desires</u> of thine <u>heart</u>.

7. Psalm 133:1–2
   Behold, how good and how pleasant it is for <u>brethren</u> to dwell together in <u>unity</u>! It is like the precious <u>ointment</u> upon the head, that ran down upon the <u>beard</u>, even Aaron's beard: that went down to the skirts of his garments.

8. Psalm 139:14
   I will praise thee; for I am <u>fearfully</u> and <u>wonderfully</u> made: marvellous are thy <u>works</u>; and that my soul knoweth right well.

9. Proverbs 3:5–6
   <u>Trust</u> in the Lord with all thine <u>heart</u>; and lean not unto thine own understanding. In all thy ways <u>acknowledge</u> him, and he shall direct thy <u>paths</u>.

10. Proverbs 30:5
    Every <u>word</u> of <u>God</u> is pure: he is a shield unto them that put their <u>trust</u> in him.

11. Isaiah 26:3
    Thou wilt keep him in perfect <u>peace</u>, whose <u>mind</u> is stayed on thee: because he <u>trusteth</u> in thee.

12. Isaiah 40:31
    But they that wait upon the Lord shall renew their <u>strength</u>; they shall mount up with <u>wings</u> as <u>eagles</u>; they shall run, and not be weary; and they shall walk, and not <u>faint</u>.

13. Isaiah 41:10
    Fear thou not; for I am with thee: be not <u>dismayed</u>; for I am thy God: I will strengthen thee; yea, I will help thee; yea, I will uphold <u>thee</u> with the right <u>hand</u> of my righteousness.

14. Isaiah 53:4
    Surely he hath borne our <u>griefs</u>, and carried our sorrows: yet we did esteem him <u>stricken</u>, smitten of God, and <u>afflicted</u>.

15. Isaiah 53:5

But he was wounded for our <u>transgressions</u>, he was bruised for our <u>iniquities</u>: the <u>chastisement</u> of our peace was upon him; and with his <u>stripes</u> we are healed.

16. Isaiah 53:6

All we like <u>sheep</u> have gone <u>astray</u>; we have turned every one to his own way; and the LORD hath laid on him the <u>iniquity</u> of us all.

17. Isaiah 55:8

For my thoughts are not your <u>thoughts</u>, neither are your ways my <u>ways</u>, saith the LORD.

18. Jeremiah 29:11

For I know the thoughts that I think toward you, saith the LORD, thoughts of <u>peace</u>, and not of <u>evil</u>, to give you an expected <u>end</u>.

19. Micah 6:8

He hath shewed <u>thee</u>, O man, what is good; and what doth the LORD require of thee, but to do <u>justly</u>, and to love <u>mercy</u>, and to walk <u>humbly</u> with thy God?

20. Matthew 3:2

And saying, <u>Repent</u> ye: for the <u>kingdom</u> of heaven is at <u>hand</u>.

21. Matthew 5:16

Let your <u>light</u> so shine before men, that they may see your <u>good</u> works, and glorify your Father which is in <u>heaven</u>.

22. Matthew 11:28–30

Come unto me, all ye that labour and are heavy laden, and I will give you <u>rest</u>. Take my <u>yoke</u> upon you, and learn of me; for I am <u>meek</u> and lowly in <u>heart</u>: and ye shall find rest unto your souls. For my yoke is easy, and my burden is light.

23. Matthew 22:37

<u>Jesus</u> said unto him, Thou shalt <u>love</u> the Lord thy God with all thy heart, and with all thy <u>soul</u>, and with all thy <u>mind</u>.

24. Matthew 28:18

And <u>Jesus</u> came and spake unto them, saying, All <u>power</u> is given unto me in <u>heaven</u> and in <u>earth</u>.

25. Matthew 28:19–20

Go ye therefore, and teach all <u>nations</u>, baptizing them in the name of the Father, and of the Son, and of the Holy <u>Ghost</u>: Teaching them to <u>observe</u> all things whatsoever I have <u>commanded</u> you: and, lo, I am with you always, even unto the end of the world. Amen.

26. John 1:1

In the <u>beginning</u> was the <u>Word</u>, and the Word was with God, and the Word was <u>God</u>.

27. John 1:12

But as many as received him, to them gave he <u>power</u> to become the sons of God, even to them that <u>believe</u> on his <u>name</u>.

28. John 3:16

For God so loved the <u>world</u>, that he gave his only begotten Son, that whosoever believeth in him should not <u>perish</u>, but have everlasting <u>life</u>.

29. John 3:17

For God sent not his Son into the <u>world</u> to <u>condemn</u> the world; but that the world through him might be <u>saved</u>.

30. John 5:24

Verily, verily, I say unto you, He that heareth my <u>word</u>, and believeth on him that sent me, hath everlasting <u>life</u>, and shall not come into condemnation; but is passed from <u>death</u> unto life.

31. John 10:10

The <u>thief</u> cometh not, but for to steal, and to <u>kill</u>, and to <u>destroy</u>: I am come that they might have <u>life</u>, and that they might have it more abundantly.

32. John 11:25

Jesus said unto her, I am the <u>resurrection</u>, and the life: he that believeth in me, though he were <u>dead</u>, yet shall he <u>live</u>.

33. John 13:35

By this shall all <u>men</u> know that ye are my <u>disciples</u>, if ye have <u>love</u> one to another.

34. John 14:6

<u>Jesus</u> saith unto him, I am the way, the <u>truth</u>, and the <u>life</u>: no man cometh unto the <u>Father</u>, but by me.

35. John 14:27

Peace I leave with you, my <u>peace</u> I give unto you: not as the <u>world</u> giveth, give I unto you. Let not your <u>heart</u> be troubled, neither let it be afraid.

36. John 15:13

Greater <u>love</u> hath no <u>man</u> than this, that a man lay down his <u>life</u> for his <u>friends</u>.

37. John 16:33

These things I have spoken unto you, that in me ye might have <u>peace</u>. In the <u>world</u> ye shall have <u>tribulation</u>: but be of good <u>cheer</u>; I have overcome the world.

38. Acts 1:8

But ye shall receive <u>power</u>, after that the Holy Ghost is come upon you: and ye shall be <u>witnesses</u> unto me both in <u>Jerusalem</u>, and in all Judaea, and in <u>Samaria</u>, and unto the uttermost part of the <u>earth</u>.

39. Acts 2:38
Then Peter said unto them, Repent, and be baptized every one of you in the name of Jesus Christ for the remission of sins, and ye shall receive the gift of the Holy Ghost.

40. Acts 4:12
Neither is there salvation in any other: for there is none other name under heaven given among men, whereby we must be saved.

41. Acts 17:11
These were more noble than those in Thessalonica, in that they received the word with all readiness of mind, and searched the scriptures daily, whether those things were so.

42. Romans 3:23
For all have sinned, and come short of the glory of God.

43. Romans 5:8
But God commendeth his love toward us, in that, while we were yet sinners, Christ died for us.

44. Romans 6:23
For the wages of sin is death; but the gift of God is eternal life through Jesus Christ our Lord.

45. Romans 8:28
And we know that all things work together for good to them that love God, to them who are the called according to his purpose.

46. Romans 8:38–39
For I am persuaded, that neither death, nor life, nor angels, nor principalities, nor powers, nor things present, nor things to come, Nor height, nor depth, nor any other creature, shall be able to separate us from the love of God, which is in Christ Jesus our Lord.

47. Romans 10:9–10
That if thou shalt confess with thy mouth the Lord Jesus, and shalt believe in thine heart that God hath raised him from the dead, thou shalt be saved. For with the heart man believeth unto righteousness; and with the mouth confession is made unto salvation.

48. Romans 10:17
So then faith cometh by hearing, and hearing by the word of God.

49. Romans 12:1
I beseech you therefore, brethren, by the mercies of God, that ye present your bodies a living sacrifice, holy, acceptable unto God, which is your reasonable service.

50. Romans 12:2
And be not conformed to this world: but be ye transformed by the renewing of your mind, that ye may prove what is that good, and acceptable, and perfect, will of God.

51. Romans 15:13
Now the God of hope fill you with all joy and peace in believing, that ye may abound in hope, through the power of the Holy Ghost.

52. 1 Corinthians 6:19
What? know ye not that your body is the temple of the Holy Ghost which is in you, which ye have of God, and ye are not your own?

53. 1 Corinthians 10:13
There hath no temptation taken you but such as is common to man: but God is faithful, who will not suffer you to be tempted above that ye are able; but will with the temptation also make a way to escape, that ye may be able to bear it.

54. 2 Corinthians 5:17
Therefore if any man be in Christ, he is a new creature: old things are passed away; behold, all things are become new.

55. 2 Corinthians 5:21
For he hath made him to be sin for us, who knew no sin; that we might be made the righteousness of God in him.

56. 2 Corinthians 12:9
And he said unto me, My grace is sufficient for thee: for my strength is made perfect in weakness. Most gladly therefore will I rather glory in my infirmities, that the power of Christ may rest upon me.

57. 2 Timothy 1:7
For God hath not given us the spirit of fear; but of power, and of love, and of a sound mind.

58. 2 Timothy 3:16–17
All scripture is given by inspiration of God, and is profitable for doctrine, for reproof, for correction, for instruction in righteousness: That the man of God may be perfect, thoroughly furnished unto all good works.

59. Hebrews 4:12
For the word of God is quick, and powerful, and sharper than any twoedged sword, piercing even to the dividing asunder of soul and spirit, and of the joints and marrow, and is a discerner of the thoughts and intents of the heart.

60. Hebrews 4:15
For we have not an high priest which cannot be touched with the feeling of our infirmities;

but was in all points <u>tempted</u> like as we are, yet without sin.

61. Hebrews 4:16

Let us therefore come <u>boldly</u> unto the throne of <u>grace</u>, that we may obtain <u>mercy</u>, and find grace to <u>help</u> in time of need.

62. Hebrews 10:24–25

And let us consider one <u>another</u> to provoke unto <u>love</u> and to good <u>works</u>: Not forsaking the <u>assembling</u> of ourselves together, as the manner of some is; but exhorting one another: and so much the more, as ye see the day approaching.

63. Hebrews 11:1

Now <u>faith</u> is the <u>substance</u> of things hoped for, the <u>evidence</u> of things not seen.

64. Hebrews 11:6

But without <u>faith</u> it is impossible to please him: for he that cometh to God must <u>believe</u> that he is, and that he is a <u>rewarder of them</u> that diligently <u>seek</u> him.

65. Hebrews 12:1–2

Wherefore seeing we also are compassed about with so great a cloud of <u>witnesses</u>, let us lay aside every weight, and the sin which doth so easily beset us, and let us run with patience the race that is set before us, Looking unto Jesus the author and <u>finisher</u> of our faith; who for the joy that was set before him endured the <u>cross</u>, despising the <u>shame</u>, and is set down at the right hand of the throne of God.

66. Hebrews 13:5

Let your <u>conversation</u> be without <u>covetousness</u>; and be <u>content</u> with such things as ye have: for he hath said, I will never leave thee, nor forsake thee.

67. James 1:2–3

My <u>brethren</u>, count it all joy when ye fall into divers <u>temptations</u>; Knowing this, that the trying of your <u>faith</u> worketh patience.

68. James 1:12

<u>Blessed</u> is the man that endureth temptation: for when he is tried, he shall receive the crown of <u>life</u>, which the Lord hath <u>promised</u> to them that <u>love</u> him.

69. James 5:16

Confess your faults one to another, and pray one for another, that ye may be <u>healed</u>. The effectual fervent <u>prayer</u> of a righteous <u>man</u> <u>availeth</u> much.

70. 1 Peter 2:24

Who his own self bare our sins in his own body on the <u>tree</u>, that we, being dead to <u>sins</u>, should live unto <u>righteousness</u>: by whose <u>stripes</u> ye were healed.

71. 1 Peter 3:15–16

But sanctify the Lord God in your <u>hearts</u>: and be ready always to give an answer to every man that asketh you a reason of the hope that is in you with meekness and fear: Having a good <u>conscience</u>; that, whereas they speak evil of you, as of <u>evildoers</u>, they may be ashamed that falsely accuse your good conversation in <u>Christ</u>.

72. 1 Peter 5:7

<u>Casting</u> all your <u>care</u> upon him; for he careth for <u>you</u>.

73. 1 John 1:9

If we confess our <u>sins</u>, he is <u>faithful</u> and just to forgive us our sins, and to cleanse us from all <u>unrighteousness</u>.

74. 1 John 3:16

Hereby perceive we the love of <u>God</u>, because he laid down his <u>life</u> for us: and we ought to lay down our lives for the <u>brethren</u>.

75. Revelation 1:10

I was in the <u>Spirit</u> on the Lord's <u>day</u>, and heard behind me a great <u>voice</u>, as of a <u>trumpet</u>.

103. Scrambled Scriptures

1. Psalm 46:10

Be still, and know that I am God: I will be exalted among the heathen, I will be exalted in the earth.

2. Psalm 118:24

This is the day which the Lord hath made; we will rejoice and be glad in it.

3. Psalm 119:11

Thy word have I hid in mine heart, that I might not sin against thee.

4. Luke 11:9

And I say unto you, Ask, and it shall be given you; seek, and ye shall find; knock, and it shall be opened unto you.

5. Luke 11:10

For every one that asketh receiveth; and he that seeketh findeth; and to him that knocketh it shall be opened.

6. John 14:6
   Jesus saith unto him, I am the way, the truth, and the life: no man cometh unto the Father, but by me.

7. Romans 3:23
   For all have sinned, and come short of the glory of God.

8. Romans 5:8
   But God commendeth his love toward us, in that, while we were yet sinners, Christ died for us.

9. Romans 10:9
   That if thou shalt confess with thy mouth the Lord Jesus, and shalt believe in thine heart that God hath raised him from the dead, thou shalt be saved.

10. Romans 10:13
    For whosoever shall call upon the name of the Lord shall be saved.

105. Names of God Part 1

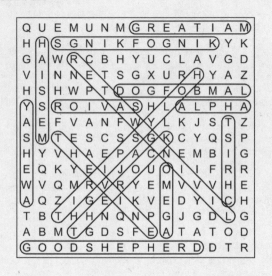

106. Names of God Part 2

107. Names of God Part 3

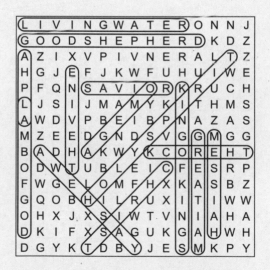

108. People and Angels Part 1

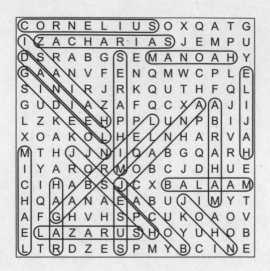

109. People and Angels Part 2

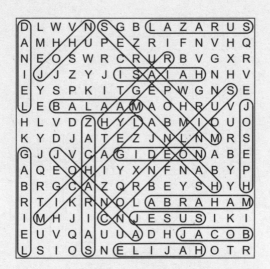

110. People and Angels Part 3

111. Abraham's Progeny Part 1

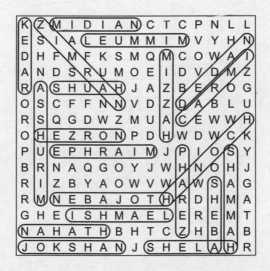

112. Abraham's Progeny Part 2

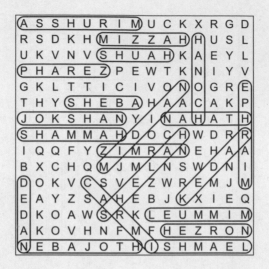

113. Abraham's Progeny Part 3

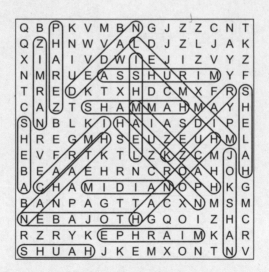

114. Cities of Judah Part 1

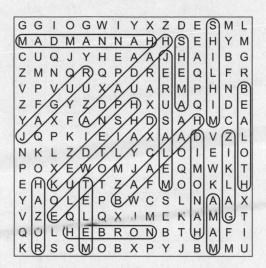

115. Cities of Judah Part 2

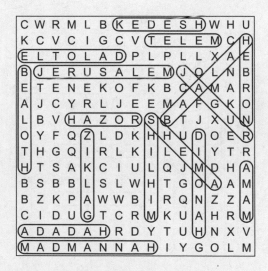

116. Cities of Judah Part 3

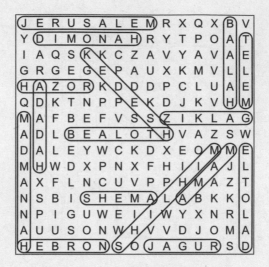

117. Women in the Bible Part 1

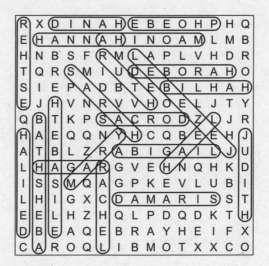

118. Women in the Bible Part 2

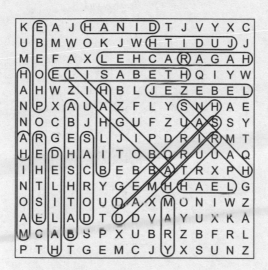

119. Women in the Bible Part 3

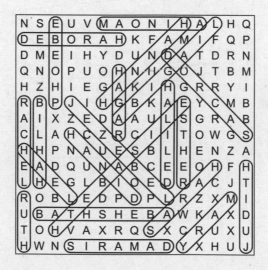

120. Paul's Journeys Part 1

121. Paul's Journeys Part 2

122. Paul's Journeys Part 3

123. Prisoners and Exiles Part 1

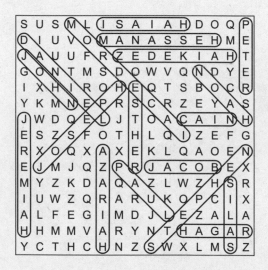

124. Prisoners and Exiles Part 2

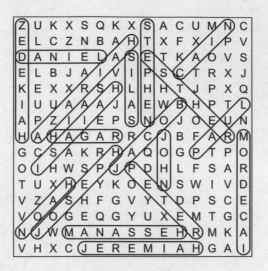

125. Prisoners and Exiles Part 3

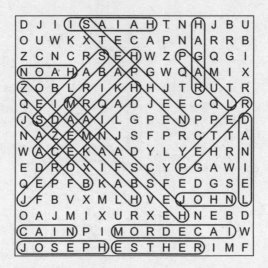

126. The Book of Genesis

Chapter 1

1. Light
2. Firmament (sky)
3. Dry land
4. Stars, sun, and moon
5. Sea animals and flying creatures
6. Beasts of the earth and humans
7. God rested

Chapter 2

1. Dust
2. The ground
3. Adam's rib
4. Garden of Eden

Chapter 3

1. The tree of the knowledge of good and evil
2. The serpent
3. The serpent would have to crawl on his belly and eat dust
4. He would be forced to till the ground in hard labor
5. She would give birth in pain and be subject to man
6. To keep man out of the garden
7. So man would not eat of it and live forever

Chapter 4

1. Because Cain did not honor God with his offering like his brother Abel did
2. Murdered him
3. Put a curse on him
4. Cain was afraid someone would find him and kill him
5. God put a mark on him that identified and protected him
6. Seth

Chapter 5

1. Shem, Ham, and Japheth

Chapter 6

1. They took the daughters of men as wives
2. He viewed it as wicked
3. He was sorry he had made man
4. Noah

5. Build an ark
6. 300 cubits long (450 feet), 50 cubits wide (75 feet), 30 cubits high (45 feet)
7. Two of each

Chapter 7

1. Two of each
2. Seven of each
3. Seven of each
4. Forty
5. Eight
6. They remained in the seas

Chapter 8

1. 150
2. Three
3. First month of the next year

Chapter 9

1. The blood of that man or that beast
2. Rainbow
3. He told his brothers

Chapter 10

1. Ham
2. On the coastlands
3. In the east
4. Noah's sons, Ham, Shem, and Japheth

Chapter 11

1. A tower that would reach to the heavens
2. For fame and so they would not be scattered
3. He gave them many various languages and scattered them
4. 292
5. Abram's nephew (the son of his brother, Haran)

Chapter 12

1. Leave his father's house
2. He would make him a great nation
3. The land of Canaan
4. Because Pharaoh took Abram's wife to his house

Chapter 13

1. There was not enough room for them all
2. They decided to move to separate places
3. Canaan
4. Sodom

Chapter 14

1. Lot
2. Abram
3. Tithed them to God
4. Melchizedek, king of Salem, priest of the most high God
5. To let him keep the spoils of war
6. So the king could not take credit for making Abram rich

Chapter 15

1. One of Abram's servants
2. They would be as numerous as the stars in the heavens
3. They would be held in bondage
4. Four hundred years
5. The land of Canaan

Chapter 16

1. Hagar, her maidservant
2. She hated her
3. He would multiply her descendants
4. Ishmael

Chapter 17

1. Abraham
2. Father of many nations
3. Circumcision
4. Sarah
5. A son

Chapter 18

1. Three men standing by him
2. Angels
3. She would bear him a son
4. She laughed
5. Sodom
6. Lot was in Sodom and would be killed when it was destroyed

Chapter 19

1. Two
2. Lot
3. The men of the city
4. To "know" (have sexual relations with) the "men" in Lot's house
5. Blinded them
6. The Lord
7. Destroy it with brimstone and fire
8. They thought he was joking
9. A small town called Zoar
10. Lot's wife
11. She was turned into a pillar of salt
12. Get him drunk and "lie" (have intercourse) with him
13. To have children since there were no other men around
14. Moabites and Ammonites

Chapter 20

1. He thought someone would kill him to have Sarah for himself
2. God
3. God healed Abimelech, and the women became capable of bearing children

Chapter 21

1. Isaac
2. Laughter
3. Cast them out
4. Make him a nation
5. They would not deal falsely but would show kindness to each other

Chapter 22

1. To test his faith
2. Isaac
3. Because Abraham was about to carry out the sacrifice of his son
4. A ram
5. The seed of Abraham
6. Bethuel

Chapter 23

1. Kirjatharba (or Hebron)
2. In the cave of Machpelah

Chapter 24

1. His oldest servant
2. Rebekah
3. She would offer a drink to him and his camels
4. Covered her face
5. Yes, he loved her

Chapter 25

1. In the cave of Machpelah
2. The twins were two nations
3. Esau and Jacob
4. Hairy and a cunning hunter
5. Esau
6. Because Esau was a hunter and fed Isaac meat
7. His birthright

Chapter 26

1. Gerar
2. His sister
3. King Abimelech
4. Depart from the land
5. Beersheba

Chapter 27

1. Abundance of the land and master over his brethren
2. To live by the sword and faithfully serve his brother
3. Kill him
4. To her brother's house in Haran
5. She did not want Jacob to take his wife from among the daughters of Heth

Chapter 28

1. Laban
2. A ladder going to heaven with angels going up and down it
3. His descendants would be as the dust of the earth
4. Bethel
5. House of God

Chapter 29

1. She was his mother's niece
2. Shepherdess
3. Rachel as his wife
4. Leah
5. Seven years
6. Reuben, Simeon, Levi, and Judah

Chapter 30

1. Rachel's maid, Leah's maid, and Leah
2. Issachar and Zebulun
3. Dinah
4. Joseph
5. Because Laban felt blessed in the presence of Jacob
6. All the spotted and speckled sheep and goats
7. Rods of green poplar, hazel, and chestnut trees

Chapter 31

1. God
2. His household idols
3. In the "furniture" (saddle) of a camel
4. Twenty

Chapter 32

1. If Esau attacked him, one company would be able to escape
2. As a peace treaty
3. God himself
4. It shrank

Chapter 33

1. He hugged him, kissed him, and cried
2. Because Jacob's people and flock were tired and weary
3. Shalem
4. The sons of Hamor

Chapter 34

1. Lay with her and defiled (raped) her
2. They were grieved and extremely angry
3. Hamor
4. Their sons marry each other's daughters and all live in the same land
5. They be circumcised
6. Killed them

Chapter 35

1. Bethel, in the land of Canaan
2. Israel
3. One who struggles/wrestles with God
4. Giving birth
5. Benjamin
6. Bilhah, his father's concubine
7. 180 years old
8. Esau and Jacob

Chapter 36

1. Canaan
2. Edom
3. Esau

Chapter 37

1. Because he was the son of Jacob's old age
2. A coat of many colors
3. Because they envied him and were jealous
4. Bowed down to him
5. Kill him
6. Reuben
7. Sold him into slavery
8. Egypt
9. He was killed by an evil beast

Chapter 38

1. God
2. Shelah
3. Two

Chapter 39

1. Egypt
2. Potiphar
3. Overseer
4. To lie together
5. He refused
6. She accused him of trying to sleep with her
7. Prison
8. He was put in charge of all the prisoners

Chapter 40

1. Pharaoh's chief butler and chief baker
2. He would be released from prison in three days
3. He would be hung in three days
4. To mention Joseph and his situation to Pharaoh

Chapter 41

1. Two
2. There would be seven years of plenty and seven years of famine in the land
3. Save one-fifth of the produce (grain) in the years of plenty to use in the years of famine
4. Pharaoh
5. Thirty years old

Chapter 42

1. Benjamin
2. Because they feared a calamity might befall him
3. Governor
4. Spies
5. Put them in prison
6. Three days
7. Because they had treated Joseph terribly
8. Simeon

Chapter 43

1. After their grain ran out
2. Money for grain
3. Because they feared being accused of taking the money they had brought to make their first grain purchase
4. He wept
5. They were seated according to their ages and birthrights
6. He gave him more of everything compared to his other brothers

Chapter 44

1. His silver cup
2. His personal servant
3. Tore their clothes
4. He would die in grief

Chapter 45

1. They were shocked and in fear
2. God
3. Pharaoh

Chapter 46

1. God
2. Asenath
3. Egypt
4. Goshen

Chapter 47

1. With livestock
2. By selling land to Joseph
3. Seventeen years
4. Not to bury him in Egypt

Chapter 48

1. Manasseh and Ephraim
2. The youngest one, Ephraim
3. One portion more than his brothers

Chapter 49

1. He would not excel
2. He defiled his father's bed
3. They would be divided and scattered
4. He would receive praise from his brothers

5. Joseph
6. In the cave of Machpelah
7. Abraham, Sarah, Isaac, Rebekah, and Leah

Chapter 50

1. Joseph would make them pay for all the harm they had done to him
2. Because he had already forgiven his brothers
3. Deliver his bones out of Egypt

128. The Miracles of Jesus

1. Leprosy
2. Servant
3. Mother-in-law
4. Sick and demon-possessed
5. Storm
6. Swine
7. Sick with palsy
8. Twelve years
9. Daughter
10. Touched their eyes
11. Speak
12. Hand
13. Blind and mute
14. Five thousand men, along with women and children
15. Water
16. Cloak
17. Daughter
18. Four thousand men, along with women and children
19. Demon
20. Fish
21. Sight
22. Wither
23. Unclean spirit
24. Hear and speak
25. Blind man
26. Simon's
27. A widow
28. Eighteen years
29. The Sabbath
30. Lepers
31. Ear
32. Wine
33. Son
34. Bethesda
35. Blind
36. Lazarus
37. Fish

129. Who Is?

1. Job (Job 1:1)
2. Jesus (Revelation 22:16)
3. John the Baptist (Matthew 3:1–3)
4. Jesus (Isaiah 11:1–5)
5. Timothy (1 Timothy 1:2)
6. Lucifer (Isaiah 14:12)
7. Jesus (1 Corinthians 15:45–48)
8. Jesus's disciples (Matthew 5:13)
9. Nimrod (Genesis 10:9)
10. The Pharisees (Matthew 12:24–34)

Section 3: The Bible Brilliant Section

130. Crossword Puzzle 2

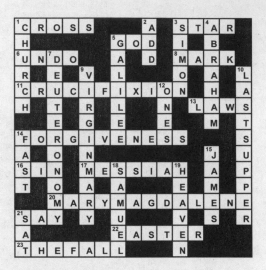

131. Crossword Puzzle 3

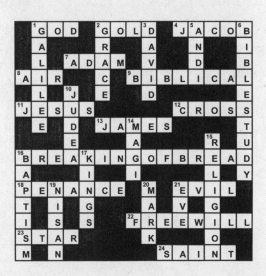

132. Group 1

1. Forty years (1 Kings 11:42)
2. They will inherit the earth (Matthew 5:5)
3. A den of thieves (Luke 19:46)
4. His father-in-law (John 18:13)
5. Water turned into blood (Exodus 7:21)
6. Psalm 23 (Psalm 23:2)
7. Tabitha (Dorcas) (Acts 9:40)
8. Visiting the fatherless and widows, and keeping oneself unspotted from the world (James 1:27)
9. Seven (Revelation 1:11)
10. On the twelve gates (Revelation 21:12)
11. A bridegroom (Matthew 25:1)
12. Interpreted his dreams (Daniel 2)
13. They rebuked them (Matthew 19:13)
14. By a well in the land of Midian (Exodus 2:16–21)
15. David
16. Samaritan (Luke 17:16)
17. An earthquake (Acts 16:26)
18. A fleece (Judges 6:37)
19. A crown of twelve stars (Revelation 12:1)
20. Midnight (Acts 16:25)
21. Samuel (1 Samuel 16:13)
22. God and your neighbor (Luke 10:27)
23. King Solomon (Matthew 6:28–29)
24. "Go ye therefore, and teach all nations, baptizing them in the name of the Father, and of the Son, and of the Holy Ghost" (Matthew 28:19)
25. Wrath (Proverbs 15:1)
26. He was killed after David instructed his men to abandon Uriah during a battle (2 Samuel 11:15)
27. Lameness (Acts 3:2)
28. Vegetables and water (Daniel 1:12)
29. He was circumcised (Luke 2:21)
30. Barabbas (Matthew 27:21)
31. Levi (Numbers 18:20–24)
32. As a sign that God had sent him (Exodus 4:6–8)
33. Two nations (Genesis 25:23)
34. He rested (Genesis 2:1–3)
35. Do not judge them and treat them impartially (James 2:1–4)
36. Jerusalem (Ezra 6:3)
37. "And thou shalt love the Lord thy God with all they heart, and with all they soul, and with all thy mind, and with all thy strength: this is the first commandment" (Mark 12:29–30).
38. A shining light from heaven (Acts 9:3)
39. Pig feeder (Luke 15:15)
40. None (Acts 27:22, 44)
41. In prison (Philemon 1:23)
42. Gilead (Jeremiah 46:11)
43. Saul (Acts 7:58)
44. The good Samaritan (Luke 10:29)
45. In spirit and truth (John 4:23–24)
46. Forty days (Jonah 3:4)
47. Ten (Exodus 7:14–12:30)
48. Fisherman (Matthew 4:21)
49. Timothy (2 Timothy 3:15)
50. John the Baptist (Matthew 3:1–2)

133. Group 2

1. The love of money (1 Timothy 6:10)
2. Potiphar (Genesis 37:36)
3. Isaiah (Acts 8:30)
4. Ananias (Acts 9:17)
5. Lazarus (John 11:41)
6. Aaron's rod swallowed them (Exodus 7:12)
7. Raised him from the dead (2 Kings 4:32–37)
8. "Put her away privily" (divorce her quietly) (Matthew 1:19)
9. Let the mother bird go free (Deuteronomy 22:6–7)
10. Tarsus (Acts 21:39)
11. Calvary or Golgotha (place of a skull) (John 19:17)
12. Paul (1 Corinthians 13:11)
13. Timothy (Philemon 1:1)
14. A lion (Proverbs 19:12)
15. Egypt (Matthew 2:13–14)
16. A parcel of land (Ruth 4:3)
17. Ten male donkeys and ten female donkeys laden with goods from Egypt (Genesis 45:23)
18. "Blessed is the man that walketh not in the counsel of the ungodly" (Psalm 1:1)
19. A ladder (Genesis 28:12)

20. Titus
21. Samson (Judges 16:5–6)
22. Levi (Deuteronomy 10:9)
23. Pharaoh's daughter (Exodus 2:5)
24. Obed (Ruth 4:17)
25. Cattle (Genesis 13:2)
26. A stone (Daniel 2:34)
27. Bethany (John 11:1)
28. Jacob and Rachel (Genesis 46:19)
29. They were killed by two bears (2 Kings 2:24)
30. A fever (Matthew 8:14)
31. Mahlon and Chilion (Ruth 1:2)
32. Uriah (2 Samuel 11:3)
33. You are guilty of breaking the whole law (James 2:10)
34. A double portion (2 Kings 2:9)
35. The death of Herod (Matthew 2:15)
36. A lion (Judges 14:6)
37. A viper snake (Acts 28:3)
38. Ahab (1 Kings 21:16)
39. Canaan (Genesis 17:8)
40. Herodias (Matthew 14:8)
41. Rachel (Genesis 31:32)
42. They wouldn't bow down to Nebuchadnezzar's golden image (Daniel 3:11–12)
43. Forty (Acts 1:3)
44. The Word of God (Luke 8:11)
45. One (Luke 17:15)
46. He was cast into darkness (Matthew 22:13)
47. Boaz (Ruth 4:13)
48. They were all left-handed (Judges 20:16)
49. Augustus Caesar (Luke 2:1)
50. They saw a star in the east (Matthew 2:2)

134. Group 3

1. Wisdom and instruction (Proverbs 1:7)
2. His long hair (Judges 16:17)
3. Red Sea (Exodus 13:18)
4. A rich man entering the kingdom of heaven (Matthew 19:24)
5. Forty (Joshua 5:6)
6. Good fruit (Matthew 7:17)
7. The tongue (James 3:5)
8. With animal sacrifices (Leviticus 4)
9. Patiently (James 5:7)
10. By his own lust (James 1:14)
11. Judah (Micah 5:2)
12. Patmos (Revelation 1:9)
13. Donkey (Numbers 22:28)
14. Jordan River (2 Kings 5:10)
15. Herod (Luke 23:7)
16. There was a famine in Canaan (Genesis 47:4)
17. Rivers of water (Psalm 1:1–3)
18. Beasts (Daniel 7:3)
19. Without ceasing (1 Thessalonians 5:17)
20. He went mad and lived as a beast (Daniel 4:33–36)
21. Malachi
22. Walking on water (John 6:19–20)
23. A famine (Genesis 12:10)
24. Warming himself by a fire (John 18:25)
25. Because only God could forgive sins (Mark 2:7)
26. A servant was sent back to Mesopotamia to choose a wife from Isaac's own family (Genesis 24)
27. One hundred years old (Genesis 21:5)
28. People who hear God's Word but have it choked out by concern for the world (Matthew 13:22)
29. He sat down on the east side of the city and built a booth (shelter) (Jonah 4:5)
30. He was thrown into the lions' den (Daniel 6:10, 16)
31. The walls fell down (Joshua 6:20)
32. Lot (Genesis 12:5)
33. Tarshish (Jonah 1:3)
34. Timothy (2 Timothy 1:5)
35. His foreign wives turned his heart toward idolatry (1 Kings 11:4)
36. The prodigal son (Luke 15:23–24)
37. That he was not sinful like other men (Luke 18:11)
38. Judah (1 Kings 11:31–36; 12:20–21)
39. They spread news about Jesus's birth (Luke 2:17)
40. "For his mercy endureth for ever"
41. He was angry (Jonah 4:1)
42. Gethsemane (Matthew 26:36)
43. Simon of Cyrene (Matthew 27:32)
44. Phoebe (Romans 16:1–2)
45. Amittai (Jonah 1:1)
46. Rehoboam (1 Kings 11:43)

47. Seventy times seven (Matthew 18:22)
48. Nazareth (Matthew 2:23)
49. Ararat (Genesis 8:4)
50. For her sons to sit on Jesus's right and left hands in the kingdom (Matthew 20:21)

135. Group 4

1. His nephew (Genesis 14:12)
2. Abram (Genesis 12:1)
3. Nehemiah (Nehemiah 2:17)
4. Samuel's (1 Samuel 2:19)
5. John (Luke 1:13)
6. As one having authority (Matthew 7:29)
7. As a little child (Luke 18:17)
8. An olive leaf (Genesis 8:11)
9. Is it lawful for a man to put away (divorce) his wife? (Matthew 19:3)
10. Marriage and divorce (Matthew 19:6)
11. Deborah (Judges 5:7)
12. Ehud (Judges 3:15–25)
13. Ephraim and Manasseh (Joshua 14:4)
14. Peter (Acts 3:6)
15. John the Baptist (Luke 7:28)
16. Works (James 2:17)
17. They were swallowed up by the earth (Numbers 16:1–35)
18. With fear and trembling (Philippians 2:12)
19. Twenty-seven
20. He tore down his barns and built larger barns (Luke 12:18)
21. "Thy kingdom come" (Matthew 6:10)
22. Sixth (Luke 1:26)
23. 120 talents of gold, spices, and precious stones (1 Kings 10:10)
24. They were cast into the lake of fire (Revelation 20:15)
25. Go with them two miles (Matthew 5:41)
26. Love (1 Peter 4:8)
27. Take no thought for it (Matthew 6:34)
28. The old bottles will burst (Luke 5:37)
29. Yeast (Matthew 13:33)
30. Charge it to Paul (Philemon 1:18)
31. Sleeping (Jonah 1:5)
32. Rebekah (Genesis 24:67)
33. Matthias (Acts 1:26)
34. Lodged in its branches (Matthew 13:32)
35. The heart (Proverbs 13:12)
36. Oil (Matthew 25:3)
37. East (Genesis 2:8)
38. Thirty-nine
39. The butler and the baker (Genesis 40:5)
40. Jerusalem (Matthew 2:3)
41. Turtledoves or pigeons (Leviticus 5:7)
42. The wood (Genesis 22:6)
43. Money for grain and a silver cup (Genesis 44:2)
44. The field of blood (Acts 1:19)
45. Sarah (Genesis 17:15)
46. Its mother's milk (Exodus 23:19)
47. A sharp sword (Revelation 19:15)
48. Esther (Esther 3:1)
49. Salt (Matthew 5:13)
50. He commanded the spirit of divination to leave her (Acts 16:16–19)

136. Group 5

1. Miriam (Numbers 12:10)
2. We have one Father, who is in heaven (Matthew 23:9)
3. He is not fit for the kingdom of God (Luke 9:62)
4. Rebuilding the temple (Haggai 1:2–6)
5. Blindness (Acts 13:8, 11)
6. Living water (John 4:10)
7. Manoah (Judges 13:24)
8. "Thou art the Christ, the Son of the living God" (Matthew 16:16)
9. Shepherd (John 10:14)
10. Rachel and Leah (Genesis 29:28)
11. Lest they be discouraged (Colossians 3:21)
12. He burned them (Judges 15:5)
13. He spit on the ground, made mud, which he placed on the man's eyes, and told him to wash (John 9:6–7)
14. Moriah (Genesis 22:2)
15. Death (Exodus 21:15)
16. Quail (Exodus 16:13)
17. Righteousness (Genesis 15:6)
18. Hailstones (Joshua 10:11)
19. Wisdom (1 Kings 3:9)
20. Tamar (2 Samuel 13:15)

21. Fine white linen (Revelation 19:8)
22. Lions (1 Kings 10:19)
23. His ring, fine linen, and a gold chain (Genesis 41:42)
24. Hitting a rock twice instead of speaking to it as instructed (Numbers 20:11)
25. Babylon (Jeremiah 29:4)
26. A brood of vipers (Matthew 3:7)
27. God (Genesis 7:16)
28. Jesus (Luke 18:16–17)
29. All sins (Proverbs 10:12)
30. From within a burning bush (Exodus 3:2)
31. Lilies of the field (Luke 12:27)
32. Bread and fish (John 21:13)
33. John (Luke 1:36)
34. A shoe (Ruth 4:7–8)
35. The plague of the death of the firstborn of Egypt (Exodus 12:27)
36. Naomi (Ruth 1:4)
37. The widow of Zarephath (1 Kings 17:22)
38. King Solomon (1 Kings 10:22)
39. Drunkenness (Genesis 9:20–21)
40. The mercy seat and two cherubim (Exodus 25:22)
41. Fish (Matthew 17:27)
42. Jesus (Luke 1:32–33)
43. Lydia (Acts 16:14)
44. Cain (Genesis 4:1)
45. Psalm 23 (Psalm 23:1)
46. Kingdoms of the world (Daniel 2:31–44)
47. Mount Sinai (Leviticus 26:46)
48. They had to marry within their tribe (Numbers 36:6)
49. Stephen (Acts 7:59)
50. Samson (Judges 14:5–6)

137. Group 6

1. Belteshazzar (Daniel 1:7)
2. Hidden (Matthew 5:14)
3. Thirty-eight years (John 5:5)
4. Eight (1 Peter 3:20)
5. Three (Judges 16:15)
6. Anoint your head and wash your face (Matthew 6:17)
7. In your closet with the door shut (Matthew 6:6)
8. Solomon (Proverbs 1:1)
9. A merry heart (Proverbs 17:22)
10. He will draw nigh to us (James 4:8)
11. He was killed by Dinah's brothers (Genesis 34)
12. Matthew (Matthew 1:1)
13. Laodicea (Revelation 3:16)
14. Sarai (Genesis 11:29)
15. Saul (1 Samuel 18:25)
16. A strong tower (Proverbs 18:10)
17. The land of Canaan (Genesis 17:8)
18. In the Jordan River (Mark 1:9)
19. An angel (Matthew 28:2)
20. Because they will be raised to life again (1 Thessalonians 4:13–15)
21. Hip or hollow of the thigh (Genesis 32:25)
22. It was eaten by birds (Matthew 13:4)
23. A room (Philemon 1:22)
24. To never flood the earth again (Genesis 9:11)
25. Mustard (Matthew 13:31–32)
26. A gardener (John 20:15)
27. A spear (John 19:34)
28. Bees and honey (Judges 14:8)
29. Spies (Genesis 42:9)
30. Joseph of Arimathaea (Matthew 27:57–58)
31. Resurrection (Matthew 22:23)
32. The new Jerusalem (Revelation 21:2)
33. Isaiah (Isaiah 7:14)
34. Angels (Acts 23:8)
35. Luke
36. He dipped a piece of bread and gave it to him (John 13:26)
37. One thousand (Judges 15:16)
38. The helm on a ship (James 3:4)
39. "They that be whole need not a physician, but they that are sick" (Matthew 9:11–12)
40. Under a fig tree (John 1:48)
41. Othniel (Joshua 15:16–17)
42. Elijah and Moses (Matthew 17:3)
43. He lifted up his rod and stretched his hand over the sea (Exodus 14:16, 21)
44. The breath of life (Genesis 2:7)
45. The eye (Matthew 6:22)
46. Blindness (Mark 10:46)
47. Obadiah
48. Matthew (Levi) (Luke 5:27)
49. Absalom (2 Samuel 15)
50. Jude

138. Group 7

1. Seven years of plenty followed by seven years of famine (Genesis 41:29)
2. It is a glory to her (1 Corinthians 11:15)
3. Scarlet or purple (Matthew 27:28; John 19:2)
4. Eli the priest (1 Samuel 3:2–6)
5. In the belly of a fish (Jonah 2:9)
6. Rome (Philemon 1:23)
7. Nicodemus (John 3:3)
8. They boiled and ate them (Lamentations 4:10)
9. Gopher (or cypress) wood (Genesis 6:14)
10. Confess your faults (James 5:16)
11. The rulers of the Philistines (Judges 16:5)
12. Red Sea (Exodus 13:18)
13. Three days (Jonah 1:17)
14. God's footstool (Matthew 5:35)
15. Father of many nations (Genesis 17:5)
16. A beam (or log) (Matthew 7:5)
17. A raven (Genesis 8:7)
18. The doctrines of the Pharisees and the Sadducees (Matthew 16:12)
19. Ravens (1 Kings 17:4)
20. The man (1 Corinthians 11:3)
21. Three hours (Luke 23:44)
22. An angel came and shut their mouths (Daniel 6:22)
23. Greek (Acts 16:1)
24. Cupbearer (Nehemiah 1:11)
25. Sea of Galilee (John 6:1–19)
26. The church (Colossians 1:18)
27. Deborah and Barak (Judges 5:1)
28. Peter's (Matthew 8:14–15)
29. An abomination (Proverbs 16:5)
30. Six hundred threescore and six (666) (Revelation 13:18)
31. It becomes corrupted and stolen by thieves (Matthew 6:19)
32. To the Unknown God (Acts 17:23)
33. Ur (Genesis 11:31)
34. Sparrow (Matthew 10:31)
35. An angel of the Lord (Matthew 1:21)
36. To be baptized (Acts 8:36)
37. Twenty-four (Revelation 4:4)
38. Ezekiel (Ezekiel 37:1)
39. Jerusalem (2 Samuel 5:5)
40. Murdering him (1 Samuel 25:34–35)
41. "Behold the Lamb of God" (John 1:29)
42. In the earth (Matthew 25:25)
43. Hannah (1 Samuel 1:13)
44. Samson's (Judges 13:7)
45. Elisabeth (Luke 1:41–42)
46. 120 years old (Deuteronomy 34:7)
47. His disciples (Matthew 8:26)
48. Make the sun and moon stand still (Joshua 10:12–14)
49. Solomon (1 Kings 3:9)
50. Naomi (Ruth 4:16)

139. Group 8

1. Joshua (Joshua 1:1–6)
2. Cows (or cattle) (Genesis 41:1–4)
3. Because blood is the life (Deuteronomy 12:23)
4. Silversmith (Acts 19:24)
5. Fifteen (2 Kings 20:6)
6. Sin (1 John 3:4)
7. Pearls (Matthew 7:6)
8. Ishmael (Genesis 16:15)
9. A criminal on a cross beside Jesus (Luke 23:42)
10. Ninety years old (Genesis 17:17; 21:5)
11. Forty (2 Samuel 5:4)
12. The tree of the knowledge of good and evil (Genesis 2:17)
13. The day of atonement (Leviticus 16)
14. His grandson (Matthew 1:2)
15. Rahab (Joshua 2:3–4)
16. Paul (Acts 23:6)
17. Thirty years old (Luke 3:23)
18. 150
19. Any man in Christ (2 Corinthians 5:17)
20. Swaddling clothes (Luke 2:7)
21. The temple (1 Kings 7:51)
22. Beautiful Gate (Acts 3:2)
23. John (John 19:26–27)
24. Four (Revelation 6:2–8)
25. If they can lead the blind (Luke 6:39)
26. Pharisees (John 3:1)
27. A molten (golden) calf (Deuteronomy 9:15–16)
28. Elijah (James 5:17)

29. They will be caught up together in the clouds (1 Thessalonians 4:17)
30. His brothers' sheaves of wheat bowed down to his sheaf (Genesis 37:5–7)
31. Jesus (Matthew 26:41)
32. So that we are not judged (Matthew 7:1)
33. A rich man entering the kingdom of God (Matthew 19:24)
34. They believed and were baptized (Acts 16:33)
35. Love your wives (Colossians 3:19)
36. Lamech (Genesis 5:28–29)
37. David (Ruth 4:22)
38. Good fruit (Matthew 7:17)
39. Stones (Matthew 4:3)
40. Pharisees (Mark 10:2)
41. David (1 Kings 2:12)
42. Carpenter (Matthew 13:55)
43. With a kiss (Luke 22:48)
44. Cut the child in half (1 Kings 3:25)
45. Isaac's (Genesis 22:9)
46. In the temple (Luke 2:42–46)
47. A ghost (Matthew 14:26)
48. The head of John the Baptist (Matthew 14:6–8)
49. He pushed the pillars over, collapsing the temple (Judges 16:30)
50. Harp (or lyre) (1 Samuel 16:23)

140. Group 9

1. Hunting (Genesis 27:1–3, 23)
2. To buy corn (or grain) (Genesis 42:2–3)
3. Jonathan (1 Samuel 18:1)
4. Ruth (Ruth 1:16)
5. His garments (Matthew 27:35)
6. God with us (Matthew 1:23)
7. Peter (Matthew 14:29)
8. Bathsheba (2 Samuel 11:4)
9. Nineveh (Jonah 3:3)
10. Abimelech (Genesis 20:17)
11. He fought to rescue him (Genesis 14:14–16)
12. "Fear not to go down into Egypt; for I will there make of thee a great nation" (Genesis 46:3)
13. Blood (Genesis 9:4)
14. He was made leprous (2 Kings 5:25–27)
15. She tied a scarlet thread in the window (Joshua 2:18)
16. Gabriel (Daniel 8:16)
17. Hiram, the king of Tyre (1 Kings 7:13)
18. Three (Acts 13–21)
19. Wine (1 Timothy 5:23)
20. Diana (or Artemis) (Acts 19:28)
21. Thirty-two thousand (Judges 7:3)
22. The fruit of the vine (Matthew 26:29)
23. Philemon (Philemon 1:10–11)
24. Psalm 117
25. As a virtuous woman (Ruth 3:11)
26. Twelve thousand (Revelation 7:5–8)
27. Elijah (1 Kings 19:5)
28. Simon the sorcerer (Acts 8:18)
29. A man clothed in linen (Daniel 10:5)
30. A band of men and officers (John 18:3)
31. Coriander (Numbers 11:7)
32. Corinth (Acts 18:1–5)
33. Eight years old (2 Kings 22:1)
34. Ishmael's (Genesis 21:21)
35. Andrew (John 6:8)
36. Righteousness (2 Peter 2:5)
37. Crispus, Gaius, and the household of Stephanas (1 Corinthians 1:14–16)
38. Nabal (1 Samuel 25:3)
39. Elkanah (1 Samuel 1:8)
40. Count it all joy (James 1:2)
41. His groanings (or roarings) (Job 3:24)
42. Judah (Genesis 29:35)
43. Gamaliel (Acts 5:34–39)
44. His brothers drove him out because he was illegitimate (Judges 11:1–3)
45. Man's (Psalm 103:15)
46. Standing in synagogues and on street corners to be seen (Matthew 6:5)
47. Frogs (Revelation 16:13)
48. Three thousand (Judges 16:27)
49. Salem (Genesis 14:18; Hebrews 7:1)
50. Ashkelon (Judges 14:19)

141. Group 10

1. Grasshoppers (Numbers 13:33)
2. Terah (Genesis 11:31)
3. Rams (Exodus 25:3–5)
4. He claimed to be the Son of God (John 19:7)
5. In a dream (Matthew 2:13)

6. Corinthians (2 Corinthians 6:17–18)
7. They cast lots (Jonah 1:7)
8. A Pharisee and a publican (tax collector) (Luke 18:10)
9. His feet (1 Kings 15:23)
10. Malchus (John 18:10)
11. Abib (Deuteronomy 16:1)
12. Philippi (Acts 16:12)
13. The doors of the gate of the city (Judges 16:3)
14. Zadok (1 Kings 1:39)
15. The Ancient of days (Daniel 7:9)
16. Seventy (Judges 8:30)
17. Obadiah
18. Philip's (Acts 21:8)
19. Treasurer (Acts 8:27)
20. "Blessed are the poor in spirit: for theirs is the kingdom of heaven" (Matthew 5:3)
21. Third (Genesis 1:11–13)
22. Philip (John 14:8)
23. Eutychus (Acts 20:9)
24. Singing (Psalm 100:2)
25. Sea of Tiberias (Galilee) (John 6:1; 21:1)
26. Cyprus (Acts 13:4)
27. She destroyed the rest of the royal family (2 Kings 11:1)
28. Elisha (2 Kings 5:10)

29. Three hundred (1 Kings 11:3)
30. It doesn't list a number (Matthew 2:1–12)
31. Tentmaker (Acts 18:2–3)
32. Og (Deuteronomy 3:11)
33. He tossed a piece of wood into the water (Exodus 15:23–25)
34. Almighty God (Genesis 17:1)
35. Sheets (linen garments, NKJV) and garments (Judges 14:12)
36. Samaria (Acts 8:12–14)
37. Paul's (Acts 19:12)
38. No, they were not ashamed (Genesis 2:25)
39. 120,000 (Jonah 4:11)
40. He was baptized (Acts 9:18)
41. Thou shall not commit adultery (Exodus 20:14)
42. Three (Deuteronomy 4:41–43)
43. A stone like a great millstone (Revelation 18:21)
44. Zarephath (1 Kings 17:9–23)
45. Ezekiel (Ezekiel 3:2)
46. Despising God (1 Thessalonians 4:7–8)
47. Julius (Acts 27:1)
48. Samuel (1 Samuel 15:22)
49. Righteous and blameless (Genesis 6:9)
50. He was lowered in a basket by the city wall (Acts 9:23–25)

142. Group 11

1. Bezaleel (Exodus 31:2–3)
2. Gravel (Proverbs 20:17)
3. Foolishness (Proverbs 22:15)
4. 127 years old (Genesis 23:1)
5. Ahijah (1 Kings 11:30–31)
6. Bread and wine (Genesis 14:18)
7. A thirty-foot flying roll (Zechariah 5:1–4)
8. She was his grandmother (2 Timothy 1:5)
9. The coming of the Messiah (Daniel 9:20–27)
10. Thirteen (1 Kings 7:1)
11. Which disciple was the greatest (Luke 22:24–30)
12. Rivers and fountains of waters turned to blood (Revelation 16:4)
13. Asher (Luke 2:36)
14. Ai (Joshua 7:5–12)
15. Onyx (Exodus 28:9)
16. Philippi (Acts 16:11–14)
17. Ammonites (Judges 11:9–11)
18. Fifty denarii (Luke 7:41)

19. Locusts (Exodus 10:4; Revelation 9:1–4)
20. Agabus (Acts 21:10–11)
21. Annas (John 18:13)
22. Eight years (Judges 12:13–14)
23. A lion, a bear, a leopard, and a dreadful and terrible beast (Daniel 7:3–7)
24. Barnabas (Acts 13:4)
25. "The lost sheep of the house of Israel" (Matthew 10:5–6)
26. Seventy (Exodus 15:27)
27. Rubies (Proverbs 8:11)
28. Four (Genesis 2:10)
29. Jewels of silver and gold and raiment (Exodus 3:22)
30. On earth (Revelation 5:10)
31. The wife of Phinehas (1 Samuel 4:19)
32. Elymas (Acts 13:8)
33. Jesus (Mark 1:14)
34. Ishmaelites (Genesis 37:28)
35. The sick (James 5:15)
36. Joseph (Genesis 41:45)

37. In the valley of Sorek (Judges 16:4)
38. Joab (2 Samuel 14:22–23)
39. Onesiphorus (2 Timothy 1:16)
40. Each would sit on one of the twelve thrones and judge the twelve tribes of Israel (Matthew 19:28)
41. That it will sprout again (Job 14:7)
42. Mist rose from the earth (Genesis 2:5–6)
43. Angels (Revelation 5:11–12)
44. Purim (Esther 9:24–26)
45. Half (Luke 19:8)
46. Rebekah (Genesis 24:14–19)
47. Eighty-four years old (Luke 2:37)
48. John (John 6:48)
49. A young goat and unleavened bread (Judges 6:19)
50. Machpelah (Genesis 23:19)

143. Group 12

1. Household idols (Genesis 31:19)
2. A crown (Proverbs 12:4)
3. Psalm 58 (Psalm 58:8)
4. Daniel (Judges 13:25)
5. To keep them from the Egyptians who thought shepherds were an abomination (Genesis 46:34)
6. A priest (Luke 10:31)
7. Numbers (Numbers 22:22–35)
8. To know understanding (Proverbs 4:1)
9. Fish and honeycomb (Luke 24:42)
10. 110 years old (Genesis 50:22)
11. Make one hair white or black (Matthew 5:36)
12. Every creature of God (1 Timothy 4:5)
13. With the fruit of his mouth (Proverbs 18:20)
14. Sun, moon, and stars (Genesis 1:14–18)
15. Bethlehem (1 Samuel 17:58)
16. A scorpion (Luke 11:12)
17. "In sanctification and honour" (1 Thessalonians 4:4)
18. Thirty (Judges 14:11)
19. Moses (Psalm 90:1)
20. 350 years (Genesis 9:28)
21. Trumpets and cymbals (Ezra 3:10)
22. 147 (Genesis 47:28)
23. Simeon (Genesis 42:24)
24. Isaiah (Isaiah 20:2–3)
25. Seventeen (Jeremiah 32:9)
26. Goats (Song of Solomon 4:1)
27. Cain's fruit of the ground (Genesis 4:3)
28. Summer (Matthew 24:32)
29. Those who do God's commandments (Revelation 22:14)
30. Lying (Proverbs 21:6)
31. Blue (Exodus 28:31)
32. Prevails with God (Genesis 32:28)
33. Build a battlement (guard rail) around the roof (Deuteronomy 22:8)
34. Hosea (Hosea 11:1)
35. A wall fell on them (1 Kings 20:30)
36. 666 talents (about 39,960 pounds) (1 Kings 10:14)
37. Benhadad (2 Kings 8:15)
38. A Hittite (Ezekiel 16:3)
39. Pray for one another (James 5:16)
40. Dorcas (Acts 9:36)
41. 1 Samuel (1 Samuel 17)
42. Gold (Proverbs 16:16)
43. Tongues of fire (Acts 2:3)
44. Those without fins and scales (Deuteronomy 14:9)
45. Reuben (Genesis 30:14)
46. He was a man of war (1 Chronicles 28:3)
47. Moses (Exodus 2:21)
48. Nebuchadnezzar (Daniel 4:1–11)
49. Jehoshaphat (2 Kings 9:2)
50. Hebrew, Greek, and Latin (John 19:19–20)

144. Group 13

1. Saul (Acts 9:17–18)
2. Moses and Aaron (Numbers 1:46)
3. John the Baptist (Luke 1:41)
4. Thirty years old (2 Samuel 5:4)
5. Joshua (Joshua 24:15)
6. Be faithful until death (Revelation 2:10)
7. Psalms (Psalm 117; 119)
8. One hundred years old (Genesis 21:5)
9. Four (Genesis 2:10)
10. Six cubits and a span (over nine feet tall) (1 Samuel 17:4)
11. Both Peter (Matthew 16:23) and Satan (Luke 4:8)
12. Antioch (Acts 11:26)

13. Love (Romans 13:10)
14. Simon of Cyrene (Matthew 27:32; Mark 15:21)
15. Levi (Exodus 2:1)
16. The new Jerusalem (Revelation 3:12)
17. Abimelech (Genesis 26:1–9)
18. Midian (Exodus 2:15)
19. Keturah (Genesis 25:1)
20. Mary Magdalene; Joanna; and Mary, the mother of James (Luke 24:10)
21. Aaron (Exodus 7:7)
22. Ruth and Esther
23. Simon and Andrew (Mark 1:16)
24. Samson (Judges 14:5–9)
25. Levi (Deuteronomy 18:2)
26. The bones of Joseph (Exodus 13:19)
27. Circumcision (Genesis 17:10)
28. Gideon (Judges 8:32)
29. Bethlehem (Luke 2:4)
30. Joseph (Genesis 46:20)
31. Pharaoh's daughter (Exodus 2:10)

32. His brother Aaron (Exodus 4:14–16)
33. A serpent (Genesis 3:1–4) and a donkey (Numbers 22:28–30)
34. His father-in-law, Jethro (Exodus 3:1)
35. Twelve baskets full (Matthew 14:20)
36. Job (Job 1:8)
37. Seven (Luke 8:2)
38. Ninety-nine years old (Genesis 17:24)
39. Matthias (Acts 1:26)
40. Nod (Genesis 4:16)
41. Satan (Matthew 4:4)
42. Four days (John 11:39)
43. Nine (Matthew 27:46)
44. His disciples (John 4:2)
45. Moab (Deuteronomy 34:6)
46. Seth (Genesis 4:25)
47. Pearls (Revelation 21:21)
48. Enoch (Genesis 4:17)
49. None (Romans 3:10)
50. 930 years (Genesis 5:5)

145. Fulfilled Prophecies about Jesus

1. Matthew 1:22–23 and Luke 1:27
2. Luke 3:3–6
3. Matthew 1:20 and Galatians 4:4
4. Matthew 3:16–17
5. Matthew 2:1 and Luke 2:4–6
6. Matthew 27:37 and Mark 11:7–11
7. Luke 1:33 and Hebrews 1:8–12
8. Luke 3:33 and Hebrews 7:14
9. Matthew 1:1 and Romans 9:5
10. Luke 4:18–19
11. Matthew 2:14–15
12. Matthew 27:38
13. Luke 1:32–33 and Romans 1:3
14. John 1:11 and John 7:5
15. Matthew 1:23
16. Matthew 27:34 and John 19:28–30
17. Acts 3:20–22
18. Matthew 2:23

19. Matthew 21:16
20. Matthew 26:67
21. John 15:24–25
22. Luke 23:35
23. Luke 3:34
24. Romans 5:6–8
25. Matthew 13:10–15, 34–35
26. Matthew 26:14–16 and Luke 22:47–48
27. John 19:33–36
28. John 20:25–27
29. Mark 14:57–58
30. Mark 15:4–5
31. Matthew 27:35–36 and Luke 23:34
32. Matthew 27:46
33. John 19:34
34. Matthew 28:2–7 and Acts 2:22–32
35. Mark 16:19 and Luke 24:51
36. Matthew 22:44 and Mark 16:19

146. 100 Common Phrases That Originated in the Bible

1. A drop in the bucket
2. A fly in the ointment
3. A graven image
4. A house divided against itself cannot stand
5. A labor of love

6. A law unto themselves
7. A leopard cannot change its spots
8. A man after his own heart
9. A multitude of sins
10. A peace offering
11. A sign of the times

12. A soft answer turns away anger
13. A thorn in the flesh
14. A two-edged sword
15. A voice crying in the wilderness
16. A wolf in sheep's clothing
17. All things must come to pass
18. All things to all men
19. Am I my brother's keeper?
20. An eye for an eye, a tooth for a tooth
21. As old as Methuselah
22. As old as the hills
23. As white as snow
24. You reap what you sow
25. Ashes to ashes, dust to dust
26. At their wit's end
27. Baptism of fire
28. Be fruitful and multiply
29. Beat swords into plowshares
30. Bite the dust
31. Born again
32. Breath of life
33. By the skin of your teeth
34. By the sweat of your brow
35. Cast bread upon the waters
36. Cast the first stone
37. Charity begins at home
38. A coat of many colors
39. Don't cast your pearls before swine
40. A cross to bear
41. Eat, drink, and be merry
42. See eye to eye
43. Faith can move mountains
44. Fall from grace
45. Feet of clay
46. Fight the good fight
47. Fire and brimstone
48. Flesh and blood
49. For everything there is a season
50. Forbidden fruit
51. From strength to strength
52. Get behind me, Satan
53. Gird your loins
54. Give up the ghost
55. Go the extra mile
56. A good Samaritan

57. Harden your heart
58. He who lives by the sword dies by the sword
59. Your heart's desire
60. Holier than thou
61. How the mighty have fallen
62. In the twinkling of an eye
63. It's better to give than to receive
64. Like a lamb to the slaughter
65. The letter of the law
66. Living off the fat of the land
67. Love of money is the root of all evil
68. Love thy neighbor as thyself
69. Man does not live by bread alone
70. Manna from heaven
71. Many are called, but few are chosen
72. My cup runneth over
73. No rest for the wicked
74. There's nothing new under the sun
75. O ye of little faith
76. Out of the mouths of babes
77. The patience of Job
78. Physician, heal thyself
79. Pride goes before a fall
80. Put words in one's mouth
81. Put your house in order
82. Reap the whirlwind
83. Sour grapes
84. Spare the rod and spoil the child
85. The straight and narrow
86. Sufficient for the day
87. Tender mercies
88. The apple of his eye
89. The blind leading the blind
90. The ends of the earth
91. The fruit of your loins
92. The root of the matter
93. The salt of the earth
94. The spirit is willing, but the flesh is weak
95. The wages of sin is death
96. The way of all flesh
97. The wisdom of Solomon
98. Wash your hands of the matter
99. Weighed in the balance
100. Woe is me

147. Imprisoned

1. B (Acts 16:25–26)
2. C (Acts 5:12–42)
3. D (Matthew 14:2–4)
4. A (Genesis 39:1–20)
5. D (Genesis 42:16–17)
6. B (Jeremiah 32:2)
7. C (Jeremiah 52:11)
8. B (2 Chronicles 16:7–10)
9. A (Judges 16:21)
10. B (2 Kings 24:15)
11. D (1 Kings 22:26–27)
12. C (2 Kings 17:4)

148. The Fast 100

1. Garden of Gethsemane (Matthew 26:36)
2. Sleeping (Jonah 1:5)
3. Potiphar (Genesis 37:36)
4. Egypt (Matthew 2:13–14)
5. The walls fell down (Joshua 6:20)
6. Canaan (Genesis 17:8)
7. An earthquake (Acts 16:26)
8. Ten (Exodus 7:14–12:30)
9. Wisdom (1 Kings 3:9)
10. With animal sacrifices (Leviticus 4)
11. A burning bush (Exodus 3:2)
12. The kingdom of God and his righteousness (Matthew 6:33)
13. Rachel (Genesis 29:30)
14. Without ceasing (1 Thessalonians 5:17)
15. The ark of the covenant (Deuteronomy 10:8)
16. In your closet with the door shut (Matthew 6:6)
17. The breath of life (Genesis 2:7)
18. John (Revelation 1:1)
19. Three days (John 1:17)
20. Ishmael (Genesis 16:15)
21. Making a false idol, a golden calf (Deuteronomy 9:15–16)
22. Abram (Genesis 12:1)
23. A pillar of cloud and a pillar of fire (Exodus 13:21)
24. Thirty years old (Luke 3:2)
25. A donkey (Numbers 22:28)
26. Leah (Genesis 29)
27. Moses (Exodus 14:21)
28. Barabbas (Matthew 27:21)
29. Sarai (Genesis 11:29)
30. John the Baptist (Matthew 3:13)
31. Gabriel (Luke 1:26)
32. Rebekah (Genesis 24:67)
33. The disciples (Matthew 8:26)
34. In the earth (Matthew 25:25)
35. Rachel (Genesis 29:28)
36. Hannah (1 Samuel 1:20)
37. Swaddling clothes (Luke 2:7)
38. Michal (1 Samuel 18:20–26)
39. "You are the Christ, the Son of the living God" (Matthew 16:16)
40. The bridegroom (Matthew 25:1)
41. Joseph (Luke 1:27)
42. Ruth (Ruth 1:16)
43. Potiphar's wife (Genesis 39:14)
44. He forced it to move on its belly and eat dust (Genesis 3:14)
45. Zipporah (Exodus 2:21)
46. Judas (Luke 22:48)
47. In the knowledge of good and evil (Genesis 3:22)
48. To take no thought for it (Matthew 6:34)
49. Jacob (Genesis 32:28)
50. Not judge them and treat them impartially (James 2:1–4)
51. In the Jordan River (Mark 1:9)
52. Peter (Matthew 16:18)
53. He draws nigh (near) to us (James 4:8)
54. Joseph (Genesis 41:41)
55. Easter Sunday
56. "He that is without sin among you, let him first cast a stone at her" (John 8:7)
57. Delilah (Judges 16:6)
58. Mary (Luke 1:46)
59. Satan (Matthew 4:3)
60. Saul, who became Paul (Acts 8:22)
61. Mother of all living (Genesis 3:20)
62. Esther (Esther 7:3)
63. Jezebel (1 Kings 19:2)
64. He climbed a tree (Luke 19:4)
65. Esau (Genesis 25:34)
66. Jochebed (Exodus 6:20)
67. Daniel (Daniel 6:23)
68. Lot's wife (Genesis 19:6)
69. Orpah (Ruth 1:4)
70. To hide his nakedness (Genesis 3:10)

71. Daniel (Daniel 1:17)
72. God with us (Matthew 1:23)
73. Gopher wood (Genesis 6:14)
74. The angel of the Lord (Matthew 1:20–21)
75. He believed God was on his side (1 Samuel 17:46)
76. The Sermon on the Mount (Matthew 5:1)
77. Almonds (Numbers 17:8)
78. A dove (Luke 3:22)
79. God the Father (Matthew 3:17)
80. They were cast into the lake of fire (Revelation 20:15)
81. Sea of Galilee (John 6:1–19)
82. He clothed them (Genesis 3:21)
83. Gomer (Hosea 1:3)
84. Hagar (Genesis 16:15)
85. He was angry (Jonah 4:1)
86. Joshua (Deuteronomy 34:9)
87. As a little child (Luke 18:17)
88. He was thrown into the lions' den (Daniel 6:16)
89. His brother (Luke 15:25)
90. God the Father (Matthew 3:17)
91. Chief tax collector (Luke 19:2)
92. Interpreting dreams (Genesis 41:12)
93. To keep the meaning from those who would not understand (Matthew 13:13)
94. Grain (Genesis 41:57)
95. Satan (Matthew 4:9)
96. He was lowered through the roof (Mark 2:4)
97. Thomas (John 20:28)
98. Benjamin (Genesis 42:4)
99. Cherubim (angels) and a flaming sword (Genesis 3:24)
100. Mustard seed (Matthew 13:31–32)

150. Fasting

1. D (Matthew 4:2)
2. C (Exodus 34:28)
3. B (1 Kings 17:2–6)
4. B (2 Samuel 12:14–31)
5. C (Acts 23:12–13)
6. A (Acts 27:33–37)
7. A (Daniel 6:16–19)
8. B (Acts 14:23)
9. A (Nehemiah 1:4–2:1–4)
10. A (Jeremiah 36:8–10)

151. Wine

1. D (Matthew 11:19)
2. C (1 Timothy 5:23)
3. A (1 Timothy 3:3)
4. A (Proverbs 31:6)
5. B (Judges 7:24–25)
6. A (Numbers 6:1–3)
7. B (Matthew 27:34)
8. C (Luke 5:36–39)

152. The Apostles

1. A (Acts 12:2)
2. C (Acts 1:25–26)
3. A (Matthew 9:9–13)
4. D (John 13:23)

153. Kings

1. D (1 Kings 18:17)
2. B (Judges 4:2–3)
3. C (2 Kings 17)
4. A (1 Kings 16:31)
5. A (Numbers 21:1)
6. B (Joshua 11:1–15)
7. D (Deuteronomy 3:11)
8. C (1 Samuel 8:1–21)
9. B (1 Samuel 16:13)
10. B (2 Samuel 12)

154. Heaven Awaits

1. A (John 14:3)
2. C (John 3:3)
3. C (Revelation 21)
4. A (Revelation 3:12)
5. D (Revelation 21:19–20)
6. B (Revelation 21:18)
7. C (Revelation 21:21)
8. A (Revelation 22:2)
9. D (Revelation 4:4)
10. B (Revelation 4:6–11)
11. D (Revelation 21:21)
12. D (Revelation 21)

155. Hairy and Hairless

1. C (Ezekiel 44:20)
2. C (Judges 16:17)
3. B (Acts 21:23–36)
4. B (Daniel 4:33)
5. C (Genesis 9:1–3)
6. D (Job 1:20–21)
7. D (2 Samuel 14:26)
8. C (Leviticus 14:7–9)
9. C (Leviticus 19:27)
10. C (2 Kings 2:23)
11. C (Ezekiel 5:1–4)
12. C (2 Kings 1:8)

156. Citified

1. A (Acts 18:24)
2. B (Acts 21:17)
3. A (Jeremiah 1:1)
4. C (Acts 11:26)
5. C (John 19:38–39)
6. B (1 Samuel 6:17–18)
7. A (Ezekiel 1:1; Daniel 1:1–6)
8. C (Acts 17:16–22)
9. B (Matthew 21:1–7)
10. B (Acts 25–26)
11. A (Acts 16:1)

157. Are You Speaking to Me?

1. A (Deuteronomy 4:33)
2. C (John 1:15–23)
3. B (Revelation 1:15; 14:2)
4. C (Numbers 7:87)
5. A (1 Samuel 1:12–13)
6. C (Matthew 2:18)
7. D (Daniel 4:14)
8. C (1 Samuel 26:17)
9. B (1 Samuel 15:22)

158. Jesus

1. C (Luke 2:1–20)
2. B (Matthew 2:1)
3. C (Matthew 1:23)
4. D (Matthew 1)
5. C (Matthew 2:11)
6. C (Matthew 2:7–11)
7. B (Luke 1:26–28)
8. A (Luke 1:46)
9. B (Luke 2:21–22)
10. C (Matthew 2:22)
11. A (Micah 5:2)
12. D (Isaiah 7:14)

159. Firsts

1. C (Acts 7:54–60)
2. A (Genesis 10:9)
3. A (Genesis 4:22)
4. A (Esther 2:1–18)
5. C (Genesis 5:21–24; Jude 14)
6. C (1 Samuel 9–10)
7. D (Genesis 4:17)
8. C (Genesis 4:22)
9. C (Acts 13:1–13)
10. D (Genesis 40:20)

160. Costly

1. D (Daniel 9:25)
2. C (John 17:12)
3. C (Acts 3:1; 4:1–4)
4. B (Acts 9:3)
5. D (Genesis 19:30)
6. B (Joshua 10:16–27)
7. B (Joshua 10:33)
8. B (Daniel 1:1)
9. C (Ezra 4:2)
10. A (Judges 16:30)

161. Women

1. A (Mark 16:1)
2. C (Judges 16:13–17)
3. A (Hebrews 11:31)
4. A (Genesis 17:16–18)
5. C (Matthew 14:3–8)
6. B (2 Samuel 21:11)
7. A (2 Chronicles 15:16)
8. B (Luke 2:36–40)
9. C (Judges 5:4)
10. D (1 Kings 1:5)
11. B (Exodus 15:20)
12. A (Luke 1:57–60)
13. B (Acts 8:27)
14. D (Acts 25:13)
15. A (Judges 4:3–5)
16. C (1 Kings 10:1)
17. A (Genesis 35:18)
18. B (Numbers 12:1)
19. C (1 Samuel 25:3)
20. A (John 4:15)
21. D (Ruth 3:7)

22. A (1 Chronicles 3:5)
23. C (1 Samuel 25:3–25)
24. A (2 Samuel 21:10)
25. C (2 Samuel 11–12)
26. B (1 Kings 16:31)
27. C (Esther 2:1–17)
28. D (2 Chronicles 22:10)
29. C (2 Kings 22:14–20)
30. D (1 Kings 16:31–34)

162. Who Asked?

1. C (Genesis 4:9)
2. B (Genesis 15:2)
3. C (Genesis 18:25)
4. A (Exodus 5:22)
5. D (Genesis 15:8)
6. A (Jeremiah 15:18)
7. B (Habakkuk 1:3)
8. A (Numbers 16:22)
9. C (Ezekiel 11:13)
10. C (Exodus 3:13)
11. B (Job 40:4)
12. D (1 Samuel 23:2)

163. Hearing from God

1. C (Genesis 6:14)
2. D (Genesis 12:1)
3. D (Exodus 28:1)
4. D (1 Kings 12:20)
5. C (1 Kings 17:17–24)
6. B (Exodus 6:6)
7. B (Numbers 25:11–12)
8. C (Genesis 37:5–8)

164. Bible Brilliant Level

1. C (John 11:35)
2. B (Job 29:6)
3. C (Acts 9:36–41)
4. A (Joshua 6:17–25)
5. A (Genesis 29:11)
6. B (Judges 9:1–6)
7. B (Judges 14:5–6; 1 Samuel 17:36; 1 Chronicles 11:22)
8. B (Judges 3:31)
9. D (Daniel 4:33)
10. A (Exodus 26:14)
11. C (2 Kings 2:20)
12. D (Luke 1:1–4; Acts 1:1)
13. C (1 Samuel 14:50)
14. B (2 Kings 18:4)
15. C (Revelation 3:9)
16. C (Ecclesiastes 2:2)
17. D (Exodus 12:40)
18. B (Revelation 21:12)
19. C (Isaiah 38:5)
20. C (Matthew 13:55; Luke 6:16; John 14:22; Acts 5:37; 9:11; 15:32)

165. Anything Goes

1. D (Genesis 7:13)
2. D (Judges 4:4)
3. B (Luke 1:26–31)
4. B (Genesis 6:16)
5. A (2 Corinthians 11:33)
6. A (Genesis 41:27)
7. C (Acts 5:1–11)
8. C (2 Kings 9:10)
9. A (1 Samuel 4:21)
10. C (Psalm 56:8)
11. D (Ruth 1:2–4)
12. C (2 Kings 21:1)
13. C (1 Kings 10:1–7)
14. A (Matthew 3:4)
15. B (Acts 9:9)
16. C (1 Kings 3:25)
17. C (John 3:2)
18. A (Acts 12:5–17)
19. B (Genesis 6:10, 18; 1 Peter 3:20)
20. D (1 Samuel 25:14–42)
21. A (Daniel 5:2)
22. B (Philemon 10–18)
23. C (1 Kings 21:1–4)
24. A (Genesis 20:3)
25. C (Genesis 8:8–12)
26. B (Esther 9:13)
27. B (Genesis 40:22)
28. A (Esther 2:21)
29. C (1 Kings 10:21)
30. C (1 Kings 11:4)
31. A (2 Corinthians 11:25)
32. B (Acts 23:8)
33. A (1 Chronicles 3:10)
34. B (2 Chronicles 11:21)
35. A (Exodus 26:14)
36. C (1 Kings 2:20)
37. B (Genesis 9)
38. D (Luke 1:1–4; Acts 1:1)
39. C (1 Samuel 14:50)
40. B (2 Kings 18:4)
41. C (Revelation 3:9)
42. C (Ecclesiastes 2:2)
43. D (Exodus 12:40)
44. B (Revelation 21:12)
45. C (Isaiah 38:5)
46. C (Matthew 13:55; Luke 6:16; John 14:22; Acts 5:37; 9:11; 15:32)

166. Royalty

1. C (1 Kings 11:3)
2. A (1 Samuel 9)
3. D (1 Kings 11:7)
4. B (Acts 18:3)
5. D (Exodus 32:4)
6. B (Luke 23:8)

7. A (2 Chronicles 36:11–21)
8. B (1 Kings 7:13–14)
9. D (Daniel 5:1–5)
10. C (Numbers 21:9)

167. More Firsts

1. A (Matthew 4:18–20)
2. B (Judges 3:9–10)
3. C (Genesis 4:6)
4. A (Genesis 8:20)
5. C (Genesis 24:65–67)
6. D (Genesis 41:42)
7. B (Genesis 4:2)
8. D (Genesis 14:17–18)
9. A (Genesis 29:9)
10. D (Acts 13:1–13)

168. More Random Bible Trivia

1. B (Acts 2:14–42)
2. A (Revelation 3:16)
3. C (Mark 2:14)
4. C (Matthew 26:75)
5. B (Numbers 20:11)
6. C (Daniel 7:9)
7. A (Exodus 16:13)
8. A (2 Kings 6:18–23)
9. B (Acts 17:28)
10. C (Ephesians 5:14)
11. B (1 Samuel 19:10)
12. A (Genesis 19:1)
13. B (Matthew 26:36)
14. C (Exodus 7:20)
15. A (Matthew 12:27)
16. D (Ezekiel 1:1)
17. D (John 11:43)
18. C (Genesis 17:15)
19. C (Matthew 8:24)
20. A (Genesis 26:34)
21. B (2 Chronicles 24:25–26)
22. A (Genesis 41:45)
23. B (John 2:1–11)
24. C (Luke 1:43)
25. D (Luke 2:36–37)

169. Encouragement

1. tower, safe
2. Proverbs, Trust, heart
3. Fear, dismayed, hand
4. John, Peace, world
5. John, me, world
6. God, refuge, mountains, sea
7. Timothy, spirit, power, love
8. Psalm, LORD
9. Cast, LORD
10. Peter, care
11. perfect, mind
12. Psalm, LORD, song
13. Psalm, hiding, shield
14. dust, word
15. Psalm, word
16. afflicted, learn
17. Psalm, distress, LORD

170. Friendship

1. friend, brother
2. Proverbs, angry, soul
3. wise, fools
4. better, kisses
5. Two, help
6. John, love
7. friend, brother
8. Iron, man
9. righteous, wicked
10. adulterers, world, enemy
11. friends, tears

171. Forgiveness

1. forgive, heavenly, Father
2. John, faithful, forgive
3. transgressions, sins
4. Acts, Repent, sins
5. Isaiah, reason, scarlet, snow
6. Christ, creature
7. redemption, blood, grace
8. sins, remember
9. rebelled
10. delivered, darkness, sins
11. Psalm, east, transgressions
12. God, sins, sea
13. Matthew, pray, Hallowed, heaven, evil
14. praying, forgive, trespasses
15. blood, sins

172. Inspiration

1. Jeremiah, thoughts, evil
2. Psalm, dwell, house
3. Psalm, taste, good
4. Proverbs, friend
5. heard, Creator, earth
6. John, Greater, love

7. things, love, purpose
8. Romans, say, against
9. God, peace, power
10. Romans, death, angels, separate
11. not, morning
12. man, renewed
13. faith, strong
14. loss, dung, faith
15. Father, world
16. heart, faith, washed
17. chosen, nation, light
18. James, joy, faith
19. Romans, faith
20. Deuteronomy, courage, forsake
21. work, Lord, vain
22. witnesses, patience

173. Anger

1. sin
2. James, brethren, wrath
3. Proverbs, fool
4. anger, transgression
5. spirit, fools
6. answer, wrath
7. Proverbs, anger
8. anger, mouth
9. anger, city
10. Proverbs, friendship
11. Psalm, anger, earth
12. Proverbs, wrath, spirit

174. Who Is God?

1. Genesis 18:14; Luke 18:27; Revelation 19:6
2. Deuteronomy 33:27; Psalm 90:2; Jeremiah 10:10
3. 1 Kings 8:22–27; Jeremiah 23:24; Psalm 102:25–27; Revelation 22:13
4. Exodus 3:13–14; Psalm 50:10–12; Colossians 1:16
5. Psalm 139:7–12
6. James 1:17; 1 John 1:4–5
7. 2 Samuel 7:22; Isaiah 46:9–11
8. Psalm 139:2–6; Isaiah 40:13–14
9. Psalm 102:25–27; Hebrews 1:10–12
10. Leviticus 19:2; 1 Peter 1:15
11. Proverbs 3:19; Romans 16:26–27; 1 Timothy 1:17
12. Deuteronomy 32:4; Psalm 11:7; Psalm 119:137
13. Psalm 31:5; John 14:6; John 17:3; Titus 1:1–2
14. Deuteronomy 7:9; Psalm 89:1–8
15. Exodus 34:6; Psalm 103:8; 1 Peter 5:10
16. Psalm 25:8; Psalm 34:8; Mark 10:18
17. Deuteronomy 4:31; Psalm 103:8–17; Daniel 9:9; Hebrews 2:17
18. John 4:24
19. John 3:16; Romans 5:8; 1 John 4:8
20. Matthew 28:19; 2 Corinthians 13:14

175. The Book of Revelation

Chapter 1

1. John
2. Jesus
3. The seven churches in Asia
4. The angels of the seven churches and the seven churches themselves

Chapter 2

1. They had left their first love, God
2. They had no current problem, but their faith would be greatly tested by the upcoming tribulation
3. Pergamos
4. Thyatira

Chapter 3

1. Sardis
2. Philadelphia
3. A lukewarm church

Chapter 4

1. God
2. The seven spirits of God
3. A lion, a calf, a man, and a flying eagle
4. Twenty-four elders

Chapter 5

1. A book sealed with seven seals
2. Jesus

Chapter 6

1. White
2. Wars
3. Famine
4. The pale horse
5. Those slain because of the Word of God
6. A great earthquake

Chapter 7

1. 144,000
2. People of all nations, kindreds, people, and tongues

Chapter 8

1. Judgment upon the earth
2. Hail and fire
3. The burning of a great mountain
4. A great star
5. One-third

Chapter 9

1. Torment them without killing them
2. Four angels that killed a third of humankind
3. Two hundred million
4. No, they did not

Chapter 10

1. That God's plan would no longer be delayed
2. It would be finished

Chapter 11

1. Forty-two months (three and a half years)
2. They prophesied about the coming judgment of God
3. The beast of the bottomless pit
4. They ascended to heaven
5. The establishment of the kingdom of God on earth

Chapter 12

1. Israel
2. Satan
3. Satan

4. Jesus
5. The ones who "keep the commandments of God, and have the testimony of Jesus Christ"

Chapter 13

1. A leopard
2. Make war with the saints
3. A beast with two horns
4. Their right hands or their foreheads

Chapter 14

1. The 144,000 survivors of the tribulation
2. The gospel to all people
3. The second angel
4. The mark of the beast
5. A cloud

Chapter 15

1. The survivors of the tribulation and those who refused the mark of the beast
2. The seven last plagues of God's wrath, reserved for those left on earth

Chapter 16

1. Horrible sores for the people
2. Blood
3. Blood
4. Excessive heat from the sun
5. Darkness
6. Euphrates River
7. A great earthquake

Chapter 17

1. The seven kingdoms that would come into power

2. The ten kings and their nations that would support the beast

Chapter 18

1. One hour
2. A millstone

Chapter 19

1. Babylon
2. Jesus
3. They were cast into the lake of fire

Chapter 20

1. The bottomless pit for one thousand years
2. Resurrection
3. He was cast into the lake of fire
4. The lost and the remainder of the dead

Chapter 21

1. Heaven and earth
2. The new heaven
3. The twelve tribes of Israel
4. The length, width, and height were all equal to 12,000 furlongs (1,380 miles)
5. Jasper
6. Pearls
7. The glory of God

Chapter 22

1. A river of water of life
2. The tree of life
3. Blessing
4. Amen

Answers

Section 4: The Bonus Section

176. Food by the Book

Dairy Products

1. Butter
2. Cheese
3. Butter
4. Eggs
5. Milk

Fruits

1. Apple
2. Date
3. Fig
4. Grape
5. Melon
6. Olive
7. Pomegranate
8. Raisin
9. Sycamore fruit

Vegetables

1. Cucumbers, leeks, and onions
2. Gourds

Nuts

1. Almonds
2. Pistachio nuts (NIV)

Legumes

1. Beans and lentils
2. Lentils

Spices and Herbs

1. Anise
2. Coriander
3. Cinnamon
4. Cummin
5. Dill
6. Garlic
7. Mint
8. Mustard
9. Rue
10. Salt

Fish

1. Seven
2. Peter

Various Grains

1. Barley
2. Bread
3. Corn or grain
4. Flour

5. Millet
6. Spelt (a form of hardy wheat)
7. Unleavened bread
8. Wheat

Various Meats

1. Calf
2. Goat
3. Lamb
4. Oxen
5. Sheep
6. Venison

Various Fowl

1. Partridge
2. Pigeon
3. Quail
4. Dove

Miscellaneous

1. Grape juice
2. Honey
3. Olive oil
4. Vinegar
5. Wine

177. The Sixty Hardest Questions

1. Methuselah, 969 (Genesis 5:27); Jared, 962 (Genesis 5:20); Adam, 960 (Genesis 5:5); Noah, 950 (Genesis 9:29); Seth 912 (Genesis 5:8); Kenan, 910 (Genesis 5:14); Enosh, 905 (Genesis 5:11)
2. Ehud (Judges 3:15)
3. Joshua (Joshua 12:9–24)
4. Sarah, 127 (Genesis 23:1)
5. Joseph, who died at age 110 (Genesis 50:22)
6. Zedekiah and Ahab (Jeremiah 29:22)
7. At the baptism of Jesus (Matthew 3:17), at the transfiguration (Matthew 17:5), and shortly before Jesus went to the cross (John 12:28)
8. Three years (Exodus 7:7)
9. Joseph (Genesis 41:14)
10. Saul (1 Chronicles 10:8–10)
11. A sheep (Genesis 4:2–4)
12. Mahlon (Ruth 1:4–5; 4:10)
13. Thirty-seven; she died at age 127 and gave birth at age 90 (Genesis 23:1)

14. Twelve (Luke 8:41–42)
15. Lamech (Genesis 4:23)
16. Joseph (Exodus 13:19)
17. Noah (Genesis 8:20)
18. Lydia (Acts 16:14–15)
19. Acts, James, and 3 John
20. Joseph (Genesis 50:26)
21. Isaac (Genesis 24:11–67), Jacob (Genesis 29:1–29), and Moses (Exodus 2:15–21)
22. Zenas (Titus 3:13)
23. Manasseh (2 Kings 21:1)
24. Er (Genesis 38:7)
25. Bow and arrow, mace, sling, sword, ax, club, dagger, and spear (1 Samuel 17:45)
26. Stephen (Acts 6:7–8)
27. Zimri (1 Kings 16:15)
28. Miriam (Exodus 15:21)
29. Gamaliel (Acts 22:3)
30. Dinah (Genesis 34:1)
31. Othniel (Judges 3:9–10)
32. Philip (Mark 6:17)
33. John the Baptist (John 1:35–37, 40)
34. Sadducees (Acts 23:8)
35. Lahmi (1 Chronicles 20:5)
36. "Where art thou" (to Adam) (Genesis 3:9)
37. The ostrich (Leviticus 11:16)
38. Abram (Genesis 14:13)
39. Aaron, the brother of Moses (Luke 1:5)
40. Rachel, while giving birth to Benjamin (Genesis 35:16–19), and the wife of Phinehas, while giving birth to Ichabod (1 Samuel 4:19–22)
41. Green (Genesis 1:30)
42. Enoch (Jude 1:14)
43. Felix (Acts 23:23), Festus (Acts 25:1), and Fortunatus (1 Corinthians 16:17)
44. Malachi, in which forty-seven of the fifty-five verses are God speaking
45. Havilah (Genesis 2:11–12)
46. Eli the high priest (1 Samuel 4:17–18)
47. Zeruiah and Abigail (1 Chronicles 2:13–16)
48. Twenty-five (Numbers 8:24–25)

49. The king of Nineveh (Jonah 3:7–8)
50. Judges (Judges 5:10)
51. James (Acts 12:1–2)
52. Joash (2 Chronicles 24:1)
53. Ruth (Ruth 4:21–22; Matthew 1:5–6)
54. Gideon (Judges 7:4–7)
55. Ur (Genesis 11:28), Ai (Joshua 7:2), On (Genesis 41:45), Ar (Numbers 21:15), Uz (Job 1:1), No (Ezekiel 30:15)
56. The feeding of the five thousand (Matthew 14:13–21; Mark 6:32–44; Luke 9:12–17; John 6:1–14)
57. Caesar Augustus
58. Moses (Exodus 34:28) and Elijah (1 Kings 19:8)
59. Elijah raised the widow's son (1 Kings 17:17–24), Elijah raised the son of the Shunammite (2 Kings 4:18–37), an unnamed man was raised after his body was set upon the bones of Elisha (2 Kings 13:20–21), Jesus raised the son of a widow (Luke 7:11–15), Jesus raised the daughter of Jarius (Luke 8:41–42, 49–56), Jesus raised Lazarus (John 11:1–46), Jesus himself was resurrected (Matthew 28), many dead saints arose out of their graves after the crucifixion of Jesus (Matthew 27:51–53), Peter raised Tabitha (Dorcas) (Acts 9:36–51), and Paul raised Eutychus (Acts 20:9–12)
60. When he fed the five thousand with five loaves of bread and two fish (Matthew 14:15–21), when the money to pay taxes was found in the mouth of a fish (Matthew 17:27), when Peter was told by Jesus to let down his fishing nets again and the nets filled with fish (Luke 5:4–11), and when Jesus told the disciples to cast their net on the right side of the boat and the net was filled with fish (John 21:4–11)

178. Crossword Puzzle 4

179. Crossword Puzzle 5

Timothy E. Parker is a Guinness World Records Puzzle Master and an ordained minister. He entertains over twenty million puzzle solvers as the senior crossword puzzle editor of the Universal line of crosswords and assorted puzzle games. He is the author of more than thirty books and the founder of Bible Brilliant. CNN calls his puzzles "Smart games for smart people," and he has created custom games for companies including Microsoft, Disney, Coca-Cola, Nike, Warner Bros., and Comcast. For more Bible puzzles and quizzes, go to www.BibleBrilliant.com.